BY DANIEL MARK EPSTEIN

POETRY

No Vacancies in Hell

The Follies

Young Men's Gold

The Book of Fortune

Spirits

The Boy in the Well

The Traveler's Calendar

The Glass House: New Poems

Dawn to Twilight: New and Selected Poems

PROSE

Star of Wonder

Love's Compass

Sister Aimee: The Life of Aimee Semple McPherson

Nat King Cole

*What Lips My Lips Have Kissed: The Loves and Love Poems
of Edna St. Vincent Millay*

Lincoln and Whitman: Parallel Lives in Civil War Washington

The Lincolns: Portrait of a Marriage

Lincoln's Men: The President and His Private Secretaries

The Ballad of Bob Dylan

The Loyal Son

PLAYS

Jenny and the Phoenix

The Midnight Visitor

The Leading Lady

TRANSLATIONS

The Trinummus of Plautus

The Bacchae of Euripides

The Loyal Son

The Loyal Son

The War in Ben Franklin's House

Daniel Mark Epstein

BALLANTINE BOOKS

NEW YORK

Published in the United States by Ballantine Books, an imprint of Random House, a division of Penguin Random House LLC, New York.

BALLANTINE and the HOUSE colophon are registered trademarks of Penguin Random House LLC.

LIBRARY OF CONGRESS CATALOGING-IN-PUBLICATION DATA
Names: Epstein, Daniel Mark, author.
Title: The loyal son : the war in Ben Franklin's house / Daniel Mark Epstein.
Description: First edition. | New York : Ballantine Books, 2017. |
Includes bibliographical references and index.
Identifiers: LCCN 2017013553| ISBN 9780345544216 (hardcover : alk. paper) |
ISBN 9780345544223 (ebook)
Subjects: LCSH: Franklin, Benjamin, 1706-1790. | Franklin, William, 1731–1813. |
Statesmen—United States—Biography. | Governors—New Jersey—Biography. |
American loyalists—Biography. | Statesmen's children—United States—Biography. |
United States—Politics and government—1775–1783.
Classification: LCC E302.6.F8 E59 2017 | DDC 973.3092 [B]—dc23
LC record available at https://lccn.loc.gov/2017013553

Printed in the United States of America on acid-free paper

randomhousebooks.com

2 4 6 8 9 7 5 3 1

First Edition

Book design by Caroline Cunningham

For Charles and Laura Jenkins

CONTENTS

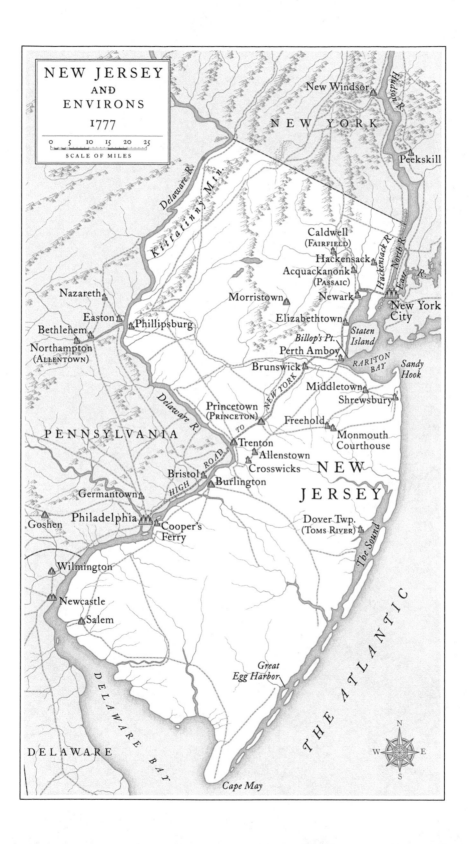

NEW JERSEY
AND
ENVIRONS
1777

0   5   10   15   20   25
SCALE OF MILES

NEW YORK

New Windsor

Peekskill

Hudson R.

Delaware R.

Kittatinny Mtn.

Caldwell
(FAIRFIELD)
Hackensack
Acquackanonk
(PASSAIC)

Hackensack R.

North R.

East R.

Nazareth

Morristown

Newark

New York
City

Easton
Phillipsburg

Elizabethtown

Staten
Island

Bethlehem
Northampton
(ALLENTOWN)

Billop's Pt.
Perth Amboy

RARITON
BAY

Sandy
Hook

Brunswick

Delaware R.

NEW YORK

Middletown
Shrewsbury

PENNSYLVANIA

Princetown
(PRINCETON)

TO

Freehold
Monmouth
Courthouse

Trenton
Allenstown
Crosswicks

NEW
JERSEY

Bristol
Burlington

ROAD

Germantown

HIGH

Goshen

Philadelphia

Cooper's
Ferry

Dover Twp.
(TOMS RIVER)

The Sound

Wilmington

Newcastle

Salem

THE ATLANTIC

Great
Egg Harbor

DELAWARE BAY

N

W   E

S

DELAWARE

Cape May

PREFACE

================

A Night Journey, 1731

WORKS OF FICTION OFTEN benefit from prefaces that are non-fictional statements. These are usually personal and sometimes historical remarks by the writer that help us find our way into the story. Is it possible that a book of history might profit from a nearly fictional preface? Might an author part from convention just long enough to favor the reader by turning the tables? I don't know if it has ever been done before; but, begging the reader's indulgence I mean to try it.

When I am done with my preface, I will resume my vocation as a historian with no constellation to guide my craft but the facts.

ON A STARRY NIGHT in April 1731, a young man in a borrowed two-wheeled shay drove along the Lower Post Road from Burlington, New Jersey, toward Cooper's Ferry, where he hoped to cross the river into Philadelphia before daybreak. There was enough of the moon in its last quarter to light the muddy road.

Beside him on the seat was a packing crate lined with blankets, and wrapped in the blankets and wound in bunting was a baby. Right now the baby was sleeping, lulled by the rhythm of the horse's hooves and the easy jouncing of the carriage upon its creaking wheels. The driver guided the horse carefully in the hope that a bump in the road wouldn't set the baby to crying again. Just eight months old, he had never been long away from his mother. She had explained a few hours ago that if the baby cried he was to pick him up, just so, and put him up on the shoulder and pat him, once, twice, and again to raise the air in his belly. Then rock him or sing to him and he would go back to sleep. He was a good baby, she said, sobbing. "He does not cry or fuss but when he is hungry or raw or has the air in his belly."

She had weaned him early in anticipation of this terrible hour. In a separate compartment of the crate were a pewter sucking pot, a silver pap boat and spoon for pabulum, and a covered jar of mixed flour, bread, and water. He knew nothing about babies but meant to figure it out.

Franklin was famously capable. In the fullness of his twenty-four years he had proved this to himself and a few other people and was sometimes frightened of his own power. The advantage was partly an inborn mental endowment, a knack for absorbing knowledge and putting it to work in useful and novel ways. In spite of little schooling he had mastered Latin, French, ancient history, and strange branches of mathematics such as the magic square. He was a wunderkind, at sixteen already demonstrating a command of language that would make him the greatest writer of topical essays in America. A precocious businessman, at seventeen he had replaced his brother as editor of *The New-England Courant*; now he was owner of *The Pennsylvania Gazette* and the colony's official printer.

All of these accomplishments might be understood as functions of intellect and a hearty constitution. But he had more mysterious talents: an ability to see things, events, objects, before they appeared to his senses; also his potent influence upon people of all ages—he couldn't account for it and preferred not to think too much about it, but this was a force he had come to rely upon without conscience.

Franklin believed in God but shunned the church. At nineteen he had published a pamphlet arguing against free will. As God was infinitely wise, good, and almighty, nothing in His creation could be wrong. Therefore vice and virtue were empty distinctions. By and by, though, he had begun to see the danger in this creed. He had allowed a large debt to a friend go unpaid. He treated his brother badly, first by running out on his apprenticeship in Boston, then by returning there in triumph a year later, flaunting his new wealth, flashing gold coins, embarrassing James in front of his staff. He had treated his fiancée, Deborah, terribly at one time, neglecting her while indulging his passion for low women.

Lacking a proper philosophy, religion, or supervision, he realized there was no end of mischief and misery he might cause the world. Look what had happened in the past year during a time when he was trying so hard to mend his ways.

The carriage hit a bump and the baby stirred in the wooden box, murmuring, and then fell silent again.

Two women were in love with Benjamin Franklin. One he loved with all his heart and soul; the other was his wife, who was waiting for him, weary and anxious, in their rooms on Market Street in Philadelphia. The woman he had left behind, weeping, at the door of a mansion on the outskirts of Burlington was the mother of the child who lay beside him.

He had met the woman at a lively dinner gathering at the home of the surveyor general in Burlington three years ago, when Franklin and his business partner were printing paper money for the province of New Jersey. She and her husband, Captain Joseph Bradford, were seated when he entered the parlor. The first thing he noticed was the sheen of her long, abundant hair, nearly black, pinned back, strands touching her bare shoulders, and eyes of china blue that made a brilliant contrast. The second thing he noticed as she rose and extended a slender hand was how tall she was, almost equal to his five feet ten inches.

They were seated together at the long table as the two youngest of the company, and because it was hoped that the twenty-two-year-old writer, with his wit and vast reading, would entertain the captain's wife, herself a woman of unusual erudition. Her father, a rich merchant and amateur scientist, had novel ideas about women and spared no expense on books and tutors for his youngest daughter, Marion. It had stood her in good stead. She had married the adoring Captain Bradford, master of two merchant vessels, who was at sea for years at a time while she managed his business affairs on land, having complete power of attorney and notable financial literacy.

After one hour in Mrs. Bradford's company, Franklin was not quite sure whether she found him entertaining or ridiculous. She smiled agreeably. At times she fairly beamed, raising an eyebrow, whether what this bachelor said was funny or not, as if she laughed at some inner joke that might be at his expense, or perhaps a distant memory awakened in her that had nothing to do with him. She was certainly the most beautiful woman he had ever seen, with the clear cameo features of a Titian Madonna. She seemed much older than he (she was then twenty-eight) and more worldly-wise, a wife, woman of affairs, and mother of a ten-year-old daughter.

At the other end of the table the surveyor general, a judge, their wives, and several aldermen sipped wine and talked business with Captain Bradford, who knew everything about the balance of trade. He was a jovial mariner of fifty with thick side-whiskers and merry eyes. He would be sailing for England in May with a cargo of tobacco and lumber, returning, God willing, in October with broadcloth and salt. Then off again on a winter run to Barbados.

Captain Bradford and his wife owned two homes, the mansion outside Burlington and a smaller house in the port city of Perth Amboy near Raritan Bay and the ship channel. She first wrote to the young printer from Perth Amboy on May 17, 1728, asking if he might call upon her in Burlington during the following week. She had questions about the currency.

There in the twilight of her book-lined drawing room, as night closed in around them, it took them all of fifteen minutes to realize they were in love—hardly enough time to light the lamps. These free spirits, unsupervised, without religion, and agreeing that vice and virtue were empty distinctions, gave in to nature and high spirits. They soon found that they could not get enough of each other.

That spring and summer, in Burlington County and in Philadelphia, in inns and courtyards, meadows, haylofts, and rowboats, they made love as lovers have done since time began and as they believed no lovers had ever made love before, with enthusiasm, imagination, and acrobatic virtuosity. They did things not to be recorded here. They were cleverly discreet. And of course they took care to see that Mrs. Bradford did not get pregnant. She knew all about that, and he trusted her to supply what he lacked in experience.

When the leaves turned and it was time for the captain to come home, they were not quite exhausted, but discovered the fire that had warmed them in the summer had given way to a glow that was inextinguishable: a sort of tenderness and deep understanding of kindred spirits. Now each must appeal to the other's highest nature. They must not meet again. They must consider not only themselves, but others.

So in November, Franklin wrote his famous "Articles of Belief and Acts of Religion" in which he embraces virtue and goodness as the only means to leading a happy life. During the next few years he would create a program calculated to achieve moral perfection, by checking off cardinal virtues one by one on a chart: temperance, frugality, justice, moderation . . . twelve in all, with the last being chastity. By concentrating on one per week, then repeating, in a year or two one might become a saint. He managed to stay away from Marion Bradford for more than eight months during which he pined for her. He took consolation in the company of his old flame Deborah Read, a handsome woman he had known since they were seventeen. She, too, was married, but disastrously; her husband had run off years ago, so she was for most purposes available, if not legally marriageable.

But in the summer of 1729 he received a letter from Marion informing him that the captain was departing upon a triangular trade route from Sandy Hook bearing rum to the Gold Coast, slaves from Africa to the West Indies, then molasses to England. Her husband would not return before late winter eighteen months hence. This was more temptation than the aspiring saint could bear, not to mention Mrs. Bradford. They picked up their affair where they had left off, but with renewed intensity after months of longing, and the piquancy of knowing that this must come to an end, the sweet torment of swearing oaths that they would never see each other again, of tearful, high-minded partings, and then delicious, wicked falls from grace.

After Christmas they made love in a damp hunting lodge, and in March she told him she was pregnant. This was a sobering development. What could she do? The pregnancy could be concealed with proper clothing until the end, and then she would travel. Her daughter would be away at school. There was a friend in Richmond who could be trusted. Her husband must never know; he wanted more children, would never forgive her. She would be ruined. Benjamin must go away and never see her again. She would write to him.

He had seen her one more time before that long night in April 1731. Drawn by an overwhelming impulse, he went to her upon her return from Richmond, learning she had been unwilling to give up the newborn until she had weaned him. He found her alone in the house near Burlington with only one servant so old and frail she appeared ready to carry Marion's secret to the grave any moment. The mother was both happy to see him and very sad. The boy child in his cradle, with the promise of a smile, was perfectly formed, as one could see when she undressed him. He did not touch the baby. He promised her that he would return when the boy was weaned and see to it that he was placed in a good home. It was the least he could do.

Franklin had been in fitful negotiations with Deborah Read for several months concerning their domestic arrangements. She wanted to marry him but couldn't until there was proof of her husband's demise. Franklin wanted a wife for all the usual reasons. He was fantastically busy. He did not want to assume responsibility for the enormous debts of Deborah's late husband should he prove to be dead, which colonial law demanded. One solution was for them to set up housekeeping together and declare themselves husband and wife, above the law, which appealed to him more than to her. They argued over it, bargaining. Now there was another pawn on the board—this baby. It might tip the balance for Deborah Read. After a heated discussion, she consented to raise the bastard under two conditions: Franklin was never to see the child's mother again, whoever she was, and "the woman's identity must never be revealed, even here, to *me*. At best the world may come to believe he is ours; at worst he will be known as a foundling orphan."

Deborah moved into Ben's house in September 1730, beginning their common-law union. Never gregarious, she served her husband, traveling occasionally to visit her siblings.

In April he crossed the Delaware River with his baby. He drove the shay along Front Street in view of the sailing ships, turning up Market Street in the dawn. It was a new world that needed good fathers. A ship's horn blared, and sounds of the city waking woke the baby beside him. At an alley between Second and Third Streets the infant whimpered. Then he began to cry in earnest. They were almost home. He did not want to bring this baby to his wife screaming and crying. He reined the horse, jumped down and tied him to a hitching post, and threw a blanket over him. He got back up on the carriage seat, gently lifted the baby from the cradle, and began rocking him side to side as he had seen women do. The baby cried. He put him up on his shoulder and patted his back, just so. He began to sing.

Hush ye, my bairnie
Bonny wee laddie
When you're a man
You shall follow your daddy . . .

Franklin loved to sing old tunes. It calmed the child, and soon he was sound asleep once more.

Leaving the horse and shay in the rising light he carried the bundle to the house and up the stairs to the bedroom where his wife was half asleep. He laid the child in the middle of the bed and got in beside him. When Deborah's eyes were fully opened, she first saw the baby sleeping between them.

"His name is William," her husband whispered.

THE NIGHT JOURNEY OF young Ben Franklin may have happened much as it is described above. The persons and the circumstances were real (excepting the Bradfords) and the events highly probable. But there is no record of them. So it is not history. It is scaffolding. Like the wooden frame that follows the form of the underside of an arch while the marble stones are laid upon it, until the last capstone is in place and the arch is self-supporting from the weight of gravity, the little story may now be taken down.

What lies ahead is the stone arch of history.

PART ONE

Sons of the Empire

CHAPTER I

Americans in London: September 22, 1761

T HE CROWD THAT GATHERED that morning in the square mile of streets, yards, and parks surrounding Westminster Abbey was the largest that had ever been seen in Europe. A million Britons had come from all over the kingdom to witness the crowning of King George III and his bride, Princess Charlotte of Mecklenburgh.

Every house, inn, and tavern was jammed. People couldn't sleep for the shouting and singing, the ringing of church bells, and the hammering of scaffolds. From St. James's Park to the banks of the Thames, nobles and peasants, merchants and plowmen, flower girls, jugglers, and piemen filled the streets in hopes of a glimpse of the royal procession. Such is the power of the British monarchy that a famous American scientist of the day might have likened the choir of the Abbey—with its ancient chair of Saint Edward in which the king would be crowned—to a magnetic pole enforcing order on the field of humanity surrounding it.

The hopes of a quarrelsome empire waited upon the young king.

Even the elements of nature were moved. It had drizzled rain upon the city since Sunday. Yet on Tuesday morning the sun dispersed the clouds and fog and shone throughout the day of the pageant, an omen inspiring the *London Chronicle*'s bard to write:

Since then, great Prince, it looks like heaven's decree
Ev'n to our sunshine we should owe to thee
Let this day represent thy future reign
Clear after clouds, and after storms serene . . .

For the nobles, gentlemen and ladies, bishops and choristers commanded to walk in the procession ahead of the king, and for those with engraved tickets that reserved places in Westminster Hall where the procession formed, there was a great deal to see. The splendor of the spectacle would exceed the expectations that had been building since the death of King George II nearly a year before.

Westminster Hall, cavernous beneath its hammer-beam oaken roof, had been emptied of all but the floor and steps of the king's law court that convened here. A new floor of planks had been laid from the North Gate up the middle of the half-acre space to those steps and covered with woven matting. Immense galleries had been erected on either side, up to the beams, three levels seating thousands of spectators. Fifty-two chandeliers, each surmounted by an imperial crown of gold, were ready to light a postcoronation banquet with a thousand candles.

There were few Americans in London, fewer who could witness the coronation of their sovereign, and only one who was entitled to walk in the procession. He was William Franklin, the thirty-one-year-old son of the famous American scientist Benjamin Franklin. The older Franklin sat on a plank in the packed gallery. He had purchased his place in the open market, where they were changing hands for five guineas or more (a workingman's wage for a fortnight).

Ben Franklin gazed down at the privileged ranks of bedecked, bedizened, and bejeweled humanity: judges in scarlet robes, choirboys with scarlet mantles, heralds in tabards, and all the nobility in their robes of state, their coronets in their hands.

And there on the edge of that rainbow of heraldry stood his son, William, in his drab coat of broadcloth, his tricorn hat in his hand. Benjamin Franklin regarded this scene with that blend of intense curiosity and amusement that often animated his bright blue eyes. He was by temperament and practice an observer of life as much as an actor in the human drama, both critical and self-aware.

William, his only son, a keen observer and student of manners himself, was more naturally a man of action, a confident frontier soldier, a man of law, a scientist in his own right, and—as his father's aide—a colonial advocate. Pennsylvania had sent father and son to England on a fateful mission. Proprietor Thomas Penn's refusal to pay taxes on his vast property had crippled defenses on the colony's western frontier. Success for the Franklins with Parliament would mean safety for their countrymen; failure would mean more Indian raids, more massacres. Success depended upon their harmonious collaboration. It would also depend upon the grace of the new king.

William was handsome, an endowment his father must have noticed served him well in his unique role on this glorious day. His face was long and lean, his nose perfect, his chin strong and prominent, his mouth in repose a bow with upturned corners; his eyes were dark with long lashes and arched brows well drawn by nature. It was a comely face saved from androgyny by the force that animated it when he spoke or laughed. A friend had written to Mrs. Franklin, soon after meeting him in London: "Your son I really think one of the prettiest young gentlemen I ever knew," in a century when the word "pretty" bore no unmanly connotations.

The Franklins' friend William Strahan was forty-six, a publisher whose circle included such luminaries as David Hume, Dr. Samuel Johnson, and Edward Gibbon, all of whom he edited and befriended. His wide-set eyes shone with humor; kindness showed in his easy smile, force in the tilt of his chin. Equally at home with lords and commoners, he covered the proceedings in Parliament, publishing his remarks in journals, including Franklin's *Pennsylvania Gazette*. In the same letter Mr. Strahan, a good judge of character, praised William Franklin's "solidity of judgment, not very often to be met with in one of his years." The English publisher, a man of the world, had never met such a father and son—strong personalities who worked in perfect collaboration, without envy or friction.

Although Mrs. Franklin might take pride in William's levelheadedness, having reared him, she took no credit for the man's beauty, an endowment (and souvenir) bestowed by the woman of mystery who had been her husband's mistress before he commenced his civil union with Deborah Read. The origins of that common-law marriage, and Deborah's adoption of its bastard issue, are noteworthy.

DEBORAH READ HAD KNOWN Benjamin Franklin from the day of his arrival in Philadelphia at age seventeen. She was the first girl to take notice of the stranger, bedraggled, disheveled, ill shod. Standing by her father's door on Market Street she watched him pass, munching a large, puffy bread roll while holding two others, one under each arm. She later recalled that the lad made "a most awkward ridiculous appearance." He may have heard her giggle. Benjamin had run away from his apprenticeship in Boston and wanted lodging. By chance this turned out to be the home of Deborah Read's father, John, a carpenter, who owned the house of Franklin's new employer, the printer Samuel Keimer. When Franklin's trunk and his clothing arrived, the boy made a better impression upon Miss Read than he had the day he passed by her door chewing the bread.

They became friends and more than friends, sharing the same hearth and table on Market Street. At eighteen he expressed his desire to marry her, soon after her father's untimely death. The governor of Pennsylvania was about to send this charming journeyman to London to purchase a letterpress and type, with the commission to set up as the province's official printer; he could leave Keimer's employment. With such prospects Franklin was confident he might start a family upon his return. As much in love with the attractive, bright Deborah Read as she was with him, he wanted a wedding, or at least an engagement, before he set sail, so as not to lose her to the tides of time and distance. Her mother, Sarah, citing those same uncertainties—their extreme youth and the long sea voyage—opposed the betrothal, arguing that a marriage "would be more convenient" after his return. By then he might be well established in his business, an enterprise she wisely considered to be founded more upon wishes than probabilities.

Minding her mother, Deborah bade Benjamin farewell. He sailed for England, where his hopes were dashed upon the ground of the governor's empty promises and a lack of credit. He toiled in London print shops for a year and a half. Enjoying the heady life of a bachelor abroad, he neglected to write to Miss Read.

When he returned to Philadelphia at age twenty-one he found his Deborah married to one John Rogers, a potter. She was married, but now alone. The shiftless potter had gone through her dowry in a matter of months. Rumor had it that Rogers was also married to a woman in London. Hearing of this, Deborah left him. Rogers then ran away to the West Indies, where he may or may not have been killed in a brawl. So Deborah was married, and perhaps a widow, living with her mother when Franklin returned from his unprofitable adventure to England.

Not married in the true sense, nor free to marry in the legal sense, Deborah was in a painful situation. Benjamin not only pitied her, he felt guilty. A frequent visitor to the Read household, where he was welcome not only as a friend but also as an adviser in the family's affairs, he found that Deborah was usually dejected, rarely cheerful, and avoided company. He believed that his own neglect and frivolity during his year in London was the cause of her unhappiness, even though Mrs. Read insisted upon taking the blame. It was she who had opposed their engagement, she who had encouraged the other match in Franklin's absence.

Deborah was grateful for his attention and loved his company. Gradually their old affection was rekindled. But now there were many obstacles to their union. If Rogers was indeed married to someone in London, Deborah's marriage was null and void. But at such a distance the fact could hardly be proved. If he was dead, stabbed in a barroom in Barbados or Grenada, then she was a widow; this was likewise unlikely to be proved. Inquiries had been made, and perhaps time would tell, but the corporal punishments for bigamy in those days were so severe that no one dared to risk it.

Meanwhile, twenty-one-year-old Benjamin Franklin was a man about town, not only in Philadelphia but in nearby Burlington, New Jersey. He and Samuel Keimer were busy there printing the official colonial currency in the spring of 1728, and doing what young men do in their spare time. He later confessed to his helplessness in managing his sexual urges: "That hard-to-be-governed passion of youth had hurried me frequently into intrigues with low women that fell in my way, which were attended with some expense and great inconvenience, besides a continual risk to my health."

About that time Franklin fell into an intrigue with a woman unlikely to pose a risk to his health, not a low woman but one who would cause him considerable inconvenience, as he did her. Although her identity remains a mystery, unknown at the time even to Deborah, the woman in question was one who could keep a secret. She was someone who had at least as much to lose as Benjamin, if not more, than Benjamin, by the divulging of the secret trysts, the affair, the pregnancy, the birth. Most likely it was someone of breeding, and perhaps a woman already married, whose husband was out of the picture for months or years, a sea captain or merchant trading in China or Africa. For the sake of discretion, so much the better if the woman in question lived at a distance, anywhere but Philadelphia, where no one could keep a secret, someplace like Burlington, over the river. Deborah would be kept wondering, as would the whole world, for the sake of that woman's honor, which was only as safe as the knowledge of William's true parentage. *Three may keep a secret if two of them are dead,* wrote Poor Richard, famously and sagely.

The woman in question was confined sometime in 1729 or 1730. The child was born and put to nurse. His father—who at the time was practicing to become a saint, or rather a moral paradigm, as his writings show—resolved to adopt this baby, William, as his own. He meant to rear the boy and acknowledge him despite the world's vain and idle opinions. This was a rare course of action for a man of Franklin's class, although not unheard of. Usually bastards were reared by their mothers, when they were not abandoned. But Franklin was no ordinary man. In 1730 he was refining his "Art of Virtue," a manual that was no less than a "project of arriving at moral perfection," and responsible fatherhood seemed as good a place as any to begin.

Now things grew complicated and inconvenient, if not expensive, for the unwed father. The mother returned home with her honor intact and a terrible grief that time might heal. Her child was lost, and the world need know little more about it than that. Franklin, the would-be saint, went back to his lodgings, after the weaning, with a bastard to mix into the bargain of his marriage contract, for he had every intention of living with Deborah Read. "Better to be married than burn," Saint Augustine advised, and Benjamin Franklin at twenty-four wanted badly to be married. He wanted a mother for this baby, and a wife. His choices were limited by his paternity, especially with respect to a dowry. Years later he would blame the limitation on his trade: As the printing business was generally thought a poor one, he couldn't expect a dowry along with a wife, unless it was such a woman as he would otherwise think disagreeable. The truth is rather that Benjamin Franklin was an eligible and engaging bachelor, talented, charming, handsome, and full of promise, with one liability—his bastard son.

This is where his needs coincided with Deborah's. They were equally damaged goods. They had been in love when they were eighteen. Six years later, sadder and wiser, they nourished a mutual affection that would ripen into conjugal love. While Deborah waited for sworn testimony of her husband's death in order to marry again, Ben Franklin faced the contingency that as Rogers's successor he would be held liable for the late husband's debts, which were considerable. He would have to accept such bad news with the good. Deborah, for her part, had to accept the role of mother to the bastard son Benjamin had sired in a passion that was neither impetuous nor insignificant, in all probability. It was a bitter pill. He had probably been in love with her, whoever she was, since he had gone to such lengths to care for the child and protect her anonymity. He had made love to her sometime after returning from England, and God only knew what he felt for her now.

Understanding these things they agreed to enter into a common-law marriage. On September 1, 1730, they invited friends and family to an informal ceremony in which they declared their intention to live together as husband and wife. They set up housekeeping in Franklin's residence at 139 Market Street about the time little William was taking his first steps. Two years later, on October 20, 1732, Deborah gave birth to a son, Francis Folger Franklin. Assisting with the delivery of the newborn as well as the care of the toddler William was Deborah's mother, Sarah, who had come to live with them. She also helped in the stationery store Deborah managed on the ground floor.

Little Frankie was his mother's darling, longed-for, prayed for in the trying presence of his handsome half brother. The new baby arrived during a year of ample fortune and prosperity for the little family. Benjamin had paid off his debts and consolidated his publishing, printing, and stationery businesses; he had brought out the first edition of *Poor Richard's Almanac,* which would soon make him rich. Perhaps it was the pressure of business or the feeling of invulnerability that comes with lavish good luck that caused Franklin to neglect inoculating this baby against smallpox. William had been treated. It was a curious oversight. He had been an early champion of the controversial experiment, studying its statistical results and sharing his opinions in the *Gazette.* In 1736, smallpox swept the city, and Frankie died of it. Now his father would have to explain to critics that the child had not died of the inoculation, but of the disease itself. He would never forgive himself. In death the little boy seemed to him to possess every human grace and promise of greatness—in any case, this was what he told Deborah and the world.

She could not wish harm to any child, but it must have seemed cruel to the grieving mother that Death would pass over the bastard son and carry off the only baby she and her husband were ever likely to have. They both came from large families that prized fecundity, and like most couples of their generation, they wanted many children. Franklin loved children. In the almanac he had written: "A ship under sail and a big-bellied woman / Are the handsomest things that can be seen common." For whatever reason, they had failed each other in this. It was not for a lack of trying. Now she was twenty-nine, and an entire decade would pass between fruitful pregnancies. On August 31, 1743, at the age of thirty-five, she gave birth to a daughter they named Sarah after her grandmother. They would call her Sally. The girl was as fine a specimen of her sex as Frankie might have been of his, with all of her parents' virtues, strength, beauty, and intelligence. William adored her. Her father was so proud of her that he joked with Mr. Strahan about arranging a marriage between the seven-year-old Sally and Strahan's ten-year-old son.

Meanwhile, the gossips of Philadelphia either did not know or did not care that William Franklin was illegitimate until the early 1760s, about the time of the coronation of King George III. In that decade the rumor would be useful to the Franklins' enemies. Until then, all the world—including Mr. Strahan—took for granted that Deborah Franklin was mother of all three children.

It was through Strahan's influence, in part, that William stood by his side in Westminster Hall, about to walk in the procession. Although Strahan had not met the Franklins until their arrival in London in 1757, he had corresponded for many years with Benjamin and had heard intriguing stories about young William as he came of age on the American frontier.

THE BOY HAD BEEN bright and headstrong, precocious like his father before him. And had he not also been charming, the task of rearing William in adolescence might not have seemed worth the trouble.

At fifteen he tried to run away from home on a privateer, longing for adventure and plunder. Benjamin fetched the boy from the ship, later protesting that no one could say it was hardship at home that prompted him, for Franklin was by all accounts not only an attentive but an indulgent father. When he himself had run away from home as a teenager, it was to escape a harsh apprenticeship to his brother James, a printer of inferior talents who whipped him to get even. William had no such complaints, being favored and coddled. He had received the best education available in Philadelphia in the 1730s and '40s: a private tutor, then a desk at Annand's Classical Academy at age eight. The boy wrote a fine hand and knew his Latin declensions. He danced, and rode well on his own pony.

Benjamin would have liked to see his son follow him in the printer's trade, but the boy declined. If he could not go to sea, he was hell-bent on being a soldier, and in no time he proved he was good at it. At sixteen he enlisted in the king's army; by eighteen he had distinguished himself, having risen to the rank of captain during King George's War. In the seemingly endless war with France, the enemy and her allies (various Indian tribes) engaged in gruesome raids upon the settlements of the New England borders, and in battles on the high seas. French-led Indians burned Saratoga in 1745 and murdered trappers and British patrols in Albany in 1746. William marched north to Albany and wintered there with his company under severe and dangerous conditions, with rusted guns, spoiled beef, and cutlasses so soft they would bend and stay bent like wax. Sixteen British soldiers were killed in a single Indian ambush.

While dozens deserted, William Franklin stood his ground, and he volunteered to join a march on French forces at Saratoga. He came home briefly in May 1747, as a captain charged with hunting down deserters and hauling them back to camp. Captain Franklin, seventeen years old, discharged this duty with a zeal and efficiency his father admired.

That year, French privateers plundered plantations along the lower Delaware. When the pacifist Quaker-dominated Assembly refused funds for arms, Ben Franklin campaigned for a voluntary defense association. Within days he gathered a thousand signatures to his proposition; weeks later he had ten thousand men armed and drilling in several companies around Philadelphia. They built a fort below the city and bought thirty-nine cannon from Boston. In all of this military business young William's advice was indispensable.

As it turned out, the kings of England and France grew weary of the distant conflict before William did, resulting in the flimsy Peace of Aix-la-Chapelle in the autumn of 1748. He returned home to Philadelphia a hero, achieving the highest rank a colonial soldier might attain without paying for a commission. Now he was welcome to dance the minuet at the Dancing Assembly of Philadelphia under the approving gaze of high society, including Dr. Thomas Graeme, whose beautiful daughter Elizabeth was soon to play a crucial role in William's life. His father was proud of the youth, who had risked his life for Crown and country at an age when most boys of his generation were serving as apprentices. With his head full of dreams of glory, he would have liked to continue as an officer, but after 1748 he had to agree with his father that the timing was wrong.

"As peace cuts off his prospect of advancement in that way," Ben Franklin wrote to Strahan, "he will apply himself to other business." The other business was not so dangerous as fighting Indians, but nearly as challenging: befriending them. Some war veterans, officers who knew William's courage and trusted his capability in the field, put his name forward for an expedition to the west. Virginia and Pennsylvania had put aside their disagreements about borders and trade, cooperating in order to negotiate a treaty with the Miami nation. The tribe had grown bitter over the high prices and shoddy goods of their recent partners, the French.

The time was ripe for the English to win the confidence of these native people, and to accomplish this, the emissaries were ordered to call upon the Indians in their own domain, the Ohio Valley territory. The distinguished interpreter Conrad Weiser had been chosen to lead the way into the Indian country on this expedition—the first ever west of the Alleghenies—and Captain Franklin was named as his personal guard.

On August 11, 1748, the embassy set out from Weiser's home in western Pennsylvania. The party included two experienced fur traders, the half-breed Andrew Montour, old Reverend Richard Peters, a Captain Trent, who had served with William in the war, and Trent's partner, a fast-talking, wily Irishman named George Croghan who would get rich acquiring land as one of the king's Indian agents on the frontier.

Franklin was fifteen years younger than any other member of this delegation, yet they looked to him for strength and leadership on the unfamiliar path. Riding ahead of a train of twenty pack horses saddled with provisions, rum, and presents for their hosts, the men took the Kittatinny path northwest through mountain passes, a trek of one hundred seventy miles in two weeks, in heavy rain. Arriving at the banks of the Allegheny River on August 25, William and several others, including Weiser, went ahead of the team in a bark canoe, coming ashore in Logstown two days later, eighteen miles down the Ohio from the Forks.

When their canoe scraped on the north bank, the delegation looked up the hill at the tepees of the trading village, and the natives in deerskin and feathers greeted them as if they had been awaiting them for weeks. The meeting with the Iroquois, Mohicans, Shawnees, and Delawares went on for days with feasting, rum drinking, and promises of friendship while the Indians waited for their presents to arrive. At last the pack horses appeared on the path curving below the escarpment, carrying the gifts of gold coins, guns, knives, blankets, and thousands of beads of wampum that sealed the pact.

"Brethren," said Conrad Weiser, "some of you have acquainted us that you had taken up the English hatchet ... and made use of it against the French, and that the French had very hard heads, and your country afforded nothing but sticks and hickories which was not sufficient to break them. You desired your brethren would assist you with some weapons sufficient to do it." The conference concluded with a peace treaty based on the king's willingness to provide weapons fit to crack the Frenchmen's skulls, an arrangement the good-hearted Weiser and his friend the Reverend Peters might not have realized could backfire, while Franklin and Captain Trent, who had fought the French and Indians above Albany, knew the danger. The Peace of Aix-la-Chapelle that derailed William's military career was only a pause in the epic war between England and France.

WILLIAM HAD KEPT A journal, which is lost. But his father's correspondence with Strahan shows that the real significance of the adventure was not in the diplomacy, or even the view of native American manners. The epiphany was the land itself, what Weiser once called "the country back of us."

From the bluffs over the Shenango, on Pennsylvania's western border, William Franklin had glimpsed the outlines of a colossus in the green vistas and panoramas of the Ohio Valley cut with silver streams, the canvas and many-colored palette upon which his generation would paint the picture of American prosperity. William was one of the first white men to see that landscape, and the impression would mark him for life. In the words of the Reverend Peters, "the moment you leave the last ridge of hills the lands are exceeding good and continue so uninterruptibly."

William realized that investment in such fertile land would make men rich. He hoped to buy acreage there in the West, farmland and timberland along watercourses for the fur trade. His father, already wealthy from the printing press that had spawned *Poor Richard's Almanac* (ten thousand copies sold per year, every year), was not so easily beguiled. Yet he agreed with William that England must not waver in laying claim to the Ohio territory.

In April 1750, Ben Franklin wrote to his mother, "As to your grand-children, Will is now nineteen years of age, a tall proper youth, and much of a beau," and was pleased to report that the youth had applied himself to his studies and would likely become a hardworking man. Meanwhile the proud father, retired from publishing at forty-five, sub-merged himself in the study of natural philosophy, of weather and elec-trical phenomena, that would soon make him one of the most famous men in the world.

In those quiet years of the midcentury, Ben Franklin engaged the aristocratic young lawyer Joseph Galloway to tutor William in the law. And he welcomed William, in his spare time, as a partner in those celebrated scientific studies. In June 1752, father and son flew the kite in the thunderstorm that has become as finely etched in our minds as the story of Isaac Newton and the apple that fell on his head. And in the summer of the following year it was William, charting the course of a lightning bolt that struck a three-story house, who ascertained that the visible electrical charge of lightning moves from the ground up and not from the clouds down, as it might appear.

All of these things and many others Ben Franklin recounted in the transatlantic correspondence with Strahan that went on for a decade before they met, letters that promised true friendship. This was instan-taneous upon the Franklins' arrival in London—for all three. Strahan was struck by William's readiness in optimizing "the daily opportuni-ties he has of improving himself in the company of his father, *who is at the same time his friend, his brother, his intimate, and easy companion.*" For four years, since their arrival in 1757, the two Americans had lived happily together in rooms on Craven Street, companions in work, travel, and study.

It was a rare chemistry indeed, a dynamic that seemed to Strahan unique—or at least uniquely American. It had been forged in a strange crucible, both military and political, a foreign climate that few En-glishmen could understand as well as he, not the lords and ladies that surrounded them, glittering, in Westminster Hall, and certainly not the young king himself.

CHAPTER 2

Colonial Contemporaries, 1753

WHILE TWENTY-THREE-YEAR-OLD WILLIAM FRANKLIN was studying law, and chasing thunderbolts as his father's laboratory assistant, the English and French had been brewing a new war.

In Europe they called it the Seven Years' War, pitting Britain and Prussia against France and the rest of Europe. In America it was known as the French and Indian War, as the Indians rekindled their affection for their old French allies, helping them drive the English trappers and traders out of the Ohio Valley and claim it for Louis XV and themselves.

Ben Franklin, having made his fortune as a printer, turned his attention to public service, science, and politics. As clerk of the Pennsylvania Assembly for years he had enjoyed a first-class seat at all its debates and deliberations. Elected a voting member in 1751, he transferred the paid position of clerk to his son. So the Franklins, as clerks and members of the Assembly, grew familiar with the pressing political controversies of the day: the tax exemption enjoyed by the rich proprietors as the descendants of Pennsylvania's founding father, William Penn, and the management of Indian affairs.

In fact, these two pressing problems—taxes and Indian affairs—

were fatally linked. William Penn had secured a grant to the Pennsylvania territory in 1681 in return for a debt the king owed his family. A Quaker, Penn claimed the land for settlement by his persecuted fellow Friends, planning to deed them parcels of it to plow. The charter that was drawn up, and a later Charter of Privileges, struck a balance of power between Penn's deputy governor and the people's elected assembly. The assembly had the rights and privilege to make laws and levy taxes "according to the rights of free-born subjects of England, and as is usual in any of the King's Plantations in America." The language was vague. The proprietors (Penn and his descendants) still held the overwhelming power to instruct deputy governors to veto budgetary bills.

The proprietary colony of Pennsylvania, still under the king's jurisdiction, was subject to a hereditary government: The proprietor and his heirs were the governors; a Penn could serve there as governor himself, or he could appoint a deputy. In 1754 Thomas Penn and his younger brother Richard were the proprietors, living in England while deputy governor Robert Hunter Morris supervised the colony in person.

The Pennsylvania charter unfairly excluded the Penns' vast holdings from the tax rolls; without such revenue the colonists lacked funds for a military defense to protect their land against hostile tribes on the frontier. When the enemy came to include the French, as it did in the 1740s and again in 1754, the lack of defense funding became so dire and intolerable that the Assembly took strong measures to address the problem.

In June 1754—while Major George Washington was already battling a French invasion below Fort Duquesne, three hundred miles west—the Pennsylvania Assembly agreed to send the Franklins up the Hudson River to Albany to a momentous conference. Convened by order of the British Board of Trade early that year, representatives from Pennsylvania, Connecticut, Maryland, Massachusetts, New Hampshire, New York, and Rhode Island were gathering to discuss Indian relations and defense measures against the French. In the new red-brick City Hall overlooking the waterfront, the bell in the white steeple called the delegates to consider their common needs and goals.

Anticipating more hostilities on the frontier, the English government wanted a pact with the Iroquois that would promise their support in the looming war. The chiefs attended. But all the diplomacy of Ben Franklin and Conrad Weiser, all the gifts of wampum, guns, and blankets, could not purchase an alliance with the Six Nations of Iroquois against the French—or anything more than sullen neutrality. The Indians' response to the English was summed up in a graceful speech by Sachem Tiyanoga: "You have asked us the reason of our living in this dispersed manner. The reason is your neglecting us for these three years past." He picked up a stick from the ground and tossed it over his shoulder. "You have thus thrown us behind your backs and disregarded us."

The great Mohawk leader in his time had looked on in amazement as the governors of Virginia and Canada quarreled over lands they knew belonged to the Six Nations. Pennsylvania had invaded Indian territory and now they were prepared to pay two thousand silver dollars for a tract of it. Surrounded by greedy white men, the Indian was hard put to decide upon an ally, but he made it clear which side had won his admiration: "Look about your country and see. You have no fortifications. . . . 'Tis but a step from Canada hither, and the French may easily come and turn you out of doors. Brethren, you desired us to speak from the bottom of our hearts, and we shall do it. . . . Look at the French; they are men; they are fortifying everywhere. But, we are ashamed to say it, you are all like women, bare and open, without any fortifications."

After hearing such a speech, no wonder Ben Franklin admitted that nothing important had been transacted there; it had not been worth the trouble. Yet one thing led to another: If the purpose of the Albany congress had been a coordinated effort by the colonies for self-preservation, and they could not count on the might of the Iroquois—the best native warriors on the continent—then the colonies must rely upon one another.

Several delegates already considered this a fine opportunity to unite the provinces, and they had arrived with plans. But the scheme that got everyone's attention was devised by Benjamin Franklin and William's tutor, Joseph Galloway. The plan Franklin put forth on July 9, 1754, included all the British North American colonies excepting Delaware and Georgia, and it called for a president general appointed by the

Crown and a Grand Council to be chosen by the representatives of the assemblies. The president would be responsible not only for Indian relations and military readiness, but also for carrying out laws pertaining to trade and finance. The number of delegates would be apportioned according to the taxes each colony paid to the General Treasury.

JOIN OR DIE read the caption beneath Ben Franklin's political cartoon: a snake broken into pieces labeled with the initials of the colonial regions: N.E. at the head, N.Y. at the neck, N.J., P., and so on down to the Carolinas at the coiled tail. The cartoon published in Franklin's *Gazette*—the first drawn by an American to represent a union of colonies—was prophetic. It would be reprinted throughout the revolutionary decade as an emblem of American strength through unity.

Franklin read his plan to the Albany congress and it was adopted the next day. The delegates submitted this program to the British Board of Trade (the parliamentary office that managed colonial affairs) and to the colonial assemblies—not only those attending, but also New Jersey, Virginia, and the Carolinas. If the king approved his plan, Franklin believed, an onslaught of turmoil and grief might be avoided. The united colonies would be strong enough to defend themselves; they would need no British troops; and there would be no pretext for Britain to levy a military tax on America.

On July 12, 1754, Ben and William Franklin, along with Reverend Peters, John Penn, and Isaac Norris (Speaker of the Assembly), set sail from Albany. The triple-sailed sloop plied the Hudson River in the spectacular green shades of the Catskills, making port in New York nine days later.

By then the news of George Washington's embarrassing defeat and the French victory in an undeclared war was the talk of the colonies.

GOVERNOR ROBERT DINWIDDIE OF Virginia had dispatched the twenty-one-year-old surveyor George Washington to invite the French to quit the territory along the Allegheny River. In the winter the French refused. In the spring of 1754, Major Washington rode out again with a regiment and orders to build an English fort at the fork of the river. By then the French had built Fort Duquesne in that very spot, and the

major's desperate efforts to build another nearby (called "Fort Necessity") on an alpine meadow led to a series of calamities and infamous
rumors.

Washington ambushed a French scouting party, and in the confusion the lieutenant in command, Joseph de Jumonville, was killed.
Soon after, the French forces overwhelmed Fort Necessity, and Washington was forced to sign a confession that he had assassinated the
young French lieutenant. The French argued that their scouting party
had been on a mission of diplomacy. We might wonder how William
Franklin would have managed the expedition to the Forks of the Ohio
given his superior experience in King George's War and his natural
equanimity. Young Washington was impetuous, and in his execution of
the business at Fort Necessity has been judged reckless.

George Washington and William Franklin were contemporaries,
William a year older. Shaped by similar forces—the spirit of the times
and comparable natural gifts—the two were marked by differences in
class and breeding. Washington was born of landed gentry, Virginia
aristocrats who owned tobacco plantations and slaves. William Franklin was a bastard, son of a mother whose identity was unknown and a
father who was a tradesman. In a world where one's family tree was
carefully charted in the family Bible it was no advantage to see half of
the branches shrouded over. Yet Franklin made the most of his natural
advantages.

While Washington was learning the art of war by trial and error,
William Franklin was toiling at his father's side to keep the peace with
the Indian tribes in the Northwest. To accomplish this, Benjamin had
proposed a "union" of colonies, the better to mount an ongoing defense.

Not the least of the difficulties in ruling an empire was the slow
communication across the ocean, the lag between command and obedience, between a petition and the verdict of Parliament. A request
that embarked on a sailing packet on August 1 would take, depending
on the weather, about six weeks to arrive in London. If King George II
himself were standing on the pier at Portsmouth to grant his grace and
turn the ship around, the assembly or congress would be waiting until
November to know his pleasure. Add to that the infernal twists and

turns of politics, deliberation, and ceremony, and it might take four months for the colonists to receive the Crown's blessing for a proposal as complex as the Albany Plan. So they waited.

In the meantime, the French, with help from the Iroquois, could swoop down from Canada and build forts near the colonial settlements, from which they could send out raiding parties of warriors to scalp the settlers. Farmers in Virginia were so frightened by the massacre of families during the previous winter, and the capture of their English fort, that they had abandoned their plantations.

Christmas came and went, and the Albany Plan was rejected on both sides of the ocean. Instead of adopting the plan, the king shipped two regiments with orders to march over the Alleghenies and take Fort Duquesne from the French. The British transports landed at Hampton, Virginia, in February under the command of General Edward Braddock, who moved them up to Alexandria, where they made camp.

Braddock was a sixty-year-old veteran who had served most of his career with the Coldstream Guards in Holland. The general had somehow risen steadily in rank without ever setting foot on any battlefield during a fight or firing a shot in anger. Steeped in the tactical theory of the Guards, innocent of gunfire and bloodshed, Braddock was an armchair general. He had a long face and a lantern jaw, and large eyes that expressed his wonder at what he was forced to endure here in His Majesty's service. With a firm sense of entitlement, faith in the chain of command, and withering condescension to anyone of lesser rank, he arrived in Virginia skeptical of Americans, and of Indians especially, an attitude that ripened into greater contempt with every passing day.

Braddock wrote immediately to the colonial governors to remind them of their duty to supply him with whatever he needed to execute his command. The Crown had already notified these governors that they would have to raise money—yet they found the general's demand high-handed. The British had not allowed for the vexing requirement that the various assemblies would have to approve of levies before they would be disbursed—it was the right of Englishmen not to be taxed by anyone but themselves. So, to expedite matters, Braddock summoned the governors of Massachusetts, New York, Pennsylvania, Maryland, and Virginia to meet with him in the State House in Annapolis, after

Easter on March 30. Then he might hear the ways and means by which his army was to be supplied and transported during their campaign against the French.

Governor William Shirley of Massachusetts, an ally of the Franklins in Albany, had been corresponding with Benjamin ever since the conference, concerning the fate of the colonial union. Shirley insisted that Franklin accompany the leaders to Annapolis. He figured the resourceful inventor, with the help of his son the captain, might do more to help the British army—by procuring supplies—than a colonial legislature with its paltry funds.

So Ben Franklin, his son, and Governor Shirley rode horseback from Philadelphia in an April downpour that washed out roads and bridges. Arriving in Annapolis a week late, they discovered that governors James Delancey and Robert Hunter Morris were likewise delayed. For the convenience of everyone, the summit was moved to Alexandria, where all repaired, on horseback, meeting with Braddock and his staff at their camp the week of April 14.

Uncertain of how Braddock would receive him, Franklin went in his capacity of the colony's postmaster general (a recent appointment), with his son William as comptroller of the postal system, to discuss maintaining the general's correspondence with the governors. But Franklin was so charming that Braddock, once in the man's company, picked his brain on every subject. And as Governor Shirley had anticipated, the Franklins thought of so many ideas for supporting the army that they became key figures in Braddock's plans, softening his prejudice against the colonists in the process.

Had it not been for the rain, and Braddock's moving the summit to Alexandria, the governors and the Franklins might not have had the pleasure of meeting George Washington when they did.

Since his embarrassment at Fort Necessity in July, the young colonel had been living at Mount Vernon, his estate on the hill a few miles away. Despite the bloody debacle in that alpine meadow, Washington still wanted a military career. He had written to Braddock's chief of staff, and the two were in negotiations concerning his accepting a position as Braddock's aide-de-camp. The general needed a soldier of Washington's experience, one who knew the terrain and the French army, and a man who understood the Indians in their shifty relation to the English. But Braddock had heard disturbing rumors concerning the disasters in the Ohio country under Washington's command, and those stories cast doubt not only on the officer's reliability but also on any hope of an alliance with the Indians.

Washington would be called to account for what happened at Fort Necessity for most of his life, but never more urgently than during that week in mid-April when he came down to meet with General Braddock and the governors in Alexandria. The incident would have been foremost in men's minds, if not the first thing they discussed in council. It was hardly dinner conversation but could not be avoided in late-night sessions when the men's tongues were loosened with wine and tobacco and rum.

Colonel Washington's efforts to drive the French from the Three Forks in 1754 had redeeming qualities to many who read his story in America and abroad. He had shown courage, worried the French, and returned with most of his men. In this he relied heavily upon an Indian ally, the Mingo chief Tanacharison, also known as the Half King. Little is known about his origins or how he came to hate the French so much. Born into a Catawba tribe at the turn of the century, he recalled, unreliably, being taken captive by French soldiers during Queen Anne's War after watching them boil and eat his father. He did not emerge as a Mingo leader until late in life, when he was designated a half king, that is, one empowered to conduct diplomacy between nations and to address the British on behalf of the Six Nations.

The French could rely upon many Indians as brothers in arms, but this leader and his Mingo warriors were not among them. When the Ohio Company began to lay the foundations of a British stockade early in 1754, it was Tanacharison who set the first log in the earth. And it was Tanacharison's scouts who alerted George Washington that a detachment of French-speaking troops was encamped in a meadow in the disputed area. The Half King implored Washington to strike first against the invaders before they could attack: "If you do not come to our assistance now, we are entirely undone." After a war council at Tanacharison's quarters, thirty-five of Washington's men and a dozen Mingo warriors set out stealthily in the dark, crossing the glen to the

French camp, forty miles south of Fort Duquesne. The commandant there, Louis Coulon de Villiers, had sent thirty-two recruits under the leadership of his half brother, Lieutenant Joseph Coulon de Villiers de Jumonville, to find Colonel Washington and order his troops out of the area. While the order could hardly be called peaceable, the Commandant explicitly forbade attacks by his men unless they were provoked.

At dawn on May 28, the British dragoons and their Indian allies came upon the French lodged in a low clearing surrounded by standing rocks. Most of the Frenchmen were still sleeping. As they stirred from slumber and took up their arms, the British fired two volleys without warning, killing nine. The rest ran but were quickly rounded up by the Indians and taken prisoner, among them the wounded commanding officer, thirty-six-year-old Canadian-born Jumonville.

There in the rising light of the alpine glen the French officer, having surrendered his arms and ordered his men to stand down, begged to read aloud the document he had been charged to deliver to Washington. The long-faced officer looked more like a priest than a soldier. As he began to read his paper in accented English, the Half King was heard to inquire if this soldier was English or French. Being informed that this was a French lieutenant reading his paper in English, Tanacharison leapt forward, his sharpened tomahawk in hand, demanding of the young Frenchman in his own tongue, *"Tu n'es pas encore mort, mon père"* ("You are not dead yet, my father"), lifted the hatchet high above his head, and brought it down in the center of Jumonville's skull, cleaving it like a melon.

Then with a shriek, before the audience of stunned soldiers, the Half King reached into the steaming red and gray matter the skull contained and washed his hands in the brains so lately filled with hope and fear. And then? No one recalled, or even wished to report much more than that the Half King sliced away the mutilated scalp for a trophy and left the scene with a battle cry of triumph, leading his Mingo warriors. He refused thereafter to serve the English, who still needed him in the defense of Fort Necessity, complaining that Colonel Washington would not follow his advice and that he had treated the Indians like slaves.

These events, and the conflicting reports that they inspired, were matters of grave concern to Braddock and the governors as they met in Alexandria a year later.

BACK IN CIVILIZATION SOME eyewitness accounts in French and English confirmed the grisly details of Jumonville's murder, and newspapers made it a *cause de scandale* on both sides of the Atlantic. Officially these two nations were at peace. Like Jumonville, George Washington had had instructions to act on the defensive. The French insisted that Jumonville was an ambassador on a diplomatic mission while Washington argued that the men were spies, an advance guard bent on ambush and guerrilla warfare. While he never confirmed the manner of Jumonville's death, he never denied it, or the fact that the lieutenant and nine other French men had been killed without warning.

Politics having its way with the facts—politics and prejudice—Washington was lauded as a hero in the colonies while he was demonized in Europe and ridiculed in England. "The volley fired by a young Virginian in the backwoods of America set the world afire," wrote the belletrist Horace Walpole, translating the words of Voltaire, who called the event "the cannon shot fired in the wilderness . . . that set Europe in a blaze." News of Jumonville's death rocked the French court. The king took note, and his ministers complained to the British ambassador that Jumonville had been foully assassinated. The English, for their part, considered Colonel Washington brave but naive and brash, reproving him for a lack of control over his troops. Naturally his standing as a villain in France made him a hero in Virginia, where the incident beyond the Alleghenies was still wrapped in a fog of contradictions, and what the French called assassination was deemed a necessary defensive tactic.

The final act of the American tragedy under Washington's command took place three weeks later: the triumph of Coulon de Villier's troops at Fort Necessity in the driving rain; the hundred Virginian soldiers dead and wounded; how the panicked survivors broke into the garrison's liquor supply and got drunk; and the crowning humiliation, the Articles of Capitulation George Washington signed, verifying the assassination of M. de Jumonville. These scenes of bloodshed and villainy were all but forgotten in the shadow of Tanacharison's act of ritual murder: the hatchet blow, the red-handed reveling in gore. It had the force of poetry that so often outlives the rude facts of history.

The facts were very important to General Braddock, the Franklins, and the five governors. And as they talked late into the night, with George Washington there in Alexandria in mid-April, and during the weeks following in Frederick Town, Maryland, the subject of Tanacharison and of Indian relations in general bedeviled Braddock as he planned his military campaign. Washington insisted that the Indians were a necessary evil in frontier warfare. During the recent conflict there had been Indians on both sides, and if the Half King had not abandoned the British after murdering Jumonville, maybe Washington would not have been crushed at Fort Necessity and forced to surrender under such terms.

In vain did Ben Franklin and George Washington commend the Iroquois and their military importance; the image of Tanacharison's deed reinforced a prejudice that ran so deep it swept up most of the white inhabitants on the continent. Braddock was stubborn. "He had too high an opinion of the validity of regular troops, and too mean a one of both Americans and Indians," wrote Franklin. The hundred braves who came from the Ohio territory and the Delaware tribe so disgusted Braddock that he made the Indian wives and children return home. When the Delaware chief Shingas asked Braddock what would become of the land when they had taken it from the French, the general replied: "The English should inhabit and inherit the land." Thinking he might not have been understood, Shingas repeated the question, once, twice, three times. Hearing the cruel echo of Braddock's original answer, Shingas explained that if his people weren't free to live on the land they would not fight for it. The general replied that he did not need their help—he would expel the French and then the Indians if need be.

After this the Indians departed, explaining that they had to protect their families back in the villages. That was the last Braddock ever saw of them, except for a dozen he paid to serve as interpreters and scouts.

Franklin and his son were more successful in raising Braddock's opinion of the colonists, who had disappointed him in their meager contributions to the expedition. The army needed pack horses, and transport wagons with teams, oats, and corn. The Franklins set out for Lancaster, where they issued circulars on April 26 asking for a hundred and fifty wagons, with four horses for each, and fifteen hundred saddle horses to be delivered to the army at Will's Creek before May 20. A footnote to the Advertisement states, "My son *William Franklin,* is empowered to enter into like Contracts with any person in *Cumberland* County." Braddock gave them £800 to disburse to the farmers. As this was insufficient, Ben advanced £200 of his own cash; within two weeks, 150 horse-drawn wagons and 259 draft horses were on their way to the camp.

As the quartermaster's agent in Maryland that spring, William Franklin would have lots of time to spend with the British officers at Frederick Town, including Braddock's new aide-de-camp George Washington, as they prepared the army for the campaign. Imagine the two young men together in the field, each of whom would have an impact on history and on each other. Both were strikingly handsome, Washington taller, with a long, lean face, athletic, hyper-erect posture, eager to command; Franklin the more easygoing. Both were men of promising character and intellect. But Washington was a genius, a fact no one at the time could have known because his was the kind of genius that must reveal itself in action.

GENERAL BRADDOCK GOT HIS horses and wagons. Yet Benjamin Franklin had grave doubts about the campaign and fears for the army. Braddock disclosed his plans with alarming confidence. Boasting he would take Fort Duquesne in three days, he said he would surely march to Niagara, knock that out, and then, weather permitting, proceed to Quebec within the week. Franklin thought of the long line the regiment must make on their march, on a narrow road that they would have to cut through the forest; he pointed out the danger of the Indians in ambush, expert in such deceptions. Braddock smiled patiently as Franklin described the plight of the column snipped like thread into pieces unable to support one another, and replied: "These savages may indeed be a formidable enemy to your raw American militia; but, upon the King's regular and disciplined troops, Sir, it is impossible they should make any impression."

As soon as Washington saw the huge cavalcade of soldiers, horses, and wagons at Frederick Town in May, he, too, saw the problem. He urged Braddock to form a "flying column" of handpicked officers and infantry, twelve hundred men who would run ahead of the wagon train directly toward Fort Duquesne. Braddock consented, but it was this column that ran afoul of a French reconnaissance detachment from Duquesne, made up of three hundred Canadians and six hundred Indians, on July 9, 1755.

The Massacre at the Monongahela resulted in more than nine hundred casualties on the British-American side: five hundred killed, including nearly all of the British officers. There were fewer than forty losses to the enemy. The Virginia troops got trapped in the crossfire between the Indians and the British. George Washington emerged as "the hero of the Monongahela" for rallying the panicked survivors, whirling on his horse, and organizing their retreat. Washington was like some Greek hero shielded by the invisible hands of a goddess as four musket balls pierced his blue coat but not his skin. Two horses were shot out from under him and he walked away without a scratch. But he would never forget the cries of the wounded, the hideous scenes of men, some still alive, being scalped by the eager Iroquois.

Braddock rode into the middle of it, caught bullets in his chest and shoulder, and fell, fatally wounded. Captain Robert Orme, also wounded, reported to Franklin the general's last words: "Who'd have thought it," Braddock muttered, as he was being carried away. "We shall better know how to deal with them another time."

When word of the defeat traveled to Philadelphia a week later, the Pennsylvania Assembly stirred from its torpor. The French commander, Claude-Pierre Pécaudy de Contrecoeur, had, in his own words, "succeeded in setting against the English all the tribes of this region who had been their most faithful allies."

Panic swept the frontier. At Penn's Creek, a hundred miles west of Philadelphia, fourteen settlers were killed and scalped; eleven others were captured to suffer no one knew what fate. At Great Cove a survivor described the horror of a "husband looking on while these Indians are chopping the head off the wife . . . and the children's blood drank by these bloody and cruel savages." From Tulpehoccon, in Berks County, news came of a massacre in which the Indians scalped even the wailing children. The German people of Reading threatened to occupy Philadelphia if military support did not arrive soon, and making good on their threat, a thousand advanced on the capital in November.

Governor Robert Hunter Morris took the part of the proprietors against Ben Franklin and his liberal colleagues in the Assembly. But in view of wagonloads of farmers demanding protection for their homes and loved ones, the Assembly voted to establish a militia on November 25, ordering a money bill for £60,000. Still refusing to be taxed in principle, the Penns granted £5000 to add to the war chest. It came none too soon.

Within the week the Assembly learned the Shawnees had attacked the settlement of Gnadenhutten, a mission twenty-five miles up the Lehigh River Valley from the town of Bethlehem, just fifty miles from Philadelphia. Sixteen Moravians were dining in their mission house when a dozen Indians burst through the door, muskets blazing, shot and killed six men, and wounded the missionary's wife. They dragged out the bleeding and dying men, scalped them, took the women as prisoners, and set fire to the house, burning all but four men who leapt out a garret window and ran for their lives into the woods. At this point William Franklin added his voice to the cries of outrage. The minister William Smith, a friend of the Penns and of Dr. Thomas Graeme, had written a malicious pamphlet attacking Ben Franklin and his militia bill; young Franklin, along with Joseph Galloway, wrote a mocking diatribe in response, *Tit for Tat*, accusing the Penns of high treason.

The Franklins were about to make more than a war of words upon the French and Indians. It was to be their destiny to pick up the pieces of the war left by General Braddock and his English regulars. More than an accident of geography cast Ben Franklin and his son in the role of soldiers—yet if they had not lived in Philadelphia in 1755, history might have taken a very different course. The Lehigh Valley of Pennsylvania was crucial to the French strategy, being the only gap in the Kittatinny mountain range broad and smooth enough to allow their cavalry and cannon to invade the great city of Philadelphia from the west.

The Assembly had voted for a militia just in time for the colonists to defend the Lehigh River Gap. And the man above all who had made this happen, through his tireless lobbying, pleading, and cajoling of the governor and the Assembly, was Benjamin Franklin. To the dismay of his enemies in the government, he was also the man most capable of mobilizing a militia on short notice.

Eight years earlier, in 1747, about the time William had enlisted in the king's army, Franklin had written a pamphlet demanding a provincial armed force for protecting the country against marauders. Drafting a charter for an "Association" of volunteers who would supply their own weapons and elect officers, he called a meeting and filled a public hall with men interested in the plan. If the British government had taken proper care of them, he protested, this would not have been necessary. He got five hundred pledges on the spot, and thousands within the week. Soon the men were organizing companies and drilling all over the province. In London, Thomas Penn denounced Franklin's militia as being founded on contempt for government: If the people could act so independently of their government as to elect officers by popular ballot, then "Why should they not act *against* it?" He called Franklin a dangerous man; yet, acknowledging that he was "a sort of tribune of the people," the proprietors chose not to interfere with his unauthorized militia.

After the Gnadenhutten massacre, the colonists were angry enough to take legal action. The Assembly appointed a seven-man Committee of Defense, with Ben Franklin as chairman, and Governor Morris was powerless to do anything about it. The new militia formed was similar to the one Franklin had conceived in 1747—but this time the Assembly of Pennsylvania had given it official legal status.

There was no time to wait for help from the king. The committee called up more than five hundred men in Philadelphia and Bucks County to serve as soldiers on the frontier on December 17. Then Governor Morris appointed a three-man commission to direct the march—Ben Franklin, ex-governor James Hamilton, and the Quaker assemblyman Joseph Fox. The Franklins accompanied the dragoons and the supply train with three Conestoga wagons bound for Bethlehem, the week before Christmas, 1755.

"Tho' I did not conceive myself well-qualified for it," Ben Franklin said, with calculated modesty, Governor Morris had actually given him a special commission with vast powers and a stack of blank commissions for any man he saw fit to appoint as an officer. The Moravians saluted him as General Franklin. He had 560 soldiers under his command, and "my son who had in the preceding war been an officer in the army raised against Canada, was my aide de camp, and of great use to me." William mustered and drilled the companies; all of Franklin's dispatches and orders from this expedition are in his son's handwriting.

By his rank as former governor, James Hamilton was supposed to command this expedition. But in late December, Governor Morris declared that the soldiers should take orders from Colonel Benjamin Franklin.

And so it was clear that Hamilton was no more than a royal watchdog sent to keep an eye on the real leader, Ben Franklin, in his civilian dress, and his son William, in his grenadier's coat of scarlet.

CHAPTER 3

Defenses and Engagements

AGAINST TOMAHAWK AND TORCH, cannon and caisson, the Pennsylvanian line of defense ran from Reading on the Schuylkill River northeast to Bethlehem and Easton on the Delaware. Beyond this chain of villages rose the verdant barrier of the Kittatinny Mountains, open only at the blue gap where the Lehigh River descended. The town of Bethlehem was nestled within the Lehigh Gap, and the settlement of Gnadenhutten lay a few miles outside it, a likely point of attack for raiders as well as a perfect bastion if fortified.

Gnadenhutten must be garrisoned, without delay, with a fort on either side of it.

In the cold twilight of December 20, the Franklins reached Bethlehem. Smoke curled, pale blue, from a hundred chimneys. Benjamin was pleasantly surprised to find the town well defended, as a new stockade guarded the main buildings. There the citizens had even gathered small paving stones and stacked them between the windows within the high houses so the women could drop them on the Indians if they tried to scale the walls. The Moravians had organized an armed watch—even though they were exempt from military duties on religious grounds.

After a night's rest at a rustic inn in Bethlehem the expedition pressed on, due north, to Easton. Farmers and hunters from all over the valley had fled to the town, overwhelming the houses and inns, depleting the food and firewood, drinking up the liquor, fighting and quarreling. The settlement was in a terrible state of disorder and panic. When the meat and rum ran low, the refugees considered abandoning the village for the rich haven of Philadelphia.

The Franklins saw that order must be restored here before they could march to the Lehigh Gap. Ben Franklin had the authority and his son the military expertise to organize these riotous refugees, punishing the troublemakers, arming the peaceable citizens. William was able to round up a hundred more recruits. They organized a military police guard with sentries at the heads of the main thoroughfares in Easton; patrols were posted around the perimeter to watch for Indians, and scouts would visit the more distant farms.

When they had secured Easton, the Franklins and their cavalry rode the fifty-five miles southwest to the stockaded log village of Reading for a conference with Governor Morris on New Year's Day. He had come from a meeting in New York with the governors from New Jersey and Massachusetts, as settlers everywhere were taking up arms. Morris meant to consider a treaty with any agreeable Indians, and to discuss other defense strategies. Conrad Weiser joined the group, and so did the Reverend Richard Peters, that other expert in Indian affairs—but it was too late. On January 3 their summit was broken up when a messenger galloped into Reading with the news of another calamity in Gnadenhutten.

The troops that had been sent recently to reinforce that hapless outpost had been attacked in darkness, on New Year's Eve, by another Indian raiding party under the new moon. No one knew how many dozens had been killed and scalped, but the eighteen surviving soldiers had been driven back through the Lehigh Gap to Allentown. The chink in the barrier was exposed again, and the frontier stood open to a full-scale invasion by the French.

One of the commissioners would have to lead the militia to rebuild the fort at Gnadenhutten—a dangerous mission that would require not only courage but skill. Above all it would require the ability to inspire confidence in a ragtag, apprehensive, and largely untrained mili-

tia. The obvious choice was Benjamin Franklin, with his aide-de-camp
William Franklin. On January 5, Governor Morris issued a commission granting Franklin dictatorial powers from the Delaware River to
the frontier, to organize, rule, distribute arms, and appoint or dismiss
officers. While Morris, Fox, and Hamilton remained in the safety of
Berks County to negotiate with the friendly Indians, the Franklins,
taking half the cavalry, rode northeast to Bethlehem in the snow, arriving the night of January 7. In eight days there they prepared troops,
wagons, weapons, and supplies for the march to Gnadenhutten.

They set out along the Lehigh River on January 15, one hundred
thirty select troops, seven supply wagons, and a kitchen wagon. The
younger Franklin led the march; his father, falling in with the surgeon
and chaplain, brought up the rear. Rangers on horseback rode ahead,
scanning the horizon from the hilltops, looking for Indians. "We shall
endeavor to act cautiously, so as to give the enemy no advantage
through our negligence," Franklin wrote. Reaching Allentown by evening, they gathered up the eighteen soldiers who had survived the
massacre and provided them with ammunition. The next morning, the
strengthened regiment marched out toward the Kittatinny Ridge in
cold rain and fog, the mud underfoot slowing the wagon wheels. One
captain wrote in his journal of the danger as "the narrow pass through
the mountains made by the Lehigh where the rocks overhang the road
on each side . . . render[s] it practicable for a very small number to destroy a thousand."

Three days later, in the afternoon, the horsemen arrived at the
charred ruin of the mission. The carnage was grisly beyond imagining,
and it was eerie to come upon the remains in bleak winter silence,
without the sound of a bird or the rustling of leaves. The Indians were
a constant but invisible menace. "All round appears nothing but one
continued scene of horror and destruction," the captain reported.
"Where lately flourished a happy and peaceful village is now all silent
and desolate, the houses burnt, the inhabitants butchered in the most
shocking manner."

After securing the camp with a rough breastwork, the soldiers
built huts of timber, then they began to bury the dead. When the rain

stopped and the fog cleared on January 20, Franklin marked out a fort plan upon the ground. By midmorning the axmen were felling trees while others with spades were digging trenches for the sharpened palisades. Within five days they had erected a stockade of 450 timbers twelve feet high and 150 yards in circumference. They hoisted a flag and fired off their muskets to christen Fort Allen. A week later and fifteen miles west they fired their guns again to inaugurate Fort Franklin, which had shot up a mere three days after the launching of Fort Norris, fifteen miles to the east. As the Indians watched from camps in the nearby hills (patrols came upon their cold campfires in the dawn), the Franklins and their carpenters established a thirty-mile bridgehead in the Lehigh Gap.

During that month the fifty-year-old Ben Franklin commanded thirteen companies, including more than five hundred militia, from the East Branch of the Delaware River to the Lehigh Valley, over thousands of square miles. Messengers galloped back and forth to headquarters as far-flung platoons countered random Indian raids and managed the care of survivors and refugees.

BACK IN PHILADELPHIA, WILLIAM's sweetheart studied the newspaper accounts of the Indian raids and atrocities in the Lehigh Valley, as they were published in *The Pennsylvania Gazette* in shocking detail. The dark-eyed lady who had captured his affections was none other than Elizabeth Graeme, daughter of the prominent physician Thomas Graeme—and a young woman of rare refinement. Her mother, remarking that Betsy was in pathetic distress over William, urged her to visit friends in Burlington to find distraction, but the girl preferred to stay in the city and wait for news of his safety.

William would return home sooner than she expected. Neither of the Franklins felt their work was quite finished when word came that Governor Morris had called the Assembly to convene on February 3, a month early. Benjamin turned the command over to Colonel William Clapham, assuring his troops that this veteran Indian fighter was "much more fit to command them than myself." The remark is comically humble. He and William had succeeded—in only four weeks—in mounting a defense of Western Pennsylvania that would be the envy of colonial militias north and south for years to come.

Ben Franklin would always insist that he had tried to avoid the public welcome that greeted him. Hearing that a party of grateful townsmen planned to hail them on the post road and escort them in triumph to the capital, the Franklins hurried on and got to town under cover of night, avoiding the fanfare and disappointing the party. But two weeks later the Philadelphia militia elected Ben Franklin their colonel, and on February 24, Morris reluctantly endorsed the commission, making Franklin's rank official. The governor's friends, the Penns, and Franklin's opponents in the Assembly were worried by the show of enthusiasm on the part of the colonel for his militia, and the militia for their commander.

Franklin paraded them on Philadelphia's Society Hill in late winter, "1200 well-looking men, with a company of artillery . . . furnished with 6 brass field pieces." The regiment accompanied Colonel Franklin to his house, where they fired off a salute. This cannot have been music to the ears of the governor, or the Penns. Franklin's adversaries had almost as much reason to fear the man who had tamed the lightning from heaven as did the Indians he had held at bay.

The day after that military review, Franklin was to leave the capital to inspect the postal routes in Virginia, and receive an honorary degree from the College of William and Mary. He opened his front door to discover "twenty officers of my regiment with about thirty grenadiers . . . on horseback . . . just as I was going to mount, to accompany me to the ferry about three miles from town. What made it worse, was, that as soon as we began to move, they drew their swords, and rode with them naked all the way. Somebody wrote on account of this to our proprietor, and it gave him great offense."

He said he was unaware of the impact at the time, feeling merely vexed by the incident. The symbolism of the guard was ominous, and the Penns' concern justified. It was hard for royal officials to believe that a man who could raise an army and inspire such zeal would choose to do anything else. "The city is in infinite distraction all owing to the officers of the militia puffed up and now solely directed by Colonel

Franklin," Richard Peters informed Thomas Penn, in London. "And the antiproprietary party will gain more ground than ever." The proprietors were relieved when Franklin left for Williamsburg on his postal rounds in March. His appointment as postmaster had been meant to buy a little of his cooperation with their deputy governor, if not the Penns themselves.

Franklin returned to the May session of the Assembly as energetic as ever in opposing the proprietors, and now he had the devotion of the militia on his side. In June, when Lord Loudon arrived to take charge as commander in chief of His Majesty's army, Governor Morris chose Colonel Franklin to brief him. He had earned the honor.

Thomas Penn would have done almost anything to block Franklin's influence; in fact he tried to have him stripped of his postmastership. Failing that, he declared to Morris that the Militia Act violated not merely proprietary control of the colony but a basic principle of imperial rule: the commissioning of officers. This was true, and the Crown repealed the Militia Act that very summer, in July 1756, canceling all its commissions.

Governor Morris was soon gone, replaced by the affable Captain William Denny in August. A small middle-aged soldier with a large nose and perpetual smile, long-necked and horse-faced, Denny would carry on the proprietors' struggle against Franklin and the Assembly with a lighter touch. Denny meant to snare with honey what Morris could not quell with vinegar, arriving in Philadelphia with a gold medal in his pocket for Benjamin Franklin: the Copley Medal of the Royal Society for scientific achievement. In fact the prize had been awarded to him in November 1753, for the lightning experiments, but it was never delivered for reasons none but the Penns might have known. Now the timing was favorable, and Franklin would never forget the surprising conversation that followed his acceptance of the honor. Denny chose to present the medal at a reception for himself, the new governor, with remarks expressing his long-held esteem and praise for Franklin's character.

When the cloth was removed from the dinner table and the gentlemen were embarked upon the customary vessels of port, wine, rum, and whiskey, Denny drew him aside into an adjoining room. Franklin later recalled that Denny confided, "He had been advis'd by his friends in England to cultivate a friendship with me, as one who was capable of giving him the best advice, & of contributing most effectually to the making of his administration easy."

The governor, a career officer in His Majesty's service, declared that his greatest desire was to have a firm understanding with Franklin; and so he promised to render Franklin any favor in his power. He then praised the Penns' good faith, and how advantageous it might be to everyone if the conflict between the proprietors and the people could be dropped and harmony restored. Who could be more influential in restoring that harmony than Colonel Franklin, who "might depend on adequate acknowledgments & recompenses & c. & c?" Franklin was being bribed. The rest of the drinkers, remarking that the guests of honor had not returned to the table, sent them a decanter of Madeira, "which the Governor made liberal use of, and in proportion became more profuse in his solicitation and promises."

Franklin assured Denny that his circumstances were such that he wanted no favors from anybody. And as an Assembly member he could not ethically accept them. In any case he had no personal quarrel with the proprietors, and whenever Denny should propose a measure that benefited the people, he would endorse it as zealously as anyone. His opposition, he promised, had only been against measures that favored the Penns' interests above the people's. In particular he hoped that Captain Denny had not come to Philadelphia shackled by "the same unfortunate instructions that had hampered Governor Morris." This sentiment, which the newcomer neither encouraged nor deterred, hung in the air between them like a wisp of tobacco smoke until they rose, with expressions of courtesy and good faith, to rejoin the other gentlemen at their table.

Franklin liked Governor Denny as a contemporary, a drinking fellow, and an engaging conversationalist, a well-read man who had seen the world. But as a royal governor, Denny had no more freedom to exercise his good judgment, even in a crisis, than did the others. He was bound by unwritten instructions to pass no bills unacceptable to the proprietors.

In September the Assembly pledged £30,000 for defense, under protest that the proprietors would not yield a shilling. But it was too little too late, as the wrangling over taxation had created a political tangle among the Indian tribes. The Iroquois of the Six Nations who had chosen again and again to fight for the French now maintained a hostile truce with the English. The Delaware tribe was dangerously divided between the Susquehanna Delawares, who said they were friendly, and the Ohio Delawares, who had declared war on the British in October 1755. The Susquehannas needed supplies from the government if they were going to join the Pennsylvanians in fighting the French. While the assemblymen had been bickering over who would pay, Fort Allen and the others Franklin had built had fallen into disrepair and confusion, compromised by inept officers and Indian double agents. The settlers on the frontier as well as the peaceable Indians lived in fear of raiding parties made up of venal warriors of every Indian nation crazed with rum.

Rum, in fact, was the unspoken demon in most negotiations and failed treaties with the Delaware nation. That evil influence has been largely expunged from the histories. Access to rum, or its prohibition, assured or canceled oaths and pacts no sooner than they were sworn. The charismatic Teedyuscung, king of the Delawares and spokesman at the historic Easton treaty conferences that began in July 1756, was not more famous for his bold protests against Penn's thievish land deals than he was for his astonishing capacity and pathetic thirst for rum. Teedyuscung was the most influential Indian east of the Alleghenies, and he was a slave to rum, the pawn of any trader or garrison officer who could provide him with a cask of it.

Soon after the first Easton conference that summer, Teedyuscung had instigated a riot and mutiny within the garrison at Fort Allen. After this, Lord Loudon, commander in chief, forbade the governors to treat with him. Nevertheless, Governor Denny—under pressure from his council, and desperate for support among the Delawares— gave in at last to the petitions of the Delaware chief, agreeing to meet with him in the autumn.

Denny chose to travel with Benjamin Franklin, who knew the military conditions better than any of the other commissioners. In the fading foliage of early November, the forty-mile journey along the river north to Easton would have been pleasant had it not been for the couriers who stopped the party with conflicting messages. Some would tell them to turn back, warning that an ambush awaited them at the next turn. Other Indian scouts cautioned that the conference was a trap set by Teedyuscung to assassinate the governor and massacre every white person in the village. A brave would pull up with his message, then turn his horse and ride away, leaving the governor and Franklin to ponder their safety as well as the lives of the parties who followed. Another Indian would appear, with more testimony: The last messenger had lied, and was in fact a sworn enemy of Teedyuscung or a friend of the French who wished to sabotage the conference and all agreements between the Delawares and the English.

Bravely the governor and Ben Franklin rode on, in peril of their lives, despite the shrieking of crows and Lord Loudon's prohibitions, their pistols primed, swords at the ready. They arrived in Easton on November 7, finding Teedyuscung royally drunk under a full moon.

The next day the meeting began under the wide blue sky: Fifty Indians faced the governor and his council, militia officers, citizens of Easton, and a group of Quakers from Philadelphia. Rising to address the gathering, King Teedyuscung was not so much imposing as he was resentful, mournful, and sentimental. He spoke, Weiser translating as needed. Then Denny spoke, exchanging ceremonial overtures and compliments in turn until Ben Franklin, hoping to bring the conversation to its point, whispered to the governor. He should ask what the Englishmen might have done in the past to offend the Delawares and provoke their violence against England.

In response, Teedyuscung brought forth a bill of complaints that went back generations, fraud after fraud that robbed the Indians of their land until now they had nowhere left to hunt—their only livelihood. This was not the speech the Indian king had planned, nor a topic the governor had come to discuss. Passions prevailed nevertheless, and the painful subject of land transactions took over.

What was supposed to be a military peace summit disintegrated into a court of equity. When it was concluded, Teedyuscung had pledged on his part a vague peace with the English in exchange for £400 sterling to be provided by the Quakers and distributed to the king and his retinue. By then it was obvious that the Delaware sachem's status as spokesman for his nation was doubtful. News had come through several channels that he spoke mostly for himself and unreliably. He returned to Fort Allen with his women and court and five gallons of rum, under the surveillance of Weiser. He knew, as did Governor Denny and Ben Franklin, that they had risked their lives and wasted time and money to forge an alliance that would be meaningless to the Delawares, the Six Nations, and the commander in chief, Lord Loudon, who had expressly forbidden it. The settlers on the frontier, the corrupted string of forts the Franklins had built in the Lehigh Valley—all were more vulnerable than ever to the French and the unreliable Indians.

Knowing the danger, Governor Denny, a professional soldier, requested £125,000 in December for defense. But once again the Assembly protested the conditions—that the proprietors would not be taxed and that the people would not control the army. They voted £100,000, on more democratic terms. The governor vetoed the bill in January, because it was £25,000 short and violated his instructions. Assembly and governor had reached a bitter impasse in which—as Franklin later recalled—the Assembly at last, finding that the proprietors had manacled Denny with instructions that violated the people's rights as well as the king's needs, resolved to petition the Crown directly against the Penns.

So the delegates appointed Ben Franklin to serve as their agent, to sail for England to present and support the petition. As the time had come for William to complete his law studies at the Inns of Court, the Assembly also agreed "That William Franklin have leave to resign his office of clerk to this house, that he may accompany his father" on his mission to London.

THE PROSPECT OF THE sea voyage lent some urgency to William's courtship of Miss Elizabeth Graeme, which had weathered several storms: parental opposition, the terror of Indians, and Betsy's own doubts. He had known her for years before their courtship began, late in 1752, during the Yuletide season. William was twenty-one years old and Betsy Graeme was an intense brunette of fifteen with large wide-set brown eyes, a high intelligent brow, a small mouth, and a shapely chin. Daughter of the prosperous physician and adviser to the Proprietors of Pennsylvania, Dr. Thomas Graeme, and Ann Diggs, her own father a baronet, Elizabeth was the youngest of four children raised in two homes—a house in Philadelphia where the family wintered, and an elegant stone mansion twenty miles north where they lived the rest of the year. Graeme Park was one of the most beautiful estates in America, a model of landscape gardening. The house featured a paneled library, fourteen-foot ceilings, marble fireplaces, and a harpsichord in the immense drawing room.

In December 1752, Elizabeth and William shared lottery tickets for a prize to be announced at the New Year. The suspense between Christmas and New Year's Day became a subject of flirtatious banter as the youngsters speculated about winning, losing, and the meaning of the lottery tickets, as reality and as poetry. William begged her, melodramatically, not to tell him their "tickets" were worthless, and she replied in verse, that the lottery tickets were "like the new fell snow / Or as the paper clear; / Before the pen, that scribbling foe, / Makes characters appear."

They themselves, the youth and the girl, were the "tickets," their characters not quite formed. Yet they would amount to something as individuals, and perhaps something greater as lovers. William's bond with Miss Graeme, from flirtation to engagement, reveals a great deal about his personality. She was, from early youth, a poet, in a culture in which poetry played an important role in shaping values. People memorized poems, reciting them in public and quoting them in private conversation, as code, to enrich an argument or express a sentiment. She wrote in her commonplace book that there was "a certain elevation of soul . . . a noble turn of virtue that raises the hero from the plain honest man, to which Verse only can raise us." William shared this notion, joining Elizabeth and her friends in an exchange of ideas in verse.

She was one of a circle of women who loved books and music. Her closest friends were Sally Denormondie, for whom Elizabeth wrote lyrics to be sung to Scottish melodies, and her best friend, the poet Rebecca Moore, whose family owned an estate in Chester County above the Schuylkill. This group shared a mystical passion for the land-scape, the fresh hills, meadows, and valleys of their country. But Eliza-beth Graeme was a mind apart, a witty, passionate writer who would one day earn her renown as the most learned woman in America.

William visited Betsy and her friends in town in the winter. In the summer he missed her. While the women in Betsy's circle were enjoy-ing a house party at Graeme Park on August 16, 1753, he wrote a poem addressed to her, "A Song by a Young Gentleman to Some La-dies in the Country at Horsham," confessing his longing for

Ye Ladies! Who are now retired
To groves and purling springs . . .

The hot city seemed dull and dreary without them. According to his poem, the men whiled away their hours in idle pursuits such as card games at which somehow everyone at the table lost—a fate they blamed on the absence of the maidens. Autumn comes to their relief, and

Rude Winter comes to end our Grief
And with it brings our Loves;
'Tis to the chilling Frosts and Snow
That we our happiest moments know.

Betsy invited him to join her friends at Graeme Park in October 1753. The entertainment the first evening was a debate in verse, and she kept a record of the dialogue. William Franklin composed or re-cited one side in the role of Damon the Cynic, and some other poet—probably Betsy herself—composed the other in the role of the tenderhearted Alexis.

What was to be resolved in this battle of wits? Whether it is better to grieve with others in their sorrow or to stand aloof, getting on with one's life, heedless, dispassionate: "Whether the feeling or insensible Minds were happiest thro' Life." Alexis is distressed that his own pov-erty has left him unable to help the needy widow and children of a friend who has passed away. William, in the role of Damon, asks why

Alexis should bear "the weight severe of others' pain," voicing the ancient stoic opinion:

> *The truly wise and happy man*
> *That's he who is not discomposed*
> *By others' pleasures or their woes.*

Alexis protests. Damon's is a perfect recipe for dullness:

> *A mind formed on this narrow plan*
> *Is dwindled to degenerate man,*
> *His life at best a waking dream*
> *In short at most a mere machine. . . .*
> *Cooly they speak, they never feel,*
> *Their souls are harden'd o'er with steel!*

But wait, Damon insists: Life is unfair. There is more pain in it than joy, so our only hope for sanity is indifference. To this argument Alexis responds in the lover's lyric triumph, invoking his mistress, Sylvia:

> *When Sylvia comes with pleasing smiles,*
> *And every anxious care beguiles,*
> *No sorrow preys upon my mind,*
> *But flies like chaff dispersed by wind.*

William—eager to give up this role as the heartless Damon—nods, acceding to this flight of sentiment, sighing. He is now convinced, and the two debaters vow eternal allegiance to each other.

The entertainment is revealing. William the soldier had a touch of the poet in him, and like Elizabeth, he was a romantic. In this attitude these young people set themselves apart from their parents who, in 1753, were steeped in neoclassicism, the age of Pope and Voltaire. Ben Franklin himself was an avatar of Enlightenment sensibility, reining in his emotions and favoring reason over feeling and imagination. The rise of Romanticism was gradual in the eighteenth century. Here we see it in its early flowering, in the lyrics of these young adults who have just discovered the verses of Thomas Gray, and soon would be singing the songs of Robert Burns.

But it was William's fate that even his romantic life in that era was roiled by war and politics. War with the French and Indians had polarized Pennsylvania as the proprietors and the elected Assembly wrangled over money. Like Romeo and Juliet, William and Betsy were star-crossed lovers, coming from families in deadly opposition. Betsy's father, Dr. Graeme, had become a close friend of the proprietor Thomas Penn when he lived in Philadelphia. The men stayed in touch after Penn returned to England, Graeme sometimes offering advice concerning business and politics in the province. Penn's sister Margaret lived nearby, the doctor's patient. The witty, charming Betsy was a favorite of all the Penns, who visited the Graemes' homes in town and country.

Meanwhile, Benjamin Franklin had become a leader of the colonial opposition, the Quaker party, the largest in the colony. It stood opposed to the Penns and their party, which included the deputy governor and his supporters, gentlemen like the Reverend Richard Peters and Dr. Thomas Graeme. Dr. and Mrs. Graeme may have admired Franklin for his success in business, science, and public service, but they were not fond of him. Nor did they smile upon a match with his son, who shared his opinions. William's pamphlet *Tit for Tat*, accusing the Penns of being allies of the French in 1755, did nothing to advance William's cause with Betsy's parents, and it put seeds of doubt in her mind about her future with this outspoken young man.

Still, by the time William returned from his dangerous mission in the Lehigh Valley—in part because of it—Betsy was as much in love with him as he was with her, although she was coy. In a letter dated February 26, he complained because a clergyman visiting her house was coming between them. There was but one service William desired from a clergyman, he hinted. "Guess what that one thing is?" With this letter he included some poetry, confessing that he had been beguiled before by pretty faces, but no maid had ever stolen his heart until now:

But now O Love! I own thy Reign
I find thee in my Heart;
I know yet bear the pleasing Pain
For Laura *threw the Dart*
Laura's *too powerful Charms have shown,*
My heart is now no more my own.

Her response in the role of Laura was sympathetic but cautious. Like him, she writes, she has been entertained by various beaux; all of them before now simply "made a jest of Cupid's Power." However, her passion for William had arisen out of their friendship, not romance. They had enjoyed the advantage of communing without the burdens of possessive courtship. And now,

There's various Reasons to be seen,
Which make it wrong to join . . .

That is, the families on both sides disapprove. Despite her "warm affection," she pretends to give him up.

Oh may he ever happy be!
In loving, or forgetting me.

The Franklins had just accepted the appointment to confront the proprietors in London. One reason for the twenty-year-old woman to resist William's suit was that he would be gone a long time. Her hope for him, in parting, is her wish that he not "long in distant Climes remain / But meet with *Laura* once again." This maiden resists her lover only to inflame him and inspire him to renew his advances. It worked. William called her his "dear Tormentor."

During the spring of 1757, before his departure, William did everything he could to persuade the Graemes to bless their union. He found some favor with Ann Graeme—later he acknowledged her "repeated acts of civility," from "the best of women." But Dr. Graeme remained opposed. In William's absence, the infatuation, he thought, would fade away. William, fearing the same, suggested a private ceremony before his departure, but the doctor dismissed this as improper. Not even Betsy suggested that she should sail with the Franklins on their mission as a new bride.

William had to be satisfied with the sweet knowledge that he had won Betsy's heart, overcoming her doubts and reservations. They considered themselves engaged. On the political score he was reassuring: The purpose of his mission to England was to reconcile all differences with the proprietors so that these would no longer be an obstacle to their happiness. She then vowed that she would be faithful to him, and constant, and true, and her love "could by neither Time or Absence be set aside or diminished."

En route to New York, where he was to embark for England, William wrote to Elizabeth on April 7 that the clouds in the morning were lowering but by midday the sky was clearing. It reminded him of their love that likewise

> is still overcast threat'ning a wrecking storm; who knows but kind Heav'n may graciously permit a charming sun to scatter these Clouds of Difficulties which hang over us, and afford a Noon and Evening of Life, calm and serene. I trust our Conduct will be such as to deserve this mark of Divine Goodness.

William was about to enter a social and political maelstrom more powerful and transforming than any experience he could imagine, where the storm raging around him would come to mirror his inner turmoil. It would take remarkable conduct indeed for this soldier to return from abroad with the "mark of Divine Goodness."

THE ASSEMBLY HAD FORMALLY resolved that William Franklin would serve as aide to the distinguished American, Benjamin Franklin—the man most likely to convince the royal authorities of the selfishness and folly of the proprietary government.

Richard Peters, the proprietors' secretary in Philadelphia, knew Franklin's power. Writing to Thomas Penn in London, he warned that the inventor/colonel meant to overturn the colonial government. His popularity, and the celebrity he had gained by his scientific discoveries, would make him a dangerous opponent indeed. Penn was unmoved. "Mr. Franklin's popularity is nothing here. He will be looked very coolly upon by great people." The philosophers and intellectuals who cared about electric experiments—and Penn knew many of them— were far removed from "the sort of people who are to determine the dispute between us." Let Franklin come when he pleases, Penn concluded. He was in "no ways uneasy at the determination."

The Franklins, with their trunks and two negro servants, boarded the sailing packet *General Wall* in early June. They arrived in London on July 27, 1757, ready to make their case against the proprietors.

CHAPTER 4

Challenges, 1757

AFTER FOURTEEN YEARS OF lively correspondence it is fair to say that neither of the letter writers—Ben Franklin or William Strahan—was disappointed when at last they came eye to eye.

On the very morning of the Franklins' arrival in London, the men shook hands in the parlor of their mutual friend the naturalist Peter Collinson in Mill Hill, north of the city. The ocean voyage of twenty-seven days had been favored by winds but perilous. They were chased twice by privateers and nearly wrecked upon the infamous granite rocks of Scilly, off the coast of Cornwall, the night before landing in Falmouth. William remarked, "Let the pleasures of the country be ever so great, they are dearly earned by a voyage across the Atlantic." And his father added, "Were I a Roman Catholic, perhaps I should on this occasion vow to build a chapel to some Saint, but as I am not, if I were to vow at all, it should be to build a lighthouse."

The hours passed swiftly for these men who had been virtual friends for so many years. They were wits for whom conversation was sport, pastime, and a necessity like air and water. Strahan was captivated. "For my own part," he wrote to Mrs. Franklin, "I never saw a man who was, in every respect, so perfectly agreeable to me. Some are amiable in one view, some in another, he in all."

By correspondence Strahan had come to know Ben Franklin, as one printer to another. Franklin had longed for a London "agent" who could keep him abreast of current events in the capital and send him books and papers. He had given Strahan a blanket order to send him any book worth reading—excepting theology. By 1745 the two publishers were exchanging crates of their books wholesale, and the American was ordering most of his printing supplies, lead fonts, press parts, and stock from Strahan. Their letters eventually became personal: from regards to wives and children (Strahan had married young and happily and had many offspring), the correspondents turned to matchmaking. By the 1750s they were referring to Franklin's seven-year-old daughter Sarah and Strahan's ten-year-old son Billy as betrothed, daughter-in-law and son-in-law, in good fun.

And when the time came to guide William Franklin's career it was Strahan who entered the young man's name in the rolls of the Middle Temple of the Inns of Court, where William would now commence his law studies. The king's printer would use all of his influence and knowledge of English politics to help these American agents achieve a goal he knew to be salutary to the whole empire—the fair enfranchisement of the British colonists.

From the time of Ben Franklin's arrival in London until the day of George III's coronation in 1761, he faced challenges that would have daunted an ambassador with much greater experience and authority. He was, in fact, not an ambassador at all but the humble agent of a colonial assembly that had little legal power apart from what the proprietary governor granted.

Franklin must base his claim upon the natural rights of Englishmen, rights promised by the ancient Magna Carta but not, at present, by the colonial charter of Pennsylvania. Underlying every point of his argument must be the potential might of the American people, the dagger beneath the cloak. If the Empire was going to thrive, then the colonies must be secure against the French and the Indians. For Pennsylvania to survive, it needed an army, and the Penns must pay for their fair share of it. What reasoning stirred on the other side of this argument was rooted in medieval history, the feudal belief in the sanctity of property rights, of private ownership.

If Franklin presumed his Assembly's powers were akin to Parliament's, Lord Granville, president of the Privy Council (the king's cabinet), was quick to correct him. Granville, born John Carteret, was as
famous at age sixty-seven for his knowledge of Greek, German, and
philosophy as for his diplomacy. The American scientist—advised to
call upon the great Lord only days after arriving in London—may be
forgiven for thinking they might be like-minded.

Perhaps he called too early. Fond of burgundy, John Carteret was
not cheerful before noon. In any case, Franklin was stunned by his
abruptness: "You Americans have wrong ideas of the nature of your
constitution; you contend that the King's instructions to his governors
are not laws, and think yourselves at liberty to regard or disregard
them ... but ... they are the *Law of the Land,* for THE KING IS THE
LEGISLATOR OF THE COLONIES."

This was news to Franklin, who recorded it, his capital letters capturing Granville's tone of voice. He understood that the king might
veto the Assembly's laws, but he believed that the king had no right to
make a law without its consent.

"He assured me I was totally mistaken," Franklin reflected, after
leaving Lord Granville's gilded chambers in dismay, painfully aware
that the president of the Privy Council was related by marriage to the
Penns. Making short work of the meeting, Granville had informed
him that the final arbiter of the dispute was his Privy Council, who
would advise the king, whose word was law.

Dr. John Fothergill, a friend of Collinson's, had advised Franklin
that he should appeal to the Penns first, but that he must also honor
Lord Granville. No more than a week in London, and the second most
important man in government had warned Franklin that his very presence in court was a presumption.

As his coach made its way through late morning traffic up Whitehall toward the center of the city, Franklin brooded in the August heat.
On his right hand rose the palatial Tudor façade of Northumberland
House, home of Sir Hugh Percy, Earl of Northumberland, and a bastion of Tory power. Two blocks past it the coachman reined his horse,
slowing to turn into Craven Street under the stone arch. It framed a
narrow passage of cobblestone out of the Strand that grew wider as the

coach put into the block of modest brick houses, twenty on the west side, fifteen on the east, the cul-de-sac fronting south on the embankment and a weathered wharf.

The dwellings looked alike, three stories high, brick fronts with recessed window openings, iron railings at the street level, iron balconies outside the second-story windows, dormers above, tiled roofs. He had liked the modest elegance of the place immediately. He liked his landlady, Mrs. Stevenson, exactly his age, fifty-one, and her bright daughter, Polly, sixteen years old.

The hackney slowed to a halt at No. 7 on the left, the east side, not far from the river. Ben Franklin carefully descended, in a state of mind as near to panic as this man—famed for his equanimity—was likely to experience. He had decided the moment he left Lord Granville that he would transcribe their dialogue verbatim as soon as he got home, so that his excitement would not subject his memory of the important matter to any distortion.

The gracious widow Margaret Stevenson would understand his haste and preoccupation now as she greeted him beneath the arch of the door, then watched her lodger pass from the paneled hall and reach for the stair rail purposefully. He was like no man she had ever seen, this American, reserved but witty, kind and resolute. The sound of his determined steps echoed as he climbed up to the rooms he shared with his son on the second floor. Up there were four paneled rooms, spacious, bright. The front room parlor looked out upon Craven Street through three large windows. If he leaned out the window he could see the river. The tide surged darkly under the white arches of Westminster Bridge. The midday light shone from the windows upon the chimney piece of carved wood with pilasters to the jambs; a few chairs, a cupboard, chests, and a writing desk where Franklin sat down, took up his quill, dipped it in ink, and wrote down Granville's words concerning the Crown's instructions to colonial governors: "They are first drawn up by judges learned in the laws; they are then considered, debated & perhaps amended in Council, after which they are signed by the King. They are then so far as relates to you, the *Law of the Land* . . ." If a man of Franklin's age could be made to feel like a schoolboy, that was precisely Granville's intention.

FRANKLIN AWAITED A NOD from the proprietors. Thomas Penn lived nearby in a mansion befitting one of the richest men in England, in Spring Gardens, a byway that gave onto St. James's Park, not five minutes' walk from Craven Street. The chief proprietor and the colonial agent could hardly avoid each other in their comings and goings in the shadow of Northumberland House, or skirting the statue of King Charles upon his horse in the center of Charing Cross junction.

Thomas Penn might have met Franklin in Philadelphia back in the 1730s, but only in passing. Their differences in station and principles made them natural enemies. Penn's business in those years was defrauding the Indians, swindling them out of their land, and attempting to banish the Roman Catholics from the colony. More recently he and Franklin had exchanged letters on the subject of electricity; but since Franklin had founded the militia in 1748, Penn had been convinced that this was a person to be avoided if at all possible.

In 1751, Penn, at forty-nine years of age, had returned to England for good. He joined the Church of England, and married the twenty-two-year-old daughter of an earl. The most un-Quakerly son of William Penn, he grew so impatient with the opposition of the Quaker-dominated Assembly that he campaigned—one year before Franklin's arrival—to remove all Quakers from office by ordering an oath of loyalty in every colonial legislature. As their faith prohibited them from swearing oaths, the law would have shut them out of the government. But Penn's lobby failed and the Quakers kept their seats. They interfered constantly with his policies and browbeat his deputy governors, and now they had sent this upstart inventor to insist that his land be taxed.

At fifty-five, Penn was slender and fine-boned, with delicate features, bright eyes, and a dimpled chin. He had an air of supercilious mischief about him, and a smile ready to turn into a sneer. His portrait shows him dressed impeccably in an embroidered silk coat of grayish lilac, dun breeches, and a long white satin waistcoat.

When Franklin had been in his neighborhood for a few days, Penn sent word via Dr. Fothergill that he would receive him in his drawing room toward the end of the third week of August.

Franklin visited his antagonist in his home with all the rituals of courtesy. Penn was civil, inquiring about friends, complimenting the inventor on his book *Opinions and Conjectures* concerning electricity. Franklin had sent it to him in appreciation of Penn's having provided the Philadelphia Library Company "a complete electrical apparatus" for his experiments. Such pleasantries soon gave way to business that Penn would have preferred to avoid, including promises of a reasonable accommodation, as Franklin recalled, adding that each side had its own notion of what was reasonable.

Franklin began by stating the Assembly's complaints. First, Governor Denny's power of making laws with the advice and consent of the Assembly, and raising funds for the country's safety, had been abridged by Penn's instructions that Denny might grant no defense funds without the proprietor's assent. In wartime this posed a great risk to British soldiers, even the total loss of the colony to the enemy.

Second, the Assembly's right to purchase supplies in wartime had been infringed by similar "instructions" that the governor refuse any bill for raising money that did not meet with Penn's approval in every particular. Thus the Assembly was forced either to lose the country to the enemy, or to give up the people's freedom to make their own laws.

Third and last, the proprietors had instructed their governor "to refuse his assent to any law for raising money by a tax, tho' ever so necessary for the defense of the country," unless their lands were exempt.

Franklin concluded by saying that the people of Pennsylvania regarded this as unjust and cruel. He later recalled that Penn justified his conduct as well as he could—which meant that he invoked his rights and duties as a *grand seigneur*. Just as Thomas Penn was responsible to King George for the colony of Pennsylvania, so was the Assembly answerable to the Penns, and the governor to his instructions. The proprietor and his governor had to protect the king's interest in every particular; the governor's control over the purse strings was standard practice.

"We now appeared very wide, and so far from each other in our opinions, as to discourage all hope of argument," Franklin later reflected. Nevertheless, before seeing his guest to the door, Thomas Penn asked Franklin to present his complaints in writing, and said that he and his brother would consider them. Franklin complied, drawing up the document on Sunday, August 20, to be delivered to Spring Gardens by one of his servants that day or the next.

Franklin settled in to his new lodgings, six city blocks distant, to await the proprietor's formal response. That was August 1757, and the Penns would keep him waiting for a long, long time, hoping he might give up and go away.

Anxious, fatigued, and far from home, the traveler got sick a week later. "A violent cold and something of a fever," he wrote to his wife, "attended by great pain in my head, the top of which was very hot, and when the pain went off, very sore and tender." Dr. Fothergill was worried and prescribed the powder of contrayerva root, Jesuit's bark (quinine), and hartshorn drops. He grew alarmed as Franklin's fits of pain continued twelve hours at a time, and once as long as thirty-six. The patient grew delirious, suffering continually from vertigo and a maddening ringing in his ears. "Too soon thinking myself well I ventured out twice, to do a little business and forward the service I am engaged in, and both times got fresh cold and fell down again."

This went on for weeks, then months. He heard the sound of bees in his head and saw faint twinkling lights. He kept trying to get up. Dr. Fothergill grew furious and denied him not only permission to leave his bed, but also the use of pen and ink. It is hard to say from this distance in time what ailed him—probably some strain of encephalitis, a brain inflammation—and he was fortunate it did not carry him off that summer. On December 15 he wrote to Deborah that he was better, "but have not yet quite recovered my strength, flesh, or spirits. I every day drink a glass of infusion of bark in wine, by way of prevention, and hope my fever will no more return."

Not until the new year would Franklin be strong enough to renew his petition. He was fortunate in having an excellent doctor who did not bleed him to death or poison him; and "the good lady of the house," Margaret Stevenson, grew very fond of him and "nursed me kindly." Above all he was fortunate in having William's attention. "Billy was also of great service to me, in going from place to place, where I could not go myself." This, like some other crumbs of praise Franklin scattered throughout his writings, is an understatement. "Billy" was not just running errands for his father as he passed in and out of consciousness. At twenty-six, he had virtually taken over the consulate his father was too feeble to command.

William wanted foremost to focus upon his law studies at the Middle Temple, one of the schools or Inns of Court, a cluster of medieval and Gothic buildings at the east end of the Strand. The Inner Temple, as the enclosure was called, lay between Fleet Street and the river, not fifteen minutes' walk from Craven Street. While his father conferred with Granville and Thomas Penn, William explored the ivy-covered haunts of his future academy: such as the Middle Temple Hall, with its stained glass windows, oak paneling, and heraldic coats of arms. Elizabeth the First had dined here, and Sir Francis Drake. The last school term was just ending, and the next would not begin until November.

So when his father was stricken, William was able to devote full time to their mission. Indeed, during the months of September and October, there was very real concern on the part of the Franklins and their friends, and mean-spirited hope on the part of their enemies, that the agent for Pennsylvania might not live to complete his task. The Penns were taking no chances, organizing a public relations campaign to discredit the colonists, placing malicious, unsigned articles in the London papers. These letters claimed that the lamentable state of the colony's defenses had one cause: the craven Quakers, whose faith excused them from taking up arms against their enemies or even offering support to those who would.

As Benjamin Franklin was in no condition to respond to these libels, his son took up his pen and wrote "To the Printer of the *Citizen*," dated September 16, 1757, beneath the casual return address "Pennsylvania Coffee-house, London." His letter of several thousand words begins by quoting a venomous paragraph from the London *Citizen* of September 9, "calculated to prejudice the public against the Quakers and people of Pennsylvania," then sets forth six paragraphs meant to set the record straight.

The slanderer called Pennsylvania a colony where Indians had overrun the country, scalping innocent people while bills to raise funds for defense sank because of the Quakers. William answered out of hard-earned experience: First, the scalping of citizens was not peculiar to

Pennsylvania but common to all the colonies. Second, the frontiers-men weren't Quakers but Presbyterians and Moravians quick with saber and gun. Third, the disputes between the governors and the Assembly were caused by a foolish law that exempted the Penns from taxes. Fourth, while the Quakers declined to bear arms, when they had dominated the Assembly they had voted along with the rest to grant funds for the king's use, which were then applied to defense.

William refuted the charge that the Indians were at the heart of the country, and that political bickering hindered efforts at defense. He pointed out that more had been done in Pennsylvania to defend the frontier than in any other colony: Fifteen forts had been raised; dozens of cannon were purchased, thousands of rifles and pistols—all of these deployed without benefit of a shilling from other colonies or the Crown.

In closing, William described himself as one who had recently left Philadelphia, was now in London, was not and never had been a Quaker, and wrote "purely to do justice to a province and people" recently abused in anonymous articles. He called upon the slanderer to come forth with proof for his charges—or to take shame upon himself. This was a persuasive letter fortified with facts. Readers unaware of Benjamin's grave illness may have believed it had originated from the father's hand and not the son's, but the writing was all William's. He took pride when the letter appeared in *The London Citizen,* then in *The London Chronicle* of September 17–20, 1757, at the cost to the writer of one pound. It soon was reprinted in *The Gentleman's Magazine,* as well as in *The Pennsylvania Gazette,* where his fiancée read it.

BETSY HAD WRITTEN HIM on the first of October, no doubt wondering why she had not heard a word since his arrival in England on July 17. His letter to her on December 9 is an apology and explanation for his delay.

William is writing by candlelight at two o'clock on a Friday morning. The faint fragrance of wax lightens the coal fumes. His father is sleeping fitfully in the bedroom next door. He can hear his heavy breathing, then the hoarse cry of the night watchman telling the hour and the weather, a cloudy morning. "No doubt you must be much surprised at so many vessels arriving at different parts of America from England, without so much as a single line from the man who has so often, and so warmly professed himself your friend and admirer." He can imagine what thoughts, what suspicions must run in her head—it physically pains him. But he has an excuse.

From the moment he arrived in London he has been so assaulted by sights and sounds, the great towers, castles, palaces, and steeples; the teeming streets, crossings and markets; bells, the cries of street vendors, the voices of ballad singers, the clatter of carriages and gilded coaches, the jostling of sedan chairs; everyone rushing who knew where in the labyrinth of the metropolis. At first it was all he could do simply to witness and adjust to the scale of his new environment.

Moreover, William had been obliged to take up his father's business in society and court, meeting with politicians, philosophers, and men of business, men like Thomas Penn, and Governor Morris of Pennsylvania, and Governor Shirley of Massachusetts; the publisher William Strahan, who knew Dr. Samuel Johnson, and the historian Edward Gibbon, and the philosopher David Hume. They heard opera at Covent Garden, visited the British Museum, saw Garrick act Hamlet.

If he could not share it with her he longed to describe the pleasure he enjoyed in visiting Windsor Castle and the other places she herself had recommended to him: "the enchanting scenes at Vauxhall," with its immense pipe organ in the center of the Garden's main space, the lamplit paths where beaux and ladies strolled and flirted, "the elegant paintings and sculptures with which the boxes, the grand hall, and orchestra, are adorned; the curious artificial fall of water . . ." Such things would have made her think of the Elysium of the Ancients, Miss Elizabeth Graeme, with her poet's soul—so would the picturesque country villages. And yet none of these things, he wrote, could rival her company.

Knowing how she disliked politics, he has less to say on that score. But since it is his business—or *was* his business before he began his law studies in November—he must inform her that he sees no prospect of any end to his father's mission for the Assembly. The lords of the Privy Council most concerned with colonial affairs are so prejudiced against Pennsylvania, and they are so preoccupied with European troubles, Prussia being at war with Russia, they have no patience with the Franklins' suit. This state of affairs, "joined with the obstinacy and wickedness of the proprietors render his task very uphill and difficult."

Now the lover has reached a point where he risks putting his pride as well as his political concerns above his commitment to her. He had promised Betsy the year before that he would not allow politics—his father's quarrel with Thomas Penn, her family's friend—to come between them. William had promised faithfully to speak of the Penns with respect.

She would admit he was justified, however, in speaking of the proprietors with something less than respect if she knew that they were two-faced hypocrites. All the while the Penns pretended to settle things amicably with Benjamin Franklin they were publishing scandalous lies against the good people of Pennsylvania. Trusting in Franklin's sincerity, while they delayed and stalled, they thought that he might not take notice of anonymous attacks in a newspaper. They may have deceived themselves in this thought, "this piece of low cunning," for a while, but not for long under his watch.

The earnest suitor steps forth in his letter, as he had in life, admitting to his Betsy, with all possible humility and without apology, that he had written the letter published in the *Citizen* that caught the wicked slanderers dead to rights. The letter did "vindicate the honour and reputation of my country when I saw it so injuriously attacked!" Manfully he put his name to the paper, and the place where he could be found, the Pennsylvania Coffee-house, as a challenge, so as to put a stop to the anonymous attacks—otherwise the public would give no more credit to one side than the other.

And the stratagem worked. No adversary came forward.

It had been more appropriate for him to publish this, as a Pennsylvanian student visiting England, than for his father as the official agent for the colony. "I am told the Proprietor is much incensed against me on that account, though he don't venture to complain as he is sensible that he was the aggressor."

William seems to be flushed with confidence that his fiancée will share his exhilaration at his eloquence, bravery, and fame. By now she will have read the piece, so will her father and mother and most citizens of Philadelphia. The letter had echoed in print all over the English-speaking world; and he would be grateful if she would report to him any comments that she might have heard. "For my own private satisfaction I ask this favor," he assures her, and for no other purpose.

The candle is nearly burnt down and his eyelids grow heavy. In haste he tells her he has taken the liberty of sending her, with this letter, some love tokens. She had sent him a silk watch chain she had braided herself. He was sending her a fashionable muff and tippet as are "worn by the gayest ladies of quality at this end of the town," and a basket for the little ivory counters used in card games, woven by "a poor reduced lady of family who has no other way of getting her livelihood." The muff was an erotic literary allusion. Betsy liked to compare him to Tom Jones for his gallantry, and Jones had a fetish for his lady Sophia's muff. Now he commits his words and presents into the care of an Irish friend who would leave the next morning bound for Philadelphia. "Farewell, God bless and preserve you, is the sincere prayer of, Dear Betsy, your truly affectionate—Wm. Franklin."

In this overdue letter William Franklin mentions, optimistically, that his father had had "several interviews" with the proprietors at Thomas Penn's house in Spring Gardens, and that each time they had treated him with great civility. This may have been true, but they certainly had done nothing in the way of answering Franklin's formal letter of complaint.

Benjamin Franklin did not realize for some time that the Penns were incensed even by the address of the letter: "To the Proprietors" should have read "To the True and Absolute Proprietaries." Franklin's omission of the glorious adjectives was taken as such an affront that Thomas Penn and his brother, for all their civility in the parlor, refused to deal directly with the complaints. They turned the letter over to their lawyer, Ferdinand John Paris. Franklin described Paris as a proud, angry man who had "conceived a mortal enmity" to him from years of antagonistic correspondence concerning the colony's affairs. When Franklin declined to discuss his business with the disagreeable lawyer, the proprietors turned the matter over to the attorney general and then the solicitor general for their opinions.

And everyone waited.

Yet Ben Franklin persisted, as soon as his health allowed, relying on his charm and the Penns' civility to get himself invited once more to the mansion around the corner from Charing Cross. Sometime in the second week of January, Franklin got out of bed, dressed formally for the battle, took up his tricornered hat and his stick, and walked to Spring Gardens. When he and Thomas and Richard Penn had finished asking after one another's health and toasting the king's, when they had passed some time and breath in banter before the fireplace, Franklin got down to business. In a letter to his friend Isaac Norris, Speaker of the Assembly, he recorded the conversation.

Franklin asked if it was not a right of the House of Commons to name officers to enforce laws, and to have those commissioners stand without a challenge. Thomas Penn admitted this was so; but, he continued, just because this was a privilege of the House of Commons it did not follow that it was the right of the Pennsylvania Assembly. Pennsylvania was a corporation chartered by the king, with no rights or privileges but those granted by its charter. The privilege you now claim, said Penn, is nowhere mentioned.

But your father's charter, Franklin pleaded, "*expressly* says that the Assembly of Pennsylvania shall have all the power and privileges of an Assembly according to the rights of the freeborn subjects of England, and as is usual in any of the British plantations in America."

"Yes," said the son of William Penn, from a chilly eminence, "but if my father granted privileges he was not by the Royal Charter empowered to grant, nothing can be claimed by such a grant."

Then Franklin's mask of good humor tightened; his eyes betrayed their insight into a long-ignored infamy. "If your father had no right to grant the privileges he pretended to grant, and published all over Europe"—the sentence had swelled beyond temper and was threatening to go off—"as granted," so that a generation or more of immigrants "came to settle in the province upon the faith of that grant and in expectation of enjoying the privileges contained in it"—Franklin, his face drawn after his illness, needed a breath, and took it—then those who came to settle in the province upon the faith of that grant "were deceived, cheated and betrayed."

"They should have *themselves* looked to that," his host responded. Franklin could hardly believe the man's words or the expressions that ensued. "The Royal Charter was no secret! They who came to the province on my father's offer of privileges, if they were deceived," Penn said, laughing, "it was their own fault."

And Ben Franklin sat wide-eyed, appalled at Thomas Penn's insolence, the very idea that anyone would "thus meanly give up his father's character." Franklin later compared the man's manner as "such as a low jockey might do where a purchaser complained that he had cheated him in a horse," a phrase that found its way into the newspapers and back to the Penns. If there had been any reserve of goodwill remaining in January 1758, this interview exhausted it. "I conceived that moment a more cordial and thorough contempt for him than I ever felt for any man living—a contempt that I cannot express in words, but I believe my countenance expressed it strongly." Penn's brother Richard, looking hard at Franklin, observed it, as well as the color the discussion had raised in the older man's cheeks. Franklin could think of no more to say in response to Penn's remark "than that the poor people were no lawyers themselves and confiding in his father did not think it necessary to consult any."

Thomas and Richard Penn forwarded Franklin's complaints to the solicitor general for his opinion, "where it lay unanswered," Franklin recalled, "a year wanting eight days." That year, 1758, passed pleasantly enough. Ben Franklin rented a good coach, stocked the cellar with fine wine, and spared no expense upon tailors and cobblers to make father and son fit for London society. The Assembly would reimburse him by and by. William began his studies at the Middle Temple, which required attending lectures, reading for oral examinations, and "dining in" six or more times in the oak-paneled banquet room of the school, with a view to being called to the bar sometime in early autumn of 1758. In this adventure he enjoyed the company of a debonair thirty-six-year-old bachelor named Richard Jackson, a brilliant lawyer and politician who had been dubbed "Omniscient" by Dr. Johnson for his vast learning. Jackson had excelled at Cambridge and now was a fixture in the Inner Temple, a writer the Franklins admired for his knowledge of colonial affairs, especially charter rights. He took an immediate liking to William and became his guide not only through the Inns of Court but to the sites and amusements of the city on the Thames.

William must have been a quick study, and well prepared by Joseph Galloway's tutorials in Philadelphia. A glance at the Franklins' itinerary shows he was on the road with his father or Jackson for much of the spring term (April 15–July 31) prior to his final examinations rather than bent over his books. As much as father and son loved London and their rooms on Craven Street, there were discomforts in the city. The grate in the fireplace burned sea coal, and the fuel burned dirty, filling the air of the sitting room with thick oily smoke. Windows and mirrors had to be wiped daily. "The whole town," said Franklin, "is one great smoky house, and every street a chimney, the air full of floating sea coal soot." The only way to get a breath of sweet, pure air was to travel miles into the country for it.

In May they rode to Cambridge to meet John Hadley, a professor of chemistry, and conduct some experiments in evaporation. Franklin wetted the ball of a thermometer, not with alcohol, which was usual in such experiments, but with ether. They took turns pumping the bellows to evaporate the ether, watching the mercury drop to twenty-five degrees below freezing. "From this experiment," Franklin wrote, "one may see the possibility of freezing a man to death on a warm summer's day."

In July the Franklins headed for Northampton and the hamlet of Ecton, sixty miles north of London. Franklin's ancestors had lived there for generations before his father sailed for America. The ancestral home had been turned into the village school. The rector of the Ecton parish brought out the church register and showed them pages recording births, marriages, and deaths in the family going back two centuries. The rector's wife led them to the cemetery and pointed out the Franklin gravestones, so mossy that the dates and words were invisible until she sent the sexton for a brush and pail of water. Peter, Franklin's servant, scoured the stones for all to read. Then William, with paper and coal, took rubbings to send home.

The inventor and his son were fascinated by the new machinery in the factories in Birmingham—the flying shuttle and the carding machines in the cotton mills. This was the wave of the future, an industry that must soon make its way to the shores of America.

Ben Franklin returned to London in late August. William stopped at Tunbridge Wells, a fashionable resort in West Kent, in the company of his friend Richard Jackson, who was there brokering a marriage contract. William wrote to his father on September 3 telling him of his plan to stay there a week until Jackson had finished his business. Then they would return to London later in the month for a few days before setting out on a pleasure tour of Norfolk, the low-lying county in East Anglia on the North Sea.

In William's letter to his father an expression of gratitude borders on abject apology: "I am extremely obliged to you for your care in supplying me with money, and shall ever have a grateful sense of that with the other numberless indulgences I have received from your paternal affection." William was twenty-eight. At that age Benjamin's income had come from his ownership of the most widely read newspaper in the colonies and his brainchild *Poor Richard's Almanac.* He was father of two boys, guardian of his orphaned nephew, and grand master of the Pennsylvania Masons.

William, by contrast, was still a student. While by no means idle or profligate, he was financially dependent upon his fifty-two-year-old father, and Ben Franklin was keeping score, pound for pound, of William's expenses: to Christopher the Tailor, Forfar for Hats, Regnier for Cloaths. Although some of these bills would eventually be charged to the Pennsylvania Assembly, Franklin would never let his son forget them.

"I shall be ready to return to America, or to go to any other part of the world, whenever you think it necessary," William promised. He would soon be thirty, an age when most men had settled down, in an era and social stratum that frowned upon bachelorhood after that age of discretion. His father wanted to see him married.

He had not forgotten Elizabeth Graeme. When he returned from East Anglia on October 24, William found a letter from her. He had last written her in December expressing his affection. He was not a prolific correspondent, yet she had not been very responsive, either. Surely it had not taken two months for the *London*, the vessel bearing his letter, to reach her with all its passion, and the tippet and muff, or more than the same time for one of her letters to reach Craven Street. Yet summer had come and gone and he had heard nothing from Betsy.

Now he broke the seal on this letter dated May 7. The contents shocked him. Her original letter has been lost, but essential passages of it have been preserved in another that William wrote to Margaret Abercrombie, a friend of the lovers, to whom he confided his heartbreak.

Betsy had read his political letter to the *Citizen* when it was published in *The Pennsylvania Gazette* on December 8, 1757, five months before. His words blaming the proprietors disturbed her, she wrote, as she remained loyal to her father's opinions and the Penns' friendship. He was forsaking his promise never to allow politics to come between them. She called him a "collection of party malice" concluding that his carelessness was proof he no longer loved her. She condemned his selfishness in not admitting that his own frivolity, or his father's conniving, or his attachment to party politics kept him from continuing "in the tender passion" he had promised her, and said she was neither so humble nor so abject that she would consider marrying anyone like that. "It would be *folly*, nay *madness* to think of running all risks" with such a man.

He was amazed by her fury. She did not understand that his goal since his arrival in London—especially his letter to the *Citizen*—had been to resolve his differences with the proprietors whom he looked upon, William wrote, "as the bane of my future happiness as well as that of my country." He had hoped that once he exposed their lies, they would come to the table and listen to proposals for a friendly and honorable settlement of the dispute. How could she doubt his sincerity? He and Betsy had agreed "that in case of any change of sentiment, or that either should think the obstacles to our proposed happiness insurmountable, to give immediate notice." Now he could not doubt it, she had changed. She had even gone so far as to dismiss his gifts of the tippet and muff as "Gawdy gee-gaws."

He had been about to pick up his quill and write to her about the hopelessness of the negotiations with the Penns. Now this would be unnecessary. He would not write to her again. It would be his burden "to learn forgetfulness." Certain that she had called off their engagement, he wrote a letter to Margaret Abercrombie in Philadelphia with the understanding that she would convey its anguished contents to his former fiancée, informing Betsy that he accepted, with deep sadness, her decision.

THIS WAS A SEASON of meaningful changes. Three weeks later Benjamin Franklin wrote proudly to his sister Jane Mecum that William had donned his gown as a lawyer and been called to the bar in Westminster Hall. Father and son marked the occasion, November 10, 1758, by having their wigs refurbished and purchasing new suits of clothes.

Then on November 27, the Penns finally answered the complaints Franklin had presented a year earlier. It was hardly what he had hoped for after so long a wait. The response to his formal complaint was not even addressed to the agent Benjamin Franklin but instead written as a "Message to the Assembly" from the Penns' lawyer, Ferdinand John Paris. Without so much as naming Franklin, Paris claimed that Franklin's original "Complaints" were vague and rude, and that ever since then, the agent had done nothing to advance negotiations, or attain the harmony they sincerely desired. In short, no sort of harmony or agreement was possible with such a person as Benjamin Franklin. "We are ready to receive the fullest information, and also to enter into free conferences on all these several subjects with any persons of candour, whom you shall authorize and empower for that purpose."

"I need not point out to you," Franklin later wrote to Isaac Norris, Speaker of the Assembly, "the mean chicanery of their whole proceeding." Nevertheless "a final end is put to all farther negotiation between them and me." The Assembly would have to recall him and appoint someone likely to be more pliant. This ought to have happened, yet somehow it didn't. Franklin's resignation was never accepted.

In that same letter to his friend Norris that might have ended in despair, Franklin offered another strategy, broader and bolder, to attain the ends for which he had sailed from America in the first place. If the

Penns would not deal with him, there were others in power who would. He had been gathering support from liberal Englishmen and Scottish intellectuals. What Franklin was about to propose to Norris was a direct appeal to the Crown to disenfranchise the Penns. He had this plan in mind previously, when he had petitioned the king in the autumn of 1757 to take over responsibility for Indian affairs from the inept proprietors.

Franklin's optimism was dazzling. He told Norris that the Assembly had advised him "to make no application to Parliament" before hearing further instructions. "Yet I shall immediately permit the publishing of a work that has been long in hand, containing a true history of our affairs and disputes." From this forthcoming book, the work of Richard Jackson and William Franklin, he has high hopes. The whole sorry, sordid tale would be told, from the time the proprietorship descended from William Penn to his sons: Thomas's tyranny; his cruel dealings with the Indians; his suppression of the Roman Catholics; finally the Penns' infernal instructions to the governors shackling the Assembly, blocking not only the taxation of their lands but every bill necessary to defend the colony. "The proprietors will be gibbeted up as they deserve," he vowed, "to rot and stink in the nostrils of posterity." *An Historical Review of the Constitution and Government of Pennsylvania*, scathingly written, was published in June 1759.

That same month, news came from America that offered the Franklins enormous encouragement. In the face of relentless Indian attacks, Governor William Denny finally permitted the Assembly to pass a supply bill appropriating £100,000, a fund for defense that levied taxes on all land—including the proprietors'. He had defied their instructions, then left office, and left town.

At last the Franklins had a formal bill upon which to mount their case against the proprietors. The lawyer, Richard Jackson, would argue that the Penns had no right to review the bill in question or appeal to the Crown, because Governor Denny, their own deputy, had signed it. Thus under the terms of the royal charter, the bill had become the law of Pennsylvania.

CHAPTER 5

Triumphs

MANY MEN IN BENJAMIN Franklin's position would have made the most of the Penns' rebuke by returning home, honorably, to their families. After all, he and William had been gone nearly a year and a half. His wife and daughter sorely missed him.

He originally told Deborah he would be home in the spring. But spring 1758 came and went and he told her his business would take him another year. She was wonderfully patient. Yet in the late summer and early autumn of 1759 he and William were touring Scotland, where he was showered with laurels, including an honorary degree from the University of St. Andrews. And there they met with such luminaries of the Scottish Enlightenment as the philosophers David Hume and Adam Smith, Sir Alexander Dick, and Lord Kames. At one gathering the Scottish church leader Dr. Alexander Carlyle was fascinated by the Franklins. He wrote that the son was "open and communicative," and better company than his father; he also observed a "decided difference of opinion" between father and son "that might eventually alienate them altogether."

On August 29, 1759, Franklin wrote from Liverpool assuring his Debby that he would "endeavor to return early next spring." On March 28, 1760, he had the pleasure to inform her that in less than a month the Privy Council would schedule a "hearing of his case against the proprietors, after which I shall be able to fix a time for my return." Then the hearing was delayed until late August. A year later, his letter to her of August 7, 1761, informs her that he and Billy are well, but "I begin to feel the want of my usual yearly journeys . . . and possibly may take a trip to Holland." He does not mention returning to America. Her letters to him are tender, dutiful, and full of news about family and friends. His are fewer and mostly brief, attending to business.

Upon hearing of the death of his mother-in-law, on March 24, 1762, Franklin wrote Deborah a letter of condolence, "being extremely sensible of the distress and affliction it must have thrown you into." The old lady had fallen into the fireplace—a not uncommon accident. He promised he was finishing up all his business in preparing for his voyage home, either immediately or by the next packet in May 1762. That is his last letter to her from London.

He would not sail, in fact, until August of that year. From the time he arrived in London until he left in 1762, Franklin was in England for four years, and he had been away from wife, hearth, and home for four and a half.

What were he and William doing there after they finished their business with Parliament and his son had been called to the bar?

They were socializing and they were making love. More precisely, they both were socializing to promote themselves and their cause— Parliament's approval of the bill to tax the Penns. And William at least was making love to two or more women. There is evidence that his father was not celibate, either, during those years of his early fifties. In fact he became so intimate with his landlady, Margaret Stevenson, that they entertained and traveled together, appearing to the eyes of many as a domestic couple. More concrete evidence of Franklin's inclinations is a drawing by Charles Willson Peale. Visiting Franklin's rooms upstairs on Craven Street, the young painter surprised the inventor in flagrante delicto with a chambermaid, seated, their clothing in disarray, the girl on top. Peale excused himself, but not before getting such an eyeful he would hasten home and record the scene for posterity in an erotic drawing that hangs now in the collection of the American Philosophical Society.

As for William, his love life after 1758 is well documented, and of consequence. Sometime in the year 1759 he began a liaison with a woman whose name, like his own mother's, is lost to history. William fathered a child out of wedlock, probably conceived in the spring of that year. By some accounts the boy, William Temple Franklin, was born in February of the following year. Not without humor, William named him after himself as well as the school that prepared him for the bar.

Legitimacy in those days was not a matter of terribly great concern among men of means. Some men and fewer women were born out of wedlock and adopted by their fathers. They might then enjoy the sort of respectability William Franklin had known in Philadelphia. But paternity was crucial. A gentleman was unlikely to adopt a love child who might not be his own blood. We know little about William Temple Franklin's mother, or his grandmother, but we do know that these were not frivolous or abandoned women. In each case the lover had to monopolize the woman's affections over a period of weeks or months, to live in such proximity there could be no doubt that the child was his.

Clues point to the child's birth in this season. On June 20, William marked a loan of twenty pounds from William Strahan, a considerable sum, the equivalent of four thousand dollars in today's money. Unlike his father, William did not let it be known that he had fathered the bastard, and few people knew the secret until years later. Temple was placed nearby in foster care, with the help of Strahan, that indispensable friend and man of the world.

William Franklin was about thirty years old, older than most gentlemen of his social class to take a wife. For a year after his disappointment in love with Betsy Graeme he had consoled himself with a mistress. Then, a little while after committing their son to foster care, William met an amiable and attractive woman in England who, like himself, was by birth a colonist.

Elizabeth Downes, two years older than William, was born in St. Thomas Parish, Barbados, in 1728, the youngest of three children, a boy and two girls. Her father, John Downes, had been a prosperous planter when Barbados was the chief source of sugar for Britain. He died in 1731 after a lingering illness, leaving his daughters £1,200 each to be distributed when they reached the age of eighteen, about $300,000 in today's currency. In addition, each received two Negro slave girls and a yearly stipend for living expenses and education, seventy pounds, worth now about $16,000. Mrs. Downes returned to England with her children, Jonathan, Hannah, and Elizabeth.

Francis Hopkinson, an American poet and musician and a friend of both Elizabeths, described Miss Downes as "a Lady distinguished by a refined education," so at least in this she resembled William's lost love. Some of that education she must have received in London. Elizabeth lived with her mother and siblings on St. James's Street, in view of the Royal Palace, a half hour's stroll from Craven Street, at the end of the broad thoroughfare of Pall Mall.

She was an heiress, not a great or distinguished heiress but with money to bring to the table should she decide, at the ripe age of thirty-two, to accept a proposal of marriage. If she had been very rich it is probable she would have married already, or married someone other than William Franklin, as she moved in high society between the Court of St. James, at the end of the street, and Northumberland House, two blocks from Franklin's residence.

William and Elizabeth met in a merry season. Tory society was enlivened by the advent of the uncrowned king and his wife—an ironic turn of events, as the Whig Party under the leadership of "the Great Commoner," William Pitt, had recently overseen the global defeat of France in the Seven Years' War. Montreal surrendered to the British in November, nine months after Quebec had fallen; General John Forbes had finally captured Fort Duquesne. Horace Walpole wrote, "Victories come tumbling so over one another from distant parts of the globe, that it looks just like the handiwork of a lady romance-writer." Everywhere France was vanquished, and William Pitt was hailed as the hero of the British Empire—until his friend King George II passed away in October 1760, and with him a government of compromise and coalition. Whigs made room for the conservative Tories. Pitt must step down, yielding to the crown prince's former tutor Lord Bute, the restoration of Tory government, and royal control. But in the months before this the dominant Whigs, who favored the colonies, were still in control.

At Northumberland House, that huge, ornate bastion of ducal wealth and authority on Charing Cross, the lights blazed brightly. Lady Percy—soon to be lady of the bedchamber to the young Queen Charlotte—entertained the nobles and their ladies and friends, all those who were pleased to celebrate the new regime. Her husband, Hugh Percy, was a Knight of the Garter.

Between St. James's Street, where Miss Downes lived during the winter social season, and Franklin's home at No. 6 Craven Street, Northumberland House was a destination where William and Elizabeth would inevitably meet. She was delicate of face and form, dark-eyed and dark-haired probably, like her American predecessor, her eyes penetrating and analytic, critical rather than yielding. There was a reason why this woman had taken no husband in her twenties. She was a perfectionist. She was waiting for someone like William, and he was hoping not to disappoint her.

With the advice and support of men like Richard Jackson and a number of Scots such as William Strahan, the Franklins had achieved success in Court circles as well as Parliament. While William's refined manners made him the favorite in Court, his father played the angles of Whitehall. Tensions in English politics in 1760 favored the Franklins' suit, as colonial America now appeared in the light that had shone for centuries upon Ireland and Scotland. When an advisory opinion came down from the Board of Trade in June favoring the proprietors, Benjamin Franklin did not lose heart. He wrote to William Pitt himself, whom he had never met ("he was then too great a man," Franklin wrote), a bold letter inviting Pitt to join forces with him against the Penns. "Between you and I, it is said that we may look upon them all to be a pack of d——d r——ls, and unless we bribe them all higher than our adversaries can do, and condescend to every piece of dirty work they require, we shall never be able to attain common justice at their hands."

By the time the final hearing was slated for August 27, 1760, the Franklins had gathered support among powerful Whigs—men who knew the danger of the Indians and the urgency of arming the provinces—and felt they might hope for a favorable verdict. Hearings of the Privy Council were held in the Cockpit, a lofty chamber so named because it stood on a site where Henry VIII once indulged his passion for the blood sport of cockfighting. The spectators—in the gallery overlooking the long council table—were sometimes treated to conflicts as violent in emotional terms as were the avian contests that gave the room its name.

Franklin's lawyers, well prepared, presented their case now with clarity, and the councilors in their wigs and capes listened more patiently, especially Lord Mansfield, William Murray. A Scot of Ben Franklin's age, Murray was a brilliant jurist known for cutting through rhetoric and red tape, enabling litigants to come to terms swiftly, saving time and money. Now the proprietors were crying that if they put themselves at the mercy of the colony's tax assessors, "being in odium with the people," they would be ruined. No, said Franklin and his lawyers, that was not true. "The assessors were honest and discreet men, under an oath to assess fairly & equitably." Any advantage one might expect in reducing his own tax by increasing the Penns' would not be worth the cost of perjury. More important, the £100,000 that Governor Denny had approved had been issued as paper money; this had passed into circulation and if it were recalled, by the repeal of the bill, Pennsylvania would be ruined.

So this was not only a legal problem, it was a matter of shillings and pence and the colony's survival. At this point, while the lawyers were wrangling, Lord Mansfield rose from his chair and crooked his finger at Ben Franklin. Franklin followed his Lordship from the Cockpit into the clerk's chamber. In his quiet, steady voice with traces of the Scots burr, he asked Franklin: "Do you really believe that if the law is allowed to stand, then the estate of the proprietors would suffer no injury?"

"Certainly," said Franklin.

"Then," says he, "you can have little objection to enter into an engagement to assure that point."

"None at all," Franklin replied.

His word sufficed. Without further discussion, Lord Chief Justice Mansfield summoned Henry Wilmot, the Penns' lawyer. Both sides accepted the proposition and the clerk drew up a contract, which Franklin signed. Lord Mansfield returned to the Cockpit table with the bill and its new bond. The next day, August 28, the Committee for

Plantation Affairs advised in favor of the act, with the amendment Franklin had approved for the Assembly. On September 2 the act went before the king in council and was allowed to pass.

At long last Franklin and the Assembly had won the right to tax all property in Pennsylvania, and there would be no more exemptions for the proprietors. The larger controversy—whether the proprietors might revoke a law the Assembly had resolved and the governor had signed—was left up in the air. Nonetheless the colonial assembly's victory was tremendous, a monument to Franklin's tenacity and cunning.

ONCE THE UNCROWNED KING had allowed the taxation bill to pass in late summer of 1760, Franklin's mission was accomplished and his official business in England had come to an end.

In the spring, he had promised his wife that he would fix a time for his return just as soon as the hearing was over. But he did not. For the twenty-four months from September 1760 until August 1762, when Franklin finally left for America, not much is known about his day-to-day life. The fact that he remained in Europe, obscurely, for two more years is a rather curious, if not mysterious, complication in a life that is, for the most part, broadly witnessed and documented.

Toward the end of 1760, the Assembly had adopted resolutions empowering Franklin and his coagent Robert Charles (who was in London, ready to replace him) to transact the colony's financial affairs in England. This included receiving the parliamentary grants reimbursing the assembly for military expenses of some £30,000, investing the money, and then disbursing it to creditors. Such a duty called for the integrity of Caesar's wife and the financial acumen of a Medici. Franklin possessed the first virtue but was lacking in the second. Most Americans trusted him, but the fact that they trusted him to manage that amount of money in the erratic stock exchange of the 1760s shows just how confident Isaac Norris and his compatriots were that Franklin could do anything.

Dozens of letters between Norris and Franklin concerning the colony's investments, debts, and payments attest to Franklin's serious attention to those finances. Closer study of balance sheets and the purchase of volatile stocks during the business cycle in peace and war; how the stocks would rise, promising profit, then fall when Franklin wanted cash to honor debts; how he was forced to seek credit from bankers when liquidity ran low—it all amounts to a comedy of errors sweeping a clever man out of his depth, one who has risen to his level of incompetence. If this was his last official duty in England, he should have declined it. His stockbroker, John Rice, proved a forger and embezzler and was hanged at Tyburn in 1763. It was a wonder that Franklin did not bankrupt the province. His ability to refinance loans and appease creditors on the strength of his illustrious name was marvelous.

FRANKLIN REMAINED A LOYAL Briton notwithstanding all his exasperation with parliamentary politics and corruption. His zealous vision for the Empire found its highest expression in a pamphlet he published that year titled "The Interest of Great Britain Considered, with Regard to her Colonies, and the Acquisitions of Canada and Guadeloupe." As the war with France concluded, England was in a position to dictate the terms of the peace, and could not decide the fate of Canada. Should England retain all of it? Or should she just secure the border at a safe distance from the British colonies, while instead keeping the recently captured sugar-rich island of Guadeloupe? Franklin argued for keeping Canada rather than restoring it to France in exchange for a sugar mill. Like the proprietors, the captains of industry regarded America as mainly a market for British goods and opposed colonial manufacture along with self-government. Retain Canada, Franklin advised, and the colonists will have so much farmland that nobody will be tempted to make buttons or broadcloth, or to work for any master.

Boldly he confronted the possibility that the growth of the colonies might render them dangerous. This seemed unlikely, given the fact they could scarcely unite for the purpose of fighting the Indians, who were burning their villages and scalping their people. Could it be reasonably supposed there was any danger they would unite against the mother nation "which protects and encourages them, with which they have so many connections and ties of blood?" But then he added this dark caveat: "When I say such an union is impossible, I mean without the most grievous tyranny and oppression. . . . The waves do not rise, but when the winds blow."

Franklin's rhetoric naturally set off alarms in certain chambers of Whitehall. This was the man who had brought the mighty proprietors to their knees. And now that he had discharged that duty, who knew what mischief he might work in his idleness, month after month, year after year? Would he never go home?

It was no secret that Maryland's House of Delegates had been at loggerheads with Lord Baltimore, the proprietor of Maryland, over the same questions of taxation and legislative authority that had racked Pennsylvania. Baltimore had somehow foiled the Maryland legislature's efforts to appoint an agent to represent their interests. In May 1761, Maryland looked to Benjamin Franklin to present their complaint or "Address" to Secretary of State William Pitt. Franklin responded: "It would be no small pleasure to me to be able to render any service to the Assembly of Maryland . . . while I reside here, you may depend no pains or care shall be wanting on my part to place your conduct in a just light." First Pennsylvania, then Maryland. Perhaps if the famous American lingered long enough in London he might achieve the voice of an ambassador.

He spent his remaining time in England traveling and pursuing friendships and scientific experiments, in this civilization he found so superior to the one to which he must eventually return. Seven blocks north of Craven Street, a five-minute walk along the Strand brought Franklin to the door of the Society for the Encouragement of the Arts, Manufacture and Commerce. It was a colorful stroll in all weather, bustling with carriages and sedan chairs in the shadow of sturdy brick houses. A chair mender passed bearing a chair frame in one hand and rushes in the other. A woman sold vegetables from a basket on her head.

The Society of the Arts, modeled upon Franklin's own American Philosophical Society, was first organized to bestow grants to scientists for new discoveries and inventions. Naturally Franklin became a corresponding member soon after the society's founding in 1756, and he paid for a life subscription. This was the main meeting place for famous Britons. A short list of members tells us a great deal about Franklin's contacts in the 1760s: Samuel Johnson, Edward Gibbon, and Laurence Sterne, authors; David Garrick, actor; Gustavus Brander, director of the Bank of England; Thomas Chippendale, furniture maker; Sir John Cust, Speaker of the House of Commons (after Pitt); the composer Thomas Arne, who wrote "Rule, Britannia" and worked with Garrick at the Drury Lane Theatre; Benjamin West—who would paint a famous likeness of Franklin—and Sir Joshua Reynolds; and a score of peers of the realm, Scots and Englishmen of various political persuasions—a love of learning transcended most prejudices.

Between 1760 and mid-1762 the society's rolls show that Franklin attended fifty committee meetings officially. How many times he visited the cozy rooms for casual conversation and a glass of port by the fire is not recorded. Other diversions included ongoing correspondence with the giants of the Scottish Enlightenment. He had enjoyed the company of Hume and others at Sir Alexander Dick's manor house when he and William sojourned in Edinburgh in the autumn of 1759, "six weeks of the densest happiness I have met with in any part of my life," he told Lord Kames. The association led to Franklin's acceptance of an honorary doctorate from the University of St. Andrews in that year.

Another beneficiary of Franklin's literary attention was Polly Stevenson, his landlady's daughter. Now twenty-one, Polly had gone to live in the village of Wanstead, ten miles distant, with her aunt, a wealthy woman who planned to settle a fortune on her while providing an education usually reserved for gentlemen. Sixteen years old when she first met Franklin, Polly formed a strong attachment to him, and after leaving home she missed him as much as she did her mother. The lodger had become Polly's mentor and greatest admirer, writing poems for her and directing her reading. He praised her "mind thirsty after knowledge and capable of receiving it." She called him her "dear preceptor" and sometimes her "ever dear saint"; he addressed her as his "dear good girl" and his "dear little philosopher" in more than a dozen intimate letters, which mostly dwelt upon natural science: the working of the barometer; the purpose of insects in the scheme of things, such as the silkworm and bee. Many of these images lend themselves to erotic or affectionate interpretations, and that seems to be his intention. His famous experiment to measure the sun's heat as absorbed by light and dark fabric (by laying patches of each upon snow in the sunshine) is described in a letter to Polly late in 1760. In closing one of his epistles that year he wrote: "After writing 6 folio pages of philosophy to a young girl, is it necessary to finish such a letter with a compliment?"

Their letters were passionate but chaste. They were not lovers then, but there was something uncommon in his feeling for the girl that impacts this chapter of the story. Franklin admired Polly Stevenson so greatly that he wanted William to marry her. If *he* couldn't have Polly, then the next best thing would be for William, whom he loved so much, to have and hold her so that he might have Polly forever as a daughter.

This idea is expressed in his letter to Polly when Franklin realized that his matchmaking effort was doomed. He called himself afflicted in knowing that Polly "whom he once flattered himself might become his own in the tender relation of a child," might never again be the subject of such hopes. If Ben and William had not been so attached to each other, then this projection of the father's desire upon the son might not have occurred. But it did. This was part of the uneasiness that was beginning to disconnect them.

All the while William was courting Betsy Downes, in 1761 and 1762, from the gay resort of Bath to the magnificent festivities at Northumberland House, he was having to apologize to his father for not courting his favorite, Polly Stevenson. This is a curious and important complication in the developing portrait of the father and son between late summer of 1760 and September 22, 1761, the day of the coronation, when William walked in the procession and his father watched the parade from the gallery. Another important factor is William's steady ascent in the political system.

As Benjamin Franklin was trading stocks, corresponding with the Scottish sages, and attending meetings at the Society of the Arts, his son was conducting all their business that required face-to-face diplomacy or negotiations. Events after the coronation, especially the resignation of William Pitt and the rise of the Earl of Bute, made the elder Franklin wary of his political status. Lord Bute was a Scot, and as young George III's mentor he would soon be prime minister. Dr. John Pringle, Ben Franklin's friend, was Bute's physician and informal adviser, a connection that might benefit Franklin if the new king lived up to expectations, or it might backfire. The future of Tory government—which Bute promised to restore—was unpredictable. In America, William Pitt was widely admired ("we almost idolize him," wrote one New Englander), and when he resigned there was a sigh of disappointment throughout the colonies. Lord Bute, an unknown quantity, made people uncomfortable.

Under these circumstances Dr. Franklin's reputation as a troublemaker at the Court of St. James did not favor his political future—nor did his Scottish friends. In England the Scottish people, and Lord Bute in particular, were largely hated and feared. Bute's short-lived influence on the government would have disastrous consequences in the first years of George III's reign.

William Franklin was in a better position. He was handsome, easygoing, more agreeable than his father by all accounts, politically shrewd, and extremely capable. Well dressed and groomed, this new barrister had the manners of a courtier and all the advantages of his father's contacts without the obligations, private or political. His father had flattered Pitt while William avoided it, harboring a lower opinion of the man.

There are several instances of William's authority during the 1760s but perhaps none is so telling as his involvement in the affairs of Maryland. The Maryland Assembly had asked Ben Franklin to approach Pitt on their behalf, but their letter to Franklin did not reach him until Pitt was about to resign. "He was always extremely difficult of access," Franklin wrote to the speaker of Maryland's assembly, Edward Tilghman.

At this moment—a turning point in British politics—Ben Franklin backed away from the colony's problem, as well as the rocky transition in the office of secretary of state, as Pitt gave way to his successors. He stood aside and turned the matter over to his son, "who knows your affair as well as I do," he assured Tilghman.

So William Franklin put on his best suit, had his shoes cleaned and his wig powdered, took up his walking stick, and made his way along Whitehall to meet with the undersecretary of state, Robert Wood. Wood had served under Pitt, and now continued in the same office under his successor who had received a copy of Maryland's Address from Pitt. Ben Franklin had failed to get an appointment there, but William had succeeded. Wood, a great Homeric scholar, launched into an epic tirade against the Maryland Assembly, expressing the ministry's vast resentment against the provincial legislature. He blamed them for the failure of military supplies during the war and their reluctance to take up arms for the Crown.

Then William, a polished advocate, began to justify the Maryland Assembly to Wood, explaining particulars he had no way of knowing because Maryland had not been allowed an agent in London—a circumstance that rather surprised the undersecretary. William had facts to prove the people of Maryland were loyal to the Crown and forthcoming in their service, military and otherwise. This convinced Wood to weigh Maryland's Address. William smiled. He turned the conversation to matters of protocol, as Maryland wished to include the business Address in a letter congratulating His Majesty on his happy nuptials and his accession. That was indelicate, inadvisable. It moved the undersecretary to advise William Franklin exactly how to couch the petition, by itself, and how and when to send it. His sympathy aroused, the official was cooperating.

"Be assured that the Address would be favourably received," Franklin told the speaker, and it would be.

In those two years after the king allowed the Pennsylvania Assembly to tax the Penns' lands, this was as sensitive a transaction with the ministry as any. And William, not his father, was best positioned to succeed in it. William Franklin was now the most influential colonist in London.

IN MID-AUGUST 1761, FATHER and son took their last European holiday together. In the company of Richard Jackson they made their first voyage to the Continent, landing in Antwerp and then touring the Austrian Netherlands (now Belgium).

They admired the cathedrals at Ghent and Bruges, then traveled by coach up the coast of Holland, visiting Delft, The Hague, and Leyden, arriving in Amsterdam in early September. At Leyden they had the pleasure of meeting the elderly Professor Muschenbrook, inventor of the electrical storage jar. It is said that he was so overwhelmed by meeting the great Franklin that he died two weeks later, having been in perfect health when they arrived. At The Hague they dined with the English ambassador, and in Amsterdam with Thomas Hope, one of the wealthiest merchants in the hemisphere, who sent his coach "to carry us to see everything curious in the city," William wrote to his sister, Sally.

William's long letter to his sister about this vacation is lighthearted and humorous. He loved most things about Holland, with the notable exception of "the continual smoking of tobacco. I don't recollect that I saw more than one Dutch man without a pipe in his mouth, and that was a fellow who had hung in chains so long that his head had dropped off. Their very children are taught smoking from the moment they leave sucking." He told Sally "the method they take to teach them is to give them when they are cutting their teeth an old tobacco pipe which is smoked black and smooth to rub their gums with instead of coral." He was most surprised to see "at one of their music houses a man genteelly dressed" lead his partner to the dance floor "and dance a minuet smoking most solemnly a long pipe during the whole time."

The voyage to Holland was pleasant. But the return five weeks later was awful, "having hard blowing contrary winds, and upwards of 50 passengers ... in a small sloop ... all crowded below." They fell seasick, "and however it might be with the lading of other vessels, I can assure you that on board ours there was no such thing as Inside Contents Unknown.

"Though we landed 60 miles farther from London than we expected, yet we made shift to get there in time enough," William wrote. On a rainy weekend they returned just in time to attend the Coronation of King George III.

At eleven o'clock in the morning, September 22, 1761, the Franklins watched the king make his entrance into Westminster Hall, preceded by the Garter King of Arms in his tabard and the Gentleman Usher of the Black Rod.

The king was tall and handsome, with prominent blue eyes, an oval face, and a strong, dimpled chin. His robes were crimson velvet furred with ermine; on his head he wore the red cap of estate, set with jewels. He took his seat beneath a canopy of golden cloth. Queen Charlotte sat on his left, conducted by her lord chamberlain, and all awaited the presentation of the regalia. From the lower end of the hall where William Franklin and William Strahan stood with nobles at attention came a procession of clergy, one bearing the Holy Bible and another Saint Edward's crown, upon a cushion fringed with gold, encrusted with diamonds, rubies, and sapphires; others carried the jeweled orb, the scepters, and Saint Edward's staff. From dean to lord, all bowing, from constable to chamberlain these precious relics were passed, until they came to rest on the table before the king.

From the gallery high above this display, Ben Franklin looked on with a worldliness that was not quite heretical. Westminster Hall was not a church, it was a courthouse. Yet overnight the English had turned it into a theater for a miracle play. All these fabulous relics had come down from safekeeping in the Tower to be transubstantiated in this civil space upon a plain wooden table, consecrated by the people before the king. The peculiar monarchy of Great Britain held religion and the state in a delicate suspension. The crown jewels, emblems of ancient power, conferred a mystical privilege upon the sovereign. Before the religious ritual that would transpire in the church of St. Peter, Westminster Abbey, the crowns must be honored in this secular space where George would legally become king.

At noon the procession set forth from the hall, blinking, into the sunlight of New Palace Yard. The King's Herb-Woman was followed by her six maids swinging baskets, strewing the way with sage, rosemary, and thyme. Then the scarlet-cloaked High Constable marched with his staff, leading musicians: a fife, drums, and eight trumpets. Then chancery clerks, chaplains, sheriffs, aldermen, and sergeants preceded the children of the choir, the deans, the Knights of Bath in their crimson mantles. Also that afternoon there were a few ladies and gentlemen who—like William Franklin—had been granted "tickets to walk" as "Foreigners of Distinction" by order of the Earl Marshal.

Queen Charlotte advanced in the shade of a gold canopy half as wide as the street, dazzling in her crimson velvet robes, crowned with a circlet of gold adorned with diamonds sparkling in the noonday light, her long red train held by a princess and six earls' daughters. The people cheered. Behind the queen came the dukes and earls and knights whose honor it was to bear the king's regalia, the scepters and the crowns.

At last the king himself came walking under his own canopy of golden cloth, following the bishops, the Holy Bible, the chalice, and the crown. They entered the west door of the Abbey, swallowed by darkness, the deep door contracting inward between pedestals in sunlit niches, the grooms and yeomen of the guards bringing up the rear. Then the guards, too, were gone, leaving outside the cheering multitude with their view of the bright buttressed towers.

Then Benjamin Franklin would make his way home through the crowds to Craven Street, having seen this much and witnessed his son as a player in the pageant, a foreigner of distinction, if a British colonist might be considered foreign. It was time for the elder Franklin to go home.

As William Franklin entered the Abbey he saw the theater built into the choir, and the two thrones raised upon it. Eastward, to his right stood the ancient Chair of Saint Edward, five hundred years old, of dark wood, with lions carved on the legs. Beneath the seat was the Fatal Marble Stone, the color of steel shot through with red, the rock whereon it was said that the patriarch Jacob had once laid his head. From his place William could see that every section of the cathedral, the nave, the transepts, was occupied by galleries, benches rising one above the other, that soon filled with peers and peeresses, officers, musicians, heralds, and a few people like himself.

When the king and queen entered the church, William Franklin heard Purcell's anthem "I was glad when they said unto me, 'Let us go into the House of the Lord.'" The monarchs were enthroned, and the Archbishop of Canterbury, the Lord Chancellor, and the Lord Great

Chamberlain all gathered on the east side of the theater where the archbishop stood at last to proclaim:

> Sirs, I here present unto you King George the Third, the undoubted King of this Realm; wherefore all you who are come this day to do your Homage, are you willing to do the same?

Then a shout went up into the ribbed vaulting of the Abbey the likes of which few people living had ever heard—the voice of many thousands of British subjects of one mind in their devotion, spiritual, patriotic, and personal, to an idea embodied in the person of the king.

The choir sang Handel's anthem "Zadok the Priest" as His Majesty moved into Saint Edward's chair. Franklin knew one of the four knights who held the corners of the velvet covering over the king's head, Hugh Percy, Earl of Northumberland. The archbishop poured oil upon his hand, then anointed the king upon his head, his breast, his hands, in the form of a cross. The custom was primeval, old as Jacob's stone pillow, mystical, prodigious, linking this king by continuity of the scented oil with the immemorial prophets and Hebrew kings, David and Solomon, Elijah and Isaiah.

How could the mortal man not be transformed, exalted in spirit, by such a ritual? As a witness, William Franklin could not doubt it.

TWO WEEKS LATER WILLIAM wrote another long letter to Sally, referring to one he had sent her in April he thinks was lost. "It was mere chit-chat," he said, but it did include an item Sally had asked for—one of Lady Northumberland's cards. She was the wife of Hugh Percy, the Earl of Northumberland, whom William had watched as he held the velvet covering over King George. Fabulously wealthy, the earl was the patron of the painter Canaletto and of the architect Robert Adam, who designed the superb neoclassical rooms of Northumberland House, which housed the finest private art collection in London.

Lady Northumberland kept a salon there with parties every Tuesday and most weekends. She was free enough with the engraved invitation cards that William had received not one but several, as early as February of that year. Lady Northumberland was fond of handsome bachelors, like the twenty-two-year-old writer James Boswell, and William Franklin. Boswell describes a typical night party in 1762, "full of the best company, between three and four hundred" mingling in three large rooms and an enormous gallery with landscapes painted on the walls and gilded moldings. On one wall was a full-length portrait of the king, on another a large painting of Lady Percy.

In good weather the parties spilled out into the garden. When the queen's brother visited in early June, Lady Northumberland held a reception for him. Not only the mansion but the garden also was illuminated, and according to Horace Walpole "was quite a fairy scene. Arches and pyramids of lights alternately surrounded the enclosure; a diamond necklace of lamps edged the rails and descent, with a spiral obelisk of candles on each hand; and dispersed over the lawn were little bands of kettle-drums, clarionets, fifes, & c, and the lovely moon, who came without a card."

It is easy to imagine William and Elizabeth strolling in that charmed garden, moving toward their wedding day, not three months off. They advanced in the midst of turmoil, social and political, in that summer after the king's coronation, trying to make plans upon several uncertainties. They were not engaged, but she was ready to marry him as soon as he had employment; he was ready to be married, but first he wanted a position in the government.

William Franklin had made progress with the secretary of state for the southern department (Great Britain, excluding Ireland and Scotland) Lord Egremont, since his meeting with the undersecretary Robert Wood in the autumn of 1761. He had been encouraged to apply for positions in colonial government, such as in North Carolina, where there was unrest, something along the lines of a deputy secretary to the colony. This paid little but would be a stepping stone. He applied for North Carolina in July 1762.

At the accession of George III, all colonial governors were required to surrender their commissions. One resignation that was accepted was that of Josiah Hardy of New Jersey, whose management of judges had offended the Board of Trade. The lords first offered the Jersey governorship to Thomas Pownall, who had been lieutenant governor there before his tenure as governor of Massachusetts Bay. But Pownall was tired of colonial life and wanted to go home and work for the Board of Trade in London. This rebuff took Parliament by surprise in 1762.

While the Board of Trade was in recess, Lord Egremont recommended that William Franklin be appointed governor of New Jersey. This was a stunning turn of events. Pownall had been a protégé of Lord Halifax, who for years had been president of the Board of Trade. Now he had risen to secretary of state of the northern department, Lord Egremont's counterpart. Halifax still had influence on the board, which was in a period of delicate transition.

In fact, after the coronation the government was in a chaotic transition, as the new king wished to establish his authority and his independence from William Pitt. Lord Bute, his prime minister and first lord of the Treasury, wanted an end to Whig dominance and eliminated every official who stood in his way. The king replaced cabinet members with Bute's choices—right-leaning politicians—many of them his fellow Scots, who would cooperate, including Lord Egremont in Pitt's place, George Grenville as manager of the House of Commons, Sir Francis Dashwood as chancellor of the Exchequer, and Lord Halifax as secretary of state for the north and first lord of the Admiralty. Some of these men were incompetent.

Yet the personalities involved in William Franklin's appointment, the nature of the governorship, and the timing of Egremont's message to the Board of Trade all suggest that the American had everything going for him except his age. The job did not pay a great deal—£800 per year, about $200,000 in today's dollars, and no expense account—but it was important and prestigious. The fact that the job had been offered to the capable Pownall, Halifax's friend, was proof. After Egremont put Franklin's name forward, Halifax—as the other secretary of state—summoned William to the Admiralty and grilled him in order to ascertain whether Franklin was capable. Egremont and Halifax agreed that this smart and likable American was a good choice to replace Hardy as governor of the increasingly wayward colony of New Jersey. Perhaps an American with good Tory instincts could temper

authority with native sympathy and serve as an example for other colonial governments.

Lord Bute must have approved of the idea, but there is no reason to
believe he originated it. Thomas Penn was horrified, fit to be tied. A
frantic letter from the defeated proprietor seven months later accused
Bute, Pringle, and the Franklins of conspiracy in engineering the
shameful appointment in late summer, while the Board of Trade was
in recess and nobody could stop it. But this defies common sense. William Franklin got the appointment because he desired it, he was the
right man for the job at the right time, and both secretaries of state,
Egremont and Halifax, wanted him for the post.

What did Ben Franklin think of his son's triumph? It is unlikely that
he had a hand in the process, and there are signs that he was not happy
about it. He left London for America eleven days before the Earl of
Egremont put William's name before the Board of Trade. And he did
not hear of the appointment until weeks after arriving in Philadelphia.

In the months before he left England, Ben Franklin put aside politics and science. In his spare time, the inventor of the woodstove and
lightning rod, the printer, author, and politician, was an enthusiastic
musician. He loved to sing, especially the Scottish ballads of the period; he played the guitar and the viola de gamba skillfully. He once
composed a string quartet—no small feat for an amateur—and an
essay on music theory. Dr. Franklin evidently had a good deal of spare
time during the winter and spring of 1762, for he found leisure then to
invent a brand-new musical instrument, one that would enjoy a great
vogue, and for which Mozart, Handel, and Beethoven would compose
chamber pieces.

In Spring Gardens, the little street of costly private homes west of
Charing Cross where Franklin had visited the Penns, there stood a
former Huguenot chapel. Given up by the destitute sect long ago, the
open space, fifty by sixty feet, became the Great Room for art exhibi-
tions and concerts by traveling virtuosi. This was the gallery leased by
Franklin's Society of the Arts for their exhibits, and often the concert-
goers enjoyed their music in the midst of colorful portraits and landscapes.

On a Thursday evening, February 18, 1762, a beautiful girl of eighteen mounted a little stage in the Great Room to the applause of several hundred music lovers. She curtseyed and took a seat before a
strange console. The girl was Marianne Davies, celebrated as a child
prodigy, having performed onstage since the age of nine, Handel concertos on the harpsichord and her own tunes on the flute. The console,
three feet long and tapering from eleven inches wide at the large end
to five inches at the small end, contained a glittering cylinder of glass.
From a distance this looked like a ribbed cannon of silver, or a shiny,
colossal caterpillar. On the left end was a mahogany flywheel, which
was turned by a pedal beneath. No one there had ever seen anything
like it. The horizontal cylinder was actually thirty-seven hemispheres
of crystal diminishing in size from nine inches in diameter to three,
fixed upon a spindle.

Miss Davies moistened her delicate fingers in a dish, pedaled the
flywheel, and began caressing the whirling edges of glass.

You have heard the sound before but not as music: a high thin tone
that resembles nothing so much as a flute but thinner, completely
without grain, like a silver bell in the cold distance just after it has been
struck. You heard it first at the dinner table when the grown-ups sipped
sherry after a feast. The crystal goblets glowed on the table and someone would wet her finger in her mouth and run it around the shining
rim. It is that sound, ethereal and rare, but multiplied into chords and
melodies by Franklin's ingenious mechanism, thirty-seven goblets
nested, set spinning by the treadle, at the service of this graceful musician who played the "glassichord" as precisely as if it had been a pipe
organ.

Franklin would not have missed this premiere, five minutes' stroll
from his doorstep; or if he did, he would have had dozens of chances
to hear Miss Davies as she played his instrument at the Great Room
daily through March 27, and sang, to wide acclaim. His glassichord
was a sensation in the intersecting spheres of art and science, capital-
izing as it did upon a fad in London of playing concertos upon musical
glasses. Dozens of glasses ranged upon a table, each filled with the
right amount of water to produce its proper tone, provided the player
with an awkward harmonium; and one could sound only two notes at

once. Nevertheless the crowds loved it, the sweet and melancholy strain that somehow captured the mood of the age, a state of mind that put time out of mind while transcending time and space.

Ethereal, "incomparably sweet," said Franklin, the music seemed to come from the void, work its magic, then die away slowly into silence. It was the sad beginning of the end of the Age of Reason, the dawn of Romanticism. Franklin called his invention the armonica, honoring the country that in those days was considered the land of music; "armonica" is derived from the Italian *armonia*, meaning harmony. Mozart played it, and so did Marie Antoinette.

For the rest of his long life, wherever he traveled, Franklin would never live out of reach of the fragile armonica. He carried one with him at great expense, with extra glasses, when he sailed to Philadelphia in 1762.

By August, William must have known he would marry Betsy Downes, and we can be sure he discussed the prospect with his father, for Benjamin Franklin expressed his sadness that Polly would never be his daughter-in-law in a note to her on August 11. He did not disapprove of Miss Downes; in fact he made a point of calling upon her and her brother, to offer his blessings and perhaps to explain why he would not attend the wedding. The wedding came so soon after Lord Egremont's order, and so soon before William kissed the king's hand in confirmation of his royal appointment, it appears that the marriage waited upon the certainty of employment.

Transatlantic voyages were not things to be entered into lightly at any age, particularly in times of war. The king had declared war on Spain, and Franklin, fifty-six, had booked passage on the *Carolina,* one of ten ships traveling in convoy under protection of HMS *Scarborough,* a man-of-war. Given the time of year, a traveler might wait six months for another such opportunity. His son and future daughter-in-law would have to understand this, as well as Benjamin's longing, at last, to go home. He would sail on August 25.

Before leaving London for Portsmouth, Franklin dined with his son at Peter Collinson's, just as they had done upon arriving five years before. They had enjoyed England, traveling and working together. Just this spring they had been up at Oxford, where Ben received an honorary doctorate and William the master of laws degree. Before embarking from Portsmouth he wrote to a friend: "My son stays a little longer in England." And to another: "He stays in England a little longer," wistfully, as if he wished it were not so. He had told William Strahan three weeks before, as his friend begged him not to go, "I feel like a thing out of its place, and useless because it is out of its place. How then can I any longer be happy in England? . . . I must go home. Adieu."

While Benjamin was at sea the king approved William's commission: "George the Third by Grace of God of Great Britain, France, and Ireland King, To our Trusted and Well beloved William Franklin Esquire Greeting . . . And further know you that We reposing especial Trust and Confidence in the Prudence, Courage, and Loyalty of you . . . have thought fit to constitute you and appoint you. . . ." William was still young enough to hear these words without cynicism, taking them to heart as few men might.

On September 4, the bridegroom wrote to Strahan, suggestively: "Your friend is this moment arrived at the land of matrimony and, (to continue the seaman's phrase) hopes to get safe into harbor this night. I know you and good Mrs. Strahan will sympathize with Mrs. Franklin, (for I am now so happy as to call her) and me in the unbounded joy this long wished for event occasions."

St. George's Church with its stately Corinthian portico looking out on Hanover Square was the fashionable place for weddings. In the colored light from the windows of Flemish glass, beneath the barreled vault, they met at the altar. Behind the priest rose the broad ornamental screen of filigreed wood framing a painting of the Last Supper.

William and Elizabeth said their vows. Soon to begin their new life in America, they did not know whether they ever would return to the city where they had fallen in love.

PART TWO

America and Her Children

CHAPTER 6

America, 1763

A GRUELING VOYAGE OF MORE than three months brought the newlyweds to Philadelphia on February 19, 1763. There the family welcomed and celebrated them during a week of thawing weather that broke up the ice on the Delaware River.

The Franklin women—Deborah and her daughter, Sally—were eager to meet the new bride, who, after her ordeal, was thankful for the fire in a hearth that did not pitch and roll, fresh meat, and a bed of down.

Even for a winter crossing theirs was exceptionally harsh. Setting out from Portsmouth in mid-November, the convoy encountered such rough seas that their man-of-war was damaged and they had to turn back to Plymouth for repairs. On December 14, William wrote to Strahan that Elizabeth was "thank God, perfectly recover'd from her fright and fatigue and her sea sickness . . . I never saw her look so hearty and well before." The voyage had been unpleasant, yet she was not so disheartened that she would not set out again. Had she known what was in store she might have quit. "I would not wish the devil," he recalled, "to experience a winter's passage like ours. We had another storm in the Bay of Biscay, when a very great sea broke through our cabin windows and did considerable damage to our stores and baggage."

They were a mile off the coast of America on February 6, but the wind kept them from landing until the twelfth. The rivers were so packed with ice that they were forced to land 150 miles from Philadelphia. They drove from Lewes-Town in an open carriage, in bitter cold. Growing up in the tropics, and then living in London, Elizabeth had never known such weather. She may not have been hardy, but she had heart.

Driving toward the town, William saw his father and his sister, with a number of other friends, standing in the road awaiting their arrival, bundled in wool coats and fur, making ghosts with their breath. Sally Franklin at twenty was pretty, full-featured, and robust, with heavy eyebrows and long, fair hair. Deborah, as usual, was at home, making the house ready and preparing a warm meal for the travelers. What her stepson and his bride had endured was her worst nightmare and one more reason for her never to cross the ocean.

When Elizabeth got her bearings she must have been fascinated with Philadelphia, and with the simple brick home with its cozy, low-ceilinged rooms and woodstoves. Then there was the wizard's laboratory with tubes and rods and pulleys, microscopes and maps, pneumatic pumps and iron-wheeled gadgets for making electricity, including bells that rang in the kitchen at the approach of lightning. There was the elegant furniture, and the fine crystal and china Franklin had sent home to Deborah during his years in England, samples from many china works to show the variety in workmanship. Bedcovers and window curtains were cut from matching cotton yard goods, a lively pattern printed from copper plates; in the dining room a similar pattern was printed upon the Chippendale side chairs.

Above all Elizabeth was taken with the women: Sally, who adored her older brother; her mother-in-law, Deborah, matronly, kind, and quietly powerful at fifty-eight. Benjamin affectionately addressed her as "my dear child" in his letters—as she did him—with tenderness rather than condescension. He once described her as "a jolly, lively dame" with bright blue eyes, and he sent her a large beer jug with the compliment "I fell in love with it at first sight; for I thought it looked like a fat, jolly dame, clean and tidy, with a neat blue and white calico gown on, good natured and lovely," that reminded him of "somebody."

While she had assumed an attitude of reverence and submission in living with the great man, during his long absences Deborah had cultivated her innate sense of authority. Now she kept house, directing the servants, seeing to everyone's comfort—especially her husband's. Toward William she showed a peculiar reserve at first. William had been in his twenties when he left home with his father, and a bachelor whose manner she found disagreeable. Now he was middle-aged, and a married man. Her feelings for him thawed like the ice on the river.

THEY HAD ARRIVED IN Philadelphia on Friday. William left for New Jersey the next Wednesday. Betsy, not yet ready to face the weather, stayed with the women in Philadelphia while William's father accompanied him on the sixty-mile journey by coach up the road through Trenton and Brunswick to Raritan Bay. "The river was hard and firm and we got well over," Ben wrote to Deborah. He had missed the wedding and his son's royal commission; now he would not miss William's double swearing-in as governor of New Jersey.

The "double swearing" wants some explaining. Before 1700, New Jersey had been a proprietary colony, like Pennsylvania. Land title disputes and revolts against their authority had caused the proprietors to return the government to the Crown in 1702. By then the colony had become polarized between east and west by economic and cultural forces—pulled by New York in one direction and Philadelphia in the other. East Jersey had taken on the stern ethic and temperament of Calvinism imbued by the Scots, as well as the patrician air of the Anglican settlers; West Jersey assumed the more individualistic character of the Quakers, farmers and workmen with an eye on the frontier.

While the surrender to the Crown had united New Jersey, the long-standing division of the two governments would require that the Assembly meet alternately in the eastern capital of Perth Amboy and the western capital of Burlington. By custom, when the king named a new governor, he would proclaim his commission in Perth Amboy first and receive his congratulations with due ceremony. Then he would travel southwest to Burlington, where the whole ritual would be repeated.

On the long journey to Perth Amboy the weather was dreadful.

Heavy snow all along the South River Road effaced the Franklins' view of the lovely port of entry at the end of Raritan Bay. There was nothing to be seen beyond their horses in the drifting snow. But they were pleased to see, several miles from the town, a troop of Middlesex cavalry and some aldermen in horse-drawn sleighs riding out through the storm to welcome them and escort them to the courthouse.

There in that stately brick building His Majesty's Council for Middlesex received William Franklin, Captain General and Governor in Chief of the Province of New Jersey, as he marched in procession to High Street behind the mayor, the aldermen, and the Common Council. The courthouse galleries were full as Franklin proclaimed his commission and took his oaths. Then Mayor Samuel Neville congratulated him on his appointment and on his safe arrival after a long and dangerous voyage. He hoped that Franklin's administration would be guided by justice and wise councils, pleasing not only to the people but to Franklin himself. At last he wished that His Excellency would choose Perth Amboy as his seat of residence, promising that the citizens here would do everything in their power to render it agreeable.

Mayor Neville had made the opening move in the chess match between east and west, endeavoring to seat the governor in Perth Amboy. Franklin's diplomatic response shows he was ready for it. After thanking everyone, he declared that "wherever I may reside, which is as yet uncertain, I shall be glad of every opportunity of showing my regard for the city of Perth-Amboy." This choice of residence, practical and symbolic, would be one of the most important of his administration. It was good policy to defer it until he had made the acquaintance of councilmen from all points of the compass.

Seven miles west along the river at New Brunswick, on March 1 the governor was treated to similar fanfare without the formal swearing-in. The next day, halfway to Burlington, the party stopped at Prince-Town, where the governor visited the college "and was received by the president and tutors with great respect." In the auditorium of Nassau Hall, President Samuel Finley formally greeted His Excellency the Governor, committing the college to his protection and hoping for his patronage.

And if we presume, what we rationally may, from your excellency's general character—from your being entrusted with so honorable and important a commission, by the Father of his country, the royal patron of religion, virtue and learning whatever is good—and from an education under the influence and direction of the very eminent Doctor Franklin your Excellency's honoured father . . .

In short, President Finley was sure the governor would view Princeton with a favorable eye.

Outside Burlington, the mayor and aldermen met the Franklins and escorted them into town. "He was received at his arrival with the greatest demonstrations of joy, and the evening was concluded with bonfires, ringing of bells, firing of guns, & c," wrote one reporter. On Friday morning, March 4, William was escorted to the courthouse, where all the formalities of the ceremony were repeated—minus the bid for residency. Benjamin wrote to Strahan on March 28, reporting that he had just returned from the tour of New Jersey, where he was glad to see his son received everywhere "with the utmost respect and even affection by all ranks of people. So that I have great hopes of his being now comfortably settled." But to his sister Jane Mecum he confided that in regard to his profession and marriage, "the lady is of so amiable character that the latter gives me more pleasure than the former, though I have no doubt but that he will make as good a governor as husband: for he has good principles and good dispositions, and I think is not deficient in good understanding."

To be a good son, a good husband, and a good governor of New Jersey—these aspirations guided William's actions during the next decade of his life. He owed his father a great deal of money. Ben had supported him in London and now was supporting his son, Temple. For reasons no one can quite understand, Franklin kept strict account of the money his son owed him, as if William had been a friend or client and not a blood relative. William, having no other father but this one whom he adored, simply accepted the condition, and with it his father's harping on the debt as it mounted. He promised to make good on it, and one day he would, with penal interest. Meanwhile, if he was a good governor, the Board of Trade would increase his salary, which would please his wife and allow him to reimburse his father. And his presence here would create opportunities to invest in that western land he had long believed would be his key to enduring wealth.

Governing New Jersey during the dozen years of William's administration presented a challenge that would make the most of his talents. For forty years the king had temporarily relegated New Jersey to the jurisdiction of New York; as New York tended to neglect New Jersey, its citizens developed an autonomous spirit. In the 1730s they asked for their own governor, and the king sent them Lewis Morris in 1738. William Franklin was the ninth governor of New Jersey in twenty-five years—most of the others inept, and many corrupt as well. He took his oaths of office in a time of relative calm. But the same tensions between the royal governor and the elected assembly that disrupted taxation and defense in Pennsylvania also simmered in New Jersey—with a difference. For generations there had been two distinct cultures in the east and west, fostering bitter political rivalry.

William's first important political decision was to reside in Burlington rather than Amboy—a wise choice. In Perth Amboy there was actually a house under construction for the governor, but it was not funded by the province; the Council of Proprietors was building it, "and as there is no good understanding between them & a great part of the people I have reason to think that my living in their house will not be a little unpopular . . . I have therefore taken a pretty good house in this town, which as it is within 20 miles of Philadelphia makes it the more agreeable."

It was a good-sized brick house facing north on Water Street with fine views of the Delaware, one block from the wharf and ferry. "I have the prospect of an easy agreeable administration, and reason to expect an increase of the salary at least 500 pounds per annum," William wrote. He did not get that much money. But he was granted, after a friendly meeting with the Assembly on May 25 in Perth Amboy, a £200 increase. Out of his salary William would be expected to pay for his housing and all expenses, including the entertainment expected of a royal governor.

Elizabeth and William were pleased to be only a day's journey from the Franklin home on Market Street. Pennsylvania was much the same as it had been six years before, apart from an increase in prices and in population (now 18,000 in Philadelphia). Ben Franklin had been gratified to be welcomed by all of his old friends and many new ones upon his return, and to learn that in the recent election he had been chosen unanimously as a representative for the city in the Assembly. His wealth had grown. He hired carpenters to begin work on the ten-room house he had designed for the lot on Market Street between Third and Fourth streets in the shadow of the jail.

POLITICS IN PENNSYLVANIA HAD not improved in Franklin's absence. The conflict between the Quaker-dominated Assembly and the proprietors was as bitter as ever, as Thomas Penn's nephew John assumed the governorship. The British victory in the Seven Years' War did not solve the Indian problem, as the Ottawa tribe under the leadership of Chief Pontiac plotted to expel the English from the territory, attacking settlements far and wide. Tomahawk and arson took more lives in 1763 than when the French and Indian War was at its deadliest. In November, Benjamin Franklin returned from a tour of the northern post offices with his daughter, Sally, to address a crisis that had been building for a decade.

Chief Pontiac's recent uprising in Ohio had caused such devastation west of the Susquehanna that a mob of Scots and Irish vigilantes from Paxtong, Pennsylvania, announced a scalp bounty, vowing to exterminate all Native Americans. On December 15, fifty-seven vigilantes swooped down upon a village of Conestoga Indians near Lancaster. These people, many of them Christians, had lived there for years subsisting on trade from crafted brooms, clay pots, and woven baskets. The "Paxton Boys" slaughtered six of them in their huts, promising to kill more. Governor John Penn offered a reward for the vigilantes' capture and placed the sixteen surviving Conestogas in protective custody in the Lancaster workhouse.

No one came forward to name the perpetrators, and two days after Christmas the Paxton terrorists broke into the "guarded" workhouse and executed six Indian men and women and eight children. The massacre sharply divided the colony. "If an Indian injures me, does it follow that I may revenge that injury on all Indians?" *Emphatically not,* wrote Ben Franklin, in his pamphlet titled "A Narrative of the Late Massacres in Lancaster County" published in January 1764. A moving elegy for the slaughtered innocents, and a historical meditation upon racism and magnanimity, Franklin's narrative condemned all prejudice. "The only crime of these poor wretches seems to have been that they had reddish brown skin and black hair."

An astonishing number of colonists disagreed with him. The incident threatened to become a civil war pitting west against east, the frontier farmers against the merchants and tradesmen of Philadelphia, Germans and Scots against sons of old England, Presbyterians against Quakers and Anglicans. The Paxtons spoke for thousands of frontiersmen mourning lost husbands, wives, mothers, and babies. They blamed the Quakers who dominated the Assembly, who had "coddled the Indians" so they could trade with them; the pacifist Quakers, they felt, had bungled the frontier defenses.

Made bold by widespread support, the Paxtons set their sights on the capital where a hundred fifty Indians were under the protection of Governor Penn in the city barracks. On January 28, a Philadelphia merchant drove from Lancaster to report that in ten days "fifteen hundred men would come down to kill the said Indians, and that if fifteen hundred were not enough, five thousand were now ready to join them." And there was a rumor that the marchers intended to kill the Quakers, too, or at least any who opposed them.

Governor Penn ordered British troops transferred to Lancaster. On February 2, he moved to extend the British Riot Act of 1715 to Pennsylvania; the Assembly approved it within forty-eight hours. As the mob approached from the west two days later, gathering strength with every mile, Penn called a town meeting at the State House on Chestnut Street. At four o'clock in the afternoon he addressed the council, the assembly members, magistrates, and a concourse of citizens numbering three thousand who stood outside in a driving rain. Penn announced the imminent invasion, proclaimed the Riot Act, and called upon the townsmen to arm themselves.

At midnight the church bells sounded the alarm. The Paxton hoodlums had crossed the Schuylkill River and reached Germantown just north of the city armed with tomahawks and rifles. And Governor John Penn, a mild-eyed, gentle scion of that formidable clan, did what other governors had done in times of clear and present danger. Shelving his politics, he ran to Benjamin Franklin's house for advice, his counselors following, and set up headquarters there. Franklin later called this an honor, humorously, although at the time the danger was so real that there would have been no levity in the gloom.

He advised Penn to send clergymen to Germantown to meet the insurgents and use their influence to turn them back, or at least delay them while Franklin organized his militia. Penn wanted him to take command, but Franklin recalled, "I chose to carry a musket and strengthen his authority by setting an example of obedience to his order." So a Presbyterian pastor, two Anglicans, and a Swedish Lutheran rode up to Germantown in the mud to talk peace. After greeting them in the name of Christ, they told the leaders, James Gibson and Matthew Smith, that a thousand men were armed for defense and if there was an attack there would surely be bloodshed. The pastors also confided that many Quakers had taken up guns and swords, which so amazed and sobered the invaders that they paused to rest the night of February 6 in Germantown so they might ponder the best course of action.

Franklin did not wait to find out. At sunrise he led a delegation that included Attorney General Benjamin Chew, William Logan of the governor's council, the mayor, Thomas Willing, his friend Joseph Galloway from the Assembly, and a couple of pastors to confront the mob in Germantown. The frightened governor had kept him up for forty-eight hours running. And for days before that "my rest [was] so broken by alarms on other nights that the whole week seems one confused space of time," the days so jumbled it was hard to say "on such a day such a thing happened."

His recollection of events understates his bravery in deciding the course of them. Franklin says he found it not too difficult to persuade this mob to go home quietly, as "the fighting face we put on made them more willing to hear reason." That is the way he recalled it in letters to Richard Jackson and Lord Kames, but in fact the conference with Gibson and Smith took several hours of that day. The timing of this meeting had been all-important, and Franklin had engineered it as well as the mustering of the troops that backed him. The Paxton leaders agreed to come into the city peaceably and present their grievances to the governor and the Assembly in a formal petition. When Gibson and Smith crossed Vine Street with an armed guard of twenty Paxton disciples, there was another alarm and rumors that the peace was a ruse—but there was no more violence.

For forty-eight hours Franklin had been a great man, he recalled. But when the sky cleared, "I became less a man than ever: for I had by these transactions made myself many enemies among the populace." His influential pamphlet was so critical of Christianity wherever racism thrived in its name that he had alienated a lot of the electorate outside his home city, and many within it. He called the frontiersmen "barbarous" and denounced "the Christian white savages of Paxtong and Donegal," meaning Irish hoodlums in general.

Governor Penn was grateful, but not for long. He had all the old reasons to fear Citizen Franklin, and he would use the full weight of proprietary influence to squeeze him out of the Assembly. First, John Penn insulted the Assembly so roundly at the end of the Paxton affair that they were aghast, after all they had done to rescue the capital. Governor Penn dropped the investigation of the murders and met privately with the rioters, deliberately excluding the Assembly. The grandson of William Penn then decreed a bounty for Indian scalps.

It was a startling deal with the devil Penn had struck with the west against the east, Presbyterians and Lutherans against Quakers and Anglicans. "All regard for him in the Assembly is lost," Franklin told Dr. Fothergill, and declared that there was no longer any hope for happiness under the government of the Penns. The Assembly quickly passed twenty-six resolutions that condemned proprietary government and called for Pennsylvania to be directly controlled by the Crown.

The Conestoga Indian Massacre had set the stage for the bitterest election in Pennsylvania's history. It pitted men like Franklin and Galloway, who desired the king to "take the people of this province under his immediate protection and government," against many others who feared a royal government might institute the Church of England, bishops, and tithes. Most Germans and Presbyterians defended the

status quo, especially the proprietary constitution that had always protected religious freedom.

In April 1764, Franklin wrote a pamphlet called "Cool Thoughts on
the Present Situation of Our Public Affairs," in which he argued that
the current miserable dissension had not been created by depraved individuals, good or bad citizens or proprietors, but by a root cause, a
flawed system:

> As some physicians say every animal body brings into the world . . .
> the seeds of that disease that shall finally produce its dissolution, so
> the political body of a proprietary government contains those con-
> vulsive principles that will at length destroy it.

The rhetoric was revolutionary; the emotions on both sides of the
question ran high. Franklin's enemies, and especially those who wanted
him out of the Assembly, desperately wanted to destroy him.

When Franklin had distributed a few hundred of his pamphlets on
the streets of Philadelphia, he rode to Burlington, where he spent the
third week of April with his son and daughter-in-law. He wanted to
share his opinions in "Cool Thoughts" with William and to enlist his
aid in the coming election. William had put on some needed weight in
the year since the sea voyage, as had Elizabeth, and they both looked
happy and well in their house on the river. Couriers from Philadelphia
had kept him up to date on the troubles there. The Indian uprisings
had been a challenge for William's government, too. He had succeeded
in raising three hundred New Jersey militiamen to join General
Thomas Gage's forces on the frontier. Like his father at the Albany
conference in 1754, William complained: "The want of union among
the colonies must ever occasion delay in their military operation."

Benjamin boasted to Richard Jackson that the two provinces where
he and his son had influence had granted more aid to His Majesty's
service "than all the other colonies put together." But his efforts in the
Assembly were not appreciated as much as William's in the governor's
house. Benjamin's pamphlet had called for an end to the established
government. When the Assembly convened in May, angry debates
broke out upon the question. John Dickinson, a young lawyer, led the

proprietors' defense; Franklin and Joseph Galloway led the attack. Thirty-three-year-old Galloway took a swing at Dickinson, who welcomed the fistfight, and the men had to be pulled apart.

In the heat of the conflict, Isaac Norris gave up his place as Speaker of the House, and Franklin was elected to the position on May 26. More than ever, Benjamin Franklin had become a lightning rod for the storm of controversy over Pennsylvania's fate. William Franklin had written to Strahan only days before that Maryland and Pennsylvania "seem to be in a state of anarchy, & unless the King takes them under his immediate government . . . the worst of consequences will probably ensue." He also confided—prophetically—that Strahan was likely to see his friend Benjamin in England soon, for the Assembly wanted to send him to argue for the change of government.

On June 18 he wrote again to Strahan: "My father seems to be preparing in earnest for a voyage to England."

THE AUTUMN ELECTION OF 1764 became the prototype of the all-out mudslinging, poll-bullying, bare-knuckle contests that have become the embarrassment of democracy. It was not a simple or polite business, removing Colonel Franklin from the Assembly he had shaped and controlled for a decade. But the Germans, Presbyterians, and John Penn would stop at nothing to get it done.

Franklin had become an easy target. For years he had ridden roughshod over the feelings of several religious denominations and nationalities. His recent pamphlet had attacked all Christians who cited scripture in support of their bloody revenge on the Indians, particularly the Scottish Presbyterians, a large part of the electorate. When he wrote another pamphlet attacking John Penn, it was answered by an anonymous riposte in the form of an epitaph for Franklin called *What Is Sauce for a Goose Is Also Sauce for a Gander*. This became the laundry list for every charge against Franklin, however far-fetched. "Here lies the man" who plotted to become governor himself; who had pilfered his electrical experiments from other scientists; who had purchased his honorary degrees; who in spite of his advanced age had been an incorrigible lecher; whose son William, the well-known bastard, was the son of a "kitchen wench" named Barbara whom Franklin had so criminally neglected that she starved to death and rested now in an unmarked grave.

William rode down from Burlington on September 24 and spent the week before the election helping his father in Philadelphia. He worked the Germantown neighborhood, salvaging votes in a community where the Franklins had few friends. John Penn wrote to his uncle Thomas recalling William's "canvassing among the Germans & endeavoring to get votes by propagating the most infamous lies he could invent. He is as bad as his father."

The polls opened at nine in the morning on Monday, October 1, and voters mounted the steps of the courthouse in a steady stream until almost midnight. The party of Franklin and Galloway, called the Old Ticket, moved to keep the polls open for another day, as they had enlisted a number of lame and aged folk who needed assistance. But the proprietary party (the New Ticket) sent a messenger to Germantown, where they mustered several hundred voters more to cast ballots. When the votes were counted, Franklin had lost his seat "by about 25 in 4000 voters," as he recalled. Franklin took it in stride—he was already looking forward to his future journey. Two years in America had been enough for him. He and Galloway had lost, but the antiproprietary party still won the majority in the Assembly. Franklin may have known all along that he could not win this election; whatever happened, he had work to do beyond the confining walls of the colonial statehouse.

It was more evident than ever to Benjamin Franklin and his son that Pennsylvania's only hope was royal intervention. William Franklin wrote to Strahan that New Jersey stood in stark contrast to Pennsylvania. Here all was peace and tranquillity, and there "the utmost anarchy and confusion. If the Crown therefore inclines to have that province under its immediate govt. there never can be a more proper opportunity for the purpose."

In the next session the Pennsylvania Assembly resolved to petition the king. On October 26 they appointed Benjamin Franklin in his old role as agent to sail to London and negotiate the complicated business. This is what he had wanted all along—he had proposed the very thing to Isaac Norris six years earlier.

A throng of three hundred or more friends and admirers escorted Franklin from Philadelphia to Chester, the port fifteen miles south on the Delaware River, on the morning of November 7. At two o'clock in the afternoon he embarked on the *King of Prussia*. As he watched and waved from the deck, the people shouted huzzas and cannons saluted, and at last a chorus sang an adaptation of "God Save the King" that had been written for the occasion:

> *O LORD our GOD arise*
> *Scatter our Enemies,*
> *And make them fall.*
> *Confound their Politicks,*
> *Frustrate such Hypocrites,*
> *Franklin, on Thee we fix,*
> *GOD Save us all.*

CHAPTER 7

A Frenzy or Madness

ALTHOUGH SHE NO LONGER had her husband, Deborah at last had her own home in Philadelphia, only a few steps from the spot where she had first spied young Ben Franklin, the scruffy runaway from Boston. The handsome three-story brick house stood in the center of a courtyard set back from Market Street. She and Sally moved into the foursquare dwelling in May 1765, six months after her husband's departure, and were preparing to paint and decorate the ten rooms that summer according to his instructions.

In the middle of August that year, as if by some prearranged signal, an appalling number of royal officers hired to implement the new Stamp Acts were hanged in effigy from Massachusetts to the Carolinas. In the words of Franklin's friend John Hughes, who became a victim of it, "a sort of frenzy or madness has got hold of the people of all ranks, that I fancy some lives will be lost before this fire is put out."

In the printing office a few doors away from the new house, Franklin's partner, David Hall, was busy gathering dispatches and setting type for the *Gazette* that Deborah and Sally Franklin would read on September 12 describing the widespread mob violence along the Atlantic seaboard. William Franklin was writing to his father on Saturday, September 7, with similar intelligence.

It began with Andrew Oliver, provincial secretary of Massachusetts and member of the colonial council. On August 14, Oliver was hanged in effigy on the ruins of the building in which he was to conduct his office. The mob had razed it to the ground. A week later in New London at four o'clock in the afternoon, angry colonists hanged an effigy of the tax collector Jared Ingersoll on a gibbet twenty-five feet in the air above the Town Commons. He had a boot fixed upon one of his shoulders and a puppet of the devil grinning out of the boot. After an hour of exhibition he was taken down and carried through the streets, attended by most of the citizens and their screaming children while cannon from the fort boomed their approval. "Between ten and eleven the effigies were consumed [burned] amid the acclamation of the people." The writer for *The Pennsylvania Gazette* approved everyone's manners and reported that "no person suffered the least injury."

On Monday morning, August 26, the citizens of Annapolis dressed up a dummy holding some sheets of paper in his hands before his face. Everyone agreed the dummy looked like the businessman Zachariah Hood, newly appointed an officer of the Crown. They placed the effigy in a horse-drawn cart and paraded it all around the state house and the cobblestone streets near the harbor until the church bell tolled the noon hour, a "solemn knell." Then they climbed a hill and hanged the manikin on a gibbet. At last the leaders set fire to a tar barrel underneath and burned the figure until it fell into the barrel. "By the many significant nods of the head, while in the cart," the reporter noted, the manikin "may be said to have gone off very penitently."

So far, the readers of the news would have noted, the demonstrations were just "rough music"—terrifying, but not in themselves dangerous. "But as is usual with mobs when they once feel their own power," William told his father, "they have gone much beyond what was desired by those who first raised them."

On August 26, local patriots calling themselves the Sons of Liberty led a mob in the attack on William Story, deputy register of the admiralty court, in charge of naval affairs in Boston Harbor. They broke his windows, rushed into the house and office there, burned his books and papers, and broke up his furniture. Pleased with the fire and noise and smoke, the revelers advanced to the house of Ben Hallowell, comptroller of customs for the Port of Boston. There were not only books to burn and furniture to crash but also a cellar of liquor and trunks of fine clothing. When they had burned and looted to their satisfaction, and stolen thirty pounds of sterling kept in the coffer, they wondered where in the town of Boston they might go to find greater plunder.

Warmed to their work by rum and stolen waistcoats, the horde marched on to the beautiful mansion of Lieutenant Governor Thomas Hutchinson, whose daughter begged on her knees not to leave it and had to be dragged away as men were shattering the windowpanes with brick shards and rifle butts. Under a gibbous moon, the mob then "broke all the windows, wainscots, &c., cut down the cupola, and uncovered a great part of the roof, leaving the house a mere shell from top to bottom." They broke up all the furniture, tore up what clothing they didn't steal, carried off the jewelry, books, and papers, and drank, confiscated, or destroyed eight barrels and three quarter casks of wine, as well as assorted crates of fine vintages. And so on and on, "riotously assembled all night," they stole £900 in sterling Hutchinson had laid up, and all his silver plate. Next they had their eyes on the custom house, and some other rich dwelling places, but the men were tired out from their labor, and went their ways to eat and sleep and divide the spoils.

The saddest part of the Hutchinson catastrophe, for him and for posterity, is that he was perhaps the greatest collector of antiquarian books and manuscripts of his generation, and all of these were lost.

In Philadelphia, Franklin's friend John Hughes was about to become a target of this outrage over the Stamp Act. This new tax passed by Parliament on March 22, 1765, required American colonists to pay a tax on all printed documents, legal and commercial papers, newspapers, even playing cards and dice. The law was to go into effect in November, and John Hughes, along with Oliver, Ingersoll, Hood, and a half dozen other citizens, had been appointed stamp distributors. When Franklin recommended him for the job back in April, he had no idea the tax was going to cause such mayhem, or he would have picked one of his enemies. On September 12, Hughes wrote: "Our clamors run very high, and I am told my house will be pulled down and the stamps burnt. To which I give no answer than that I will defend my house at the risk of my life."

Deborah Franklin, a few blocks away, was not about to let terrorists near her new house. Her husband came under fire as John Hughes's patron. William Franklin rode down to Philadelphia the weekend of September 10, after dealing with the resignation of his own terrified tax man, William Coxe. He meant to take Deborah and Sally away with him to the safety of his home in Burlington. Sally went with him, but Deborah refused to budge.

A ship had arrived from Londonderry on September 16 with good news: There had been a change in the ministry. The Duke of Newcastle had replaced the Duke of Marlborough as Privy Seal (an important cabinet office), and the colonists saw this as an occasion for celebration and heavy drinking. They built bonfires in squares, graveyards, and parks and danced around them waving hats and cheering. John Hughes's home on Fourth Street bordered a cemetery, where he heard the mob talking about roping the chimney and pulling down his house. Hughes thought he might not live to see the sun, and wrote to Franklin by candlelight telling him so, and that he was "well-armed with fire-arms and determined to stand a siege." They would have to kill him first before wrecking his house and then Franklin's new mansion around the corner.

For a week William and other relatives and friends in town had begged Deborah to leave the house for shelter elsewhere. But Mrs. Franklin declined. "Cousin Davenport [Josiah] come and told me that more than twenty people had told him it was his duty to be with me. I said I was pleased to receive civility from anybody so he stayed with me . . . Towards night I said he should fetch a gun or two as we had none."

As the crowd and their shouting increased, so did the number of men who rallied to guard Mrs. Franklin, including her brother John Read, David Hall, and many neighbors, until there were more than a dozen under her command. "I sent to ask my brother to come and bring his gun also. We made one room into a magazine. I ordered some sort of defense upstairs such as I could manage myself."

As the raucous volume increased, they pleaded with Deborah

Franklin to leave the house. But she stood her ground. She declared she was very sure her husband had done nothing to hurt anyone, nor had she herself given offense to anybody, nor would anybody make *her* uneasy. "Nor would I stir or show the least uneasiness but if any one came to disturb me I would show a proper resentment," said the sixty-year-old housewife, armed with a flintlock musket.

By nine o'clock John Hughes reported that several of his friends patrolling the neighborhood between his dwelling and the London Coffee House at the end of Market Street near the river came to tell him "the collection of rabble begins to decrease visibly in the streets and the appearance of danger seems a good deal less than it did."

This was only the beginning of the turmoil.

DEBORAH'S HUSBAND HAD GONE to England primarily to persuade Parliament to rescue Pennsylvania from the Penns and place the colony under the king's protection. In this he had become a royalist. He was also supposed to lobby for the repeal of the Stamp Act, but he had considered that matter secondary.

To his alarm, letters from David Hall and others from home informed Franklin that "nothing [was] talked of but the Stamp Act, with which the people are much displeased." On July 11, Franklin had written, defensively, to Charles Thomson, leader of Philadelphia's Sons of Liberty, that he had done everything in his power to prevent the passing of the Stamp Act. "Nobody could be more concern'd in interest than myself to oppose it, sincerely and heartily. But the tide was too strong against us. The Nation was provok'd by American claims of independence. . . . We might as well have hinder'd the Suns setting."

Never was the agent Franklin more wide of the mark than he had been during those mild days of midsummer in London, enjoying a diet so rich it was inflaming his gout. William, in Burlington, had been closer to American reality, although he presided over a peaceable session of his assembly there in the spring, calmly recessed on June 4 when William led the legislators to his mansion for a party. It was King George III's birthday, and the crowd gathered to drink the king's health. A brass cannon had been rolled down Pearl Street, and right outside the governor's door it fired salutes. Then the company went indoors to take refreshment and to view the new full-length portraits of the king and queen in their coronation robes, recently arrived as a present from the Crown to the governor.

Everyone in town had heard about Patrick Henry's speech in the Virginia House of Burgesses on May 29 denouncing the Stamp Act and taxation proposals of Parliament: "Caesar had his Brutus, Charles I his Cromwell, and George III ..." Patrick Henry's voice had been submerged in the many cries of *Treason!* His conclusion, "George III may profit by their example," was hardly audible in the riot of dissenting voices. The Virginia resolutions declared that the General Assembly alone had power to levy taxes upon a colony. Yet when the New Jersey delegates met in the courthouse at Broad and Main streets that day in June, there was not a word about the Stamp Act. William reported to the Board of Trade in July that his recent session had been "very amicable.... The utmost harmony subsists between the several branches of the legislature.... All is peace and quietness, & likely to remain so."

A mere month later, William Coxe resigned in terror as distributor of stamps in New Jersey, while Bostonians gutted Governor Hutchinson's mansion. In London, Ben Franklin heard of Patrick Henry's speech and wrote to John Hughes on August 9, "the rashness of the Assembly in Virginia is amazing," promising he would try to get the Act repealed. Meanwhile Hughes might be unpopular, but "firm loyalty to the crown and faithful adherence to the government" was always the wisest course "whatever may be the madness of the populace." But Franklin was wrong again. John Hughes would have been better advised to follow Coxe and Oliver, or Augustus Johnson of Rhode Island, who fled to HMS *Cygnet* after witnessing his form in effigy hanged and burned in the town square. The colonists were protesting not merely because of the financial burden the Stamp Act promised but because it violated their right as Englishmen not to be taxed without consent.

The street protests and bonfires of summer prompted a Stamp Act Congress to be held in New York in the autumn. The Sons of Liberty were ready to use force against tax collectors who refused to resign, so Royal governors without clear direction from Parliament were in a ticklish situation. William Franklin blamed Coxe for resigning, calling it a betrayal, but in the face of so much public furor he was not sure he ought to replace him. What should he do with the stamps when they arrived? He considered sending them to New York, or leaving them on a ship at sea, then decided to guard them in the Burlington barracks.

For the rest of that year William Franklin was caught between his duty to Parliament and the sentiments of the New Jersey assembly members who now wanted to attend the Stamp Act Congress. In June, a calmer time, the Assembly had voted to avoid the congress, and now everyone blamed the governor for the vote not to attend. Emotionally the colonists regarded Parliament the way Pennsylvanians regarded the proprietary government, and it must have been strange for William to find himself the butt of that resentment.

When a group of lawyers met in Perth Amboy in September to consider the legal status of the Stamp Act, they agreed to work for its repeal and not to purchase the stamps when they arrived. As the autumn elections approached, Governor Franklin endured harsh criticism from Philadelphia to Burlington as the New Jersey liberals accused him—son of the man falsely rumored to have invented the Stamp Act—of intercepting invitations to the Congress and making "*strong efforts* to subdue the *spirit of liberty* in his government." Tempers ran so hot that Sally was persuaded, once again, to escape to William's home in New Jersey for safety.

The violence never spread to New Jersey, largely because of William's careful management of the crisis. He wanted to keep the peace there as an end in itself, and so that his father might point to this province as a shining example of government under the Crown. On September 24 he met with seven members of the New Jersey council and asked for their advice. They told him time was on his side: He had no stamp distributor, and no instructions from Parliament as to what to do about it; finally, he had no stamps. Calling for troops would merely alarm the citizens and occasion turmoil; by delaying, one could maintain the peace.

Delay was a good idea. Franklin would make the most of this strategy, sometimes declining to convene the Assembly for longer than a year. Despite demands for a convention that would revisit the question of sending delegates to the New York Congress, William did nothing. When the speaker, Robert Ogden, called a rump gathering of thirteen anti–Stamp Act members at Sproul's Tavern in Perth Amboy, William did not interrupt—although he thought it his duty to dissolve the unconstitutional meeting. As he explained to his superiors, "There was great reason to apprehend that I should thereby have thrown the province into the utmost confusion."

At the rogue meeting in Sproul's Tavern, the members had chosen two of their company to attend the Stamp Act Congress on October 7. During that twelve-day session in New York's City Hall, the twenty-seven delegates from nine colonies framed resolutions petitioning the king and Parliament to repeal the law. The Franklins, father and son, reached the same unhappy conclusion in the same span of five days in mid-November—as if they were of one mind despite Benjamin's distance from the turmoil. As there was a lag of several months between England and America when it came to events and round-trip responses, it is fascinating to see two letters of the Franklins crossing on ships passing in the North Atlantic in November, letters with identical sentiments concerning the Stamp Act.

"The general execution of the Stamp Act would be impracticable without occasioning more mischief than it was worth, by totally alienating the affections of the Americans from this country, and thereby lessening its commerce," Benjamin wrote to William on November 9. And William wrote to his father on November 13: "For any man to set himself up as an advocate for the Stamp Act in the colonies is a mere piece of quixotism, and can answer no good purpose whatever. And if he is an officer of government he not only becomes obnoxious, but is sure to lose all the authority belonging to his office."

In Philadelphia, Franklin's enemies were using the Stamp Act as a blunt instrument to batter his name and his son's, linking their so-called colonial agent with the parliamentary forces that sought to profit by this unlawful tax. They said that the Crown had bribed Franklin with promises of a high post in the government and that he had gotten money by recommending Hughes. In the same breath they accused

William of curbing protests in New Jersey. Friends tried to defend Benjamin, but the slanderers who began their campaign in the summer found a public eager to think the worst of him. "My father is absent," William wrote, in a defense published in October 1765, "but he has left friends enough on the spot who are both capable and willing to clear him from any aspersions which the malice of the proprietary party can suggest." In the heat of the autumn elections, such words scattered in the wind. Ben Franklin came as close to political ruin in America as he ever would in his long life.

While never doubting which side he was on, Franklin made the short-sighted decision to tolerate the Stamp Act until the situation became so dire that he was called upon to attack it. At last he did this in a series of letters to the press in the New Year, and in private conversations with British officials. Commerce had begun to suffer—English merchants, manufacturers, and shippers—from an American boycott of all transactions requiring the hated stamps, instituted by the Stamp Act Congress. In a matter of months the cost had become more than the Empire could bear.

In the second week of February 1766, the House of Commons called for a hearing to consider all problems resulting from the Stamp Act. A number of experts, English and colonial merchants, were interviewed before Franklin was called to testify on Thursday the thirteenth. But his role as agent, his celebrity, and his profound understanding of the colonies made him the star witness. Everyone was waiting to hear what he had to say.

Franklin dazzled the members of Parliament with logic, eloquence, and humor. In all, he answered 174 questions. He knew that most of his questioners were friendly, men who had opposed the act in the first place.

> Q. What was the temper of America towards Great Britain before the year 1763?
> A. The best in the world. They submitted willingly to the government of the Crown, and paid, in all their courts, obedience to acts of Parliament . . . they cost you nothing in forts, citadels, garrisons, or armies to keep them in subjection. They were

governed by this country at the expense only of a little pen, ink, and paper. They were led by a thread. They had not only a respect but an affection for Great Britain . . . They considered the Parliament as the great bulwark and security of their liberties and privileges, and always spoke of it with the utmost respect and veneration. . . .

Q. And have they not still the same respect for Parliament?
A. No, it is greatly lessened.

Q. To what causes is that owing?
A. The restraints lately laid on their trade by which the bringing of foreign gold and silver into the colonies was prevented; the prohibition of making paper money among themselves, and then demanding a new and heavy tax by stamps. . . .

Strahan reported that some lord had commented "that he never knew truth to make so great a progress in so very short a time." It was two hours of incomparable theater.

Q. Can anything less than a military force carry the Stamp Act into execution?
A. I do not see how a military force can be applied to that purpose.

Q. Why may it not?
A. Suppose a military force [is] sent to America, they will find nobody in arms; what then are they to do? They cannot force a man to take stamps who chooses to do without them. They will not find a rebellion; they may indeed make one.

Q. If the Act is not repealed, what do you think will be the consequences?
A. The total loss of the respect and affection the people of America bear to this country, and of all the commerce that depends on that respect and affection.

When the Stamp Act was repealed eight days later, on February 22, Strahan wrote to David Hall, who published the dialogue, "To this very examination more than anything else, you are indebted to the *speedy* and *total* repeal of this odious law."

Benjamin Franklin went from being a scapegoat to a hero in a matter of weeks. William did not do as well in New Jersey. He had yielded to public pressure for a special meeting to discuss the Stamp Act in November; then, once the official session convened in Burlington, he had little to do with it. On the last day he did rebuke the members for their "late unprecedented, irregular and unconstitutional meeting at Perth Amboy." His criticism of the offending members was rigorous, yet it was meant more for the record, to show his superiors he was upholding the law, rather than to take charge of a situation that had spun out of control. Privately, William blamed his troubles not on the people of New Jersey but on Parliament. They had failed to foresee the furor the Stamp Act would cause, and then had given him no guidance through the storm that followed.

Still, he had survived the Stamp Act crisis with his dignity and his property unspoiled. No other colonial governor had handled the matter so skillfully.

WHAT PARLIAMENT GAVE WITH one hand it took away with the other. The Stamp Act was gone, but in its place a month later the Declaratory Act confirmed Parliament's right to legislate for the colonies. In addition, the so-called Mutiny Act had been on the books for a year, demanding that every colony furnish quarters for the British troops, bedding and pots and pans, candles and firewood, beer and rum. And then there was the renewed Currency Act, which made money so scarce that obeying the Mutiny Act was infeasible. In these infringements glowed the embers of rancor that the Sons of Liberty would soon blow into a bonfire.

But for a while at least—until the bad news arrived on the heels of the good—there was peace in William's colony. He began building a three-story townhouse of brick, with broad lawns and gardens, on the Delaware River. He bought five acres of woods nearby, and eleven more acres five miles south on Rancocas Creek, where he built a farmhouse. Always interested in crops and planting, now he accumulated a shelf of books on agriculture and husbandry. He hired an English farm manager and experimented with new plows and windlasses. He cleared a park that could graze a hundred deer, and a plantation that would cover six hundred acres by 1770.

It is obvious from Elizabeth's relations with all the children in the family that she loved children, and there is no reason to believe she would not have wanted a child herself. As for William's inclinations, there is proof in his letters that he was prepared to have more children after Temple, and that he found in his wife an attractive mate. The year they came to America she was thirty-five and he was two years younger. As she was not a woman of robust health, it seems probable that she was infertile and it was a matter of some frustration, and disappointment, that she would pass her childbearing years without giving birth.

As governor, Franklin was expected to host banquets for visiting dignitaries, and to entertain councilmen, mayors, and assemblymen on state occasions; and as a representative of the Crown, he was expected to be a member of the Church of England. The governor and his wife attended Sunday services in St. Mary's Church on Broad Street in Burlington. The white sanctuary with its cupola and gable, its low door with sash windows on either side, was sixty years old and in poor repair; William made donations to the church fund for remodeling it.

Yet during these years, nothing was more important for William than the well-being of the three women in his life. When his father departed in 1764, he left his son as surrogate head of the family. Deborah relied on him. She, who rarely had left her neighborhood, rode back and forth to the governor's house in all kinds of weather, and Sally spent weeks at a time there. William and Elizabeth, accompanying Sally home, would pass pleasant weekends at the new house in Market Street, going to horse races and enjoying the other amusements of the city, the concerts and theater and chophouses. William and Sally's affection for each other deepened during these years. Her visits were frequent during the Stamp Act crisis and for years after, and Elizabeth's bond with Sally combined the joys of sisterhood and motherhood. Sally found freedom as well as opportunity in the governor's mansion, under the First Lady's supervision. Elizabeth would chaperone her at the balls, suppers, and other entertainments.

So it was with proper concern that William heard, in March 1767, that twenty-three-year-old Sally had fallen in love with a thirty-year-old dealer in European and East India goods in Philadelphia. Her suitor, Richard Bache, looked a little like Benjamin Franklin. This resemblance was disarming, more than his manners, those of an English squire whose favorite pastime was riding to the hounds. Their courtship was peculiar, as Bache had been engaged first to Peggy Ross, Sally's best friend. Miss Ross became ill in the summer, and "bore a long and lingering fit of sickness with *patience*," according to the *Gazette*. Sally faithfully attended Peggy in her last days, and heard her dying request that Richard Bache marry her best friend. This request he took to heart upon the lady's death on August 19, proposing to Sally sometime in the next year.

Deborah's letter to her husband of May 16, 1767, includes a little-known and revealing anecdote: "I went up to see our children at Burlington on Saturday and Billy come down with me on Monday and returned yesterday and Sally went up with him and I expect her down this day or tomorrow." Deborah encouraged her daughter to go with her brother to Burlington because she looked pale and unwell, she said. It was not unusual for Sally to have allergies or headaches this time of year, but still it worried her mother, and the trip to see her brother and his wife always did her good. "Besides," Deborah said, "I think she has been made uneasy about her brother who was challenged on Monday night." William had been challenged to a duel—a serious thing in 1767—the week before while he was in Philadelphia. "I should not a said one word to you but I think somebody will tell."

William Hicks, a political enemy of Franklin's, had challenged him. Hicks believed that William was responsible for a letter that appeared in the newspaper on behalf of the Franklins, Galloway, and the Old Ticket, accusing Hicks of beating his aged father and ridiculing Hicks as a second-rate lawyer. The men tried to negotiate a disclosure. When William kept stonewalling, Hicks put him on notice that the next time he stepped outside New Jersey he would have his choice of weapons. William boldly replied that if called out of his province "I shall not postpone my going on account of your menaces."

Not long after William entered his mother's house, Deborah later recalled, Hicks's challenge arrived in the hands of a young doctor, who was drunk. Sally was so terrified that she would not let her brother leave without her. Brother and sister were fiercely loyal to each other, and mutually protective. Nothing came of Hicks's challenge, which dissipated in meaningless exchanges, but if William had reached the dueling ground, his sister would have stood right by him.

Writing to Ben in May 1767, Deborah reported that Sally and her brother in Burlington were "very happy together indeed but I long to see her back again as I could not live above another day without her as I am . . . a mind flustered . . . sometimes glad then depressed and so on. O that you was at home but be assured no little family ever had more harmony in it than yours has and I trust will have."

Sally's father was not coming home. And in response to letters from her, Deborah, and Richard Bache proposing the marriage, Ben Franklin had advised his wife in May that he was leaving the matter to her and William "for at this distance I could neither make any enquiries into his character and circumstances, nor form any judgment." William *was* in a position to make inquiries, and what he discovered was unsettling. Bache had come from Yorkshire in 1760 to join his older brother Theophylact in the importing business in New York. In 1766 he moved to Philadelphia to strike out on his own. By June he was running ads in the *Gazette* for his store in Chestnut Street, to capitalize on the sale of the first yard goods to reach America after the Stamp Act's repeal and the end of the boycott. Bache also owned a trading vessel, heavily mortgaged to finance his retail business.

Somehow Bache's line of credit got tangled in England. William reported to Benjamin in May that "the amount is greater than the sum he is worth by his own account, which account too I am credibly informed must be greatly exaggerated." His "bills are come back protested," and Richard and his brother were bound to pay them with interest. Theophylact ran up debts for goods Richard had purchased and not paid for, even after selling the ship. And this was not the worst of it. Continuing his inquiries into Bache's character, William learned that John Ross, the late Peggy's father, recalled that Bache "had often attempted to deceive him about his circumstances." Ross was convinced that even before the misfortune of the protested bills, Mr. Bache was useless even if his debts were paid.

"In short," William told his father, "he is a mere fortune hunter, who wants to better his circumstances by marrying into a family that will support him." William confessed he did not know what to make of all the different accounts he had heard of Sally's beau. But he was sure the man's debt load was more than his assets and that if Sally married him they would both be entirely dependent upon Franklin for subsistence. "For if he should get forward in the world he must repay his brother. Do burn this."

After reading William's report, Benjamin wrote to Bache in August a letter of condolence for his bad luck. Being young, Franklin advised, Mr. Bache would with industry replace what he had lost. However, it would be wrong to take on the expense of a family before he had recovered. "I am obliged to you for the regard and preference you express for my child . . . but unless you can convince her friends of the probability of your being able to maintain her properly, I hope you will not persist in a proceeding that may be attended with ruinous consequences to you both." The same day, he wrote a letter to Deborah, responding to hers of May 16: "The harmony you mention in our family and among our children gives me great pleasure."

But the harmony that gave everyone so much pleasure was disturbed by the marriage proposal when both Franklin men took sides against the women. Elizabeth raised her glass in a toast "to brother Bache" as Sally sat writing to him in mid-May. Deborah understood the futility of standing between Sally and the man she loved. Then her father gave in, writing to Deborah that he "would not occasion a delay of her happiness if you thought the match a proper one." William was dismayed that after all his efforts he had been shut out of the decision, his careful research on the suitor ignored. His visits to Philadelphia became less frequent. And when Sally and Richard said their vows on Thursday, October 29, in Philadelphia, William was not present.

Time and grandchildren and Bache's innately good character would soon mend the breach, restoring harmony to the Franklin households. But for the present, William felt distanced not only from his mother and sister, but also from his father. True to character, he had accepted his daughter's choice, knowing that there was no way of preventing it.

ON A MORE PLEASANT note, William corresponded with his father about land speculation in the west. In November 1765, two old friends of his had visited him in Burlington, the merchant Sam Wharton and George Croghan, the Indian trader from Conrad Weiser's expedition into Indian country. They proposed acquiring a million acres of good farmland beyond the Ohio River. The idea rekindled William's youthful dream of making his fortune in the west. He was inspired.

Why not form a colony in the Illinois territory? He understood enough now about history, law, and politics to know how it might be done. His friends agreed this was a capital idea and planned to travel to New York and discuss the prospects with the superintendent of Indian affairs, William Johnson. Franklin sat down to draft an agreement for the creation of a land company, and then wrote a persuasive pamphlet, "Reasons for Establishing a British Colony at the Illinois," meant to convince the British ministry to approve his proposal. The territory, he claimed, was a "terrestrial paradise" that would serve as a supply base for the army, as well as a rich source of hemp, flax, and beaver and raccoon fur. He mentioned the idea in a letter to his father on April 30: "The company shall consist of 12 now in America, and if you like the proposals, you will be at liberty to add yourself and such gentlemen of character and fortune in England, as you may think will be most likely to promote the undertaking."

On September 12, 1766, Ben Franklin received Sir William Johnson's letter with William's proposal for the colony and forwarded it to Secretary of State Henry Conway. Ben wrote to William enthusiastically. "This is an affair I shall seriously set about.... The plan I think is well drawn, and I imagine Sir William's approbation will go a long way in recommending it." Here at last was an idea that was wholly William Franklin's creation, in which his father was eager to have a part. If the grant were approved, the vast wealth it would guarantee to both men would erase any balance of debt on the ledger.

"I thank the company," said his father, "for their willingness to take me in, and one or two others that I may nominate.... I wish you had allowed me to name more . . . by numbers we might increase the weight of interest here." Nearly a year later, on June 13, 1767, he wrote to William: "The Illinois affair goes forward but slowly. Lord Shelbourne . . . highly approved it, but others were not of his sentiments, particularly the Board of Trade."

The same day, Dr. Franklin reported to Joseph Galloway ominous events in the Parliament, a "general prejudice against the colonies so strong" that no favor to them was likely to pass. The chancellor of the Exchequer, Charles Townshend, had decided to support Lord George Grenville's motion that America pay for the British troops sent to defend it—and then pay for all judges, governors, and other crown employees. The resulting Townshend Acts, passed between June 15 and July 2, began with the suspension of the New York Assembly until it complied with the quartering act, and culminated in revenue acts levying duties on "glass, china ware, paper pasteboard, painters colors, tea & c."

This legislation revived the fury that had greeted the Stamp Act. The Franklins' old rival John Dickinson began writing his elegant "Letters from a Farmer in Pennsylvania," a series of essays widely published in colonial papers. This Philadelphia lawyer argued that the colonies were sovereign in all internal affairs, and whenever liberties were menaced, "English history affords frequent examples of resistance by force." Predictably, organized protest began in Boston. In December 1767, Sam Adams of the Massachusetts legislature drafted a letter to all colonial assemblies requesting their cooperation in a conference and joint petition to rescind the Townshend Acts as unconstitutional.

There was a new colonial secretary, and his response was stern and swift. Lord Wills Hill, Earl of Hillsborough, bull-necked, beetlebrowed, fifty years of age, was an effective speaker in Parliament. And he had been president of the Board of Trade and Plantations for several years under Grenville before being made first secretary of state for the colonies in January 1768. But Benjamin Franklin considered Hillsborough arrogant, dogmatic, and, worst of all, incompetent. King George himself once said he knew no one with less judgment than Lord Hillsborough. His overreaction to Sam Adams's circular letter was stupefying. On April 22 he demanded that Massachusetts withdraw the letter, and he ordered all governors to dissolve their assemblies if they responded to it.

When the Massachusetts House voted 92–17 *against* revoking the letter, in June, citing their right to petition, Governor Francis Bernard dissolved the legislature. The empty chamber of the Massachusetts House of Commons produced an ominous echo. Colonial legislatures were the symbol of self-government, and within a few months Lord Hillsborough nearly wiped them out. Governors of New York, Maryland, and Georgia adjourned their assemblies, while Virginia, in defiance, sent out its own circular letter. In Boston and New York, people feared a recurrence of the mob violence of 1765, and with good reason.

As outdated news of Hillsborough's demands reached America, a British battleship sailed into Boston Harbor, the fifty-gun frigate *Romney,* part of a squadron sent to enforce the Townshend Acts. Ships had been unloading taxable tea, glassware, paper, and wine in defiance of the revenue act, and Captain John Corner had come to put a stop to it. Needing more able-bodied seamen, the captain began to impress local sailors, declaring he would target crews aboard vessels suspected of avoiding duties.

The sheer size of the ship, the largest in the North American fleet, was meant to strike fear in the hearts of the Sons of Liberty. Captain Corner's report to the admiral boasted that "the sight of the *Romney* silenced Boston." Samuel Adams, in a rage, told his cousin John Adams "the country shall be independent, and we will be satisfied with nothing short of it." Far from being silenced, friends and relatives of the threatened mariners began attacking the press gangs. The conflict escalated on June 9 when customs officials under armed guard boarded John Hancock's merchant sloop *Liberty.* They accused Hancock of having unloaded a cargo of Madeira wine without paying the required duty. On the evening of June 10, Ben Hallowell, comptroller of the port, drew the king's mark, in the shape of an arrow, on the main mast of Hancock's sloop, then confiscated it, ordering that the *Liberty* be cut loose from its moorings and hauled alongside the *Romney* for protection.

A furious mob chased the officials and the seamen preparing to tow the sloop up against the battleship, throwing stones, potsherds, and oyster shells. When the navy had been driven out of range, the protesters turned and headed toward the customs office. There, according to a letter from Lieutenant Governor Hutchinson, a gang surrounded the remaining officers, "tore their clothes and bruised and otherwise hurt them until one after another they escaped. The mob increased to 2 or 300, chiefly sturdy boys and negroes, and broke the windows of the Comptroller's house and then the Inspector['s]."

While that mob was breaking the last of the windowpanes, another squad of marauders searched for a customs boat to capture in exchange for the seized *Liberty*. They found one, hauled it to the Boston Common in a parade, and burned it to cinders there, crying death to all enemies of liberty.

AT A SAFE DISTANCE from the violence in Boston—though not from the withering surveillance of Lord Hillsborough—William Franklin was once again on the horns of a political dilemma.

The New Jersey Assembly convened early in April, ignorant of the fact that Hillsborough had sent restraining orders. The governors had been commanded to obstruct assemblies protesting against the Townshend Acts and to use their "utmost influence to defeat this flagitious attempt to disturb the public peace." By the time William received these instructions, in June, it was too late: on April 15, Speaker Cortlandt Skinner had laid the Massachusetts circular before the Assembly, and the next day they appointed a committee to draft a reply. William had been ill, and the whole business of the circular seemed at the time so harmless that Skinner never showed the letter to him. Subjects of the Crown had a right to petition. When Franklin found out about it he was confident that the Assembly's response would be a humble request for repeal that would not embarrass him and he turned his attention to other matters. Then all hell broke loose.

When William received Lord Hillsborough's orders, he scrambled to control the damage, writing immediately that his assembly had sent a perfectly legal petition directly to the king. At the same time, he assured his superior that the legislators had not answered the circular directly, and the people here were not disposed "to enter into any unwarrantable combination" with the unruly mobsters in Boston. Unfortunately for William, Speaker Skinner had misinformed him. Skinner had indeed actually written to the Massachusetts Assembly approving their initiative. Franklin would have to write to Hillsborough again in July, embarrassed, promising that his colony had no intention of further uniting with the others.

Over the next year, Lord Hillsborough's displeasure, a blend of anger and contempt for New Jersey's governor, was humiliating to William Franklin. It also seemed out of proportion. Hillsborough lambasted the governor and the Assembly, complaining that their petition meant "to draw in question, the power and authority of Parliament to enact laws binding upon the colonies in all cases." This was true, but what of it? Furthermore, the secretary complained, one could no longer say that New Jersey was simply following the lead of more wayward provinces. The people of William's colony now marched arm in arm with the rebellious Sons of Liberty in Massachusetts.

In vain would William protest that this was not his fault, that it had been a quirk of fate that his assembly had been in session when the circular arrived. He wrote that there was hardly a legislator here "but what either believes that the Parliament has not the right to impose taxes for the purpose of a revenue in America, or thinks that it is contrary to justice, equity, and sound policy to exercise that right." If other assemblies had been in session, he knew they would have done the same as his. But nothing he said mattered, as Hillsborough continued to single him out for criticism. Perhaps it was his name that marked him—Franklin, the son of a colonial agent whose critique of Parliament was growing more strident with the passing days.

Benjamin had written to his son on July 2, "I apprehend a breach between the two countries. . . . you see a turn of the die may make a great difference in our affairs. We may be either promoted or discarded; one or the other seems likely soon to be the case."

In response to the Boston riots, the Privy Council voted on July 27, 1768, to send two regiments, each with five hundred men, to subdue the unruly colonists. Fifteen warships arrived in Boston harbor on September 28, and the red-coated Irish soldiers under command of Colonel William Dalrymple went ashore. They made a great show of marching, guns on their shoulders, bayonets gleaming, the full mile down Long Wharf to the Boston Common. With the assembly dissolved, they made quarters of Faneuil Hall and the chamber of the House of Commons. The Bostonians refused to comply with the quartering bill; their response to the military occupation was sullen rage and an expanded boycott of British goods.

Ben Franklin wrote to Joseph Galloway on January 9, 1769: "I am glad to hear that matters were yet quiet at Boston, but fear they will not continue long so. Some indiscretion on the part of their warmer people, or of the soldiery, I am extremely apprehensive may occasion a tumult; and if blood is once drawn, there is no foreseeing how far the mischief may spread."

Eleven days later, Thomas Hutchinson, the new governor of Massachusetts, wrote to the British official Thomas Whately in England: "There must be an abridgment of what are called English liberties" in order to rescue the colony from chaos. Hutchinson had seen his house demolished; "I wish to see some further restraint of liberty rather than the connection with the parent state should be broken."

Those letters of old friends, Franklin and Hutchinson, crossing on the high seas in January 1769 had a power of prophecy and transformation that now seems demonic. Fate would deliver Hutchinson's letter into the hands of Franklin, who should never have read it. Not only did he read the private letter, he left it where the whole world could see it, making both of them infamous for a while.

THAT WINTER WILLIAM FRANKLIN had his hands full with family troubles.

While Sally was pregnant with her first child in March 1769, Deborah suffered a severe stroke. Dr. Thomas Bond of Pennsylvania Hospital wrote to Benjamin Franklin on June 7: "Your good Mrs. Franklin was affected in the winter with a partial palsey in the tongue, and a sudden loss of memory, which alarmed us much . . . her constitution in general seems impaired." He had to learn this from Dr. Bond. William would not mention it.

Six months later Deborah wrote to him that her illness had been brought on by a series of misfortunes: her niece Debby Dunlap nearly died after giving birth, while her husband, the Reverend William Dunlap, fell deathly ill at the same time ("such a helpless family"); then her cousin Betsy Mecum "was taken ill, and so much distress so soon that added to my own . . . distress at your staying so much longer that I lost all my resolution and the very dismal winter both Sally and my-self live so very lonely [Bache was away in Jamaica on business] that I had got in so very low a state and got into so unhappy a way that I could not sleep a long time."

She and Sally were visiting a neighbor, and while she was there, Deborah lost her memory. She appears to have lain semicomatose for days or weeks during Sally's pregnancy, waking to sharp pains in her abdomen. "This time I was very ill . . . very mortally, and thank god . . . I have my memory in some measure returned. . . . I did grow very thin so much that Billy said he had never seen so much changes in me."

Her son rode back and forth to Philadelphia with Elizabeth at his side that spring and summer (the Assembly was adjourned from April 1768 until October 1769) doing whatever he could for his ailing mother and pregnant sister. All the while he was shielding his father from any news that might upset him. Deborah wrote to him long after her stroke, "I am in hopes I shall get better again to see you . . . I often tell my friends I was not sick. . . . It was only more [than I could] bear . . . and so I fell down and could not get up again indeed it was not any sickness but too much disquiet of mind but I had taken up a reso-lution never to make any complaint to you or give you any disquiet."

William wrote to his father when there was good news: Sally's first child, Franklin's first legitimate grandchild, was born on August 12, 1769. "I came to town with Betsy on Monday last in order to stand for my little nephew." They drove from New Jersey with the Reverend Jonathan O'Dell, the rector of the Burlington mission, met Deborah, Sally, and Richard at the house on Market Street, then carried the baby around the corner to Christ's Church. With Betsy and Deborah stand-ing as godmothers, the Reverend Richard Peters christened Benjamin Franklin Bache at the same font in which William Penn had been baptized in 1644.

"He is not so fat and lusty as some children at his time are, but he is altogether a pretty little fellow, and improves in his looks every day," William wrote. Deborah was proud to say "I was well enough to stand for myself." She thanked God that Sally was well and "in a way of making a fine nurse."

CHAPTER 8

Blood and Money

A S THE DECADE OF the 1760s came to an end, father and son had every reason to believe they were of one mind about the British Empire, the place of the American colonies in the scheme of things, and their constitutional rights as Englishmen.

Just as William was defending his assembly upon the grounds that the Townshend Acts were illegal, writing to Lord Hillsborough that "no force on earth [could] make the assemblies acknowledge that the parliament has a right to impose taxes on America," his father was petitioning the House of Commons and writing letters to the newspapers "against the *Right* of Parliament to tax the colonies." Both men detested Hillsborough as the embodiment of all that was reckless in the government. While William dealt with him from afar, Benjamin engaged with him daily, as he worked to depose the proprietors and lobbied for the Ohio land grant. William was so intimidated by Hillsborough that he sent all letters intended for him first to his father for review, relying upon him to edit the texts before forwarding them to their destination.

While Benjamin was stalled in his efforts to bring Pennsylvania under the king's government, he was making fitful progress in gaining support for the new colony, which now was called Vandalia. To under-

stand the time, money, and energy the Franklins spent on this grandi-
ose scheme one must grasp the scope of it, the vast wealth promised,
and the real likelihood of success. It would be fruitless to try to esti-
mate the value in pounds or dollars, then and now; the records are too
confusing. It is more meaningful to consider the size of the land grant.
In ongoing negotiations it grew from 2.4 million acres in 1769 to 20
million acres in 1770, a property three times the size of Maryland including all of present West Virginia from the Ohio River to the Green-
briar, and land north almost to Lake Erie. Twenty partners promised to
advance £200 each as "first adventurers who have proposed to purchase
from your Majesty lands in the continent of America and to make a
settlement there."

There seems to have been no sense of irony in any of the players
that they were seeking to become what they had so long despised: proprietors. The petitioners and their heirs and assigns, including silent
partners like Strahan, William Franklin, and Croghan, would be in a
position similar to that of the Penns and Lord Baltimore in the seventeenth century—proprietors with feudal rights to dispose of the land.
Of course, there was a difference. This land was worth a lot more to
settlers in the late eighteenth century than was the wilderness along
the Delaware a hundred years before. The owner of a twentieth part of
Vandalia would possess a million acres which he might rent, sell, or
cultivate as he saw fit. For this privilege the partners would have to pay
only a share of what it cost to buy the land—a pittance.

The wealth promised was almost unfathomable, inspiring not only
ambition but competition, and greed. "One half of England is now
land mad & everybody there has their eyes fixed on this country," wrote
Croghan. The land belonged to the Indians, who would sell as it suited
them to the highest bidder, who then must have a charter from the
king before he could formally claim it. In the case of Vandalia, the
Franklins' competition came from the self-named Suffering Traders, a
party of bankrupt frontiersmen, victims of Indian massacres in 1763
who demanded compensation in acreage. Also there were the Virginia
veterans of the French and Indian War. Colonel George Washington
spoke for his soldiers, to whom Governor Dinwiddie had promised
two hundred thousand acres of farmland in 1754.

Success in creating the colony required vigilant cooperation between traders and financiers in America, and shrewd negotiators in
London. Someone in America would have to purchase the land from
the Indians, securing it with a treaty and paying with cash and loans.
Then the London agents must persuade the Board of Trade, Parliament, and the king to approve the treaty and the incorporation of the
colony. This was a complex maneuver, considering the competing
claimants as well as Parliament's resistance to the consolidation of colonial power thousands of miles away.

Ben Franklin and Richard Jackson, as agents in London, had everything to gain and little to lose in the endeavor apart from their valuable
time. William Franklin, on his side of the Atlantic, was devoting not
only his considerable energy to the scheme, but everything he owned
and all he could borrow as well. It had become a monster with a hundred arms and fifty heads that was also known as the Walpole Company, briefly the Vandalia Company, and then the Grand Ohio
Company after it had consumed the Indiana and the Illinois Companies and other land grant partnerships of the moment.

The western landscape that William had beheld with such excitement when he was a teenager on Weiser's expedition became an obsession in his middle age. He worked with Croghan and Sam Wharton
on purchasing land from the Indians, negotiating treaties, and raising
money to finance the operation. Sir William Johnson, superintendent
for Indian affairs in America, acted as a go-between, a friend of the
colony on both sides.

William Franklin did his part with remarkable skill and alacrity.
Looking at the record years later, one wonders how he could serve as
governor of New Jersey and pater familias to the clan in Pennsylvania
while negotiating this colossal land deal in the Ohio Valley.

To secure the land, he used all the advantages of his position as
governor and his education as a lawyer as well as his lifelong experience
in dealing with the Six Nations. When Sir William Johnson called a
conference of colonial delegates and Indians, Franklin journeyed there
to Fort Stanwix, near Albany, New York, in August 1768. The agenda
was to extend the western boundary of Indian territory southwesterly
along the Susquehanna River to the Allegheny and then persuade the

Six Nations to cede this land by treaty to the Crown. This seems absurd until one understands that the Indians were legally bound to make amends for their marauding in 1763. So a portion of this land, 1.8 million acres, was to be given in trust to Captain William Trent as representative of the Suffering Traders.

Fort Stanwix became the location for a summit for thirty-two hundred Indians and official delegates from New York, Pennsylvania, Connecticut, Virginia, and New Jersey. The white men had made sure that twenty boatloads of presents, blankets, wampum, firearms, and silver and gold pieces—treasure amounting to £10,460 sterling—were prominently displayed on the fort's parade.

Governor Franklin had earned the lasting respect of all the tribes for his relentless pursuit, and prosecution, of men who had murdered some Oneida Indians in his province. So his presence at the council was crucial, and his signature on the Treaty of Stanwix definitive. In an elaborate ceremony soon after the conference began, the tribes bestowed on the governor the Indian name Sagorighweyoghsta, meaning Great Arbiter of Justice.

As Franklin left the conference in early November, he knew that he and Sir William Johnston had achieved a major victory for the Grand Ohio Company. The treaty depended on the Crown's acceptance of the land transfer, so the ministry must accept it as a whole or forgo the articles of peace. On December 17, 1768, Governor Franklin wrote to the Board of Trade: "If the boundary is speedily ratified by His Majesty, I have no doubt it will . . . contribute more towards securing a permanent and lasting peace with them than any other matter whatever."

Franklin, Wharton, Croghan, and Trent understood the significance of this new treaty as few Americans did, having arranged it in order to incorporate a colony. The £10,460 had come from the king, who had empowered Johnson to buy the land from the Indians; now the Company had to use their influence to get the king to sell it to the Grand Ohio Company. Meanwhile, the Treaty of Fort Stanwix and its likely ratification set a precedent worth trillions to bold men who knew how to act upon it—the sooner the better. Land in New York adjoining the Vandalia grant would appreciate exponentially. While Governor Franklin was in New York on October 24, he contracted to buy thirty thousand acres of land at the upper springs of the Susquehanna River. His partners were Galloway, Trent, and Amos Ogden. Galloway rendered the purchase, Franklin as master partner pledged to pay three-quarters of the purchase price for a commensurate share of the profits, and the others accepted smaller shares.

This marked the doorway of a winding passage in William Franklin's life in which an ambitious man's sense of adventure overwhelmed his innate good judgment. He followed the lead of Croghan and Trent, old friends who were greedier and no less beguiled than he was. All of them, in fact, were taking a well-calculated business risk. By 1769, Trent and Croghan had invested all their cash to purchase land in the west, and had mortgaged the property they owned to purchase more. Overextended, they persuaded William—whose name and prestige secured him credit—to help them raise money to patent more land in the country around Lake Otsego, New York. Croghan already owned a huge tract south of the lake. He pledged fifty thousand acres to William Franklin in exchange for his promise to raise £3,000 for the purchase of the new tract north of the lake, which was even larger. William then formed the Burlington Company, eight investors who put up £300 each for the privilege of owning the fifty thousand acres in New York.

This was only the beginning of a tangled web strung upon the loom of the Stanwix Treaty, which hypnotized investors. It was like nothing so much as a gold rush, for men in the know. They were fascinated, and so were their bookkeepers. There was not much hard money in America, so land deals relied on shaky currency, bonds, and collateral. The financial specifics are convoluted, labyrinthine, mind-numbing. The main enterprise called the Grand Ohio Company in England led William down byways of side deals, and in roundabouts in search of spinoffs and creative mortgaging, borrowing from Peter to pay Paul as his name was frequently put forth to secure loans, his own and others'. He would end up in the same mess as Trent and Croghan—mortgaged up to his neck—all in the rosy prospect of the wealth that must come when the king ratified the treaty and approved the formation of the Grand Ohio Company. William even pledged to pay 20 percent of the expenses for Trent and Thomas Wharton to go to London as lobbyists for the grant.

In all of this wheeling and dealing, his father—a few months behind events in America and ahead of William in his knowledge of Parliament—encouraged him. Progress was slow but steady, triumph an eventual certainty. Upon learning of the success at Fort Stanwix, Ben Franklin began organizing the new land company that would pay the full cost of the treaty, £10,460, when its prospectus was approved. If he was able to interest enough English investors with influence, ratification would be guaranteed. For Franklin this was not difficult. The articles of the company's organization, drafted in June 1769 and submitted to the Privy Council in July, bore the signatures of members of Parliament, lawyers, and diamond merchants.

Lord Hillsborough took one look at the petition and exclaimed, to Franklin's surprise, that the gentlemen were asking not too much of the king but not enough. When we first asked for two and a half million acres, Franklin recalled, Hillsborough advised: *ask for enough to make a province,* were his words, pretending to befriend our application.* A little suspicious, Franklin nevertheless revised the grant to include 20 million acres. And on December 27, 1769, under a new moon for luck, he convened a meeting of an expanded Grand Ohio Company, in a spacious room at the Crown and Anchor Tavern in the Strand. The larger grant called for more, and more influential, partners. So now the subscribers included members of the House of Lords, several members of the Privy Council, and a secretary of state. William Strahan and his son Andrew joined the group; William Franklin, Joseph Galloway, Sir William Johnson, and George Croghan were now official shareholders as well.

Then in the New Year, January 4, 1770, the proposal was laid before the treasury, who agreed to it, somewhat to Hillsborough's surprise. Now the final approval of the company's plan awaited the Board of Trade's hearing. The wheels of Parliament ground slowly, yet this petition looked too good to be denied. There was not a man in the Grand Ohio Company who doubted he would be rich—it was only a matter of time.

TIME FAVORS THE YOUNG, the healthy, and those who possess that much-praised and little-cultivated virtue, patience. Ben Franklin had a great reservoir of it, a benefit from all his sixty-three years on this earth, and all sorts of experience, the real kind that shows that good things come to those who wait. This is particularly true in business negotiations; the advantage often goes to the side that can hold out the longest. It was this fund of patience that supported Franklin's other gifts of character and made him the most effective mediator of his age.

It was not so hard to be patient for an American in London in the early 1770s, living the good life on Craven Street on a government salary, with his adoptive family, the Stevensons. When his beloved Polly married Dr. William Hewson, Franklin gave her away; when their first child was born in April 1771, he stood as godfather. Only minutes away, in the Strand, was the Royal Society (formerly the Society for the Arts), and there he would resume his conversations with the British wits and sages. Wealthy, and with little official business in those years, Dr. Franklin also had leisure to travel widely in England, Ireland, and Scotland, communing with old friends like David Hume in Edinburgh and Lord Kames at Blair-Drummond.

In the summer of 1771, visiting his friend the bishop Jonathan Shipley's country house called Twyford, he had the leisure to begin writing the memoir that would become the immortal *Autobiography*. It was dedicated, in the form of an affectionate hundred-page letter, to William Franklin: "Dear Son, I have ever had a pleasure in obtaining any little anecdotes of my ancestors. You may remember the enquiries I made among the remains of my relations when you were with me in England . . ."

William did not receive this long letter, because his father would not post it then, or ever. What he did receive, around the time the *Autobiography* was under way, was a letter enclosing Benjamin's "account against you for money advanced and paid here since my being in England." William's bill includes all kinds of items from 1765 through 1771, including books and prints. "The heaviest part is the maintenance and education of Temple," but Benjamin was sure no one would begrudge him that when they saw the results. The next sentence of this letter of reckoning is "The Ohio affair seems now near a conclusion. And if the present ministry stand a little longer, I think it will be completed to our satisfaction." This must have been a great comfort to William, who was mired in debt—to Wharton and Trent, among others. On July 21, the lobbyists wrote to remind him his portion of their expense money was overdue: "We are under an absolute necessity of drawing on you in favour of Mr. Thomas Wharton for two hundred pounds sterling [$32,000]."

William could not, and would not, pay it. Across the sea in New Jersey, it was not so easy for William to be patient, as his debts increased in the tantalizing view of that land bonanza. To be a good son, a good husband, and a good governor was becoming more difficult in the 1770s. It would be impossible without a great deal more money.

In those days, New Jersey itself was poor, almost beyond imagining. Bounded on the south and west by the Delaware Bay and River, and vaguely by the Hudson River on the north, the whole province contained fewer than 5 million acres and 120,000 settlers. More than a fourth of it—the whole length of the land along the Atlantic and thirty miles inland—was untillable pine barrens, undrained meadows, and marshes. Millions of acres had yet to be surveyed. The Delaware River, from the headwaters down to Trenton, had not been improved for navigation because there were few settlements that far west.

Despite its situation on the Atlantic the colony provided no harbor for shipping other than Sandy Hook on Raritan Bay—very near New York. The southern inlets down to Cape May stood mired in salt meadows and swamps and buffeted by winds out of the northeast. In a few settlements along the coast, herders raised cattle in the meadows, and loggers cut down the pines and red cedars for subsistence. There were plenty of fish and oysters for watermen to sell in the New York and Philadelphia markets, so a man might live that way if he knew boats and nets and tonging.

The province had little foreign trade from its own ports, and produce for sale went to Philadelphia or New York. New Jersey was known to the world chiefly as the concourse between those thriving cities. With such a limited economy and tax base, Governor Franklin's realm was constantly struggling to meet its own financial obligations, apart from any additional duties levied by Parliament. Disagreements over the budget were more heated and bitter than in wealthier colonies. Franklin longed for a better appointment—or at least an increase in salary.

So a bizarre crime that occurred in 1768, perpetrated upon the coffers of the treasury of New Jersey, rocked the government and altered the course of Franklin's administration for years afterward. During the night of July 21, someone very skillfully stole into the Perth Amboy home of Stephen Skinner, the treasurer of East Jersey, while Skinner and his wife, his four children, and their servants were sound asleep upstairs from his first-floor office.

"About six o'clock on Friday morning he was waked up by his Negro boy who told [Skinner] that the office window was broke open, the iron chest opened and the money taken out." Skinner drew his sword and hurried down the stairs. He found the east window of his office open and the shutters broken, the room in disarray. All the desk drawers were ajar. The chest had been opened with a key that was kept locked up in the drawer of a desk that stood in the same room. The money was all gone, paper money and gold coins that now would be worth $150,000. One of the curious details of the story is that the key that was used to open the chest was a type Skinner recognized but did not know that it worked in the treasure chest lock. His own key he kept secure in the drawer of a secretary desk in a back room.

Naturally the theft was a source of anguish and fury among the citizenry in a time of financial distress, limited credit, and a dire shortage of currency. Few people suspected that Skinner himself had been an accomplice, but most agreed he had been negligent. He was, after all, the man to whom the public funds had been entrusted. His response to the disaster could not have been more honorable or reassuring. Dispatching a posse to catch the thieves, he reported the details of the crime to Governor Franklin, and submitted an affidavit four days later to Chief Justice Frederick Smyth in Perth Amboy. He offered a £100 reward for information leading to the capture of the culprits. His friend Governor Franklin added fifty pounds of his own money, and he notified the governments of New York and Pennsylvania of the theft, including a description of the stolen currency to discourage its use. Justice Smyth conducted an investigation of the robbery while the Assembly pursued its own independent inquiry.

Despite all these efforts, there were no arrests. Governor Franklin was obliged to convene the legislature in the autumn of 1769 deprived of a quarter of its liquid assets. While the Assembly's investigation was still open they gave Skinner a vote of confidence: Without proof of guilt it would be libelous "to impeach the conduct or character of the said Treasurer."

Skinner was an honorable member of a prominent and wealthy family. His brother Cortlandt was speaker of the house and a key ally of Governor Franklin. A prosperous merchant when he became treasurer, in 1761 Skinner had married Catherine Johnston, daughter of Andrew Johnston, an even wealthier merchant, trustee of Princeton, and East Jersey's previous treasurer. Catherine and Betsy Franklin were good friends, and the Franklins and Skinners were members of the provincial high society. So the governor and the legislators warned Skinner to take greater care of their money in the future and put him and his western counterpart, treasurer Samuel Smith, under security bonds for all funds entrusted to their care.

Wary but resigned, the lawmakers got on with the difficult business of colonial government, now made more difficult by the shortage of cash. In some other decade this might have been the end of the sorry affair. But these were volatile years in which the merest chink in a supporting wall drew the crowbar of faction. Skinner, recently appointed to the upper New Jersey Council, was regarded as landed gentry. The Assembly, for the most part, represented the humble farmers and mechanics of West Jersey.

Just one year after their vote of confidence, in the autumn session of 1770, a bolder assembly revived the hearings in Skinner's case, calling more witnesses and changing the tone of the inquiry: First, the money was gone and not likely to be recovered; second, it had been stolen "for want of that security and care that was necessary to keep it in safety." The majority said Skinner was responsible, and they wanted him to reimburse the colony every cent it had lost in the burglary. He protested he was innocent, and besides he could not afford to pay such an exorbitant sum; it would be the ruin of his family, including children hardly out of swaddling clothes. Franklin took Skinner's side in a controversy destined to polarize the governor and the Assembly, a power struggle between east and west, men of privilege against tradesmen and farmers.

Men would seize upon any excuse to choose sides. The year 1770 had seen a resurgence of the fury the Stamp Act had provoked five years earlier, and now it was even more violent, with mobs taking to the streets to protest against greedy lawyers and corrupt judges in New Jersey.

There was no doubt in Governor Franklin's mind that the protests in his province were part of a larger pattern of defying authority. On February 7, he summoned his council, who suggested a special meeting of the legislature to address the problem. Protests against the courts had been going on for at least six months before the council saw fit to respond; now the rioting and vandalism had forced their hand.

The timing of the special session of the New Jersey Assembly, mid-March, happened to coincide with a signal event in British-colonial relations: a bloody melee in the streets of Boston.

THERE HAD BEEN REPORTS of clashes between redcoats and civilians since the arrival of the British troops from Halifax in October 1768. By year's end the animosity between the troops and the people had reached a tipping point, and the English soldiers felt in constant danger of their lives.

When a league of merchants calling themselves "the Body" met in Faneuil Hall to renew their ban on importing any articles subject to duty under the Townshend Act, eight mercantile firms refused to sign the agreement. And on January 23, 1770, the Body published an incendiary broadside denouncing the dissenting merchants as traitors. One of these merchants, Theophilus Lilly, had recently caused a stir by publishing a letter denouncing all those who invoked the principle of Liberty in order to deprive others of the liberty to make a living.

On February 22, some patriotic boys put up a sign in front of Lilly's shop, with cartoons of the Tory merchants who had defied the ban.

Ebenezer Richardson, a neighbor who was friendly to Lilly's cause, tried to tear the sign down. So the boys made him a target, chasing him down the street, where they proceeded to barrage his house with sticks and stones, breaking his windows and striking Richardson and his wife. Grown men joined the boys, shouting, according to the *Boston Post*, "Come out, you damn son of a bitch, I'll have your heart out." That was when Richardson loaded his musket. He fired into the mob, hitting two boys. Christopher Seider, twelve years old, died of his wounds, and Richardson was charged with murder.

The boy's death brought anti-British sentiment to a boil. Two thousand people formed the funeral procession. John Adams wrote: "The ardor of the people is not to be quelled by the slaughter of one child and the wounding of another," a prophecy soon to be fulfilled.

The evening of March 5 was clear and cold. Private Hugh White stood guard near the Custom House, near the military command post. About eight o'clock Edward Garrick, a wigmaker's apprentice, passed by and shouted an insult intended for one of White's friends. The affront came to include the honor of all of Captain White's regiment, and he would not stand for it. He confronted the wigmaker in the street, and the next time Garrick taunted him, White hit him in the head with the butt of his musket.

The British guard returned to his post muttering and growling. Soon after that, a church bell began ringing the alarm for fire. Garrick's cries had attracted more apprentice wigmakers and nine other young men, and the company soon swelled to a throng of fifty, pointing at the sentry, challenging him to step up and fight. "There's the son of a bitch that knocked me down," cried Garrick. "Lousy rascal," someone called.

Frightened, Private White fled to the curbed front stoop of the Custom House, climbed the steps, and loaded his musket.

"Kill him," they shouted, while pelting the soldier with snowballs packed with stones. He leveled his musket and they dared him to fire. He knocked on the big door but it did not open, then he cried for help, begging the Guard to turn out. As the church bells rang, the crowd in King Street swelled to a riot of four hundred, many of them armed. At last the commandant, Captain Thomas Preston, decided to lead a relief party, six tall grenadiers and a corporal, on a rescue mission. As the soldiers moved through the mob, their bayonets pricked anyone who came too close. The crowd, led by a heavyset mulatto named Crispus Attucks, wielding a bludgeon, pressed forward, swinging at the redcoats with clubs and cutlasses.

Preston may have given the order to fire or not, but there is no doubt the mob demanded it. "Fire if you dare, God damn you, we know you dare not," the rioters yelled. Fire they did, about the same time that four redcoats started shooting from the windows of the Custom House. Attucks, and a sailor named James Caldwell, and the rope maker Samuel Gray fell dead on the spot. Two men died of their wounds hours later and six others were badly injured.

The Boston Massacre would soon be acknowledged as the first battle of the American War of Independence. As Governor Hutchinson's counterpart in a more orderly colony, William Franklin was alarmed and apprehensive when the news reached New Jersey two days later. This was one week before the special session of the General Assembly he had called to address "the late tumultuous and riotous proceedings in the County of Monmouth."

The weather was foul. The lawmakers were hardly prepared to convene in Burlington so soon after their last session ended in December, but they dutifully answered their governor's request to report on Thursday, March 15. That day there was no quorum, so Franklin had extra time to work on his speech. In light of the recent events in Massachusetts, he had taken great pains with the address—an eloquent plea for the rule of law and civility.

He began by apologizing to the gentlemen for summoning them so soon. The recent riots in Monmouth had made it imperative. An armed mob there "did, by their threats and outrageous behavior, so insult the magistrates and officers . . . that they judged it neither safe nor prudent to attempt opening the court." Only an act of this assembly—expensive and inconvenient as it was—could reconvene the court. The leaders of those deluded people had convinced them that their lawyers had been overcharging their clients in suits for debt. True or not, it did not justify their offense. "If the people are aggrieved, there are legal methods of complaining—there are legal methods of obtaining redress." He then described the avenues of complaint and appeal, right up to the governor's office and application to the king himself, "the fountain of Justice." The truth of the matter was that some people would prefer not to pay their debts, and the "licentiousness of the times," that is, the Boston riots, had encouraged this sort of behavior.

The governor then proposed several acts designed "for the better preventing tumults," and for punishing rioters: continuing the militia, and providing emergency plans for the courts. Without such measures the administration of justice would be impossible; anarchy and confusion would then ensue, and "the most despotic and worst of all Tyrannies—the Tyranny of the Mob—must at length involve all in one common ruin." On March 17, every act their governor had proposed passed his assembly and became law.

If William's father had known of these acts of constraint it would have surprised him, and caused him to reflect upon his obligations to that Assembly. For Benjamin had gotten word just recently that they had chosen him to be their agent in London. He had been their obvious choice. Yet his actual awareness of what was going on in the colonies in March 1770 was as vague as William's grasp of what transpired in London. The day of the carnage in Boston, Lord North was introducing a bill in Parliament to repeal the Townshend Acts that had sparked the violence. Ben Franklin did not hear about the Boston Massacre until May; by this time the Repeal Act (April 12, 1770) had nullified most of the Townshend Acts—all but the tax on tea and the plan to fund the salaries of colonial governors.

While William Franklin was using his powers of persuasion to manage the wild emotions of street gangs, his father at that moment was writing a fiery letter to Charles Thomson, the leader of Philadelphia's Sons of Liberty. Franklin's letter, urging all merchants' associations to stand firm in their nonimportation agreements, would, once published, provoke accusations that Postmaster Franklin had ceased to be a loyal officer of the Crown.

Unknowingly, father and son had taken conflicting positions.

Dr. Franklin's comments upon the recent dispute over the Repeal Act roundly condemned the Parliament and the Bedford Party (an anti-American faction led by the Duke of Bedford) in particular. The majority in the House of Commons wanted to repeal the Townshend

Acts altogether, but the Bedford Party was so powerful they made moderation impossible. "Rebels and traitors are the best names they can afford us, and I believe they only wish for a colourable pretence and occasion of ordering the soldiers to make a massacre among us." On the other hand, William Pitt, the Great Commoner, and other liberals would favor America if they returned to power. America had—on her side—all sorts of dissenters in England, and more in Ireland, and the rest of Europe, "applauding the Spirit of Liberty." But these had no votes. The colonists' greatest support came from British merchants, as ships were returning from Boston to Bristol laden with precious cargoes of nails and glass, unsold. "In short," Franklin concluded, "if we do not persist in this measure [the nonimportation agreements] until it has had its full effect, it can never again be used on any future occasion with the least prospect of success."

When this letter arrived in America, passages were published immediately in Philadelphia and Boston. Three days after writing to Charles Thomson, Franklin wrote Joseph Galloway a more formal polemic he wished Galloway to lay before the Pennsylvania Assembly: The success of Parliament in keeping the tax on tea while repealing the rest of the Townshend duties was, to Franklin, an unbearable setback, proof that Parliament would continue to tax the colonies without their consent. Should the colonies accept the compromise, cease the boycott, and make peace with England? Or should they keep up the policy of nonimportation, holding out for complete victory and repeal?

If asked his opinion, Ben Franklin would advise Americans to stand by their nonimportation agreements until their object had been *fully* realized. Lord Hillsborough and the Bedford Party believed, Franklin wrote, that "the colonies were a rope of sand, and could not long hold together for any one purpose; and that a little firmness shown by government here, would infallibly break us all to pieces. . . . If we give way, they and their friends will exult."

He was not feeling generous, or friendly. What Franklin had been witnessing in London, from coffeehouses to newspapers to Parliament and the court, now amounted to a moral and civil bankruptcy. "The public affairs of this nation are at present in great disorder," he observed. Great Britain, as he saw it, was on the verge of civil war between a jealous aristocracy and a power-hungry, factious Parliament. The nation was neither strong enough nor noble enough to deserve the colonies' indulgence. The time had come for them to stand firm, trusting in their own sense of justice—whatever the cost—even at the risk of a permanent break from the mother country.

He had come to prize American independence above peace and harmony. Dimly aware of the chaos in America, he now believed that no place where English was spoken was more corrupt and chaotic than England itself.

WORDS OF WARNING CAME to Governor Franklin in the summer of 1771. It was fitting that the personal advice should come from William Strahan, the man who of all men knew the Franklins best, and loved them.

His letter was borne under the sails of an April packet that reached William in mid-June. Strahan's unadorned sentences seem chilling, a portent of doom. Although the events of the past year may have prepared William for his friend's confidences, they still must have come as a rude awakening.

Strahan began by discussing the land grant proposal that had lain neglected before the Board of Trade all that year, under its new title, the Walpole Company. William was eager to know the status of the project upon which such high hopes depended, and his father had not been forthcoming. Strahan explained: "Your father could not stir in this business as he is not only on bad terms with Lord Hillsborough, but with the *Ministry* in general. Besides, his temper is grown so very reserved, which adds greatly to his *natural inactivity,* that there is no getting him to take part in *anything.*" In other words, Franklin had been angry and depressed. His outgoing correspondence slowed to a trickle soon after he got word of the Boston Massacre. He spent hours in his room, buried in books. His marginalia during this period are the most profuse of his life. Upon a wide-margined pamphlet by Dean Josiah Turner, *Letter from a Merchant in London to His Nephew in North*

America, Franklin's comments nearly equal the word count of the text: "This then is the *spirit* of the Constitution, that taxes shall not be laid without the consent of those to be taxed." And "While the colonies were weak and poor, not a penny or single soldier was ever spared by Britain for their defence." And when the pamphleteer offers British troops as one example of the Empire's largess to the colonists, Franklin scribbles, "To oppress, insult, and murder them, as at Boston!" And so on in that vein.

Benjamin Franklin had grown up in Boston. His anger had turned inward and he withdrew, neglecting business or losing all confidence in it, as with the Walpole project. "Of this he is himself so sensible," Strahan continued, "that I have heard him at my house propose to Mr. Wharton to strike his name out of the list, as it might be of prejudice to the undertaking. *But all this to yourself.* My *sole motive* for writing you thus freely, is to *put you upon your guard,* and to induce you to be as circumspect in your conduct as possible."

Strahan put it plain: "It is imagined here, that you entertain the same political opinions with your father, and are actuated by the same motives with regard to Britain and America." Those motives had begun to fascinate and then worry Strahan after the Boston Massacre, as he watched his friend's behavior up close. He told David Hall how far Franklin's opinions had diverged from his own: Strahan believed the colonists should pay their taxes first and then seek redress later, and he saw nothing *in principle* in the tea tax that violated American rights. "I am sensible that what I have just advanced," he continued, "differs widely from the opinion of our worthy friend, Dr. Franklin. As I most highly esteem him, I am sorry for it."

But it was Dr. Franklin's actions, more than his opinions, that alarmed Mr. Strahan. On June 8, 1770, Franklin had written a letter to the Reverend Samuel Cooper, pastor of Boston's Brattle Street Church. Cooper's flock included John Hancock, the Adamses, and other Sons of Liberty. Though not himself a member of the Massachusetts Assembly, Reverend Cooper was influential, as well as nonpartisan. It was Cooper who had first sent Franklin news about the Boston Massacre. Franklin's reply was both a letter of condolence and a political argument against a standing army in America as well as other violations of colonial charters by Parliament. "Let us therefore hold fast our loyalty to our King," Franklin wrote, "as that steady loyalty is the most probable means of securing us from the arbitrary power of a corrupt parliament, that does not like us, and conceives itself to have an interest in keeping us down and fleecing us."

He also enclosed a copy of a letter he had written to Strahan answering some queries about his sentiments concerning the Townshend duties and their repeal. The tone of these letters was as troubling as their content. The idea of royal independence and superiority of the Crown to Parliament had been odious to Lords and Commons for almost a century—since the Glorious Revolution—and Franklin's harping on the theme seemed paradoxical, if not perverse. His final prophecy was chilling: "Mutual provocation will thus go on to complete the separation; and instead of that cordial affection that so long existed, and that harmony so suitable to the circumstances, and so necessary to the happiness . . . of both countries; an implacable hatred . . . will take place."

His obvious purpose in writing to Cooper—his first recorded response to the Boston Massacre—was to convey his opinions to the leaders of the Massachusetts House, who were in the process of choosing an agent for their affairs in London. Cooper shared Franklin's thoughts immediately, although with great caution and delicacy. The delegates were enthusiastic about retaining Franklin, notwithstanding certain reservations—that he was already an agent for other provinces, and that he and his son held royal offices. Yet they held such a high opinion of his abilities and integrity, Cooper reported, that "a majority readily confided the affairs of the province at this critical season to your care." Benjamin Franklin's ambition to serve the Bay Colony, and their desire to have him, sent a powerful signal to Strahan, to Hillsborough, to all of Parliament, and to William Franklin, who of course knew of the appointment months before his father.

Massachusetts was not like Pennsylvania, New Jersey, or Georgia. It was the cradle of the Sons of Liberty; Boston was, by 1770, a cauldron of insurrection. Franklin's transparent eagerness to add the troubled colony to his list of clients might have been taken as a gesture in service of the Empire, striking at the heart of the problem, if he had shown any recent signs of moderation in regard to Parliament. But he had grown more radical every year. His new alliance with the Assembly of Massachusetts would set him in direct opposition to the most controversial governor in America, Thomas Hutchinson.

CHAPTER 9

Rebellion, 1772–73

DURING ALL OF 1771 there was only a single, querulous letter from Benjamin to his son, mostly concerning William's debts to him, the bitter winter in England, and the status of the land grant, full of promise as always, but uncertain.

The year had gotten off to a bad start for Dr. Franklin when Lord Hillsborough refused to accept his credentials as agent for Massachusetts. The conversation at Hillsborough's house on January 16 was so startling and ominous that Franklin went home afterward and recorded every word of their dialogue in the manner of a stage play. It is not known exactly where he sent the script, although the contents were surely intended for his new employers, the Massachusetts Assembly. One reader (who made notes on the surviving copy) referred to the document as "a singular conversation," meaning it was at once private, exceptional, and whimsical.

Strahan had advised Franklin to call upon Hillsborough at his home to present the credentials. In the receiving room Franklin found Governor Bernard, ex-governor of Massachusetts, and several other gentlemen waiting. Franklin was flattered when Thomas Pownall, another ex-governor of Massachusetts, now a member of Parliament, emerged and invited him to enter first. He had been known to wait three or four hours for an audience with Hillsborough. This courtesy made it much easier for him to put on the cheerful countenance Strahan had advised him to wear that day.

Lord Hillsborough had been dressing to go to Court, but hearing that Franklin was in the house, on business, he now approached him cordially. Franklin replied that his business was not much: merely to pay his respects and acquaint him with his appointment as agent by the House of Representatives of Massachusetts Bay. Hearing the long name of that province, his lordship winced and his features darkened.

L.H.   I must set you right there, Mr. Franklin, you are not Agent.

B.F.   Why, my Lord?

L.H.   You are not appointed.

B.F.   I do not understand your Lordship. I have the Appointment in my Pocket.

L.H.   You are mistaken. I have later and better Advices. I have a Letter from Governor Hutchinson. He would not give his Assent to the Bill.

B.F.   There was no Bill, my Lord; it is a Vote of the House.

L.H.   There was a Bill presented to the Governor, for the purpose of appointing you, and another, one Dr. Lee, I think he is call'd, to which the Governor refus'd his Assent.

B.F.   I cannot understand this, my Lord. I think There must be some Mistake in it. Is your Lordship quite sure that you have such a Letter?

L.H.   I will convince you of it directly. *Rings the Bell.* Mr. Pownall will come in and satisfy you.

B.F.   It is not necessary that I should now detain your Lordship from Dressing. You are going to Court. I will wait on your Lordship another time.

L.H.   No, stay. He will come in immediately. *To the Servant.* Tell Mr. Pownall I want him. *Mr. Pownall comes in.* Have not you at hand Govr. Hutchinson's Letter mentioning his Refusing his Assent to the Bill for appointing Dr. Franklin Agent?

Sec. P. My Lord?

L.H.   Is there not such a Letter?

Sec. P. No, my Lord . . .

B.F. I thought it could not well be, my Lord, as my Letters are by the last Ships and mention no such Thing. Here is an authentic Copy of the Vote of the House. . . . Will your Lordship please to look at it? *(With some seeming Unwillingness he takes it, but does not look into it).*

L.H. An Information of this kind is not properly brought to me as Secretary of State. The Board of Trade is the proper Place.

B.F. I will leave the Paper then with Mr. Pownall, to be—

L.H. *(Hastily)* To what End would you leave it with him?

B.F. To be entered on the Minutes of that Board, as usual.

L.H. *(Angrily)* It shall not be entered there. No such Paper shall be entered there while I have any thing to do with the Business of that Board. The House of Representatives has no Right to appoint an Agent. We shall take no Notice of any Agents but such are appointed by Acts of Assembly to which the Governor gives his assent. . . .

B.F. I cannot conceive, my Lord, why the Consent of the *Governor* should be thought necessary to the Appointment of an Agent for the *People*. It seems to me, that—

L.H. *(With a mix'd look of Anger and Contempt)* I shall not enter into a Dispute with you, Sir, upon this Subject.

B.F. I beg your Lordship's Pardon. I do not presume to dispute with your Lordship: I would only say, that it seems to me, that every Body of Men, who cannot appear in Person where Business relating to them may be transacted, should have a Right to appear by an Agent; the Concurrence of the Governor does not seem to me necessary. It is the Business of the People that is to be done, he is not one of them, he is himself an Agent.

L.H. Whose Agent is he? *(Hastily)*

B.F. The King's, my Lord.

L.H. No such Matter. He is one of the Corporation, by the Province Charter. No Agent can be appointed but by an Act, nor any Act pass without his Assent. Besides, This Proceeding is directly contrary to express Instructions.

B.F.   I did not know there had been such Instructions, I am not concern'd in any Offence against them, and—

L.H.   Yes, your Offering such a Paper to be entered is an Offence against them. *(Folding it up again, without having read a Word of it.)* No such Appointment shall be entered. . . .

There were a few more cross words. Franklin reached out for the paper, and Hillsborough returned it to him. Franklin apologized for having taken up so much of his lordship's time and took his leave, with this parting shot: "It is I believe of no great importance whether the appointment is acknowledged or not, for I have not the least conception that an agent can *at present* be of any use, to any of the colonies. I shall therefore give your Lordship no farther trouble." *(Withdrew.)*

He had told Hillsborough, in so many words, that as long as he was secretary for the colonies, he, Franklin, could do no more business with him. And he didn't. That year he enjoyed his surrogate family in London, the Stevensons and their in-laws, the Hewsons. He traveled in England, Ireland, and Scotland, and at the end of the year he entertained his son-in-law, Richard Bache, in London. He wrote very little apart from the opening section of his memoirs, and conducted no business that year of any consequence.

Resuming communication with his son in 1772, Franklin wrote some of the most intimate and revealing passages to be found in all of his papers. In the first, posted on January 30, Franklin described Lord Hillsborough's surprising behavior recently in Ireland. William had informed his father that Hillsborough in his letters had begun to show signs of desiring better relations with him, after years of hostility. His father remarked that "his behavior to me in Ireland corresponds exactly." Invited to dine at Lord Lieutenant Viscount Townshend's home in Dublin, Franklin and Richard Jackson came upon Hillsborough, seated alone in the parlor. "He was extremely civil, wonderfully so, to me whom he had not long before abused to Mr. Strahan as a factious turbulent fellow, always in mischief, a Republican, enemy to the King's service, and what not." Afterward Hillsborough insisted that Franklin and Jackson stop at his home on their way north. "Does not all this seem extraordinary to you?" Franklin asked his son. "I knew not what to make of it, unless that he foresaw a storm on account of his conduct in America . . ." and wanted the colonists to think better of him.

In the same letter Franklin recalled the time spent with his son-in-law, especially their conversation about his career. Bache wanted a political office in the colonies. Franklin was against it, saying he preferred his friends and relations to be more independent, self-employed. So he had advised Bache, who had brought £1,000 sterling to England, to use it to buy goods he could sell at retail in Philadelphia and thus "get forward in the world."

His grandson, Temple, now twelve, had come home from school to spend his Christmas vacation with him and the Stevensons on Craven Street. Now his proud grandfather wrote that the boy "more and more engages the regard of all that are acquainted with him, by his pleasing, sensible, manly behavior."

And at last, in a rare moment of sentiment, he confessed that he was homesick, and at the age of sixty-six he was afraid that illness might prevent him from ever returning to America. "I have also some important affairs to settle before my death, a period I ought now to think cannot be far distant." For the time being, he suspected, Parliament was uninterested in America, unlikely to institute or repeal any taxes. Franklin supposed he might leave for a year without missing any business of consequence. Yet once at home, he would probably never see England again. He closed with the words:

> I have indeed so many good kind friends here that I could
> spend the rest of my life among them with great pleasure, if it were
> not for my American connections, and the indelible affection I re-
> tain for that dear country, from which I have so long been in a
> state of exile. My love to Betsy. I am ever your affectionate father
> B Franklin

BEN FRANKLIN HAD BEEN correct when he told Strahan that he had grown so unpopular among the ministers that the affairs of the Walpole Company would fare better if he kept his distance. On April 15, the Board of Trade rejected the Walpole petition. But on July 1, the

Board reversed its decision upon the order of its Committee on Plantations—much to Franklin's satisfaction, and in spite of Hillsborough's resistance. Hillsborough had suspended his courtesies to Franklin in the New Year: "He threw me away as an orange that would yield no juice, and therefore not worth more squeezing. . . . I have never since been nigh him, and we have only abused one another at a distance." It did not matter.

British politics, a hornet's nest in 1772, had stung the secretary of state that summer while Franklin was on vacation in Scotland. On August 17, Dr. Franklin wrote in triumph to his son: "At length we have got rid of Lord Hillsborough, and Lord Dartmouth takes his place." William might think that the Walpole Company and their friends had ousted his lordship, but in fact Hillsborough's colleagues disliked him so much they longed for a chance to trip him up, and "so seeing that he made a point of defeating our scheme, they made another of supporting it, on purpose to mortify him, which they knew his pride could not bear."

When the Committee on Plantations overruled the Board of Trade, approving Franklin's petition, Hillsborough, irate, offered his resignation. To his surprise, Lord North accepted it, and on August 14, the Privy Council endorsed the Walpole grant. Franklin was guardedly optimistic: "Therefore let us beware of every word and action, that may betray a confidence in its success, lest we render ourselves ridiculous in case of disappointment." Parliament was capricious, and vicious—regardless of the merits of any human endeavor—and therefore not to be trusted.

Some letters to William that August, of unusual intimacy, express Franklin's affection for his son as well as great trust in him as a confidant. On August 19 he refers to William's letter of May 14, now lost, and how distressed he was by his son's recent illness. He is pleased that William has followed his advice and is taking more exercise, suggests horseback riding, walking up and down stairs, and lifting dumbbells to increase his heart rate. The entire communication is tenderly sympathetic. His inventory of his life at sixty-six is difficult for us to imagine his sharing with any other man:

As to my situation here nothing can be more agreeable, especially
as I hope for less embarrassment from the new minister. A general respect paid me by the learned, a number of friends and ac-
quaintances among them with whom I have a pleasing
intercourse; a character of so much weight that it has protected
me when some in power would have done me injury . . . my company so much desired that I seldom dine at home in winter, and
could spend the whole summer in the country houses of invited
friends if I chose it. Learned and ingenious foreigners that come
to England almost all make a point of visiting me, for my reputation is still higher abroad than here. . . .

Ambassadors sought him out "as one of their *corps*" from the desire to
learn of American affairs. Even King George himself "has been heard
to speak of me with great regard."

It is an extraordinary outpouring of self-affirmation and self-
congratulation whose every line invites the curious reader to wonder:
What is the occasion? Does Franklin suppose his son has grown so far
removed that he does not know these things, and more, about his celebrated father? Is Franklin, at age sixty-six, still hungry for approval? Is
he perhaps simply reassuring his distant son that life in England is
comfortable, and fulfilling, and that he need not be concerned if his
father stays away a little longer?

The answer comes obliquely in a postscript to this long and revealing letter dated August 22, a Saturday. "I find I omitted congratulating
you on the honor of your election in the Society for Propagating the
Gospel." Back in 1770, William was proud to inform his father that he
had been elected to membership in a society aimed to advance the
Christian ministry overseas, and in America to evangelize the non-
Christian races, especially the Indians. This was a distinct honor for
William, who was not a minister or missionary, but who had done so
much to support the Anglican parish in Burlington, and had fostered
peaceful relations with the Indians.

More than two years later, Franklin extends his congratulations, and
adds, "But you are again behind, for last night I received a letter from

Paris of which the inclosed is an extract, acquainting me that I am chosen *Associé etranger* [foreign member] of the Royal Academy there." Franklin was one of eight foreigners, "the most distinguished names for science."

Now this would be much like one's father writing: Congratulations, my son, on your success in the marbles tournament in Perth Amboy two years past. It puts me in mind of my more recent victory in the Olympic Games in Athens, where I brought home the gold medal in the pentathlon, jumping, throwing the discus and javelin, outrunning and outwrestling the greatest athletes of Europe.

The passage removes any doubt that might remain about the dynamic between father and son—in this particular. Benjamin Franklin is in open, unabashed competition with his forty-year-old son. Yet William, on his side, confident in his own considerable abilities, secure in his convictions, does not now, and will never, play that game. He honors his father, loves and admires him. He knows he will never be his father's equal as an inventor, writer, or mechanic; but he puts more stock in filial pride than in jealousy. Both men have cause for concern about their political futures, although the recent developments in the ministry, particularly Dartmouth's accession (Lord Dartmouth had always favored Benjamin), look very promising. William needed his father's support more than Benjamin needed William's. That had usually been the case, the natural order of things; but the two had nonetheless been partners, in politics and in family life—since the French and Indian War.

William was pleased to inform his father, on September 1, that his health, and Betsy's, were much improved. "I am glad," his father replied, "and I think as you do that Amboy Air may possibly agree better with you both than that of Burlington." This is the first he has heard of his son's desire to leave the western town on the Delaware River, so near Philadelphia, to settle in Perth Amboy, the port of entry on Staten Island Sound. No doubt the air was fresher there. But there were political and social considerations that weighed as heavily upon William and his wife that year as did their health.

Resentment over the treasury robbery had festered over the past three years, polarizing the colonists during a period when William felt his authority was waning. When he requested more money to supply the king's troops, the legislature balked. Insisting that they meant no offense to His Excellency, they declared the colony was insolvent; they might only fund the troops by raising taxes, and this they refused to do. There was no paper currency, land values were depressed, and New Jersey was still suffering from the blow to the treasury. Governor Franklin, usually calm in the face of adversity, lost his temper and for the first time questioned the legislators' motives, calling them short-sighted, tight-fisted, and selfish, impugning their patriotism. Further-more, he engaged in a misguided argument claiming that New Jersey was not in distressed circumstances, but in fact was gradually improv-ing.

Indignant, immovable, the governor adjourned the Assembly of 1771. He wrote to London, hoping to get funds from the ministry in the form of a Loan Office Bill (a float of currency); but by simultane-ously assuring Hillsborough that the province was on the road to re-covery he sabotaged his own appeal. He would not be able to buy cooperation with fresh funds. The controversy over the burglary, and Stephen Skinner's part in it, was bound to blow up in the heat of the colony's financial crisis. And for once, Governor Franklin's reliable tac-tic of delay worked against him. He did not convene the Assembly again until September 1772, and by that time a new election had al-tered the fabric of the legislature. Franklin had lost many of his allies, and now more than half the thirty members were newcomers.

Again the treasurer entered his plea of innocence. But this time the legislature voted that Governor Franklin enforce an order that Skinner reimburse the colony in full. The lawyer who drafted the in-structions to Franklin, James Kinsey, was a freshman delegate from Burlington, and he did not soft-pedal his message: Kinsey censured not only the treasurer but the governor himself, saying the whole business would have been better managed if the Assembly had been empowered to impeach the negligent treasurer in the first place. A politician more artful or cynical than William might have seen James Kinsey for what he was: an ambitious Quaker lawyer who used the Skinner affair to grab power in the momentous populist, anti-imperial movement. As far as Franklin was concerned, Kinsey's demand was outrageous. He could not enforce such an order—Skinner had not been convicted of any wrongdoing.

On September 18, 1772, the Assembly demanded that Stephen Skinner be dismissed from his post. They requested that he be replaced, and that the new treasurer bring suit against the old one to reimburse the colony. Franklin saw this as an attack upon the Crown's prerogative to appoint, or remove, government officials, pledged his loyalty to Stephen Skinner, affirmed his duty to make appointments, and would hear no opposition.

"Controversy," he told the peevish legislators, is "really disagreeable to me; and though I never seek it, yet I never avoid it where it is necessary to my character, let the consequences be what they may." At a time when compromise would have served every faction—compromise in the form of asking for Skinner's resignation—Franklin dug in his heels. Chief Justice Smyth, a man of good judgment who knew Franklin well and liked him, was alarmed at what he saw as having become a "violent contest." He wrote to Hillsborough on October 5 that he was disappointed in the governor, whom he knew to be diplomatic by nature, engaging in an unseemly squabble with the lawmakers that left his government "much degraded." And he feared that Franklin's "extraordinary attachment" to Mr. Skinner would lead to his downfall. William denied it. "I pretend not to infallibility, but I do to principle."

Principle had been its own reward. William had been New Jersey's governor for a decade, since he was thirty-three. While not a man of enormous ambition, he desired a better living for himself and his wife than he was getting. His salary was frozen and they were living in a rented house in Burlington. There were advantages, to be sure, in living so near his mother and sister in Philadelphia, only twenty miles away, during his father's long absence. But now it appeared his father would be coming home to take over, and William could consider the possibility of living in the east.

He had every reason to be proud of his record as governor, and he was disappointed that Hillsborough had not promoted him. On October 13 he wrote to his father of the death of William Spry, late governor of Barbados, a superior office. "I wish I could succeed Govr. Spry, but I stand no chance of any promotion or enlargement of my salary, I imagine, while Lord H. is at the head of the American department, and is so much displeased with your conduct."

Hillsborough was gone, as William would learn, but meanwhile he was frustrated and weary. At forty-five Elizabeth was past childbearing age. She had expected to live in a manner more becoming to an heiress and a first lady of His Majesty's American dominions. William asked his father to have made for him a dozen mahogany parlor chairs with horsehair bottoms, "made in a fashionable taste," at the cost of 25 shillings sterling apiece. Also, "I must likewise beg you to send me a handsome tea urn, I can't afford a silver one, and therefore must be contented with a plated one, or a copper one with silver spout and handles.... Send me that which you think best." His father would oblige by commissioning the urn from Matthew Boulton, the premier manufacturer of Sheffield plate.

All that week he had been in Philadelphia with the family, and he "had dined at Governor Richard Penn's, with whom I am become very sociable." He could not have thought his father would welcome such news, yet it appears boldly near the end of his letter, just above the closing, "Betsy joins in duty, with, honored Sir, your dutiful son, Wm Franklin."

Soon after hearing that Lord Dartmouth had taken over the American office he wrote to him, explaining his predicament: "Whilst others in my station have made considerable fortunes, been promoted, or received considerable honors and rewards, my own private fortune has been really lessening, and I have as yet only the satisfaction of having served His Majesty faithfully and to the best of my ability." This was partly because the governor of New Jersey could make no money from granting land. And with two capitals, he bore the burden of entertaining a stream of dignitaries in both, in a colony known as the great corridor between the two cities of New York and Philadelphia.

William had made the decision to live in Burlington at the time he took his oaths of office, largely out of consideration for his West Jersey constituency. This had been a wise decision, and the government had benefited from it. But all the while the proprietors of East Jersey had been constructing a beautiful mansion on a deep lot of twelve acres on the west side of High Street in Perth Amboy. It would be the honor of the proprietors, they declared, to provide "a convenient house for the residence of the Governor," the cost not to "exceed three thousand pounds," about $600,000 today. The builders used the finest white pine and red cedar boards, hewn stone and white brick, and oak and ashlar stone for finishing. On that cold day in February, so long ago, he and his father had seen the shell of it, the cornice complete around the two main entrances—the promise of grandeur.

Since then he had seen Proprietary House completed and refined: the broad hall with its marble chimneypiece, the sash Venetian doors to the banquet room, the drawing room with pilastered fireplaces. He saw the mansion become a showplace, and it tempted him. Whenever the governor chose, he could have the keys. William Franklin had worked hard, and he had good reason to believe he would soon be rich.

By the autumn of 1772, it seemed that all that could be gained from his choice to live in the western capital had been gained. It was a fool's bargain to remain in a town where he was daily losing favor when most of his friends and allies, including the Skinners, lived in Perth Amboy on Raritan Bay, a few miles closer, as the crow flies, to England.

In England, Ben Franklin's involvement in the affairs of Massachusetts had taken a curious turn: The king now wished to pay the governor's salary. For a year, Parliament had intended to assume the payment of the colonial governors' salaries, a measure the Americans opposed because it would curb their assemblies' influence. The law was challenged in both England and America, but nowhere was the contest more feverish than in Boston. There the Sons of Liberty waged a war of words with the formidable governor, Thomas Hutchinson. In the spring of 1771, awaiting formal orders from London, Hutchinson began to refuse the usual Assembly grants that provided his salary, without explanation. When rumors that the king would pay Hutchinson's salary were confirmed in July 1772, a House committee condemned the act. If Hutchinson wished to show good faith, he would ask the Crown to reverse its decision.

Hutchinson would do nothing of the kind. Instead he delivered an argument of twenty-five hundred words analyzing the Assembly's attack on the royal salary, explaining the checks and balances of colonial government and the importance of the governor's freedom from the legislature's financial pressure. A few days later the members heard rumors that their judges also would soon be funded by the Crown, and their fury knew no bounds. A Boston town meeting demanded that Hutchinson confirm whether rumors of this innovation "to complete the system of their slavery" were well founded. When he refused to discuss the Crown's intentions, the members—under the leadership of Samuel Adams—issued a manifesto of the rights of colonists "as men, as Christians, and as subjects" and published it under the title *Votes and Proceedings of the Freeholders of Boston* on November 20, 1772. The provocative pamphlet was circulated in every town in Massachusetts.

The same month that Adams wrote his rabble-rousing pamphlet, Franklin in London received the Assembly's petition to the king denouncing the royal salary for the governor. After showing the petition to Lord Dartmouth, Franklin agreed to withhold it until the time might be more favorable. What this delay meant to Franklin is difficult to say. We do know that by the time he met with Dartmouth he possessed some documents that Thomas Hutchinson and others had never wanted him to read. These were the very letters of Governor Hutchinson to one Thomas Whately that passed Franklin's own on the high seas, in January 1769. They included Hutchinson's fateful words *"There must be an abridgment of what are called English liberties"* and *"I wish to see some further restraint of liberty rather than the connection with the parent state should be broken."*

Exactly how Ben Franklin came to possess these private letters of Hutchinson no one knows. There is an even greater mystery: Why did Franklin make these private letters public when he did? As to the first perplexity, he never answered, and he and his unknown confederate carried their secret to the grave. As to the second, his answers were so odd and contrary to common sense they seem unworthy of Poor Richard, who had made a fortune from that simple virtue.

America was in turmoil. Massachusetts in particular had been on the verge of insurrection, on and off, since the Stamp Act in 1765, and after the Boston Massacre of 1770 had bred a group of inspired and well-organized radicals including Sam Adams, John Hancock, Paul

Revere, Deacon Philips, Benjamin Church, and others. Twenty-one of them created the "committee of correspondence" at Faneuil Hall on November 2, 1772, the meeting that published the rights of the colonists to the world. Since the British regiments had arrived in Boston in 1768, mob violence had grown so threatening that at times the soldiers were ordered to seek shelter in the stone fortress of Castle William Island in the Harbor.

Knowing all of these things as well as any man in England or America, on December 2, Ben Franklin sent Governor Hutchinson's letters of 1768–69, along with a few by his secretary, Andrew Oliver, to Thomas Cushing, Speaker of the Massachusetts Assembly.

The letters had originally been addressed to a friend in London, MP Thomas Whately, a protégé of George Grenville, the king's first minister during the framing of the Stamp Act. The letters pointed to the violence against royal officials during the late sixties as proof that something must be done to keep the peace—even if it meant abridging "what are called English liberties." Hutchinson's home had been destroyed; the customs officers had been harassed. Andrew Oliver proposed that they receive their salaries from the Crown, and both men urged that the government be removed as far as possible from popular control. Whately's connection with Grenville left little doubt that Hutchinson had provoked Grenville's repressive policies.

Franklin's letter to Cushing, in which he enclosed the packet of purloined Hutchinson letters, begins with a report on the status of the Assembly's petition concerning the governor's salary. As friendly as the new secretary was to America, Dartmouth believed that presenting it to the king right away would only offend him. Only a severe reprimand to the colonial assembly would come of it, and this would cause more discontent and unrest in the province. Tempers were inflamed on both sides, but Dartmouth trusted "those heats are now cooling" and was averse to adding fresh fuel.

Under these warm circumstances Franklin saw fit to acquaint the Speaker of the House "that there has lately fallen into my hands part of a correspondence, that I have reason to believe laid the foundation of most if not all of our present grievances." Franklin sent those explosive papers to Cushing, on the condition that they would not be printed, nor any copies made of them in whole or part, but that they "be seen by some men of worth in the province for their satisfaction only." He holds Cushing under a strict injunction *not* to allow the letters to be published, while in the same breath he asks they be shared with men of worth there, that is, every man of importance including the Adamses, Hancock, Church, and Revere.

Three may keep a secret if two of them are dead, he had famously written in the *Almanac.* Franklin knew the letters would be published. They were published almost immediately upon arriving in Boston, and widely read.

Franklin's motive, as set forth to Cushing, was based on his own experience: His resentment against England for its harsh government under Hillsborough had softened since he read these letters, which had convinced him that the measures he loathed "were projected, advised and called for by men of character among ourselves," namely, Americans such as Hutchinson. Also, Hutchinson's advice had been misleading, Franklin argued—the governor and his men had never really been in danger. "My own resentment, I say, has by this means been considerably abated." So he wishes he might "make the private letters public," to share this abatement and good feeling, but he cannot in good conscience; so he must be content to share them only with gentlemen of the Committee of Correspondence.

It is possible but unlikely that Franklin felt any such "abatement"— nowhere else does he express it. What is not possible, although generations of historians have swallowed the bittersweet dose of Franklin's account, is that he actually believed that the people en masse would feel less resentment—that the display of Hutchinson's letters would ease the tensions between America and England. On his desk he had a petition from the Massachusetts House proving that the lawmakers were furious with Hutchinson for obeying Parliament's orders. Focusing more anger on Hutchinson as instigator of the doctrine behind those orders would not deflect anger from the British ministry that had embraced the odious policies and then told the governor to enforce them. The editors of the *Papers of Benjamin Franklin* suggest, "Anyone familiar with the situation in Boston must have known that the letters would arouse particular fury against the governor."

If it had truly been Franklin's aim to reconcile the colonies to the mother country by this peculiar experiment, then "he was not thinking clearly," the editors conclude, charitably. Franklin habitually thought clearly about important matters; it is fair to say that reconciliation was not his aim here. At age sixty-six he had spent more time and effort in the study of natural science than he had in the realm of international diplomacy. The scientist might have lit a grease fire in a pot and poured water upon it to see how many drops it would take to create a fireball, a geyser of exploding steam and blazing oil—but not in his own kitchen.

The letters arrived in Boston on March 24, 1773. The Speaker of the House immediately showed them to members of the Committee of Correspondence, the Adamses, John Hancock, Deacon Philips, and the rest. All agreed that if the letters were to serve the purpose for which Franklin had sent them, he must lift the restrictions. So Cushing wrote Franklin to ask, disingenuously: If they could not *publish* the letters, at least they might be permitted to *copy* them? It took weeks for this request to reach London, and months for the response to arrive— that Franklin would first have to get permission from the gentleman who had procured the letters. On June 4, Cushing was still waiting to find out whether the consent would be granted when Franklin wrote to report on the debates in Parliament over the American duty on tea:

> It was thought at the beginning of the session, that the American duty on tea would be taken off. But now the scheme is, to take off as much duty here as will make tea cheaper in America than foreigners can supply us; and continue the duty there to keep up the exercise of the right. They have no idea that any people can act from any principle but that of interest; and they believe that 3 pence in a pound of tea . . . is sufficient to overcome all the patriotism of an American!

And by the way, he says, months after being asked, he has *not* been able to obtain leave to make copies or publish Hutchinson's letters; however, the House might keep them as long as they served any purpose.

The letters by now were in wide circulation, fanning the flames of rancor Governor Hutchinson had inspired weeks before their arrival. "Upon convening the General Assembly," Samuel Cooper reported, "the Governor opened with the long speech in defence of the absolute supremacy of parliament over the colonies, inviting both houses to offer what they had to object against this principle." They had plenty to offer against Hutchinson and his principles. In the New England spring of that year, everyone who was anyone was reading and talking about the Hutchinson letters. John Adams took copies of some of them with him as he rode the muddy circuit of the superior court and shared them with interested folk in the countryside.

When the Assembly at last convened on May 26, people could talk of little else. On Wednesday, June 2, Sam Adams strode into the great redbrick Massachusetts Town House, seat of the government. He passed the seven-foot-tall figures of the lion and the unicorn in wood, emblems of the monarchy, and entered the central chambers. Waving his arms, he cleared the public galleries. When only the legislators remained, Adams announced he had "perceived the minds of the people to be greatly agitated with a prevailing report that letters of an extraordinary nature had been written and sent to England, greatly to the prejudice of this province." They were then read aloud, as if every man in the hall had not already studied them, and the House then voted 101 to 5 that the intention of Hutchinson was to overthrow the constitution of the colonial government.

On June 15, printers began rolling out copies of the letters despite the restrictions that had been placed upon them—claiming they had an independent source—for members of the Assembly, and then for the world at large. The next day the House adopted a resolution establishing their authenticity and declaring the letters "had a natural and efficacious tendency to interrupt and alienate the affections of our most gracious sovereign King George the Third from his loyal and affectionate province ... and to suppress the very spirit of freedom." The document concluded with the request that the king remove the governor and his secretary from office immediately and forever.

Before year's end the offending letters and the resolves had gone through ten printings in America and England. Editorials in the Boston papers called the letters "footsteps stained with blood." John Adams, seething, wrote of Hutchinson, "Vile serpent, bone of our bone, born and educated among us." The governor was strung up and burned in effigy in Philadelphia and, to William Franklin's dismay, in Princeton, New Jersey. Reverend Cooper wrote to Benjamin Franklin that "nothing could have been more seasonable than the arrival of these letters. They have had great effect."

On July 7, Ben Franklin addressed a long discourse to Cushing that was intended for the House; it became widely known before it was read aloud there. Published in *The Boston Gazette,* choice passages warmed the hearts of Sam Adams and other radicals. Franklin had succinctly stated the argument for a congress of all the colonies, "to engage firmly with each other that they will never grant aids to the Crown in any general war till those rights are recognized by the King and both Houses of Parliament," that is, the same rights granted to citizens in the mother country. Hutchinson thought the letter was treasonable, and he sent a copy to Dartmouth, seeking revenge.

Franklin received the Resolves of the Committee of Correspondence on July 25, and he expressed relief "that no person besides Dr. Cooper and one of the Committee know they [the letters] came from me." In the line of duty he had acted "regardless of the consequences. . . . However, since the letters themselves are now copied and printed, contrary the promise I made, I am glad my name has not been heard on the occasion."

He waited until Saturday, August 21, to send the Assembly's resolution, with its grievances and request to remove the governor, to Lord Dartmouth. Nothing would be done at present, as most of the Privy Council had gone to their country estates for the summer. Months would pass before Lord Dartmouth would return from his country seat in Staffordshire. Moreover, Governor Hutchinson had requested leave to return to England, according to some, including William Franklin. According to others, there were influential persons in the Court who had read the letters and did not believe they justified the Assembly's desire to remove the governor. He would be allowed to resign, and provision would be made for him in England. If there were to be a hearing, Ben Franklin advised Cushing, he would hire a lawyer from the province and advance him whatever money might be necessary. Such suits were costly.

In the summer of that year, Benjamin Franklin amused himself, and the friends of American liberty, in writing two of his greatest satires, "Rules by Which a Great Empire May Be Reduced to a Small One" and "Edict by the King of Prussia," works worthy of a Swift or Voltaire. His twenty "Rules" begin with the premise that "a great empire, like a great cake, is most easily diminished at the edges." So first get rid of your remote provinces. To assure this, take care that they do not enjoy the same rights, and "are governed by *severer* laws, all of *your enacting.*"

His "Edict by the King of Prussia" is a proclamation, in the voice of Frederick II, that England, as a German settlement, owed him obedience. Frederick had fallen out with Britain over the late Peace of Paris, and he had recently threatened to occupy the island and be king of England himself. He had in fact sent regiments to subdue his Polish provinces, and he once issued an edict annexing part of the Netherlands.

Franklin's hoax was so cleverly conceived that he actually had the pleasure of seeing friends taken in by it. He was staying in West Wycombe, at the famous estate of Frances Dashwood, Lord Le Despenser, his superior as postmaster. Franklin had spent most of the summer there, and he probably wrote his satires in the mansion. They were coming down to breakfast with the writer Paul Whitehead and other guests when the morning papers arrived. Whitehead would often skim the papers first.

"We were chatting in the breakfast parlor," Benjamin wrote to William, "when he came running in to us, out of breath, with the paper in his hand. Here! says he, here's news for ye! *Here's the King of Prussia, claiming a right to this Kingdom!* All stared, and I as much as any body; and he went on to read it."

After hearing two paragraphs, one gentleman cried, *"Damn his impudence, I dare say, we shall hear by next post that he is upon his march with one hundred men to back this."* Whitehead soon grew suspicious and, looking at Franklin, said, *"I'll be hanged if this is not some of your American jokes upon us."* The reading continued, amid gales of laughter, and Dashwood and others reached a verdict that it was a direct hit.

The postmaster, Lord Le Despenser, was a Tory Member of Parliament from 1741 to 1763 and chancellor of the Exchequer in 1762–63, a post that was said to be given him "for his skill in casting up tavern bills." He was made postmaster general in 1766, two years after Franklin arrived in London. Dashwood's principal claim to fame, however, is as the founder of the Knights of St. Francis of Wycombe, also known as the Medmenham Club. This secret fraternity of lords and gentlemen was devoted to drunkenness, sexual orgies, and blasphemy. The meetings twice a month in Medmenham Abbey or the Caves of West Wycombe featured mock religious ceremonies, sacrifices, and ritual costumes. The motto inscribed over the door was *fais ce que tu voudras,* or *Do As You Will.* As host of these revels, Le Despenser was known as the most careless libertine of his age.

Franklin wrote to his son from West Wycombe on August 3, 1773, "I am in this house as much at my ease as if it was my own, and the gardens are a paradise." The landscaped park with its little Doric temples and Roman arches surrounded a huge man-made lake in the shape of a swan, whose waters cascaded into a lower canal pond. Nearby, up the hill, stood Medmenham Abbey. Under the building, Dashwood had carved out a series of caves to provide the knights with greater darkness and privacy for their annual general meeting in September. "But a pleasanter thing," Franklin continued, "is the kind countenance, . . . and very intelligent conversation of mine host, who having been for many years engaged in publick affairs, seen all parts of Europe, and kept the best company in the world is himself the best existing."

Franklin took his ease in a summer suit of light gray, adorned with buttons of natural sea-carved slate, from Button-mold Bay in Vermont. William had sent him the buttons, and in his letter Franklin thanks his son for the gift.

Whatever went on in West Wycombe, it was surely a devil-may-care atmosphere in which Franklin composed and published his superb satires that September. The writing of satires is an idle exercise of virtuosity, unlikely to change people's minds, but likely to provoke anger in the closed-minded. Franklin knew this. Yet he was so eager to draw attention to imperial folly, he was willing to risk heightening the conflict and bringing down the wrath of Parliament on his own head. As he explained to his sister Jane Mecum in a letter months later, "I had used all the smooth words I could muster, and I grew tired of meekness when I saw it without effect. Of late therefore I have been saucy, and in two papers, *Rules for reducing a great Empire to a small one;* and *An Edict of the King of Prussia,* I have held up a looking-glass in which some ministers may see their ugly faces, and the nation its injustice."

Many readers were amused, "and a few very angry, who I am told will make me feel their resentment," which he would suffer in the interest of the common good. William read these works, and he watched his father's progress with curiosity and concern, perhaps even dread, not knowing the extent of Benjamin's involvement in the imbroglio in Massachusetts.

On his way to Albany for a summer vacation with Betsy, "who wanted a jaunt this summer on account of her health," William stopped in New York to transact some business. He posted a letter to his father from the city on July 29. This letter, written in haste, records his awareness that Benjamin had sent the Hutchinson letters to Boston, and that he had also written a letter to Cushing in which "you went so far as to advise the colonies" to be so bold as "insisting on their *Independency.*" This was of course the seditious letter of July 7 that had gone on wings to America and had been taken up and broadcast by the Sons of Liberty.

William did not express his concern over these matters specifically, but there is enough general anxiety in this letter to indicate he was none too happy about any of it. And William could hardly believe his father's reports that the Walpole grant was still in limbo: "By the May packet Wharton wrote that everything would be completed so that he should certainly leave England by the end of the month." William's business in New York had to do with land and financing. He was beginning to fear that the quickening political crisis might doom the all-important land grants.

Benjamin Franklin usually wrote to his son at the beginning of the month. So in late September, William had his father's dispatch from the gardens of West Wycombe, with its tribute to his charming host, Lord Dashwood, as well as the first mention of the importance of making a will. Temple Franklin had just gone back to school after vacationing with his grandfather. "He always behaves himself so well, as to increase my affection for him every time he is with me. As you are likely to have a considerable landed property, it would be well to make your Will . . . and secure this property to him." Their friend Galloway the lawyer would advise William; no doubt the boy will be worthy of the inheritance if his character does not strangely alter.

Then, in October, William received a sprawling letter from his father concerning some resolutions of New England townships endorsing the Boston Town Meeting and reflecting upon Irish politics. Most important, however, is Benjamin's confiding to his son that he *was* the man who had sent the Hutchinson letters to Boston. "It is as well that it should continue a secret. Being of that country [Massachusetts] myself I think those letters more heinous than you seem to think them"— and here William could detect a note of disapproval—"but you had not read them all." He offers the same explanation of his actions that he had provided Cushing and others. Now, he says, he means to return to America, and so has written declining to serve another term as agent for Massachusetts. He may stay one more winter, in order to promote the land grant business.

Before he heard from his father again, William Franklin knew of upheavals in America that would transform their lives forever. The British East India Company, an imperial mainstay and pillar of the economy, was near collapse. To rescue it, Parliament had almost erased the duty on tea to make the English product competitive with Dutch tea. The Tea Act appeared to repeal the Townshend duty on tea, but the appearance was deceiving. Although Parliament considered removing the last shred of the Townshend duties, they decided to keep a slight import tax on tea in order to fund the customs commissions in America, and to uphold Parliament's power to tax the colonies.

That autumn protest was widespread. William could read about it in *The Pennsylvania Journal* of September 29, in a letter from a colonist in London claiming the Tea Act was Lord North's plot to enforce the Townshend duty on tea. If effective this would become a "precedent for every imposition the Parliament of Great Britain shall think proper to saddle us with." *The New York Journal* printed a letter on October 7, purporting to be from London, declaring "I have told several of the East India Company that the tea and ships will all be burnt...as I think you will never suffer an Act of Parliament to be so crowded down your throats." A public meeting in Philadelphia on October 15 resolved that the Tea Act was an attack "upon the liberties of America which every American was in duty bound to oppose."

On the ocean at that moment, breasting the waves, Francis Rotch's ship the *Dartmouth* was under sail with one hundred and fourteen chests of East India Company tea stowed in the hold, headed for Boston.

THERE WAS NO MAN in America who could understand Hutchinson's agony as well as his fellow governor in New Jersey, William Franklin. He would not have traded places with him for all Hutchinson's riches.

The *Dartmouth*, shipping its cargo of East India Company tea, approached Boston Harbor on November 27. She anchored in Broad Sound outside the hooked peninsula that night and entered the inner harbor the next day, a Sunday. She rode at anchor there while the customs officers boarded her on November 29 and was officially entered at the customs house the next day, a Tuesday. Still technically in limbo, the *Dartmouth* would not be tied up at Griffin's Wharf until December 1.

Meanwhile, word of the ship's anchorage had come to people gathering in churches all over the town for Sunday worship on the twenty-ninth. At noon the Committee of Correspondence convened in Faneuil Hall to decide what to do. They sent for the consignees—two of them Hutchinson's sons—hoping to make one final appeal to them to resign their commissions. But none of them would leave the safety of the great stone fortress at Castle William Island.

Disheartened but resolute, Governor Hutchinson left town to ride out the storm at his country house. On November 14, he had received the longed-for letter granting his request to step down as governor and leave this pandemonium. Now he was so far carried away in the tide of troubles that he told Dartmouth "I should have feared the King's displeasure if I had left my government."

He faced a momentous but clear-cut decision regarding the tea duty and the cargo ships crossing the sea nearing Boston Harbor. The law was clear, and the governor had the might of the British navy to help him enforce it. He had tried to avert the crisis by advising his sons and the other tea consignees to prevent the ships from entering the harbor. Once cargo ships out of Broad Sound had rounded Deer Island, it was against the law for them to put to sea again until the duty was paid. Hutchinson believed that the Sons of Liberty, in dispatch boats, had forced Captain Rotch at gunpoint to enter the inner harbor and register the tea. Be that as it may, the governor had a choice of either issuing an "exit permit" allowing the ships to sail away, or risking one more awful conflict in his province. The exit permit would be unprecedented and technically illegal. According to Bernard Bailyn, Hutchinson's biographer, in view of Hutchinson's humiliating confrontation with the Assembly earlier in the year, and "the fearful trauma of the disclosure of his letters ... he seems to have welcomed the black-and-white simplicity of the issues in the tea controversy."

Monday morning the church bells tolled to summon a mass meeting at Faneuil Hall at nine o'clock. Posters and handbills hastily printed proclaimed the agenda to prevent the landing of the tea. Faneuil Hall, with seats for thirteen hundred, could not accommodate the thousands who thronged the streets and marketplaces surrounding the square red building, grumbling and shouting. So once the citizens indoors had voted for the tea to be returned to England, their leaders adjourned to meet again that afternoon, in the Old South Meeting House with its great bell tower fronting Marlborough Street. The long building, under the high steeple, could seat three thousand in the light of its arched windows. And that afternoon, three thousand saw and heard the long-faced patriot Sam Adams propose in his voice of doom "that the tea should not be landed; that it should be sent back in the same bottom to the place where it came ... and that no duty should be paid on it!"

With a single booming voice, the crowd adopted the motion. The meeting appointed twenty-five men to guard the *Dartmouth* and its cargo, a watch that included Edward Proctor and Paul Revere. On the meeting's instructions, Sam Adams ordered Captain Rotch to unload all the cargo aboard his ship excepting the damned tea.

The next morning, when the meeting reconvened in Old South, Sheriff Stephen Greenleaf presented the people with an order from Governor Hutchinson to disperse. Samuel Adams rose in a fury and in a fifteen-minute speech made no effort to conceal his contempt for the man who had just signed this proclamation to disband the meeting.

On December 2, another ship, the *Eleanor*, laden with tea, entered the harbor; and on Wednesday, December 15, the *Beaver*, also bearing East India tea, joined the other two ships at Griffin's Wharf. Law required that the ships be unloaded and duties paid upon the cargo within twenty days after it entered the harbor. The grace period for the *Dartmouth* was about to expire, on Thursday, December 16. On the seventeenth the governor would enforce the law despite the mob's rage and volume, with naval ships and harbor cannon, and confiscate the cargo. Rumor had it that the tea on all three vessels was about to be taken under the protection of the British navy and deposited at Castle William Island. There the consignees would pay the duties and sell the tea. Samuel Adams stood up and addressed the meeting in Old South with grim finality: "This meeting can do nothing more to save the country."

The ship's log for the *Dartmouth* records that the mob at the wharf that night, December 16, 1773, numbered about a thousand, many of the men "dressed and whooping like Indians." A Boston merchant recalled that the meeting at Old South went on until "the candles were light," and that the men boarding the tea ships were "clothed in blankets with head muffed, and copper-colored countenances, being each armed with a hatchet or axe, and pair of pistols," and that "by nine o'clock . . . every chest of tea . . . was knocked to pieces and flung over the sides."

Three hundred forty-two chests of tea, valued at £9,659 ($1,408,826 in today's dollars) according to the board of directors of the British East India Company, rippled and stained the waters of Boston Harbor.

CHAPTER 10

A Thorough Government Man

WHEN WORD OF THE vandalism reached England six weeks later, all of society there—excepting a few of his friends—laid the blame for the Boston Tea Party at Benjamin Franklin's door. He was then known as the "infamous man of letters" who had violated Hutchinson's correspondence and sent it to Boston. Franklin had been driven to admit his complicity. When William Whately, brother of the late recipient of the letters, accused one John Temple of stealing them, the men had fought a duel. Whately had been shot, and called for a rematch. In order to prevent more bloodshed, Franklin published a letter of confession in Strahan's newspaper on Christmas Day.

Meanwhile he had been scheduled to attend a hearing in Whitehall at which the Privy Council would consider the petition to remove Governor Hutchinson from office. The timing was unfortunate, and would prove disastrous. At a preliminary hearing on January 11, Franklin had realized he was being set up. Although no one believed Hutchinson would be dismissed, what mattered was how the government handled the petition and the agent presenting it. That day he was surprised to find that the opposition was bringing legal counsel, and strongly advised to engage his own. The reason? Hutchinson's letters and Franklin's misuse of them. What he considered to be a political question, the governor's qualifications, had become a legal—possibly a criminal—case. Franklin had enemies, and after Christmas 1773 they had enough damaging evidence to make a fool of him.

Even Franklin's friends were perplexed by his actions that year, and doubtful of his apologies. In addition to the threadbare explanations he had provided Cushing and William Franklin, he justified his use of Hutchinson's letters by saying they were not really private communications between friends. As letters "written by public officers to persons in public station, on public affairs," they forfeited the usual sanctions. Apart from the fact that the letters really *were* private, this was an argument difficult for an Enlightenment philosopher such as David Hume or Lord Kames to swallow, not to mention the host of enemies Franklin had made in Parliament.

News of the Boston Tea Party reached London on Thursday, January 27, 1774. The following Saturday morning, Franklin, accompanied by his lawyer, entered the crowded Cockpit. He was wearing a suit the color of dried blood. There is a famous painting of the scene. Christian Schussele's rendering is formal and lofty, showing Franklin facing his tormentors, standing in a posture of superior dignity, left foot forward, right hand behind his back, left hand clutching his lapel. His high-domed head rises above the crowd, framed by a blank square of panel. Most of the councilmen and their ladies are seated around the long green-baize-covered table in armless plush chairs before the high dais and seat of Lord President Gower in his red robes.

Lord Gower is enthroned under a red-curtained baldachin whose royal crest ascends to the wooden balcony running along the walls to the clerestory. A few periwigged gentlemen look down on the scene: the thirty-five peers of the realm in their black robes, perukes, and red surplices; their ladies in low-cut satin dresses, hair piled on their heads, fluttering fans and eyelashes.

At the head of the table, his figure inclined like a question mark or scythe, rises the dark figure of the solicitor general, Alexander Wedderburn, a lawyer famed for eloquence and malice. A short, delicate, hawk-nosed man, Wedderburn pointed his finger at Franklin and pounded the table. He had come on behalf of Governor Hutchinson, Lord North, and the rest—the king, the Empire, and the very principle of decency—to call Benjamin Franklin to account.

The colonial agent had come to petition the Privy Council to remove Hutchinson from the governor's mansion, indeed? Well, what about these letters that had produced such an uproar and scandal on both sides of the ocean? The petitioners did not cite a single action of the governor as a matter of complaint in the four years while he was in office, only these letters, written before he took office. The governor and his lieutenant then owe "all the ill will that has been raised against them, and the loss of that confidence, which the Assembly themselves acknowledge they heretofore enjoyed, to Dr. Franklin's good office in sending back these letters to Boston."

Franklin later likened the mood in the Cockpit to a bullbaiting. Wedderburn held the floor, delivering a tirade against Franklin so scurrilous it had no precedent in any judicial proceeding. Abandoning the question of the petition, he attacked Franklin's character, calling him a thief and a liar who had "forfeited all the respect of societies and men."

Wedderburn asked the assembled lords to "mark and brand the man, for the honor of his country, of Europe, and of mankind," as one who had violated the sanctity of private correspondence. Where in the world can he go now without shame? "Men will watch him with a jealous eye; they will hide their papers from him, and lock up their escritoires. He will henceforth esteem it a libel to be called *a man of letters; homo trium literarum!*" At that, the crowd chuckled, guffawed, laughed aloud, beyond any decorum. The solicitor went on in this vein for more than an hour, in English, Latin, and French, so that his jokes would echo all over the Continent.

He meant to demolish Franklin's character, to show that he and a few radicals in Boston had conspired to alienate the king's subjects and spoil the peace of the whole province. And Franklin stood there, in his dress suit of Manchester velvet, "conspicuously erect," as witness Edward Bancroft observed, his face having been "composed so as to afford him a placid, tranquil expression"—and never altered his posture during the entire barrage. When Wedderburn had exhausted himself he called upon Franklin to stand as a witness. The American did not respond, but declared through his own counsel that he did not choose to be examined. At last he stirred and left the Cockpit. So did the spectators. And then the Privy Council dismissed the petition.

He returned to Craven Street, removed the suit of velvet, carefully folded it, and put it away in the clothespress. He vowed not to wear the garment again until such an occasion as might recompense him for the humiliation he had suffered. To say that he was outraged would not do justice to his feelings or his state of mind that day and night, or during the months that followed. It had been a life's study for him to contain and conceal his emotions when the expression of them served no purpose.

The next morning at breakfast he told the scientist Joseph Priestley that never before had he been so aware of the power of a good conscience, because the thing for which he had been so disgraced he considered "one of the best actions of his life." And if he had it to do over again, in the same circumstances, he would do it again. Priestley's judgment of his friend's rationalization is nowhere recorded. Franklin had been humiliated, pilloried, and disgraced, and would never again be welcome in English society. The newspapers called him "traitor," "old Doubleface," a "grand incendiary," and the "living emblem of iniquity in grey hairs."

England had been his home for nearly twenty years. Overnight his familiar rooms at Mrs. Stevenson's became known as "Judas's office in Craven Street." There he had grown old, lauded, laureled, gaining *a character of so much weight that it has protected me when some in power would have done me injury.* Now his name was vilified here, beyond redemption. He had no reasonable choice but to go back to Philadelphia.

On Monday, recovering in his rooms in Craven Street, he received notice from the postmaster general that he found it necessary to dismiss Franklin from his duties as deputy postmaster for America. That very day, by coincidence, an advertisement appeared in *Dunlop's Pennsylvania Packet* offering for sale William Franklin's six-hundred-acre farm. He was leaving Burlington, and in need of money.

On Thursday, February 2, Dr. Franklin found the composure to take up his quill and write to his son in America, "just to acquaint you that I am well, and that my Office of Deputy-Postmaster is taken from me. As there is no prospect of your being ever promoted to a better government," and New Jersey had never covered William's expenses, "I wish you were well settled on your farm. 'Tis an honester and a more honourable because a more independent employment."

His father wished he were settled on his farm. Reading this note in the spring of 1774, William must have thought it one of the more curious letters he had ever received from the old man, maddening in what it implied and concealed. There were only two lines more: "You will hear from others the treatment I have received. I leave you to your own reflections and determinations upon it, and remain ever, Your affectionate Father, B. Franklin."

What treatment had his father received? When would William hear of it in the village of Burlington? The full report was not mailed to *The Pennsylvania Gazette* until January 31. It must have arrived just before April 18, so that a bard on that day could publish a little poem lamenting the incident:

> *Blush, Albion, blush at the unmanly rage*
> *The sons assume in this degenerate age;*
> *Where worth, like Franklin's meets a vile reward*
> *And infamy, like Wedderburn's regard. . . .*

The poem was included in the Wednesday, April 20, 1774, issue of the *Gazette* that published a summary of the proceedings. There is no evidence that William knew of his father's embarrassment before that date. On May 3, while he and Betsy were visiting the ailing Deborah and the Baches in Philadelphia, he wrote to his father that his popularity in America, "whatever it may be on the other side, is greatly beyond whatever it was." The citizens had proposed burning "in effigy, a certain counsellor with whom they are highly irritated." They had made up effigies of Wedderburn and Hutchinson, drawn them on carts through the streets, and hanged and burnt them "by electric fire."

William had reason to be alarmed. His father's comment upon his career, "no prospect of your ever being promoted," hinted of worse things to come. He had just received another note Benjamin had written two weeks after the last, stating that "some tell me it is determined to displace you likewise" and advising him not to move his residence from Burlington to Perth Amboy, a useless expense. He went on to speculate that the Dartmouth ministry expected William to resign in protest of his father's treatment, "to save them the shame of depriving you whom they ought to promote." He counseled against this with the epigram *One may make something of an injury, nothing of a resignation.* Dr. Franklin could not resist the stinging aside "let them take your place if they want it," adding that the governorship had never paid him enough money to keep him from running behind in his debts.

Governor Franklin had no intention of retiring. And the exasperating affair of the treasury robbery, which had ended with the forced withdrawal of his friend Stephen Skinner on February 24, only strengthened his desire to leave Burlington for the welcome society of Perth Amboy. He seemed hardly aware that the shifting political landscape that had brought about Skinner's downfall now threatened his own authority.

KING GEORGE WAS SO furious over the Tea Party he had demanded that Parliament restore order by any means—and their means were predictably antagonistic. In March they passed the Boston Port Bill, closing Boston Harbor to trade until reparations were made. Then they drafted the Massachusetts Government Act, nullifying the colony's power to govern itself—removing the government to Salem and suspending the right to public assembly. In April, General Thomas Gage, in command of four regiments of redcoats, set sail for America to succeed the exhausted Thomas Hutchinson, and to enforce these new laws that the colonists would soon rename "the Intolerable Acts."

The new military governor arrived in Boston on May 13, ten days after Hutchinson and Wedderburn were hanged in effigy and two weeks before the official closing of the port. By that time the punitive actions of Parliament had inspired protests that spread from Boston to meetings in Providence, Philadelphia, Baltimore, and Richmond. In Virginia the House of Burgesses denounced the Port Act, proclaiming a day of fasting and mortification on June 1, the day it was to go into effect. In New York and Rhode Island there were calls for a congress that would represent all thirteen colonies.

Opinion was still divided. Many in England and America believed that the Port Bill was altogether tolerable, as it would be revoked as soon as the ruined tea was paid for. On May 21, Governor Franklin wrote a letter to William Strahan that expressed his support of the Crown and his opposition to the Massachusetts Assembly. Strahan carelessly shared this letter with the conservative Whartons, supposing it would strengthen his friend's position. When excerpts of the private letter appeared in a Philadelphia paper, it caused the governor considerable embarrassment and loss of goodwill among his countrymen. In any case William Franklin could not conceal his feelings much longer. "His Majesty may be assured," he wrote to Lord Dartmouth on May 31, "that I shall omit nothing in my power to keep this province quiet. Let the event be what it may, no *attachments or connections* shall ever make me swerve from the duty of my station."

He meant, of course, that his attachment to his father would not sway him. As agent for the Massachusetts Assembly, Dr. Franklin had become identified with their radical sentiments and was, some believed, the source of them. Franklin had written to his son just before the Boston Tea Party, stating that after long consideration he believed "that the parliament has no right to make any law whatever, binding on the colonies." And as recently as July, William had heard that Dr. Franklin had advised the Assembly to be bold "in insisting on their Independency." He admitted that his sentiments differed from William's on these subjects. "You are a thorough government man, which I do not wonder at, nor do I aim at converting you," he wrote. "I only wish you to act uprightly and steadily, avoiding that duplicity" that in Hutchinson's case made him not only offensive but contemptible to the colonists.

In the same month that General Gage landed in Boston with his troops to enforce the Intolerable Acts, as the assemblies in six colonies clamored for a congress to organize resistance, William Franklin worked to foster conservative opinion and take on the radicals of the newly formed New Jersey Committee of Correspondence. The task was daunting. This committee sided with the Bostonians, informing their brothers there that they would join them in any measures to secure their rights. They asked the governor to call for their assembly before August, declaring, to William's alarm, that "the Committee is well disposed in the Cause of American Freedom." On June 6 a larger gathering took place in Lower Freeport, demanding a boycott of British goods. In Newark a conference invited every county to form a caucus to choose delegates for a provincial council if Governor Franklin refused to convene the regular assembly. Then they scheduled a meeting to be held in New Brunswick on July 21.

William reported these events to Lord Dartmouth on June 28, declaring that he had no intention of convening the Assembly under compulsion and no sympathy with these radicals clamoring for an unauthorized congress. Franklin must have known the risk he was taking in this "secret" correspondence, after his letter to Strahan had strayed. Informing Dartmouth that the Port Act was fraught "with the most dangerous and alarming consequences," he allowed that there was no telling what might come of a congress such as the one so many colonies were demanding. William advised that the king instead design his own congress, with governors and members of the assemblies in each province. This might benefit the Empire in its distress, "especially if they were assisted by some gentlemen of abilities, moderation and candour from Great Britain commissioned by His Majesty."

At last it had dawned upon William Franklin—to his horror—that he was reaping a whirlwind sown by the vandals in Boston Harbor. The ensuing turbulence might unravel the Walpole Company and the promised land beyond the Ohio, the bounty of the Vandalia territory— for which he had gone so deeply into debt he might never recover. Along with the tea, the red-painted Sons of Liberty had drowned his lifelong dream of riches, the means by which he might pay his old debt to his father and make Elizabeth comfortable in this wild country, so far from her home in London.

He copied his report to Dartmouth in a letter to Benjamin five days later, on July 3. William told his father he was surprised that neither the people of Boston nor the Massachusetts Assembly had shown any desire to compensate the East India Company for their losses, or the customs officials for their trouble. By doing those things "consistent with strict justice," and by agreeing never again to hinder goods legally imported, they would see their harbor open again swiftly, whereas if they waited until their proposed congress met, and "the grand question is settled between the two countries," their trade would have gone elsewhere, and their merchants and manufacturers would be ruined. "Besides they ought first to do Justice before they ask it of others, and the business of the Congress may be carried on as well after the port is opened as it can be when it is shut."

William did not suppose that his father would disagree with such self-evident reasoning. Nor could he have imagined that this letter would cross, midocean, with one his father had written on June 30. "I hear a non-importation agreement is intended," Dr. Franklin wrote, excitedly. "If it is general, and the Americans agree in it, the present ministry will be knocked up, and their Act repealed; otherwise they and their measures will be continued, and the Stamp Act revived."

Compensation for the tea was the last thing on Benjamin Franklin's mind. The minute he got William's letter discoursing upon justice, and reparations, and "the grand question," he composed a closely argued, withering response. After acknowledging William's recent payment on his interminable debt he launched into a critique of his son's plea for compensation. "I do not, so much as you do, wonder that the Massachusetts have not offered payment for the tea." First, the Port Act was vague about when the port might be reopened after payment was received, and the amount owed. And then no one was sure what would satisfy the customs officers; and finally it rested in the king's power to decide just what part of the port should be opened, if any.

Benjamin reserves his most caustic remarks for William's high-minded demand for justice: "As to 'doing Justice before they ask it,'" Parliament should have thought of that long before they demanded it of the colonists. They had extorted tens of thousands of pounds from America in unlawful taxes, and by an armed force. They ought to make restitution for those funds. "But you who are a thorough courtier, see everything with government eyes," declared Benjamin Franklin.

There, at last, his father had said it—in a tone that could not be mistaken. Feelings he could not express elsewhere he reserved for his son.

No doubt he had been disappointed, then peeved, that William had not expressed more sympathy, more rage over the way his father had been abused. In a little less than a year's time William had fallen—in his father's estimation—from "a thorough government man" to "a thorough courtier," the sort of tool of government that had enfeebled the British Empire and humiliated Dr. Franklin in the eyes of Europe.

THE MOBILIZATION OF THE colonies, as William feared, was a juggernaut. Try as he might there was very little he could do to slow it. By the end of June *The Pennsylvania Gazette* was swelled with supplements publishing statements of solidarity from Newport, Philadelphia, Newark, Annapolis, Yorktown, Reading, Hunterdon County, New Jersey, New York, Charleston, and elsewhere, all crying out against the Port Act and embracing the nonimportation pact and a colonial congress in late summer, in Philadelphia.

Governor Franklin would not even consider convening the New Jersey Assembly. The regional committees went forward with their plan and met on July 21 in New Brunswick. Seventy-two delegates began by avowing their loyalty to the king and rejecting independence. But they ended by passing resolutions to "procure redress for their oppressed countrymen . . . and the re-establishment of the constitutional rights of America," denouncing Parliament's taxation and the Boston Port Act, and appointing a committee to raise relief money for Boston. Finally, like the other provinces, New Jersey resolved to support nonimportation and exportation measures—and to send delegates to the colonial congress in September.

All of this was done without royal authority. Their governor was working on his own business, attending an Indian conference at Sir William Johnson's grand estate west of Albany. Sir William, superintendent of Indian affairs—and a key figure in the Walpole Company— had called upon his friend to help negotiate a treaty with the Shawnees, who trusted Franklin. During a conference with six hundred Indians on July 11, Johnson died of a stroke. After serving as a pallbearer, Governor Franklin took over for the late peacemaker and settled the treaty. As he sailed home down the Hudson River in the heat of summer, the

July 27 *Gazette,* his father's old newspaper, published the resolutions of the Freeholders of Burlington, approving the colonial congress.

It was time for the governor and his wife to pack their belongings and move to Perth Amboy. The congress was inevitable; his own colony would send delegates to it. His only hope was that cooler heads would prevail there, men like Joseph Galloway, in his prime at forty-three, with whom William was in regular communication. Speaker of the Pennsylvania Assembly, Galloway had agreed to attend, and backed the selection of other moderate delegates such as George Washington, whose military stature and long service to the Crown would lend force to any resolution that bore his signature.

On the morning of September 5, Galloway joined the Adamses, Roger Sherman, John Jay, and other delegates from twelve colonies in Philadelphia as they gathered at Smith's Tavern, on Second Street near Walnut. Many of them lodged there during the seven weeks of meetings. From there, the gentlemen strolled the two blocks west on Walnut to Carpenter's Hall, a fine two-story brick building with high arched windows and a white belfry on Chestnut Street used by Ben Franklin's Library Company to house its collection. Conservatives from Pennsylvania and New York would have preferred the spacious State House nearby, but most agreed that the Carpenter's was more appropriate—having no political history, and being, in any case, more discreet.

Next day the members resolved that the doors would be closed during hours of business, "and that the members consider themselves under the strongest obligations of honor, to keep the proceedings secret" until the majority agreed to make them public. This promise was one that Joseph Galloway did not intend to honor. From the beginning he kept his friend Governor Franklin, over in Burlington, apprised of the goings-on, writing at once that he was not pleased with the choice of Carpenter's Hall, or of Charles Thomson, a local radical, as secretary for the congress. On September 6, Franklin mailed Galloway's notes to Lord Dartmouth, along with his friend's pamphlet "Arguments on Both Sides of the Dispute." It was his duty, he assured Dartmouth, to keep him well informed of the proceedings, and he begged him to keep the letters a secret. Otherwise a "stop will be put to my obtaining any farther intelligence from that quarter."

Galloway's hope for an early reconciliation with England rested upon his Plan of Union, modeled upon Franklin's Albany Plan twenty years earlier. The assemblies would choose delegates for an American parliament; then the king would send a governor general to preside over this body, which would regulate commerce and legal affairs that involved more than one colony. While the American parliament was to have veto power over the English Parliament's colonial legislation, the English would have similar power over the Americans. The Sons of Liberty paid no attention to this idea. It was read into the minutes in late September, and then erased from the record. Galloway was mortified, then inconsolable—it was the beginning of the end of his influence.

Then the delegates got on with their main purposes: resolving to ban imports from Great Britain, and opposing the harsh acts of Parliament. The details of these secret discussions in Carpenter's Hall, Governor Franklin reported to the colonial secretary as soon as Galloway delivered his notes. While Franklin believed this correspondence was his civic duty, many of his countrymen in 1774 would see it in a darker light, particularly after the embarrassing publication of William's letter to Strahan of May 21. That scandal, erupting as it did only a week after the congress came together, must have seemed a nightmare to William and his wife, and to all of the Franklin family from Boston to Philadelphia.

The contents of the damaging letter, as well as the circumstances by which it emerged in Philadelphia, are unknown and can only be inferred from men's reactions. It must have been a hearty endorsement of the Crown in general, and a reproof of the people in Boston rallying against the Port Bill and the arrival of the soldiers. It must have included bellicose language advocating the use of force in order to have drawn such ire from Thomas Wharton. On September 23 he wrote to his cousin Samuel, and to Thomas Walpole, in London: "What shall I say with respect to Gov. Franklin? He certainly must be lost to every principle which his aged and honoured father has been for years supporting." News of the letter had spread rapidly in the city, Wharton reported, and William Franklin's character "is treated with great freedom."

How in the world had William's letter gotten from the privacy of Strahan's study to the streets of Philadelphia? Through whose hands had the document passed?

Strahan certainly meant William no harm. The Tory publisher, who loved the Franklins, could have had only one motive: to burnish William's image in the eyes of the ministry, and of anyone else who might think William was in sympathy with his disgraced father. But this was a tangled web, and shifty, as men's politics were blowing right to left and back again, as fortune dictated. It suited their fortunes to save the Walpole Company, which depended upon the stability of the empire and so many peers of the realm. So it would help to show Governor Franklin's letter defending the rule of law to men like Thomas Walpole and his circle—even Samuel Wharton, who had lobbied tirelessly for the land grant.

Mr. Strahan, however, did not know how much money William Franklin owed Samuel Wharton, or how violently the Franklins had quarreled with him over Virginia's claims to the Ohio territory. Distrust had grown on both sides, with Thomas Wharton at one point declaring that the Franklins' actions were "as mean and despicable, as my brother's behavior, was generous and laudable." In short, Strahan was imprudent when he decided to share his friend's opinions with men who, reading them three months later, within a stone's throw of the Continental Congress, might see the letters as traitorous. Thomas Wharton, a highly respected Philadelphia merchant, had been elected a member of the Committee of Correspondence on May 20. No wonder the man joined the chorus of patriots who frowned upon the reports of Governor Franklin's opinions.

In Boston, Jane Mecum, Benjamin Franklin's favorite sister, wrote to her brother after reading the embarrassing news in the *Boston Gazette:* "I must just mention the horrid lie told and published about your son & with such plausibility . . . that at first it struck me with a fear that it might be true and I can't express to you the pain it gave me on your account." Although Benjamin never recorded that he was aware of William's letter, even in his correspondence with Jane, others informed him of it. Whether the matter pained him would depend upon what he read.

What Jane Mecum read in the *Gazette* of October 3, 1774, is the only surviving paraphrase of the document: "mention is made of a letter from Governor Franklin dated the 21st of May, advising the ministry to send more Men of War to batter down the capital towns, which would bring them to submission." The piece also claims that some gentlemen in Philadelphia "received a letter from Dr. Franklin, where he says, he never knew what pain was, until he saw his son's letter to the ministry." Dr. Franklin wrote no such thing; he never saw his son's letter to the ministry, because the letter was to Strahan and not to the ministry. Also, there are several letters from Dr. Franklin to his son in this time frame, and none express any pain caused by any such letter. Either he never saw it, or what he read was not objectionable to him. Nonetheless, Governor Franklin was in trouble. His reputation was damaged, just as Hutchinson's had been when his letters were exposed a year earlier. "The inhabitants have sent for the Governor to clear the matter up. . . . The matter makes much stir at Philadelphia," the *Gazette* concludes.

Nobody would have to send for him. As soon as William heard the gossip he saddled up and rode posthaste from Burlington to his mother's house. There he conferred with his brother-in-law, Bache, and Captain Nathaniel Falconer, a family friend often trusted, in his capacity as packet boat captain, to carry messages and goods back and forth from London. The three of them decided to call upon Thomas Wharton at his country house in Twickenham, ten miles to the north, where they would ask to see the letter that had disturbed the peace. Wharton agreed. He invited two friends, one of whom, William West, was a fellow merchant and budding patriot, to witness his part in the critical meeting in the parlor of his three-story mansion.

It was October. The leaves of the maples and chestnut trees shone in golden glory outside the seven sash windows across the grand façade. Wharton, a long-faced, balding man of thirty-nine, extended his visitors due courtesy, as lord of the manor, relieving them of hats and canes. Franklin had been in partnership with the Whartons in an enterprise that would have made him nearly as wealthy as any of them; his wife, Betsy, might have been the lady of such a manor had it not been for the scourge of politics, party strife, and factions.

Now he confronted his old friend turned enemy, one who would publicize a private letter without warning him, without first giving him the chance to respond man to man. In a lofty parlor at Twickenham the governor demanded that this letter be read aloud. The gentlemen took their seats. Given the nod from their host, William West unfolded the letter from Thomas Walpole and began to read it. There were passages purporting to be quotes from Franklin of the kind paraphrased in the *Gazette,* advocating the use of force to repress rebellion. Wharton later recalled William's being furious until West came to a passage that mentioned his willingness "to make peace with the Administration." His original letter had been even-handed in criticizing the British ministry and the riotous colonists. William smiled. When West finished reading, the governor remarked that the letter did not contain as much offensive content as had been reported. Yet he had already been judged in the court of public opinion.

Why, he asked his host, would not a friend have done him the courtesy of showing him such a letter before making it public? They were neighbors; they lived not eight miles from each other across the Delaware River!

The question, provocative enough, sparked more provocative dialogue that would have been humorous had the subject been less fatal.

Did your father, Wharton asked, take that step with the correspondence of Governor Hutchinson?

Distressed by the comparison, William Franklin pointed out that their "circumstances were different, his father being an agent."

To this, the portly host self-righteously replied, "if the liberties of America were to be injured it was no matter whether Hutchinson or he did it, but who ever did it ought to be known."

And William cried out, bewildered, "*O, Mr. Strahan has used me ill!*" In fact, Mr. Strahan had no such intention, he had rather wished to show his friend in a flattering light to the ministry, as a moderate representative of the Crown, one who could strike a balance. Strahan had simply blundered. The temperature in the colonies was warmer than anyone in England could have known.

Wharton, by no means an unkind man, suggested that William might restore his good name by requesting a certified copy of his letter to Mr. Strahan and then publishing that, instead of fretting over some other letter containing quotes claiming to be his words. Wharton was convinced that William would do this, and "wipe himself blissfully whole." And yet William did not. If he ever tried, the glacial movement of the mails across the sea, as Captain Falconer knew, would make publishing the original six months hence more damaging, in reviving the scandal, than it would be redeeming. Also, he had to consider the effect that any criticism of the ministry would have upon the security of his job as governor. He might lose his royal seat and still be held as treacherous by his countrymen.

So instead William placed a brief notice on the third page of his hometown newspaper, *The Pennsylvania Gazette,* on October 12. Still the most influential journal in America, it was one he might count upon for support.

> We have authority to assure the Public, that the reports which have been circulated respecting a neighboring Governor having wrote to the Ministry recommending certain hostile measures against America, are without any just foundation.

This was printed among the obituaries, shipping news, and ads for dry goods and spirits. So the defense of one's honor was no less important than mortality, yet no more significant than the clearing of the sloop *Peggy* or the schooner *Sally* from the port bearing Jamaica spirits, broadcloth, or ground ginger in kegs. For a few shillings a man might purchase a few words in his favor, or promote a flask of lamp oil.

Meanwhile, in the conclave of Carpenter's Hall that week, the Continental Congress, as it came to be called, was putting the finishing touches on a letter to General Gage protesting the British actions against Massachusetts. On the eleventh of October the president, Peyton Randolph, signed this letter and the delegates prepared a proclamation for the people of British America, inviting them to unite behind the congress. And on Friday, October 14, as the *Gazette* bearing William Franklin's negligible defense fluttered through the coffee-houses, and Smith's tavern, where George Washington breakfasted with the Sons of Liberty, the congress resolved that from December 1 there would be "no importation into British America, from Great Britain or Ireland of any goods, wares, or merchandise whatsoever."

By what authority did these men issue such resolutions? No legal authority that William Franklin or Joseph Galloway could discern, except by the inalienable rights of men, and the "constitutional rights" these particular delegates claimed for the colonists at large. They were, de facto, a revolutionary body, and such bodies demand prominent and vivid personalities like Thomas Hutchinson on whom they can focus their righteous fury. Hutchinson was long gone. Governor Franklin, in his mansion just across the river, was the natural heir to Hutchinson, a godsend. The notice Jane Mecum read in the *Boston Gazette* of October 3, with all of its errors, aimed to slander her nephew in a city eager to think the worst of him. There is something like glee in the tone of that article, with its references to Dr. Franklin, and the comment that "this matter makes much stir at Philadelphia." The plot to demonize William would naturally take root in radical Boston from intelligence gathered in Philadelphia by the Sons of Liberty meeting there.

Before leaving the city in mid-October, after that terrible interview with Thomas Wharton, William went home with Bache to visit his mother. He found Deborah weak and disoriented after the series of strokes, and her spirits as well as her health in decline. She missed her husband terribly. Benjamin had written to her on September 10 complaining that it had been nine months since he had heard from her. "I have supposed it owing to your continual expectation of my return," he surmised. "I have imagined anything rather than admit a supposition that your kind attention towards me was abated." He need not have worried over that possibility. The truth was that Deborah Franklin could no longer write to him or anyone else.

William stayed by her side as long as he was able. As he rose to take his leave, she confided to him that she never expected to see her husband again unless he came home this winter, as she could not expect to live until the next summer. After placing his notice of protest in *The Pennsylvania Gazette,* William turned to other things. He went home to Elizabeth.

THERE WAS A GREAT deal to be done. That week they were packing trunks with clothing, blankets, and bed linen and directing servants to load the wagons with their furniture, glassware, silver, and other household goods for the move northeast to Perth Amboy. Elizabeth's trousseau, all the things that had come with her from St. James's Street a decade ago, and the valuables they had acquired since, must be made ready: portraits of the king and queen by Alexander Ramsay, the wine cellar, the leather-bound books on husbandry and the arts; mahogany chairs upholstered in yellow silk and red damask; the chased silver tray that held four china cups and saucers and a cream pot; the quart tankard with its hinged top, the pint and half-pint cans, very plain but made by the king's goldsmith, Thomas Jeffries, who also made the silver salt mills; and the great tea urn of Sheffield plate with silver spout and handles.

There were the portraits of the Franklins, father and son, oil paintings in gilt frames rendered by such artists as Benjamin Wilson and Mason Chamberlin. There was no painting of Elizabeth. It is a telling reflection upon Mrs. Franklin's faint vanity that no likeness of the first lady ever hung upon the walls of the governor's mansion or any other place. There is no evidence any likeness was ever drawn. So of all the women who pass through these pages, Elizabeth's figure leaves the most to one's imagination.

All of these beloved artifacts, household mementoes of a shared life in London and Burlington, England and America! How many times, by wine and candlelight, after supper, had the couple wished "we could put Great Britain under sail, bring it over to this country and anchor it near us," for all the comfort that delightful island afforded. Now, as if the fanciful wish were to come true, they were moving their worldly goods to a port on the seaboard, where the packets dispatched mail direct to Europe.

Whatever Franklin might do to maintain his authority and keep the peace would be more easily accomplished from the safer distance of Amboy, in a friendly enclave upon the Raritan Bay. Burlington now seemed like a suburb of Philadelphia, where men like Charles Thomson, Thomas Wharton, and William West distrusted him. His correspondence would certainly be more secure in this eastern port.

On Wednesday, October 12, Burlington's mayor, recorder, and aldermen invited the townspeople to an entertainment at the courthouse at Broad and Main streets—to honor the governor and his lady. And before they departed the next day, the mayor delivered a valedictory that was heartfelt in its praise and candid in its envy of the eastern capital. Thanking Franklin for his decade of "kind deportment and courtesy," the corporation expressed "deep concern . . . on your departure, both for the affection we bear your Excellency, and for the benefits we should reap, had this city been continued the seat of government." Wishing the governor and his lady every happiness, the mayor concluded: "If your inclination should again favor us with your residence here, we shall feel the most sensible satisfaction." Not only was the village taking leave of one of its most illustrious, wealthiest residents, but western New Jersey would be losing influence with the British ministry during a perilous time.

"Gentlemen," Franklin replied, "I return you my hearty thanks. . . . It gives me very particular satisfaction to find that my deportment, during my long residence among you, has merited your approbation." No matter how far away his future residence might be, he assured them, he would always "reflect with pleasure on the many happy days I have enjoyed in this city."

CHAPTER 11

Two Roads

A S THEY SETTLED INTO the house on the hill, the fragrance of ripe apples mingled with the salt smell of the sea. The windows on all three floors, from the dormers above the classical pediment to the eight-paned casements lighting the main rooms, overlooked the Raritan River; and in back the west garden gave upon the orchards.

Mounting the cascade of sandstone steps, the governor's wife opened the great Venetian door under a fanlight, entering the broad hall with its marble chimneypiece. To the right lay her dining room under a dazzling chandelier; to the left a drawing room, more fire-places with tabernacle frames. The staircase from the grand foyer, yellow pine steps with an oaken balustrade, led to the upstairs hall, master bedroom, dressing room, and guest bedrooms.

The four levels, basement to attic, offered eighteen rooms, sixteen fireplaces, a wine cellar, two book-lined studies on the main floor, a breakfast parlor, and butler's and housekeeper's quarters. The tile roof was equipped with lead gutters and lightning rods. This was a house to compare to Twickenham, or Graeme Park. The governor wished his father could see it now that it was finished and he and Betsy had made it their home.

In fact, William Franklin wished, more than anything else, that his father would come home. Deborah was dying. He ought to be here to comfort her in her last days. His father's effort to maintain peace between England and America was important, but it might be managed more efficiently from this side of the ocean. While he had lost credibility in England, he was more popular and respected than ever in America. He alone could use his authority and good reasoning to bring the congress to its senses. There might still be time to broker an agreement that would satisfy the radicals while preserving the Empire.

Governor Franklin had not given up hope of reconciliation or the dream of Vandalia. There were many intelligent men, like Galloway, who urged moderation. If all of them remained prudent and calm, they might end up on the right side of the civil dispute. On October 29, 1774, Franklin dispatched a secret letter to Lord Dartmouth with a full account of the congress's proceedings, sounding a note of optimism: He felt confident the people of New Jersey would not support the congress's resolutions.

Now William and Elizabeth were ready for Temple to join them. William had recently received a letter from his father concerning the boy's education and prospects. Temple had just turned fourteen. His headmaster, James Elphinston, William Strahan's brother-in-law, praised the boy's learning and his behavior, arguing he should remain in the little school in Kent, although Dr. Franklin wanted to send him to Eaton, then Oxford. Benjamin thought he would make a fine lawyer, "as he has a good memory, quick parts, and ready elocution." He might also make an excellent painter, being fond of sketching, and talented, "but I do not find that he thinks of it as a business." Temple hinted he might like to be a surgeon, but he did not appear to hold that vocation in high esteem, either.

His grandfather wanted Temple to acquire some art or trade he could count on to earn his bread. "And after that, if anything better could be done for him, well and good. But posts and places are precarious dependencies," Franklin averred, with a nod to his own place, and his son's. "I would have him a free man." And so, he concluded, "we should turn him to the law," as a profession worthy in itself, and useful no matter what else he chose to do.

He expected they would sail in September, which would bring them home by Christmas. "But I begin to have my doubts," he added. "With love to Betsy, I am, ever, your affectionate father." In fact, William, Deborah, the Baches, and friends had curtailed writing to Franklin after his humiliation in the Cockpit because he had assured them he was on his way home. But he was not, though his reasons for staying never seemed as compelling as the reasons William saw for him to come home.

To be sure, Dr. Franklin was engaged in backstage diplomacy with the various lords, generals, and admirals and their friends, Whigs interested in the American cause—or at least in avoiding war. He spent months conferring with William Pitt, Earl of Chatham, and preparing the still influential politician to present a conciliatory plan to Parliament on February 1, 1775. Chatham wanted a plan that would allow Parliament to send troops to the colonies and also to regulate imperial trade. But he believed that Parliament must also recognize the authority of the Continental Congress, and the exclusive right of the colonial legislatures to impose taxes upon their people. Franklin frowned upon the first two points but welcomed the last two. And he agreed to accompany Chatham to the House of Lords when the Great Commoner, renowned for eloquence, presented the proposals.

Yet that day in Whitehall, in the chamber teeming with peers, nothing seemed much more important than abusing Dr. Franklin. He was seen as the evil genius behind all this radical rhetoric. When Chatham had finished, Lord Sandwich, first lord of the Admiralty, took the floor. Arrogant and peevish, he attacked Chatham's bill before fixing his attention upon Franklin, seated in the gallery. Lord Sandwich would not be persuaded that the points of Chatham's proposal had come from such a distinguished English peer.

"I have in my eye," he announced, staring at Franklin, "the person who drew it up, one of the bitterest and most mischievous enemies this country has ever known." He said it had all come from Franklin's lobbying and undercover plotting with Whigs and lords and admirals in and out of favor. So Chatham's bill was treated with no more respect than they might have afforded "a ballad offered by a drunken porter," Franklin wrote.

For this Dr. Franklin had remained in England during months

when he might have been sailing home to comfort his wife in her last days, or using his charm and common sense to disarm the Sons of Liberty, who wanted to smash the fragile vase of the British Empire.

WILLIAM KNEW NOTHING, AT the time, of his father's dealings with Lord Chatham or his other affairs. He did not know then of his father's intimate friendship with the beautiful and eccentric American sculptor Patience Wright, whose career he championed in London. In the autumn of 1774 William and Elizabeth were settling into their home upon the Raritan River, unpacking their trunks and preparing that magnificent mansion for the holiday season. Mrs. Skinner, the former treasurer's wife, who had a knack for it, would help with the decorations.

The center of interest and master stroke of the Franklins' design was to be seen when visitors entered the front hall: from the cornice molding of the ceiling to the chair-rail paneling, the walls were papered with black-and-white panoramas of Passaic and Cohoes Falls, printed on a buff-colored ground. A matching panorama on the stair wall depicted the Horseshoe Falls of Niagara. The American landscape suggested the hypnotic sound of rushing water, violent power rendered peaceful by the painter's art.

In such amusements and reflections the time passed pleasantly for the governor and his wife, despite the gathering clouds of war. The situation was troubling but not desperate: there was still time for the colonists to come to their senses and for cooler heads to prevail—especially if Benjamin Franklin were to join the conversation in Philadelphia. He was expected any day.

Surrounded by books in his green study, William wrote candidly to Lord Dartmouth on December 6. While many colonists disdained the proceedings of the congress, he was sure their resolutions would be carried because "few have the courage to declare their disapprobation publicly" and risk becoming targets of popular resentment. This had happened to him, and even royal officers—except in Boston—had no protection from the mob. William joined Dartmouth in hoping that the actions of the congress would not remove the last promise of union with the mother country. But even the most moderate among us, William admitted, the most hopeful, understand that the Continental Congress has left Parliament no choice but this: "consent to what must appear humiliating in the eyes of all Europe, or *compel obedience to her laws by a military force*." The congress might have avoided the dilemma by embracing Galloway's Plan of Union, but they buried it. William enclosed a salvaged copy. He signed and sealed this letter, entrusting it to a courier who would assure it was conveyed, confidentially, via the next packet bound for England.

A week later, Wednesday, December 14, Deborah Franklin suffered a massive stroke paralyzing most of her body. Sally and Richard summoned Dr. Thomas Bond, Franklin's partner in founding the Pennsylvania Hospital at the west edge of town. He would have come prepared to bleed or purge the patient to reduce the pressure on her system. The doctor gave them reason for hope. Then, on Sunday night, as the full moon peeked in the windows, she took a turn for the worse. Without showing signs of pain she continued breathing until Monday morning at eleven o'clock. "Then," Richard Bache wrote to her husband, "without a groan or even a sigh, she was released from a troublesome world, and happily relieved from all future pain and anxiety."

He sent an express rider to Perth Amboy, who reached the governor's mansion Tuesday night. William set out in a snowstorm the next morning, crossing the river at dawn and posting along the lower road through Allenstown and Burlington. It was slow going in the blizzard, the horses breathing hard, bogging down in drifts. He did not reach Philadelphia until four o'clock Thursday afternoon, an hour before the body was to be moved to Christ Church for the funeral. Following the casket to the snowy churchyard as chief mourners were Richard Bache and William. Several of Benjamin Franklin's best friends, charter members of the Philosophical Society, served as pallbearers.

"A very respectable number of the inhabitants were at the funeral," William reported to his father on Saturday, Christmas Eve. He had decided to stay in Philadelphia to comfort his sister in the house where mother and daughter had lived together for a decade. Betsy was snowbound in Perth Amboy, so they would spend this sad holiday apart, the first they might have enjoyed in their new home.

William gazed out at the snow-covered yards and streets of his hometown. Upstairs was the library, and through another door the dusty relics of a laboratory—glass tubes and retorts, magnets, copper wires, rods, and Leyden jars. He had a great deal to say to his father. By daylight and candlelight, as Sally played with her boys, five-year-old Benny and the toddler Billy, named after him, William Franklin composed a long and passionate letter describing his journey through the snow and the funeral procession. He did not dwell upon the details of his mother's illness, saying only that "her death was no more than might be reasonably expected after the paralytic stroke she received some time ago, which greatly affected her memory and understanding." Then William told his father of his mother's pathetic words back in October, when she prayed he would come home in the winter to see her while she was still alive. He could not conceal his resentment: "I heartily wish you had happened to have come over in the fall, as I think her disappointment in that respect preyed a good deal on her spirits." At the moment, to William and probably the Baches, his failure to return home seemed contemptible. Resorting to irony, he continued: "It gives me great pleasure to find that you have so perfect an enjoyment of that greatest of blessings, health." William was baffled that despite his father's recent words that he could not "in the course of nature" long expect such good health to continue, he still postponed returning to his family.

"If there is any prospect of your being able to bring the people in power to your way of thinking, or those of your way of thinking's being brought into power, I should not think so much of your stay." But by now "neither can be expected," he wrote, and "you are looked upon with an evil eye in that country, and are in no small danger of being brought into trouble for your political conduct."

Sitting in his father's chair, in his father's house, with Deborah Franklin's ghost over his shoulder and the snow edging the windowpanes, he admonished the old traveler: "You certainly better return, while you are able to bear the fatigues of the voyage, to a country where the people revere you, and are inclined to pay a deference to your opinions." His countrymen "ardently" wanted him to return for the last meeting of the Continental Congress. "I have since heard it lamented by many that you were not at that meeting." They believed Franklin might still devise a plan of reconciliation that would subdue the radicals.

The world was out of kilter, and his father knew only half of it, the country that had abused him. "However mad you may think the measures of the ministry are, yet I trust you have candor enough to acknowledge that we are no ways behind with them in instances of madness on this side of the water. However, it is a disagreeable subject, and I'll drop it." William turned then to the agreeable subject of his son. He agreed that Temple ought to study the law and suggested he attend the New York College for a year or two. In closing, William looked forward to seeing them both in the spring. He was happy to say that he and Betsy were well settled in their new house, and they would always have a fine room prepared for him.

There was a knock at the door. A messenger informed the family that the packet was about to sail and he must have all their letters at once. So William bade his father a hasty adieu, and turned his thoughts again to his grieving sister.

WILLIAM RETURNED TO PERTH Amboy in the new year and began to prepare for a difficult session of the Assembly. This would be the first meeting in nine months, since those rogue gatherings in Lower Freehold, Newark, and other townships had declared their solidarity with Massachusetts, endorsed the embargoes, and appointed delegates to the Continental Congress.

Thirty assemblymen and twelve executive councilors from every county in New Jersey gathered in the stone courthouse on Market Street on January 11, 1775. Their chief concern was the actions of the congress, and whether this province would endorse the boycott and the congress's other measures. Franklin figured the House would be divided: Burlington and the western counties would favor the nonimportation pact; moderates in Bergen County, and Quakers in Salem would resist the radicals. The upper house would be pitted against the lower, and it was the governor's task to diffuse the conflict. His language must confirm loyalty to the Crown as well as everyone's shared desire to preserve their constitutional rights.

On Friday, the thirteenth of January, Governor Franklin left his wife at the door of the mansion, his speech rolled in his hand, and walked east toward the river. He was forty-three years old and the winters had begun to weigh upon him. His greatcoat and his tricorn hat scarcely kept him warm. He knew what he would say to the fractious legislators, but it would be his tone of voice and his composure that must win them over. He walked two blocks north and mounted the stone steps of the courthouse. Inside, several dozen lawmakers seated at their desks in a half circle awaited him in the dry, smoky council chamber where he had been sworn into office eleven years before.

"Gentlemen of the Assembly," he began, warmly, welcoming them and inviting all to continue in supporting their government. On this day it would be a grave oversight to "pass over in silence the late alarming transactions in this and the neighboring colonies." He called upon the good people of New Jersey to resist any further "mischiefs to this country." He did not presume to resolve the dispute between Great Britain and her colonies, and he had no desire to censure anyone who sought to redress a grievance, a duty the people "owe themselves, their country, and their posterity." Upon this note the lawmakers might have applauded the governor, if he had paused.

"All that I would wish to guard you against is giving any countenance or encouragement to that destructive mode of proceeding which has been unhappily adopted in part by some of the inhabitants in this colony, and has been carried so far in others as totally to subvert their former constitution." All these unlawful congresses had usurped the powers rightfully owned by the provincial assemblies. He urged the lawmakers to petition the Crown by legal means. Otherwise you will "destroy that form of government of which you are an important part." There is no greater threat to a free society, he declared, than that the chief men of a country might "show a greater regard to popularity than to their own judgment." Franklin would make no such mistake, and now he asked the assemblymen also to be leaders and not the pawns of demagogues.

"You have now pointed out to you, gentlemen, two roads—one evidently leading to peace, happiness, and a restoration of the public tranquility—the other inevitably conducting you to anarchy, misery, and all the horrors of a civil war." It was his best speech, written in heat by winter light and candlelight—the culmination of his life's work as a lawyer, a governor, and a patriot. As he stepped down and made his way to the door, Franklin could tell from the look in the men's eyes, and their congenial murmuring, that his words had touched them. It was up to them to choose the proper road.

Days passed, then a week, as the legislators discussed and debated the congress's petition. Franklin had cause for hope. His Council (the higher chamber of the legislature) backed the governor, promising "Your excellency may be assured that we will exert our utmost influence, both in our public and private capacities." But the greater force lay on the side of the new congress and its resolutions. On January 25, not two weeks after Franklin had given his "Two Roads" speech, he received a bill of resolutions from the House. The proceedings of the Continental Congress had been approved unanimously; three delegates were to be named to attend the next congress in May; and a copy of these resolutions was to be sent to the assemblies of New York and Philadelphia, so that they might act likewise.

This was a sad day for the governor and his wife. For the first time, they had reason to fear for the security of their home. An assembly that pledged allegiance to an American congress before promising it to their English king might soon do without a royal governor. The Franklins took what comfort they could in playing cribbage and sipping wine in the company of sympathetic friends like the Skinners and William Coxe, Franklin's old friend from Burlington and fellow parishioner from St. Mary's; David Ogden, the judge from Newark; and Francis Hopkinson, the witty poet and composer whose friendship had spanned decades encompassing both Betsys—the bluestocking ingénue from Philadelphia and the delicate wife from Barbados. Hopkins was good company despite his waxing sympathy with the radicals, and the old judge, a Yale graduate, was a match for him in conversation.

All agreed that the Assembly had at least kept up an appearance of loyalty to the king: Every communication began with the formulaic oaths. In a hollow gesture to placate their governor, after his speech they did prepare a separate petition to send to King George, in the same language as the congress's petition—requesting relief for taxation, and other intolerable acts. Under the circumstances it made William angry. He refused to forward the petition and left it to them to send it via their agent, Benjamin Franklin.

The governor adjourned his assembly on Monday, February 13, to convene again exactly a month later. On the eighteenth, measuring the danger of the situation, he wrote to notify Dartmouth that he would enforce His Majesty's order concerning the importation of arms. The custom officers would seize any guns or ammunition imported without the king's license.

In Philadelphia, Governor John Penn echoed many of Franklin's sentiments, advising his assembly on February 21 "that any grievances, which his Majesty's subjects in *America* have reason to complain of should be humbly presented to His Majesty by the several assemblies." In the debates in the Pennsylvania Assembly, Joseph Galloway was one of the moderates who supported Governor Penn. But he so enraged the Independent Party that they threatened to throw open the doors of the State House and turn the mob loose on him. Learning of this in advance, Galloway was able to gather friends to guard him.

He had driven down from Trevose, his country estate, and was staying at an inn near the State House. One night the porter informed him that a box had been delivered addressed to him. Prying the lid off the nailed box, Galloway found a hangman's noose and a letter. The letter suggested how he might use the noose if he did not mend his opinions. He read and reread the unsigned note, nailed up the contents of the box, and locked it in the trunk of his carriage. On March 26 he wrote to William that the time that had been bought by the adjournment was useless, the Assembly would vote against them, as even Governor Penn's speech had been no more than a charade "to save appearances." Like William Franklin, Galloway longed for Benjamin Franklin to come home. Perhaps he would find a way to set things right.

And at last Dr. Franklin was on his way. He left London on March 20 a step ahead of the sheriff, as he was threatened with a civil suit regarding the Hutchinson affair. He embarked with his fifteen-year-old grandson from Portsmouth on the packet *Pennsylvania* the next day.

Franklin had spent his last day in London with his friend the chemist Joseph Priestley. They sat in the sunlit parlor on Craven Street as Mrs. Stevenson, sad and distracted, bustled around them. She must deliver the broad copper plate at the head of the garret stairs to Mr. Pownall. She must return another print to Captain Walsingham, MP, and a number of borrowed books. Much of that Sunday was passed in reading the American newspapers, especially the accounts of how the Boston Port Bill had been received. "And as he read the addresses to the inhabitants of Boston," Priestley recalled, "from the places in the neighborhood, the tears trickled down his cheeks." Distressed by the specter of civil war, he told his friend he had done all he could do to prevent it. America would win, surely, but the war would take a decade and he would not live to see the end of it.

There is no other record of Franklin's ever weeping. Were those tears really shed over the prospect of war, or some other, more private grief? He had learned of his wife's death only three weeks earlier. He never wrote a line to any friend or relative about Deborah's passing. But on board Captain Osborne's ship he spent hours each day in his cabin, for six weeks, composing a two-hundred-page letter to his son. Known to scholars as the "Journal of Negotiations in London," it is the chief source of information concerning those secret meetings with the Howes, Chatham, and others that took up several months of Franklin's time late in 1774. All of it may have happened as Franklin recalled, although he confessed, at the end, that in his own confusion from "discoursing with so many different persons about the same time on the same subject," he may sometimes have forgotten who said what to whom.

It is the only letter he had written to William since receiving William's of Christmas Eve, informing him of Deborah's death and taking him to task for his absence. The two-hundred-page screed is, among other things, an apology—a rhetorical defense of his actions. The reason he was not at his wife's side was that he was toiling, day and night, to turn back the tide of civil war. Nothing less would excuse him; and the more he made of the story, the more likely William was to forgive, or at least understand him.

Benjamin Franklin's timing in returning to America on Captain Osborne's ship was uncanny. It was natural for a superstitious man to think him a wizard; it was difficult for a reasonable person to think him anything else. His movements upon the Continent during the last decade had been capricious, instinctive. Now instinct had placed him and his grandson upon the high seas, taking the daily temperature of the water, mapping the Gulf Stream, just as news of the bloodshed at Lexington and Concord on April 19, 1775, raced from Massachusetts to South Carolina as fast as a man on horseback could travel.

Governor Franklin heard news of the fighting on Sunday evening, April 23. He was beside himself with fury at General Gage for initiating such an action—sending seven hundred infantry and grenadiers across the Charles River to attack Concord. Until then there had been no violence in New Jersey, only the calm enforcement of the non-importation agreement and the measure to approve the proceedings of the Continental Congress. Now Gage had put him and the other governors in a devilish position, reducing their chances to negotiate a conciliation. In the coming week, town meetings from Newark to Burlington would call for voluntary militia as well as delegates to a provincial congress, set for May 23.

William had no idea his father was on the ship bound for Philadelphia, nor did anyone else in America. Dr. Franklin had put himself out of reach of his enemies on both continents, blameless for the violence on one shore and the tyrannical policy on the other. He said of himself, "I do not find that I have gained any point in either country except that of rendering myself suspected for my impartiality: in England, of being too much an American, and in America of being too much an Englishman."

The *Pennsylvania* lowered its anchor in the Delaware River on Friday, May 5, in fine weather. As their longboat lunged toward the Market Street wharf under a waxing moon, the first news the Franklins would have heard from the oarsmen was of Lexington and Concord, the shots heard 'round the world. Half a hundred American militia had been killed, and sixty-five British regulars, a little more than two weeks ago. New England was in mourning and all of America was up in arms.

FOR THE FIRST TIME, he entered the courtyard through the brick arch on Market Street and beheld the house he had designed, three stories high.

Ben Franklin in London, circa 1760, age fifty-four, as colonial agent of the
Pennsylvania Assembly. He and his thirty-year-old son would petition Parliament
for authority to tax the rich proprietors of the colony.

Deborah Read Franklin, Ben Franklin's wife, circa 1759, age fifty, dressed in her finest silks for her portrait by Benjamin Wilson in Philadelphia. While her husband served in diplomatic posts in Europe for twenty-three years, he could never persuade her to leave Philadelphia.

Sally Franklin (Mrs. Richard Bache), Franklin's daughter, in 1793, age thirty-nine, draped and coiffed "a la mode" for her portrait by John Hoppner. Devoted to her father, mother, and brother William, Sally was the heart and anchor of a quarrelsome family.

Governor William Franklin in retirement in London, circa 1785, age fifty-five. Painting by Danuta Wyszynski after a portrait by Mather Brown.

Benjamin and William Franklin's London residence on Craven Street. Father and son were lodgers in rooms on the second and third floor, rented from the widow Margaret Stevenson from 1757 to 1762. Benjamin returned to live here during his second mission to Parliament, 1764 to 1775.

Joseph Galloway, a wealthy lawyer and William's tutor, in militia coat of Pennsylvania regiment, circa 1760, age twenty-nine. A political partner of Benjamin's before the Revolution, he remained a staunch Tory, and so the friends grew apart.

Benjamin Franklin with "friend" on Craven Street, circa 1761, surprised in a private moment by the artist Charles Willson Peale.

Thomas Penn, proprietor of Pennsylvania, 1752, age fifty, dressed to receive company in his London mansion. His refusal to pay taxes upon his vast land holdings brought the Franklins to London to petition against him. Portrait by Arthur Devis.

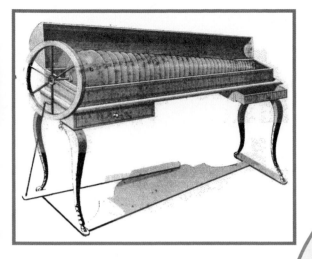

Glass armonica, Franklin's musical invention, 1762. Mozart, Beethoven, and others composed works for the instrument, fashionable in its time.

Lord Stirling (William Alexander), 1770, in militia uniform of New Jersey regiment, age forty-three. Wealthy merchant, astronomer, winemaker turned Patriot soldier, this friend of William's became his archenemy during the Revolution.

George Washington in 1772, age thirty-nine, dressed in his dated uniform from the French and Indian War. Painting by Charles Willson Peale.

Benjamin Franklin being interrogated by the Privy Council after the Boston Tea Party, 1774. His chief inquisitor, the lawyer Alexander Wedderburn, called him an "incendiary" and "the prime conductor" of the trouble between Great Britain and the colonies. Painting by Christian Schussele.

Marquis de Lafayette, Major General in the Continental Army, friend of George Washington and Benjamin Franklin, in 1790, at the age of thirty-three. Lafayette was privileged to carry Franklin's private correspondence by hand between Philadelphia and France during the war. Portrait by Jean-Baptiste Weyler.

The great diplomat in France,
1778, age seventy-two, by
Joseph Siffred Duplessis.

William Strahan, publisher of
Gibbon, Hume, and Dr.
Johnson, and the Franklins'
most devoted friend, in 1780,
age sixty-five. It is difficult to
imagine either Ben or
William Franklin's diplomatic
success in England without
Strahan's support. Portrait by
Sir Joshua Reynolds.

Benjamin Franklin returns to America, 1787, age eighty-one, by Charles Willson Peale.

William Temple Franklin, William's son, in America, 1790, age twenty-nine. Charming, handsome, and talented, Ben Franklin's grandson, who served as his aide in France during the war, struggled to fulfill his promise. Painting attributed to John Trumbull.

His homecoming after more than a decade was bittersweet. His wife had been dead half a year. Upon the furniture, the draperies, the bed linens and colored counterpanes he saw her shadow, her fingerprints upon the silver. The home they had planned together now belonged essentially to his thirty-two-year-old daughter, who had lived there for years, her husband, and their children. He came upon the little boys drilling up and down the hall with toy muskets.

They made up a bed for Temple and embraced him as a member of the family. After a night's rest in his old bed and an early breakfast, Franklin opened his doors to a stream of friends, relations, and dignitaries eager to welcome him home and brief him on the state of affairs. This would have included his oldest friend, Hugh Roberts, a merchant who had helped him start the library, the philosophical society, and the university, and had served as a pallbearer at Deborah's funeral; Charles Thomson, secretary of the recent congress; John Morton, Speaker of the Assembly; and politicians of every stripe eager for news of England as well as Franklin's opinions. Governor Penn himself might have paid a call, embattled as he was and in need of advice and support.

News of his return was widely celebrated and put to use. One New York correspondent quoted Franklin as saying the colonies had no favors to expect from the ministry, as "nothing but submission will satisfy them" and they expected no opposition to their troops. "Dr. Franklin is highly pleased to find us arming and preparing for the worst events, he thinks nothing else can save us." While this was not the opinion he wanted published so soon after his arrival, it was foremost in his thoughts on Saturday evening as he sat down to write to a friend in London, David Hartley. He said he was pleased to learn that the colonies were in agreement; even New York—which the ministry was so sure would defect—appeared as courageous as the others. Before the day was done, the Assembly had chosen Franklin unanimously as a delegate to the Continental Congress. He was all the more a hero in America for having made himself a villain in England.

William learned of his father's and son's arrival on May 7—a happy surprise. He could not go to them immediately, as he had called his assembly to convene the following week. In view of the recent turmoil, the session promised to be challenging, perhaps defiant, so the governor had to be well prepared. He sent word by return courier that he would be in Burlington on May 15; if he could not ride that afternoon to Philadelphia, he wished his father and son would come to him.

Meanwhile, Benjamin Franklin was getting his bearings in a new world that was full of surprises, most of them deeply disturbing. He wrote again to Hartley on Monday the eighth: "You will have heard before this reaches you of the commencement of a civil war; the end of it perhaps neither myself, nor you, who are much younger, may live to see." What seemed six weeks ago in England to be a dark possibility, here and now was reality. He wrote on the same day to his protégé and partner in politics Joseph Galloway, eager to share information and frame a plan of action. At the moment it would be safer to be seen with Galloway than with his own son.

Galloway had sent a note down from Trevose, Pennsylvania, twenty miles to the north, welcoming Franklin home and congratulating him on his accomplishments as agent for the Assembly. He also confided his recent decision to retire from public life, troubling news. Galloway offered to send his carriage to bring his friend up from the city. On a Monday, Franklin replied, accepting the kind offer for later that month, adding that a man of Galloway's talents was greatly needed and that he hoped he would change his decision to retire.

Franklin's timing, as one has observed, was uncanny. On Tuesday, May 9, 1775, George Washington, Peyton Randolph, Patrick Henry, Richard Henry Lee, and the rest of the delegation from Virginia arrived in Philadelphia, along with those of North Carolina, Maryland, and Delaware, for the meeting of the Continental Congress. Washington had packed his uniform, the blue cutaway with gold buttons over the scarlet waistcoat. And on Wednesday, John Hancock, the Adamses, and Thomas Cushing rode in from Massachusetts. Ben Franklin could not have planned his entrance upon the scene more perfectly if he had possessed a flying machine and mental telepathy.

He received a hero's welcome in the State House, although the delegates gathering there on May 10 were not sure quite what to make of him. Quiet, old, and rather mysterious, he was a celebrity, but many held him in suspicion. No one really knew whether he would side more with his son and Joseph Galloway than with Sam Adams and Patrick

Henry. Galloway's situation had become so problematic that the once revered legislator felt compelled to publish a letter in his own defense on May 12. He stood accused of insulting a provincial council, declaring that their meeting was unlawful "and that the magistrates ought to disperse them." More serious was the charge that he had written letters to Parliament harmful to America, an act potentially treasonable. "I have, neither directly nor indirectly, any such correspondence . . . injurious to the rights and freedom of America," he wrote. He went on to say he had not recommended any measures to resolve the present dispute between the two countries.

This, of course, was not true. And Franklin must have wondered at the contradiction, even as he was looking forward to his carriage ride to Trevose that weekend in mid-May. Galloway himself had sent him the ill-starred Plan of Union back in February so that he could share it with Lord Chatham. A few weeks later he was surprised to hear that his friend had already sent it directly to Lord Dartmouth. Parliament cited it in censuring the Continental Congress. In a careful letter to his "dear friend," Franklin offered a word of caution: "It is whispered here by ministerial people that yourself and Mr. Jay of New York are friends to their measures, and give them private intelligence" of what the radicals are doing in America. Although *he* doesn't believe it, Franklin thinks it a duty of friendship to let Galloway know the English regard him as a spy.

What really had happened is that *William* had sent the Plan of Union, with other bits of intelligence, to Dartmouth, after receiving it from Galloway first. The day Franklin arrived home, May 6, William was writing secretly to the colonial secretary, Lord North, in his ongoing role as an informant: "Alarms are spread, which have a tendency to keep the mind of the people in a continual ferment . . . and prevent their paying any attention to the dictates of sober reason." A New Jersey militia, he said, had marched toward Perth Amboy armed with firelocks to protect the treasury upon a mere rumor that a British man of war had anchored off Sandy Hook. Hearing it was a false alarm, the men turned back; but they made a point of parading through the town past the governor's house "with colors, drum, and fife."

He knew very well that his son the governor was Dartmouth's chief spy. His own sister Jane, and his friend the Reverend Thomas Coombe, Jr., had written to him about the scandal over William's letter to Strahan, which somehow got reincarnated as a letter to Whitehall. He feared for William, a royal officer, even more than he did for Joseph Galloway. But he must not mention this concern to anyone; above all he must not write to William about it, for fear that such a letter, falling into the wrong hands, might be construed as proof of collusion between father and son. That would be fatal.

So instead he wrote to Galloway, his son's friend and confederate, knowing he would share the burden with William and that both would stand warned. He addressed his friend and his son as one man, with vehemence and fire, in terms that could not be mistaken: He desired no reconciliation with Britain.

> I have not heard what objections were made to the Plan in the
> Congress, nor would I make more than this one, that when I con-
> sider the extreme corruption prevalent among all orders of men in
> this rotten state, and the glorious public virtue so predominant in
> our rising country, I cannot but apprehend more mischief than
> benefit from a closer Union. I fear they will drag us after them in
> all the plundering wars their desperate circumstances, injustice
> and rapacity, may prompt them to undertake; and their wide-
> wasting prodigality and profusion [will] devour all revenue and
> produce continual necessity in the midst of natural plenty. I ap-
> prehend therefore that to unite us intimately, will only be to cor-
> rupt and poison us also.

This letter must have put the fear of God in Joseph Galloway and his friend the governor of New Jersey, arriving when it did, only days before the carnage at Lexington and Concord, and weeks before the appearance of the old wizard himself, in his doublet jacket and cocked hat, on the Market Street wharf. It never occurred to them that his would be anything other than a voice of reason.

PART THREE

War

CHAPTER 12

Trevose, 1775

TREVOSE, THE ANCESTRAL HOME of the Galloway family, commanded a hilltop in Bucks County above the bend of Neshaminy
Creek. More than a century old in 1775, the two-story mansion of
pointed fieldstone with its high-pitched roof, nine windows wide, enjoyed a view of forests, fields, and orchards. The traveler could see it
from miles away.

The air was sweet with apple blossoms. As the carriage rolled and
jolted along the curving lane between columns of chestnut trees, Benjamin Franklin admired the classic façade, the white portico and pillars
of the venerable dwelling. There were few houses in America older
than he was, and this was a very fine one. He had fond memories of his
friend's hospitality in an easier time. Mrs. Galloway's grandfather had
built the house in 1680, and she had inherited it from her father in
1770. As the law prohibited wives from owning property while their
husbands lived, it became Joseph's. So the great estate would be held
hostage to his political choices.

After the coachman reined his horses to a halt, got down, and offered a hand to help his famous passenger to the door, the old man
stretched his limbs and paused. His friend Cadwalader Evans had informed him that Galloway had collapsed from sunstroke while work-

ing in his father-in-law's fields some time ago. He had not recovered from the shock to his nervous system, the vertigo, the anxiety. Perhaps this explained his erratic behavior, his self-sabotage in politics, his ranting in the press. Franklin really had no idea what to expect more than the warmth of friendship in the handshake, the embrace, the smile of welcome. He had a great gift for friendship and believed the man would still care for him, even after a decade of confusion.

He was unprepared for the change in Galloway's appearance. Hollow-eyed, gaunt, and pallid, his cheeks sunken, the forty-four-year-old still had his hair, now silver, lank, and carelessly unbound; his face had narrowed strangely, as if it had been pressed in an invisible vise, the wide-set eyes somehow too close together. As they stood together in the high center hall, the lord of the manor greeted his old mentor. Franklin was a vigorous gentleman of nearly seventy, with an air of confidence and humorous serenity in his blue eyes, a figure that stood in awkward contrast to the younger man's premature frailty and agitation.

The men were fond of wine, and after the long carriage ride Franklin would not have declined a glass as he took his ease in the airy parlor. Mrs. Galloway and her pretty fourteen-year-old daughter Elizabeth came and went, smiled and curtsied, and retired. Whatever might happen that day, in conversation or argument, Franklin could not look toward Grace Growden Galloway for any expression of sympathy for his Whiggish pleas for independence. She was more royalist by breeding than her Quaker-born husband, who had joined the Church of England in order to marry her. And if the woman wielded any influence in this house she had inherited, it would never be on the side of a revolution.

There are women whose character blooms in adversity, but Grace Galloway was not one of them. She had been a great beauty (as a bride, she had resembled an earthy Mona Lisa) and was the daughter of one of the richest men in America, Pennsylvania chief justice Joseph Growden. Reared in abundance, pampered and adored, Grace looked forward to a life of security and good fortune as a birthright. She did marry a man almost as wealthy as she was, a brilliant lawyer and politician, charming and powerful. But they had been unlucky in parenthood. Three of her children died in infancy, leaving only the girl, and Grace had neither the faith nor the resilience to recover from the series of disappointments. Then he got heatstroke, and she became a gloomy and disagreeable woman. This was one of the cares that weighed upon Joseph during that year when he suffered such political setbacks, such humiliations.

Franklin had been home just long enough, at the hub of politics, to understand that his friend was in danger, and so were his family and his fortune. During that weekend in mid-May 1775, no one in his right mind would have been so bold as to guarantee what the congress would decide in the coming weeks. Faction divided wealthy landholders from workingmen, aristocracy from what Franklin called "the middling men," divided conservative and radicals; it came between the south and north. The congress was still considering whether they should send one more petition to the king reiterating their grievances, while its delegates could not even agree to declare for or against independence, or what military measures should be taken.

Benjamin Franklin had been sitting among them for two weeks, in the foursquare assembly room of the State House, taciturn, his bald, shapely head nodding now and then in assent, or in slumber, no one was certain. He was so quiet, so chary of his opinions, that some of the delegates thought he might be a spy. In a sense, he was—not a spy for England, but a spy for the America that was yet to be born. Everyone came to town with an opinion except this old philosopher. At first it appeared that he had no opinions apart from the slowly waxing consensus, which he did not challenge.

As a good scientist, he was gathering information before acting upon it. He was taking the temperature of the delegates, as he had of the seawater—Jefferson, Adams, Henry, Washington, Dickinson, Lee, and then of the whole body in order to determine its composition and underlying currents. Franklin understood, as Galloway did not, that the nation of people represented by the delegates downtown was a colossus capable of monstrous destruction and cruelty. It had already shown that it would not be guided solely by the voices of reason. Like Niagara's waters, gravity transformed its drops from a clear stream flowing toward the precipice to a cataract tumbling and crashing to the rocks below to demolish anything that was not already rock or water. So were the furious, grieving citizens of Massachusetts, and now all of the colonies were tributaries to that flood. A hundred twenty men had died at Lexington and Concord. Franklin knew history well enough to see that only more bloodshed would satisfy the desire for vengeance. If you were not clearly a friend, the nearsighted mob would take you for an enemy.

Franklin wanted to explain these things. If he could convince Galloway, then he might convince his own son. But the rich man was moving in a bubble, subject to a common delusion. Wealth was a great leveler. The rich Whig and the rich Tory, in their habits and morals, were more like each other than they were like the poor and working men of their own political parties. Mr. and Mrs. Galloway could rely upon Thomas Wharton and his wife nearby in Twickenham for any kind of help in a crisis. Neither family would dream of doing the other any harm. The idea that the popular party of mechanics and farmers could amass so much power that it might deprive a Galloway or Wharton of his life and property seemed not only irrational to the wealthy but downright impossible.

Galloway had little to say that was of much interest to Franklin. Like a spurned suitor he harped upon his Plan of Union, a British and American legislature in the colonies with a president general appointed by the king. His plan had been shouted down. Stunned, crushed, he was uncertain what to do. He had stayed to sign his name to the congress's resolutions, under brutal pressure for all to act unanimously. The triumph of the anti-British faction in the Pennsylvania election of 1774 further damaged Galloway's prospects. Speaker of the House for eight years, he was unseated, and while he still had influence, being named to important committees, he felt discouraged and ill. Not long after he received the death threat he submitted his resignation to the Second Continental Congress, ending his own career. He told one friend, "I hope I have retired in time from the distressful and ungrateful drudgery of public life. The want of health was one great motive, and I had many others." He had stood too long in the sun and been badly burnt. Some rapscallion had tried to kidnap his daughter. The world had gone mad, and sometimes he feared that he, too, was losing his mind.

Such tales of personal woe found a sympathetic audience in Benjamin Franklin, his loyal friend, nodding and sighing and sipping from his glass. It was his long-standing custom never to be confrontational in arguing with a person, and he would make no exception here, in Joseph's parlor. He would prefer to present the facts of a case and let his counterpart discover his own error. Franklin asked if he might call upon Joseph again here, after a few days of reflection. Perhaps then he might have something to say that would shed light on the gloomy state of affairs that was still not hopeless for men of resources. On board the ship bound for America he had scribbled a journal he would like to share with him. He might find it helpful.

Franklin stayed the night in Trevose. The next morning he was mostly silent. At last, looking his host in the eye, he said, "Well, Mr. Galloway, are you really of the mind that I ought to promote a reconciliation?"

"Yes," said Joseph Galloway.

And without further conversation, Franklin bade him farewell.

The men would not meet again for five weeks. While the congress conferred in Philadelphia, Franklin had to be circumspect in his dealings with Galloway—even to the point of avoiding being seen with him. It was dangerous now to be on the wrong side, or even suspected of it, and while Franklin held his peace and formed his strategy, the rumors flew. "I can however (inter nos) inform you," the Philadelphia lawyer William Bradford wrote to James Madison, "that they begin to entertain a great suspicion that Dr. Franklin came rather as a spy than as a friend, & that he means to discover our weak side and make his peace with the minister by discovering it to him." One reason they distrusted him was that he was William Franklin's father. Recalling the scandal over William's letter to Strahan, they naturally wondered if the Franklins were in league against them.

For a while he let everybody wonder, preferring to buy time to win Joseph Galloway and William Franklin over to his side, an outcome he might accomplish by degrees, but not abruptly or by force. The tide of events, and rational dialogue, might bring them to their senses. So during those weeks in May and June, while quietly joining forces with the congress as they raised troops to fight at Bunker Hill, Franklin led

Galloway to believe he had yet to decide whether to follow or oppose the radicals. William Franklin told Galloway that his father had avoided discussion of the political crisis. At one point his father's evasiveness provoked William to say "he hoped, if he [Benjamin] designed to set the colonies in a flame, he would take care to run away by the light of it," a sentence so fine and moving that it must have come from much thought by a man we know had a touch of the poet in him.

THE WEATHER WAS FAIR, the roads between Burlington and Perth Amboy firm and bright with new leaves on the spring boughs. William was eager to see his father and son, as they were to see him and his wife in their new home. But he could not go to Philadelphia until he had delivered his message to the Assembly on May 16. Ordered to present Lord North's new offer of conciliation, as the first governor to introduce the plan, Franklin was under pressure; if he did not succeed in New Jersey, a moderate province, it would send a message to the others that devotion to colonial unity was greater than loyalty to the king.

The king, Governor Franklin told his legislators, was happy to comply with every reasonable wish of the colonists. North's plan was simple and it was just, he added. As long as a province agreed to contribute a fair share to the common defense, to the king's satisfaction, as well as support of its civil government and its judiciary, Parliament would levy no more internal taxes apart from what was needed to regulate commerce.

That was it. North's plan of reconciliation produced a leaden silence in the courthouse. There was not a word about parliamentary supremacy, reparations for prior damages, quartering of troops. Parliament would remain sovereign and its judgments final. Governor Franklin insisted this was inescapable—the supreme power had to reside somewhere, as an arbiter of conflicting colonial claims. In any event, England would end up paying the lion's share of the Empire's expenses. In the future, as in the distant past, Parliament would come to the colonies in the usual manner—by making specific requests, he explained. If taxation was really the cause of the current disorder, "when that point is once settled, every other subject of complaint. . . . will, no doubt, of course be removed."

Lord North meant well. So did Governor Franklin in putting the best frame on a bad picture, but it was too little too late. Taxation was no longer the real source of the conflict. Now it was Parliament's supremacy that disturbed the peace, and Franklin insisted this was non-negotiable. In his calm, firm voice he told them that if they did not consider North's plan as a basis for conciliation, if they dismissed it outright, they might as well announce their desire for independence. This was their choice, and it was not, he pleaded, in America's interest to choose independence. England had supported and protected her colonies "at the expense of her blood and treasure." This was not, however, the phrase these people wished to hear a month after the bloodshed at Lexington and Concord.

"God grant," he said in concluding, "that the colonies may manifest the same laudable disposition, and that a hearty reconciliation and harmony may take the place of the present confusion and dissension." He gathered his papers and stood aside.

Just then a terrible thing took place, as if bats had flown into the room and blocked the light. Fifty-four-year-old Sheriff Samuel Tucker, a radical freeholder who would serve in the new and independent Provincial Congress a week later, demanded to be heard. In his hand he raised a document, a pamphlet called *The Parliamentary Register No. Five*, that had arrived on a recent packet from England, forwarded by friends of America. They had called Sheriff Tucker's attention to a curious item; it purported to be an excerpt from a letter Governor Franklin had written to Lord Dartmouth on February 1. In it the governor had denounced the Assembly's determination to endorse the Continental Congress, calling it an artful scheme prepared by the men who favored the resolution to bully the moderates who opposed it.

The sheriff read the letter aloud, and the legislators were vexed and furious by degrees. They demanded to know whether the excerpt was authentic. William knew that it was and could not believe that Dartmouth could have been so careless. Taken by surprise, fearful, and weary, the governor launched a counterattack on what he considered the wicked partisans who conspired to blacken his name and sow dissent in order to further their selfish political aims. "It has been my unhappiness almost every session during the existence of the present Assembly that a majority" have been "persuaded to seize on every opportunity of arraigning my conduct, or fomenting some dispute, let the occasion be ever so trifling or let me be ever so careful to avoid giving any cause of offence."

He denied writing any such nonsense, which had appeared in a paper known for sensationalism. Furthermore, the specimen was too badly written to have come from his hand. Surely they still respected the governor's style, he quipped, if they no longer revered his character. It was not his, but even if it were, the Assembly had no right to read any of his private letters.

The lawmakers swiftly rejected Lord North's plan, and they then rededicated themselves to the common cause, the resolutions of the Continental Congress. On the nineteenth they were ready to pack their bags and return to their homes. Many were preparing to attend the Provincial Congress on May 23. In taking his leave of them, William declared he had done his duty. "The times are indeed greatly altered. I lost no time in laying before you propositions for an amicable accommodation. . . . I could have no suspicion that you did not think yourselves competent to the business."

William rode directly to Philadelphia the weekend of May 19, and that week the entire Franklin family was united. The Continental Congress adjourned without business until Friday, May 25; at least that is what the Journals of the Congress reported. In fact there was a great deal of committee work going on behind the scenes. News of Benedict Arnold's capture of Fort Ticonderoga had reached the delegates on the eighteenth; and reports of the British attack on Ethan Allen's American forces near St. Johns arrived soon after. Hopes for peace were fading, and the need to establish defensive posts and mobilize troops could no longer be denied.

Such was the climate of anxious concern as William came to call upon his family in Market Street, so soon after his failure in Burlington. It should have been a joyous occasion as he was introduced to the son he had scarcely known. And so it was at first, as grandfather and the Baches exclaimed over the resemblance between father and son, as if fifteen-year-old Temple were William Franklin reborn. When the children had gone to bed, William wanted to talk about Parliament, and the colonies, and the Empire's troubles. He wanted to sound his father out on Lord North's plan. But his father was evasive, as he had been for a while, turning the conversation toward other topics—shipping, crops, music, the Gulf Stream, the grandchildren, especially the fine youngster Temple Franklin, who was destined for greatness.

Had his father given up hope for reconciliation, some sort of plan of union that would save the Empire? He would not discuss it. For his part, William let it be known that he had not given up. On the evening of May 23, he left his father's house to dine with several men moderate enough to listen to his arguments in favor of Lord North's plans, some of them members of the Continental Congress, including young Silas Deane of Connecticut, and William Moore, a loyalist from Chester County. Governor Franklin's long speech promoting Lord North's plan was published on the front page of *The Pennsylvania Gazette* the next morning. This augured well for the forces of compromise, as the delegates might still see the virtue of William's arguments set forth in cold type.

Whatever hope William's words offered to those who wanted reconciliation was battered in the days ahead. The next day, May 25, the congress emerged from its adjournment and convened in the State House, a committee of the whole that included the great men: John Hancock succeeding Peyton Randolph as president, George Washington, Patrick Henry, Silas Deane, and the Adamses; the whole pantheon of patriots. Doctor Franklin maintained the stillness of the Sphinx. Their business that Thursday was not what William or any other loyalist would have wished. They called upon the Committee for Military Preparations to report. Proposals, read aloud and approved, authorized the establishment of a thorough military defense of New York: a fort near King's Bridge on the lower Hudson, and two others in the hills on each side of the river; and a resolution that the New York militia be trained and ready to march on a moment's notice.

The congress was planning for war. There was no discussion of Parliament's olive branch, or Governor Franklin's appeal just published in the newspaper. William Franklin's name was not mentioned in the congress that day. But the next day, the first order of business was introduced by a New Jersey delegate. Mr. Richard Smith had come to lay before the congress Lord North's plan for the "accommodation of the unhappy differences between our parent state and the colonies." New Jersey could not adopt it, Smith explained, under the present circumstances, yet since His Excellency Governor Franklin had laid it before their assembly, desiring to leave no stone unturned, they now felt obliged to lay the same plan before the congress. The peace plan was read into the minutes because he, William Franklin, had insisted upon it at the moment when the Continental Congress was arming for war. They did not bother debating it; rather, they returned immediately to matters of military defense.

And on Saturday, after a report on affairs in Canada and a consideration of arming the colonies there, the congress formed one more resolution. Brief and grim, it appeared almost as an afterthought to their affairs before adjourning. Yet it must have seemed to the historians among them like a death's-head, the high-handed overture to martial law. Resolved: "That where any person hath been or shall be adjudged by a committee, to have violated the Continental Association," that is, the Continental Congress, then the offender would be arraigned, called to account, and required to promise to conform to the Association or suffer penalties to be determined. "The committee may settle the terms." There were hundreds of local committees from Maine to Georgia, and this terrible decree would license them, each in its arbitrary way, to tyrannize and terrorize suspected loyalists into submission.

THERE WAS LITTLE MORE that William Franklin could accomplish in Philadelphia, and there were signs he was not welcome there. Sometime toward the end of May he helped his sister pack up Temple's things, his clothing, schoolbooks, and drawing pencils, his sword, and his pet Pekingese named Pompey.

They set out in a carriage, crossing the Delaware at Trenton Ferry, then following the Raritan River to Perth Amboy. Elizabeth Franklin welcomed her stepson to his new home, his room under the dormer of that magnificent house on the hill. Years of correspondence between the two show affection on both sides. Elizabeth was grateful—as she had been for Sally's company and the Bache children's—for the chance to be a part of Temple's life. She was, of the Amboy Franklins, the more indulgent and gentle parent. Mrs. Franklin took pride in introducing Temple to their friends and their children; he enjoyed playing games in the summer days and twilights.

Mornings were for study. William in his new role felt some need to compensate for time lost in shaping this promising lad. Temple had confidence and charm aplenty but little sense of order. He could not keep track of his shirts and stockings. William would insist that his son adhere to a schedule in his lessons and order in his closet. Above all, William made sure that he and his son enjoyed this time getting to know each other. The governor needed relief from his political troubles; the English boy was enchanted with his father's home in America, his title, and the mansion. He had never known such luxury in the midst of wilderness. Both of them were fond of drawing. And the countryside around Amboy was a tapestry of grain fields and oak forests, meadows freshened with creeks and inland rivers, marshes, and beaches along the bay. They rode out on horseback, sightseeing until they agreed upon a view, and then took turns with the telescope. The boy was gifted with the crayon. Later they would ride home and unroll their works for Elizabeth to admire.

So the days passed pleasantly in that safe haven on Raritan Bay. They read books and crossed swords. News from Philadelphia, reports of the proceedings of the Continental Congress, newspapers, were two days distant, their effects agreeably muted in the warm sunlight of late spring.

But on June 16, a Tory postman delivering *The Pennsylvania Gazette* would find it difficult to conceal his concern. On page 3, at the end of a half dozen reports from committees from Virginia to Philadelphia and New York, appeared the notice of a proceeding against Judge William Moore by the Committee of Chester County. He had been arraigned there on June 6 and charged with being "inimical to the liberties of America . . . [having] expressed a design to oppose the present Association." That last resolution of the congress on May 27 had borne fruit. The seventy-six-year-old judge, too ill to respond to the charges in person, wrote a pathetic apology to his accusers for anything that he might have said, unguardedly, to offend them, "for, believe me, I have no interest but what is in America; I wish well to every individual in it and pray that its liberties may be preserved."

Joseph Galloway had put himself in a position as dangerous as Judge Moore's. Sometime that week, Galloway had arranged to meet with Benjamin Franklin, as they had planned to do following their visit in mid-May. Much had happened since then. Galloway, up in Trevose, lacked Franklin's knowledge of the progress in the Continental Congress, and he looked to the old man for advice. Franklin had been buying time to evaluate the situation in the colonies as a whole, as well as the dynamics of the congress, in order to balance the needs of his family, his friends, and the body politic. And now that he had made up his mind to cast his lot with the congress, he was apprehensive about associating with Galloway—not to mention his son the royal governor. Yet he must. The door of opportunity to save them was creaking shut.

Franklin preferred that Galloway come to him at home in Philadelphia. He was too busy to travel just then, and the visit from a friend on a summer night might not arouse so much suspicion as the spectacle of Benjamin Franklin setting out in the rich Tory's carriage for a weekend at Trevose. So Galloway drove down the second week of June to talk to Franklin but even more to listen, having done most of the talking during their last meeting. Franklin, for his part, would not argue with Galloway. That was not his way. Having made Joseph at home with a glass of Madeira and a comfortable chair, he would read aloud to him in his soft, expressive, sometimes musical voice.

He read to Galloway from his *Journal of Negotiations in London*, the two-hundred-page letter he had written to his son. William had not yet seen it. The reading was offered to the lawyer as evidence that no more was left to be done in bargaining with Parliament. The ministry was mostly composed of madmen, fools, and villains whose conduct had "made their claim of sovereignty over the millions of virtuous, sensible people in America seem the greatest of absurdities, since they appeared to have scarce discretion enough to govern a herd of swine."

When Franklin had read three-quarters of his journal, someone knocked at the door and the papers were set aside. Galloway never heard the rest, mostly letters pertaining to Franklin's schemes for reconciliation—all of them ignored no matter how he packaged them.

Galloway remained unconvinced but open to further discussion. Dr. Franklin was famously persuasive and nowhere more charming than in his home by his own hearth, over a bottle or two of wine. It was proposed that they invite William to join this conversation as soon as possible. Maybe he could shed light on the problems that could not penetrate the shutters of the State House, Galloway suggested. Or perhaps William might respond to an appeal to instinctive filial piety, Franklin reasoned, where Galloway stood rigidly defending the British rule of law.

In any case they agreed that a meeting was necessary. It could not be here in Philadelphia because the governor's person had become obnoxious to the citizenry, a symbol of everything the congress had come to fear and despise. So the meeting place would have to be Trevose. Galloway would send for the governor so that the three could come together at their earliest convenience.

By mid-June 1775, the Continental Congress had chartered the Continental Army, resolved to raise companies in Pennsylvania, Maryland, and Virginia, and appointed George Washington commander in chief. He signed his commission on June 17, the same day as the Battle of Bunker Hill. Under these circumstances the meeting of the Franklins and Galloway at Trevose (most likely in the third week of June) required the strictest secrecy.

Benjamin Franklin had come to tell them in person what he had tried to convey in his letters for at least a year: the British Empire as they had once known it was no more. What had taken its place in England was corrupt, bankrupt, and not worth saving. Furthermore, and most important, the older man had come to explain to these idealistic lawyers that America was arming itself for war. Martial law and not civil law would be the order of the day, and it was not going to be a pretty business. He peered at one, then the other, over his wire-

rimmed eyeglasses, imploring. They had wives and children and property to consider. A hard-bitten realist, he had come to warn them, to
save his son and good friend from courts-martial and ruin.

Two of the men who conversed in Galloway's book-lined parlor
drinking wine and spirits were lawyers skilled in debate. The third, Ben
Franklin, had no appetite for it and not much skill. One thing we know
about that night so near the summer solstice, as the crickets and tree
frogs trilled through the open windows, is that a great deal of liquor
was consumed. Galloway recalls it, and wine assuaged the agony of the
quarrel while loosening everyone's tongue. Then an uncommon thing
occurred. Benjamin Franklin, known for his reserve, his gentle voice,
began to argue. He argued quietly at first, but as the liquor flowed and
the clock struck longer and later hours he raised his voice in excitement or desperation; he grew strident. He exclaimed "against the corruption and dissipation of the Kingdom." He swore that the lack of
union in the British government, opposition there to war, and the
enormous resources of the colonies would cause them to prevail. He
urged Joseph Galloway to return to the Continental Congress.

And it may not have been until that late hour that the younger men
felt in their bones the chill of doom. This was the first time William
had heard his father speak on the subject. Either the old philosopher
was ill informed, or his son and Galloway were ruined. They argued
with him, the two lawyers, on every point, as if their lives depended on
it. It is not possible, they reasoned, that America could raise an army,
much less a fleet of battleships, that could stand up to the mighty force
of British regulars, cannon, and that invincible navy! As for Parliament's disagreement over the war, Galloway cited the well-known
fable of the two bulldogs and the cat. The two dogs were "tearing each
other to pieces, yet, on the appearance of their common enemy, their
enmity instantly ceased, and their whole powers became *united, and
exerted to reduce him*," that is, the cat.

The elder statesman stood his ground. Gravely he "declared in favor
of measures for attaining to independence," namely, mustering soldiers,
printing money, uniting the colonies. And with these words, the hopes
that William Franklin and Joseph Galloway had hoarded and nursed

for all these months, while they prayed for the great man to come home, dissolved like the waning moon in the morning light.

Galloway recalled that the two old friends "parted as they had met, unconverted to the principles of each other." The embattled lawyer would later waver in his loyalties, much to Dr. Franklin's pleasure, falsely regaining the old man's trust. As for William, his relation was more profound and complex. As he bade farewell to his father the next day, riding north toward Bristol as Benjamin turned south on the High Road, his thoughts were in a whirl. He watched the sunrise over the Delaware River. Galloway could retire to Trevose for six months to sulk and rail. William was still royal governor. And he must see his father again and again for the family's sake, and take up the terrible argument where it had left off.

CHAPTER 13

The Last Word

BENJAMIN FRANKLIN RETURNED TO Philadelphia in late June knowing he had done everything he could to persuade his son and his friend to change—or at least moderate—their positions. Now he focused his energies on the Continental Congress, the consolidation of the colonies, and preparation for war.

One of the more taciturn delegates, he quietly assumed positions of power and authority. At the end of May 1775, he was appointed chairman of the committee to establish the postal system. As a scientist he was put in charge of the committee to promote the production of saltpeter for gunpowder, and as a draftsman/printer another panel to design colonial currency. Learning of the scarcity of gunpowder he designed a pike that infantrymen could use against British bayonets. That summer, as the congress resolved to consider the sovereign state of America, Franklin read aloud a revision of his Albany Plan for Union—which would serve as the model for the Articles of Confederation, our first constitution.

At eleven o'clock on the night of June 24, an express rider arrived with terrible news from Boston. Above the city a bloody battle had been joined to defend Bunker Hill and many men had been killed and wounded on both sides. The British had rained red-hot cannonballs upon the Boston suburb of Charlestown, burning four hundred houses to the ground.

It took a full week for this news to travel the three hundred miles from Boston to Philadelphia—evidence of the confusion the battle created there on the seventeenth. On a moonless night near the stroke of twelve, a hundred men gathered in the long gallery at the City Tavern on Walnut Street to hear the news the express rider brought from Boston. These included nearly every member of the Continental Congress who was awake at that hour on a Saturday night—John Adams, his cousin Sam Adams, John Hancock, and other Sons of Liberty. These first reports of the casualties were disturbing and unclear; the burning of Charlestown after the battle the delegates denounced with horror as an atrocity against civilians. Charlestown was nothing now but chimneys, rubble, and ashes.

They sent for the members of the local Pennsylvania Committee of Safety, including Benjamin Franklin, who was too old to be stirring at such an hour, to consider the urgent need for gunpowder. Much of Franklin's time during the next few days was spent in hectic collaboration with the Adamses in procuring gunpowder to send to Boston, and in exploring means to produce saltpeter. On Tuesday the twenty-seventh, John Adams was pleased to write to James Warren and other Sons of Liberty in Boston that ninety quarter casks of gunpowder were on their way to Massachusetts.

The Bunker Hill defeat and the burning of Charlestown had a profound effect on Franklin, tapping whatever reserve of patience or tolerance he may have held out for the royal government. From the day of the battle until July 5 he wrote only two letters—both to bankers in London, registering his desperation. On June 27, he wrote to Browns & Collinson ordering them to pay all of his balance there to John Sargeant, Esquire, a private banker who was one of his oldest friends in England. The same day, he wrote to Sargeant informing him of the transfer and instructing him to keep it for Benjamin Franklin or his children, explaining that it might soon be all he would have left, "as my American property consists chiefly of houses in our seaport towns which your ministry have begun to burn, and I suppose are wicked enough to burn them all."

This scenario had haunted him for half a year. Now he saw the conflagration actually happening. It would require great wisdom on England's side to prevent a total separation, and he hoped they would discover it. "We shall give you one opportunity more of recovering our affections and retaining the connection . . ." This resolution, aptly named the Olive Branch Petition, was a last-ditch appeal to the king. Franklin and John Dickinson humbly asked for easier taxes and trade accommodations, but they left the details to the imagination of the ministry. The petition was approved by the Continental Congress on July 8, and the wry comment of several delegates was that this alone, this letter professing undying loyalty to the Crown, could convince the peace faction that the king would settle for nothing other than war.

On July 5, Franklin wrote the now famous letter to William Strahan, known to everyone but the addressee, who never saw it.

Mr. Strahan,
You are a member of parliament and one of that majority which has doomed my country to destruction. You have begun to burn our towns, and murder our people. Look upon your hands! They are stained with the blood of your relations. You and I were long friends: You are now my enemy, and I am, Yours, B. Franklin

The complimentary close above the signature is clever and poignant: the men are bonded in enmity as they had been in friendship. And in fact the friendship continued because Franklin kept the letter, pigeonholed it as a memento of his anguish, and three months later wrote to Strahan again, as his affectionate servant.

Washington formally took command of eight thousand soldiers before the walls of Harvard College on July 4. Within days another fourteen hundred troops arrived from Virginia, Maryland, and Pennsylvania, to be arrayed on the city heights from Roxbury to the Mystic River. During the rest of July, the congress focused upon mobilizing troops, raising funds for weapons and wages, and passing resolutions to strengthen the Continental Army. The British ministry had stirred up the Indians to attack colonial outposts, inviting them to form an alliance with the English and in response, the congress appointed three commissioners to neutralize the tribes; Franklin was one of these. And at the end of July, he accepted the appointment of postmaster general, the most powerful position in the fledgling government after General Washington's command. In the days before the telegraph, the flow of information we now take for granted for all purposes, military, social, and private, was facilitated and controlled by the U.S. Postal Service and the postmaster general.

At last the congress rejected the proposal for reconciliation received from Lord North—the proposal William Franklin had defended in print. The next day they adjourned for the month of August, a time they needed to go home and prepare for war. Their final business was voting funds for the paymaster general: a half million dollars for the army in Massachusetts; $200,000 more if the funds should run out before Congress returned; $100,000 for the New York forces under General Philip Schuyler. Much of the money would come from private financiers such as Robert Morris. And five tons of gunpowder were to be shipped at once to General Washington from the magazine in Philadelphia.

Anyone with the least knowledge of the Continental Congress's deliberations in these days knew that peace was only a distant hope. Yet two days' journey on horseback separated the commercial and political nerve center of Philadelphia from the sleepy, peaceful haven of Perth Amboy on the bay. For the little family of three Franklins, it was far enough away to muffle the sound of war drums, saber rattling, and the harsh rhetoric of the Sons of Liberty. Temple was a pleasant young man whose presence in Amboy was altogether natural and innocent, whatever his father's politics. If one needed an excuse in a time of suspicion, Grandfather Franklin might go back and forth to Amboy freely, visiting his son and his grandson, as was his right.

Already the Franklins had enemies on both sides ready to think the worst of them—together or apart. There were cynics who would always believe that father and son conspired to take opposite sides of the conflict so that whoever won might save the other and the family fortune. For the time being, William enjoyed the summer days with his son, riding out through the countryside, sketching the meadows and creeks, the butterflies and cattails. He dreamed of peace. And he waited to hear from his father, or see him riding up the road to the mansion from Long Ferry in the afternoon. He sent a note by stagecoach on August 10; receiving no reply, he wrote again on the fourteenth, a longer letter.

Benjamin Franklin received his son's longer letter on August 18, when he was working day and night for the Committee of Safety amassing gunpowder and sending wagonloads of it to Generals Schuyler and Washington in Albany and Boston in exchange for lead to make bullets. William's letter was odd. The content and tone of it were so far removed from current events that his father must have wondered if the writer was losing touch with reality. As the Committee of Safety consulted the generals as to whether the redcoats would first attack Boston, New York, or Philadelphia, William Franklin's letter revisited the old subject of the Walpole Company. Since his father had offered to do what he could for William concerning the land transactions, he wanted to know Benjamin's opinion concerning the validity of one purchase from the Indians. "Since you left England they [Walpole and Co.] have received the *strongest assurances* that as soon as the present great dispute is settled *our grant shall be perfected.*" In other words, then they would be rich.

William had leapt, fancifully, over the barricade of the present great dispute and was dreaming of El Dorado on the other side. The rest of his letter enters the labyrinth of the transaction and the debt structure, entreating his father to contact a neighbor, a bookkeeper familiar with the accounts, and to pressure him to arrange for a fair settlement. William watched as his son Temple copied this letter, admiring the youth's careful hand. Proudly William informed his father that this was Billy's work—implying that intelligence of this nature could be entrusted to him, and that the boy ought to understand the business, as it affected his own future. In a postscript William said he would be glad to receive a line as to when his father might visit, or if Benjamin approved of his going to Philadelphia sometime soon, and when Temple should move there in order to start college.

Benjamin Franklin did not answer this letter or any other letter from William for many years. What he did do, as soon as his duty to the army allowed, is set out for Perth Amboy. When the covered wagon of gunpowder left for New York on Sunday, August 27, he packed his bag. The next day he overtook the wagon on the High Road at Trenton, trotting at a good clip to Brunswick, and arrived at the governor's mansion on Tuesday the twenty-ninth.

Of all of them, Elizabeth would have been most deeply moved to see the great man at her door at last, smiling and bowing, the father-in-law she had seen so rarely since she left England thirteen years before. She was proud to welcome him, to show him the home they had made for each other and for Temple. Notwithstanding the fatigue of his journey, he appeared a vigorous gentleman, and the soul of politeness, despite arriving unannounced.

But Grandfather would not stay long in Proprietary House. He would not linger in that village, which William's secretary once praised as the only place in America where a friend to American liberty is considered a disgraceful character. He had come to collect his grandson from that outpost of royalism—that much is certain. He did not think the boy was safe there, and he could not have approved of his father's influence, or of his engaging Temple in the affairs of the Walpole Company. Dragging Temple into business affairs was one of many bones of contention. They had disagreed about the boy's education. William wanted his son to attend the high-toned King's College in New York, but it was expensive, and so he gave in to his father's preference for his Academy in Philadelphia, a college free of Tory bias. Now they disagreed over the boy's living arrangements. Temple was happy as he could be in his father's house, and it cannot have been easy for his parents to part with him that day. College, after all, did not begin until mid-October.

William and his father were at odds. They would honor the family bond, the rites and courtesies binding upon wife and daughter, father and son, host and guest—at least for a day or two. But there were differences that must be addressed, and one question, underscoring all others, was crucial. When Elizabeth and the boy had gone upstairs to bed, the bottle passed back and forth across the table, and the men's voices carried out on the night air.

The barometer plunged ahead of a gale out of the northeast, a hard wind from Long Island Sound that would soon cause a monstrous high tide. A wall of water would overflow the wharves of the port cities, ruining the stores of sugar. It would wreak havoc upon the low country here, washing away the riverbanks, swamping the meadows, sweeping away bridges, mills, and milldams. But first there were the heat and the heavy air and sweat of late August. And in their shirtsleeves, by candlelight, the men drank fortified wine and argued with each other, as only two persons who deeply love each other might plead, each for the other's life.

Perth Amboy was then a village of a hundred dwellings, three churches, and a barracks housing the provincial militia. The presence of Ben Franklin in the governor's mansion was a matter of keen interest to most of the several hundred inhabitants there. A young man in the neighborhood—old enough to have held the impression but young enough to recall it half a century later—eavesdropped outside the windows. He was probably not alone. He discreetly informed the local historian how the Franklins quarreled in the heat, how the older man "strove zealously to draw the Governor over to the side of the colonies" and how their arguments became so violent that they could not continue in any reasonable manner.

Benjamin Franklin left Perth Amboy with his grandson on Friday, the first of September, just ahead of the gale, which would overtake them. No pleading from Elizabeth or William to wait for better weather could hold him a day longer. He had asked William to send him a copy of his first, and more moderate, exposition of Lord North's peace proposal, as well as the minutes of the last sessions of the New Jersey Assembly, and most important, a record of the clash between William and Sheriff Tucker over his letter to Dartmouth. With these papers he might attempt a defense or apology for his son if the Continental Congress should charge him with hostile conduct, opposing the measures of the united American colonies, or other wrongdoing.

William's anxiety after his father's visit is evident in his letter to Lord Dartmouth four days later explaining he was loath to abandon his post, as his continuing in it was the best means of keeping up an appearance of government. A turn of events might make it possible for him to be of service. However, "it would mortify me extremely to be seized upon and led like a bear through the country to some place of confinement in New England as has lately happened to Governor

Skene." Lieutenant governor Philip Skene of Ticonderoga had been arrested for treason—the warrant signed by Benjamin Franklin himself, who had shared the cautionary tale with his son the night of their argument.

MORE CRACKS IN THE scaffolding of his frail government worried William Franklin that month. His old friend William Alexander (who called himself Lord Stirling, pending claims to an earldom) had accepted a colonelcy in the New Jersey militia. Stirling, an East Jersey landowner, had been a member of the Governor's Council since 1762, so the news of his commission came as a blow. Four years older than Franklin, Lord Stirling was one of the most talented men of his generation, heir to a fortune who made a greater fortune retailing dry goods, tools, and cannon. He lived like an earl in a neoclassical mansion in Basking Ridge, Somerset County. An accomplished mathematician and astronomer, he also received a medal from the Royal Academy for improving winemaking in America. Perhaps he would have liked to be governor himself. In any case, Franklin counted Stirling's friendship among his triumphs as governor. The loss of Stirling's support in the Council would be a major setback to the moderate cause.

Governor Franklin wanted to hear from the man himself. So on September 7 he had the clerk of the Council address a letter to Stirling in Basking Ridge, notifying him of a meeting on the fifteenth. At the same time he had the clerk inquire if it were true that he had accepted a commission in the provincial militia. A week later word came down that Lord Stirling begged to be excused from the meeting on account of an attack of gout. And he admitted that he had accepted the colonelcy, confident of having the governor's blessing, as he recalled Franklin's declaring in public and in private that the rights of the people and of the Crown were equally dear to him.

William responded the next day, upbraiding Stirling for his duplicity, quoting back at him his own statement that "a man ought to be damned who would take up arms against his sovereign" at such a time. The correspondence degenerated into an imbroglio, which led to Lord Stirling's resignation from the Council. Then on October 3, treasurer

Samuel Smith also resigned, pleading old age, and the governor was embarrassed to report that he could not find any man sufficiently qualified who would accept either post.

These were problems his father would have thought trivial if he troubled to think about them at all. Benjamin Franklin was packing for a long journey north to confer with General Washington at his headquarters in Cambridge. Responding to a letter from William Strahan arguing for conflict resolution, inviting him to go to London in person, Benjamin wrote that he was too busy to write much, and going to England was impossible. The ministry there was prosecuting him with a frivolous lawsuit that had been brought by William Whately over the Hutchinson letters, and Franklin's lawyer assured him that he would be imprisoned the moment he arrived in England. Nevertheless, Franklin added a request for Strahan to send him his peace proposals, "for I make it a rule not to mix personal resentments with public business"— a rule not always honored in the observance.

At the moment, Franklin's business was with the congress as it rushed toward establishing an independent government, and with the American army preparing for war. He informed his English friend that the thousand dollars per year he had been voted to serve as postmaster would be donated to wounded soldiers, so that no one might suspect him of having a material interest in keeping the war alive.

The next morning, October 4, 1775, Franklin would be setting out with his delegation. As soon as he left town, the congress passed a resolution that all local councils were to arrest and detain anyone whose freedom might endanger a colony's safety or America's liberties. William Franklin's name came up; he was judged not dangerous. This was, to be sure, a matter best deliberated in his father's absence.

The delegation the congress appointed included Benjamin Harrison of Virginia, Thomas Lynch of South Carolina, Franklin as chairman, and three servants. The trip by the High Road to New York, then the post road to Boston, took the travelers two weeks, stopping at night in the better inns. Arriving at Washington's headquarters the night of October 15, Franklin wrote a note to his sister Jane. Once they were finished with their business, he informed her, he would purchase a carriage and horses, then call for her in Warwick, where she had taken refuge with their old friend Catharine Ray Greene and her husband, William. Then they would travel south together.

He arrived in Cambridge on a Sunday; the conference with General Washington would not begin until Wednesday, October 18. The delegates were charged with instructions concerning military action, expenses, and the army's organization. During four days the council directed that the army should be increased to more than twenty thousand. They authorized the death penalty for mutiny and lashing or fines for drunkenness, sentries caught sleeping, and officers AWOL; they discussed rations, pay, and standards for firearms. Finally Washington asked permission to attack Boston before Christmas. Although the congress had discussed this and given the committee authority to approve the action, Franklin, Lynch, and Harrison now balked, saying the decision was too consequential for them to determine, so they would refer it to the Honorable Congress.

The conference ended on the twenty-second, but Franklin did not leave for Rhode Island until the twenty-sixth. First he had to settle his accounts with the Massachusetts House of Representatives for expenses incurred during his years of service as agent, and purchase a carriage and horses. He also had social obligations in his native province. One evening he dined in company with Abigail Adams, John Adams's thirty-one-year-old wife. She later reported that she found him sociable but not talkative, although whenever he did speak he said something useful. He agreed to deliver one of Abigail's letters to her husband in Philadelphia.

Franklin's plan was to pick up Jane Mecum and her belongings in Warwick and bring her home with him to live under his protection as long as was necessary. His sister Jane, sixty-three, had gone to Rhode Island after the fighting in Lexington, so near her Boston home. She had told him of her distress as the sound of fighting came nearer and nearer her door, the gunfire and battle cries, and then the litters of dying and wounded soldiers being borne through the streets. Fortunately, she was able to escape, and now was with the Greenes. Despite their assurances that the old lady was no burden, her older brother felt obliged to send for her. William had informed his father that he had invited Aunt Jane to come to Perth Amboy. Benjamin said that that might be a safer retreat than Philadelphia, but "God only knows," he told her.

It was hard to know where one might be safe. Two days after he had left home, his Committee of Safety uncovered a plot to occupy the city. They arrested a Dr. John Kearsley and others who had written to Lord Dartmouth promising to raise a loyalist army man for man upon the appearance of five thousand British regulars. Word of the treachery reached Franklin only days before his leaving Cambridge. He wrote hurriedly to Bache that he had heard of the Philadelphia plot but had no doubt of the citizens' ability to defend the city bravely in the most difficult times.

These were indeed trying times. His postscript to Bache dated October 24 states his plan to set out the next day, as well as the frightening news of the burning of Falmouth in Casco Bay, Maine, and the warning that from England orders had come "to burn, ravage and destroy all the Sea Coast; such is the government of the best of princes," wrote Franklin, sarcastically. He gave his son-in-law instructions for the care of Sally and the children, as well as for safeguarding the account books and writings stored in trunks in his library, in case the people of Philadelphia should see fit to evacuate their city in order best to defend it.

Such was his state of mind on October 26 when he set out in his carriage to meet Jane Mecum at the Greenes'. When Franklin was middle-aged he had been more than a little in love with the beautiful Catharine Ray. He had met the girl at his brother John's home outside Boston, where she was visiting in 1755, and the two remained devoted friends. What such devotion meant in those days is clear from the care they took of each other's kin. The Greene house, ten miles south of Providence, had become a sanctuary for Boston refugees including Jane and her granddaughter Jenny Flag, a charming and industrious seamstress of eighteen. Jenny had befriended the Greenes' daughter and wanted to remain in the Greenes' care; in return, Franklin agreed to take ten-year-old Ray Greene with him to Philadelphia and oversee his education.

As fond as he was of the Greenes, Franklin did not linger in Warwick. The carriage bearing Franklin, his sister Jane, and the Greene boy rolled south along the Lower Post Road at the end of October, through Wethersfield, New Haven, and Bridgeport en route to the crossing at Kingsbridge into New Jersey. Jane told Catharine Greene that the carriage was comfortable and the journey pleasant. "My dear brother's conversation was more than an equivalent to all the fine weather imaginable."

That conversation during ten days' journey would not have gotten far, as the carriage lurched along the road in view of Long Island Sound, without referring to Franklin's son. Jane had known her nephew since he was nineteen, when he had traveled to Boston with a letter from his father entrusting the young soldier to her motherly care and wisdom. This had been the beginning of a long and affectionate connection. Recently William had made her an offer of his hospitality in his home in Perth Amboy—for a visit, or a refuge if she liked. And now they were about to pass through that village on their way to the crossing at Brunswick bridge.

William had tried his father's patience with politics that flew in the face of common sense, endangering the whole family. Franklin had tried and failed to reason with him. Perhaps his aunt Jane's presence, her eyewitness account of the violence around Boston and the brutal occupation of her hometown—added to his father's report from the Continental Army—would move William to reconsider his options. She wanted to see him, and to meet the wife she had heard so much about.

So they drove to Proprietary House in the third week of November. Without this line in Mrs. Mecum's letter to Mrs. Greene we would not know that William and Elizabeth had received them at all, the visit was so discreet. She wrote: "I expected Master Ray would have given you some description of what he saw on the journey especially at Governor Franklin's house which was very magnificent." Ray did not write because he was under the weather, with a mild case of smallpox that did not show until the party arrived in Philadelphia.

During this brief visit the presence of the ladies would have smoothed any rough edges to the conversation between Benjamin Franklin and his rebellious son. But one can be sure that the older Franklins, brother and sister, with their worldly wisdom, knowledge of human frailty and suffering, and recognition of the importance of family loyalty, made the best case for William to step aside—out of the line of fire—and assume a dignified neutrality. It was their duty to do this, as it was his to listen respectfully. Their kind presence in itself, on that day in November, made a heartfelt plea.

What impression Jane Mecum made upon her nephew and his wife has not been recorded. But his father's intelligence concerning the army, as well as the measures that were being taken against traitors like Dr. Kearsley and Governor Skene, and how such men were led away in chains to jails in Connecticut, was frightening. Every issue of *The Pennsylvania Gazette* was crammed full of news of troop movements, skirmishes, and the organization of militia from South Carolina to Maine. The arraignment of private citizens for expressing their opinions was becoming routine, especially in New Jersey.

William certainly was on his guard. About this time he recommended to Elizabeth that she return to England, to her relatives there, or to Barbados. But she refused to leave him. It is also certain that his father feared for William, even as the carriage headed home. During the next month, from November 16, when the governor addressed his assembly in Burlington, until December 13, when his final speech appeared in the *Gazette,* Governor Franklin was the most controversial character in the mid-Atlantic region. His every word to the New Jersey legislators, and their passionate responses, were boldly published on the front page of the newspaper, in banner headlines above the military dispatches.

As the last royal governor conducting the king's business in America, William Franklin had become a public spectacle. In April, Governor John Murray of Virginia had fled in a British warship; Governor Thomas Gage had been recalled after the Battle of Bunker Hill in June. Governor William Tryon of New York took refuge in a man-of-war in October, while Jonathan Trumbull of Connecticut had happily adopted the cause of the Sons of Liberty. Governor John Penn, predictably, had assumed a docile neutrality, quietly deferring to the new provincial government. Dr. Franklin still hoped his son might learn from Penn's example, as he watched William's drama unfold in the pages of the newspaper he had founded.

During the weeks when Governor Franklin dominated the news, his father practically vanished from public view. His signature did not even appear on the printed notices from the Committee of Safety and no letters in his hand left Philadelphia from the time he returned from New England until December 9. Then he wrote to Charles-Guillaume-Frédéric Dumas, a Swiss philosopher living in The Hague. He did not post the letter until after December 12, because it had to be approved by his fellow members of the Secret Committee of Correspondence. The official purpose of this long letter, which began by thanking Dumas for various books, was to employ the cosmopolitan philosopher in the cause of liberty. Franklin asked Dumas to inquire discreetly at The Hague, which housed ambassadors from all the courts, if there were any that might favor "assistance or alliance, if we should allow for the one, or propose the other." This letter would serve as Dumas's credential. Enclosed was a check for a hundred pounds to defray expenses, with a promise that future services would be rewarded by the Continental Congress.

Meanwhile, Governor Franklin's conduct in Burlington was curious and disturbing. He was ill and so was Elizabeth. In all fairness there was almost nothing he could have said to his legislators then that would have pleased them. But what he did say in his first speech to the Assembly on November 16 was so offensive that his father must have known what would come of it.

After welcoming everyone to this meeting to conduct public business, and promising he would not endanger the harmony of their session by persisting in unwelcome arguments for peace, he read the latest message from the king. "His Majesty laments to find his subjects in America so lost to their own true interest, as neither to accept the resolution of the House of Commons of the 20th of February, nor make it the basis of a negotiation." As they chose to revolt, His Majesty had decided to take vigorous measures by sea and land "to reduce his rebellious subjects to obedience." Every man in that courthouse knew what this meant. "His Majesty's squadrons in America have orders to proceed . . . against such of the sea-port towns and places, being accessible to the King's ships, as shall offer violence to the King's officers," such as Governor Franklin—and against any town where troops had been raised.

It would have been awkward enough if William had simply read the message. But then he went on, as if in response to his father's warnings, to express concern for his own safety: The times were in such mad disorder, he confessed, that if he had followed the advice of his best friends, he would already have sought asylum on one of the king's ships, as Murray and Tryon had done. The governor congratulated himself, his assembly, and his province for his risky decision to remain here, because he loved them and they had shown him so much respect and affection for a decade. Should he abandon his province now, it would prove that the fear of violence was well grounded, and thus would subject New Jersey to punishment as being in actual rebellion.

"Let me therefore, gentlemen, entreat you to exert your influence," he told them, so that the people "may not, by any action of theirs, give cause for the bringing of calamities on the province."

He was matching them threat for threat. "No advantage," he continued, "can possibly result from the seizing, confinement or ill treatment of officers" that would be worth the calamity it would call down upon their colony. At last he begged them, if they were of a different opinion, and could not guarantee his safety, to let him know in plain open language that could not be misunderstood.

This speech was printed as the lead column on the front page of the *Gazette* on November 22, 1775. That week, the Continental Congress formally established an American navy and passed a resolution authorizing the seizure of British vessels—warships and transports as well. Governor Franklin had good reason to fear for his safety, on land and sea.

HE HAD ONE LAST stratagem and put his faith in it five days later. His Majesty had approved bills of credit for £100,000, a grant the Council and Assembly had been requesting for a decade. The king had finally consented, asking that the money be used to increase the salaries of civil servants and to build a hall for the legislature, and roads and bridges. It came, naturally, as "evidence of His Majesty's gracious inclination to give them *every indulgence*" when they were inclined to think the worst of him.

Suddenly the Assembly thought so well of King George that they formed a committee to express their feelings to him in a separate petition—at Franklin's request. They asked the king to interpose to prevent bloodshed, and proclaimed their desire to restore harmony with England upon constitutional principles. The same day, November 28, the Assembly resolved that their delegates to the Continental Congress would not cast any votes that would separate their colony from England.

Governor Franklin was jubilant.

His elation did not last very long. While he waited for the petition to the king to be drafted, Congress sent three of its most forceful leaders to Burlington: John Dickinson, George Wythe, and John Jay. Privately William begged his friends not to allow these intruders to speak, but to no avail. Dickinson announced that colonial forces had subdued Canada and soon France would lend its support. Wythe and Jay spoke in their turn, calling Lord North's resolution a ploy for reducing their union to a "rope of sand." So the Assembly voted against sending the new petition, and tabled the resolution to muzzle their delegates to the congress.

Meanwhile, Franklin's Council—what was left of it—turned against him. This opera played out in apologies and accusations that passed between the Council and the governor stemming from his first speech, in which he had expressed fear for his safety. In a "Humble Address to His Excellency" on November 25, the members said they were sorry that, despite their assurances, "Your Excellency expresses some degree of apprehension as to the safety of your own person and the persons of other officers of the Crown." They promised they were dedicated to peace, Great Britain, and constitutional government. Franklin replied he was much obliged for their words, but he was aware of the congress's resolutions and their effects on other governors, and even Crown officers in New Jersey (such as Lord Stirling). Men who have "done their duty here must of course have *some* reason to expect the same fate with those who have done their duty elsewhere." What he meant was that an official might choose safety out of cowardice, or face danger honorably; but one would be a fool to think the governor's present situation here was not fraught with danger.

The Speaker of the House took offense. And on November 29, he spoke for the legislators, protesting they were innocent and ignorant of any threats to the governor's safety. Franklin replied that their surprise that anyone would advise him to seek asylum when so many governors had been forced to do the same was unbelievable. Then every word of this quarrel was published on the front page of *The Pennsylvania Gazette*. On December 4, the Council, indignant, defended its honor: "Your reply, Sir, though rather darkly penned, contains, we apprehend, some reflections and innuendos, which our consciences tell us we do not deserve." How could he suggest that any one of them had left office out of cowardice or for a commission in the militia? They would have thought he would congratulate them on the serenity that still existed here rather than dampening their hopes with veiled threats.

His father, or his aunt Jane, reading these words in the paper on December 13, would have agreed that if William meant to continue as governor there, it would have been wise of him to congratulate them on the degree of serenity that continued in New Jersey. He did not. Whether he was ill, confused, or frightened, he continued on his collision course. He would have the last word today, even if it were the last word of his anyone would ever read in Philadelphia.

He did not apologize. Reaffirming everything he had said before, he defended himself against their willful insistence on misunderstanding him. Then he could not resist bringing up Lord Stirling, that traitor and aspiring general, for special censure, saying, "That *some* have actually departed from their line of duty, from some motives or other, is a matter too publicly known to justify any attempt at concealment."

In closing, the governor asserted his right to his own opinion and his duty to express it. If they only knew the pains he had taken privately to avoid this public quarrel, no one could mistake his sincerity. "But of this circumstance, though well known to some of your members, you, as a body, may, perhaps with specious propriety, declare yourselves 'totally ignorant.'"

That was Governor Franklin's last word to them as an official body.

CHAPTER 14

The Reckoning, 1776

BAYBERRY CANDLES FLICKERED IN the windows of the finer houses from Perth Amboy to Philadelphia, and the dining tables and chimneypieces were trimmed with holly and fragrant pine branches. From Christmas Day until Twelfth Night, January 6, the Christians of the mid-Atlantic colonies held banquets and balls and fox hunts. A French traveler recalled a great deal of carousing, and that in one home he saw several fiddlers, a jester, a tightrope walker, and a tumbling acrobat.

December 25 itself was set aside for prayer and quiet dining. But Twelfth Night was a hell-bender. An English visitor in 1775 described a ball at which the fiddles and squeezebox played all night. "About 37 ladies dressed and powdered to the like, some of them very handsome . . . all of them fond of dancing. . . . Betwixt the country dancers they have what I call everlasting jigs. A couple gets up, and begins to dance a jig (to some Negro tune), others comes and cuts them out . . . as long as the fiddler can play." It appeared more like some Bacchanalian dance than one you might expect in polite company. The old, the young, mothers with children bouncing on their knees, "widows, maids, and girls come promiscuously to these assemblies which usually continue til morning." The Englishman noted there was rum punch, Madeira, a cold supper, coffee, and chocolate, but no tea. Tea was under embargo. Exhausted, he went home after two, but he heard the next day that most of the company stayed and got drunk, and a fight broke out before dawn.

THE DAY AFTER TWELFTH Night, Lord Stirling, aka Colonel William Alexander, in charge of all provincial forces in New Jersey, sent a troop of militia to Perth Amboy. At noon on Sunday, as church bells chimed in the cold, the soldiers rode in, under command of Lieutenant Colonel William Winds, to arrest Governor William Franklin and Speaker Cortlandt Skinner, Stephen's older brother.

Knowing that certain letters of his had been intercepted, Franklin suspected what was afoot. So did Skinner, who had fled after Twelfth Night to the safety of a man-of-war in New York harbor. Franklin had decided to stand his ground. The soldiers milled about between the barracks and the taverns all that day and evening awaiting orders how to proceed. They were probably hoping the governor would make a break for it so they could catch him in flight, but he did not stir from the mansion.

He watched the streets from an upstairs dormer and did the best he could to calm his wife. They went to bed without hearing from anyone at the barracks, and rested until after midnight. About two o'clock in the morning they were startled awake by pounding on the front door, the sound of sword pommels or rifle butts fit to splinter the boards of solid chestnut. The racket so alarmed Elizabeth, William later recalled, "I was not without apprehensions of her dying with the fright." It was terrorism in its purest distillation, premeditated, cruel, and vengeful; Lord Stirling had given specific instructions to his soldiers as to how and when to go about it.

William leapt out of bed and went to the window. In the light of the waning moon he could see that armed men had surrounded his house, and told his servant Thomas to answer the door. A soldier handed him a letter, saying that it came from Colonel Winds and was to be answered immediately. Thomas struck a light and gave his master the letter, which asked for the governor's assurance that he would not leave New Jersey until he was notified of "the will and pleasure of the Continental Congress." By lamplight William scribbled his reply. He had no intention of leaving the province, and would not unless he was compelled by violence. To act otherwise would be inconsistent with his duties to the Assembly and his regard for the good people of New Jersey.

The day after New Year's, 1776, Congress had passed a resolution with regard to any faithless Americans who "regardless of their duty to their Creator, their country, and posterity, have taken part with our oppressors . . . by traducing the conduct and principles of the friends of American liberty. . . . *Resolved:* That it be recommended to the different Assemblies, committees in the *United Colonies*" immediately to restrain such villains. Congress believed that they ought to be disarmed and arrested.

On receiving this news, Lord Stirling ordered that the governor's mail be intercepted. Stirling's headquarters was in Elizabethtown, ten miles to the north, so he was just in time to seize William's letter of January 5 en route to New York, a report to Colonial Secretary Dartmouth marked "Secret and Confidential." This included an account of a meeting of the legislature, and a report on the state of affairs in New Jersey. Franklin said he still believed the majority were opposed to independence and would not support a governor or general who wanted it; yet he sensed a clear danger. "The design will be carried on by such degrees and under such pretence, as not to be perceived by the people in general until too late." He enclosed newspapers full of rebel "propaganda." This would have been enough to indict him. But there were also reports of proceedings in the congress, as well as news about a band of Tories in the hills of Sussex County arming for defense.

There was no doubt in Stirling's mind that these papers proved that William Franklin was violating the principles of the friends of American liberty. When William heard that the packet had been seized, he wrote another note to Dartmouth predicting that this mishap would create a great noise and likely result in his arrest. Despite William's assurance that he would not quit the province, Colonel Winds kept a guard of sentinels around Proprietary House until dawn, then all were dismissed except one sentry who kept watch at the front gate. Servants were allowed to come and go. One told William that he had overheard two officers saying they meant to seize the governor and shut him up in the barracks until the will of the congress should be known.

What happened next is a study in confusion of command as well as a failure of resolve on the part of Lord Stirling to make an example of the Tory governor. Although Stirling has not yet appeared, it is important to describe William's former friend at this point. Of average height, Stirling had a noble bearing and features, a high forehead, large, dark eyes, and a small mouth with a prominent lower lip. What was memorable was the incongruity of the strong and weak sides of his face; turning, he could suddenly look like a different man.

Lord Stirling's hatred of Governor Franklin had gotten the better of his judgment. Also, he had reckoned without considering his enemy's courage and conviction, as well as the good character of the officer in charge, William Winds. Colonel Winds, fifty, was a very large, loud, and impulsive gentleman farmer from Dover, a veteran of the French wars; he was also a God-fearing Presbyterian, a pillar of the Rockaway Church. The squire truly felt sorry when he learned that his soldiers had frightened poor Mrs. Franklin out of her wits with their banging on the door in the night. It made him question the motives of his superior officer.

Winds sent words of apology to William via a servant, saying he had been obeying a strict order to deliver the letter at that hour. His men had behaved rudely. Nonetheless, the next day, January 9, he requested a formal letter of parole from Franklin to give his word and honor not to leave the province until further orders from the congress. Franklin refused. He wrote to the colonel warning him that if he did not remove the guards from his house and leave him and his wife in peace, he would be opening himself to a charge of treason. Franklin had already promised he was not going anywhere. Furthermore, he would continue to represent the king. When Winds heard all of this he was not sure what to do next, so he sent a rider to Elizabethtown to ask Stirling his opinion.

Lord Stirling sent orders then to seize William Franklin by whatever force was required and transport him under a strong guard to Elizabethtown. There he would stay in the lawmaker Elias Boudinot's home, where Stirling meant to detain him until receiving direction from the congress as to what he ought to do with him. Franklin had known Boudinot his whole life and might feel safe there.

One hundred soldiers led by four officers rode up from the Amboy barracks to escort the governor, in his carriage, to Elizabethtown. Upstairs he was gathering some clothing and personal articles and trying to reassure his wife all would be well—a pathetic scene, because by now Elizabeth was in hysterics. Their old friend Stephen Skinner stood by, intending to go with Franklin as a witness to his arraignment before Colonel Alexander.

Meanwhile, their neighbor Chief Justice Frederick Smyth had been studying the situation, and he was worried. Upon hearing that Governor Franklin had been taken prisoner, the judge had penned a letter of protest to Colonel Winds at the barracks. He warned him of the dire consequences—to the province as a whole and to this town in particular—if one of the king's warships stationed in New York Harbor should demand the governor's person. He begged Winds to countermand the order to transport Franklin to Elizabethtown.

While Colonel Winds was thinking it over, Smyth went to the governor's mansion to see how things stood, to measure William's state of mind, and talk to the officers. He told them the same things he had told the colonel, and that Winds was considering the matter. He asked them to take no further action until he returned from the barracks, where he was now going in order to confer with their commander. William was the picture of cool indignation, noting he was perfectly indifferent at this juncture. Telling Judge Smyth he preferred not to leave home, he called it an equal offense to be under arrest in his house or in Elizabethtown. The damage was done. They had come with an armed guard to take him prisoner. Determined to ask no favors he would not interfere in the matter. Given fifteen minutes' notice he would leave whenever they liked. "You may force me," he declared, "but you shall never frighten me out of my Province."

Chief Justice Smyth went up to the barracks and was gone for more than an hour. The lieutenants, thinking it unlikely that Winds would have any success in revoking Lord Stirling's orders, grew restless as the winter day drew to its end. They decided to proceed as they had been told. William himself was unwell and weary, and he wished to get going if they were to undertake this journey in the freezing cold. The coach stood at the door of the mansion, and the soldiers ordered him and Mr. Skinner to step inside.

The horses drawing the coach, surrounded by cavalry, had not gone more than a few hundred yards up High Street when they met Judge Smyth and an officer coming down Dock Street from the barracks. Signaling for the horsemen to stop, the officer announced that Colonel Winds had consented for Governor Franklin to remain in his house. The chief justice was going alone to Elizabethtown to protest the impropriety of removing Governor Franklin, and to persuade Lord Stirling to recall his orders.

William Franklin later wrote, "I was accordingly brought back to my house, where Winds soon after came," in a posture of apology, or humility in any case, for Franklin always spoke of him with respect. There was no reason for Winds to call upon the governor in his home apart from courtesy. He had come to tell him about his conversation with their friend Smyth, and to let Governor and Mrs. Franklin know that he was doing everything in his power to leave them in peace. As to sending an embassy to Lord Stirling, Governor Franklin replied, with dignity, that he wanted them to remember that "it was a matter entirely between themselves; . . . I considered myself as in illegal confinement, and should therefore neither approve nor disapprove the measures."

Judge Smyth's arguments before Colonel Alexander (Lord Stirling) must have been very persuasive. Returning from Elizabethtown the next day he reported to Colonel Winds, who immediately removed the guards from Propriety House. "And I have continued unmolested ever since," Franklin wrote to Lord Germain, the new British secretary of state, on March 28. He had heard that many members of the congress had not approved of Lord Stirling's conduct in the affair, although they did not officially censure him.

From his seat in the congress, Benjamin Franklin was aware of all that was going on in relation to his son's arrest. Dr. Franklin's activities by this time had become so important, and so secret, that his name rarely appeared in the official minutes. On November 29, he had been appointed chair of the Committee of Secret Correspondence— officially to establish a network of foreign allies and spies, but with even more clandestine goals in handling arms, gunpowder, prisoners, and counterespionage. Much of this activity was so covert that there is no detailed record of it. The Continental Congress had made him the head of America's first central intelligence agency.

He became a sphinxlike figure in the State House. But he was there almost every day. He heard the letters from Stirling and the interchange between William and Colonel Winds as the reports were read aloud. On November 9 they had received the intercepted letter to Lord Germain, and the next day they read Stirling's letter of intent to detain the governor in Elizabethtown. Evidently, on the record, the congress did not interfere with the colonel's handling of the matter—although they did send a strong signal in ordering the arrest of Cortlandt Skinner. Not until January 15 did they appoint a committee to consider what to do about William Franklin. Chaired by the New Jersey patriot William Livingston, whom Governor Franklin had condemned as a "Demogogue [sic] of Faction," the committee did nothing, and the irksome business died there.

So William was allowed to live in peace, as much as he could under an informal house arrest in Perth Amboy. His wife had not recovered from the shock. On January 22, Franklin wrote to Temple that Elizabeth's nerves were so on edge that the least sudden noise would throw her into hysterics; he was afraid that another such alarm would kill her. They were disappointed that no one in the family had inquired about the recent ordeal; there was no sign that any of them knew about it. When Temple received the letter from his father he replied at once, apologizing for his ignorance and expressing his sympathy. There had been no mention of the arrest in the Franklin-Bache household. William could hardly believe that any of their friends or family could have been ignorant of what everyone was talking about—or he would have informed them at once.

Although Benjamin Franklin's communication with his son had come to an end, they remained connected through Temple, and one other concern, namely, the everlasting machinations of the land grant companies—Grand Ohio, Walpole, Indiana, and the rest. William seems not to have known, but just after Christmas his father attended a meeting of shareholders and lawyers in Philadelphia. Somehow the promoters in London had secured rights to sell parcels of land in the Indiana Company upon its being converted into a joint stock enterprise. Benjamin owned none of it, but William was entitled to one-twentieth of the stock in the reorganized company. His father represented his interests at that meeting and others in the new year, and he signed documents as William's agent. When the legal bills came due, Franklin paid his son's share. Again, there is no evidence that William knew of this. If Benjamin held a power of attorney, there is no record of it. Later events suggest that by protecting William's share, his father was acting in the interest of the whole family and not of William alone.

William Franklin had isolated himself. Even his best friend, the gentleman bachelor Judge Frederick Smyth, who was said to be Franklin's first mate on the ship of state, feared that the captain had lost his bearings. Smyth was one of many loyalists who preserved a dignified neutrality throughout the war. He did not understand or support the extremity of William's position. Sally Bache, as fond as she was of her brother and sister-in-law, was unable to go and see them under the circumstances. She had a new baby. Writing to Elizabeth soon after hearing the distressing news from Temple, she expressed her deep concern. Reporting on the birth and christening of her daughter Sarah, she promised she would visit just as soon as her father or husband should see fit to escort her. Elizabeth's response, penned on February 5, is moving, and a rare reflection of that lady's character:

> Dear Sister:
>
> Your favor of the 30th of last month was as welcome as it was unexpected, for I had long since despaired of the pleasure of a letter from you; and I confess it gave me many hours concern; for as I have no relations or connections of my own in this country and but few that I look on as friends, I was very unwilling to lose one who held first place in my affections and esteem; but I am very glad to find that your neglect was rather owing to accident than design.

The third pregnancy had been difficult. And the pressure on the men as officials in a tumultuous time—Bache was Franklin's deputy in the American postal service—had been overwhelming. Elizabeth continued:

> My thanks for your kind concern for me. I have, indeed, suffered a good deal of late and have been so thoroughly frightened that I believe I shall never recover my strength or spirits. Your brother and I have been scandalously treated, but it is too long a story to relate now; but when I have the pleasure of seeing you, will acquaint you with all the circumstances.

Much of her letter offers congratulations, greetings to the family including Aunt Jane, and special thanks for the honor of being named the baby's godmother. But the last passage yields to sorrow: "Everything is now changed; and instead of those joyous, social evenings we used to pass with each other, we only meet now to condole together over our wretched situation. But I will stop my pen lest I should infect you with vapours and dejection of spirits."

ELIZABETH AND WILLIAM GOT most of their family news from their regular correspondence with Temple. William's letters express his ongoing affection for his father; after all, the decision to break off relations had been one-sided. In every letter he sends his regards to his honored father and inquires after his health. William understood that the pressure of current affairs was more than most men could bear. Ben Franklin was no ordinary man, but even he admitted to fatigue and doubts about his usually robust health. He stopped attending meetings of the Pennsylvania Assembly in the new year, resigning on February 26, pleading frailty, although he had not quit his many other duties to the Continental Congress. And on February 15, the congress appointed him one of the commissioners to Canada, which would require a grueling journey to Montreal in late winter. Alarmed, William wrote to Temple on March 14 that if he had thought it would do any good, he would have tried to dissuade him from it, at his age, and in the middle of winter.

Sixteen-year-old Temple was frightened of staying in Philadelphia while his grandfather was gone. The city was overwrought. As the grandson of America's most famous patriot and the bastard son of its most notorious Tory, he faced taunting and abuse wherever he turned. He would not denounce his father, yet, living in a rebel household and attending a liberal college, he somehow had to mediate or rise above the controversy. William agreed that Temple's situation would not be easy in his grandfather's absence, "but let it not be your fault if it is not. However others may behave to you, be careful that your conduct is as polite, affectionate and respectful as possible."

So Grandfather gave his consent for Temple to visit Perth Amboy while he was away in Canada, during the spring break in April, and this prospect came as a relief. The letters between Temple and William that winter were affectionate and even collegial. Temple sent his father books and newspapers, Thomas Paine's *Common Sense* in a new edition, and the Connecticut poet John Trumbull's mock epic *McFingal.* This work was all the rage in Philadelphia, hot off the press there, a parodic dialogue between a Scottish loyalist and a patriot based upon John Adams. William needed a good laugh and said he was grateful, for he appreciated good writing on either side of a question. Trumbull was not a Tory, but William appreciated his wit.

William was very interested in his son's education, everything from mathematics and language studies to athletics. Short on cash, he still sent Temple money for fencing lessons, and he advised him to improve his horsemanship. The only apparent friction between them was over money. William had just so much to send the Baches to cover the boy's personal expenses, and when Temple ran out, time and again, Mr. Bache would not give him any more. William was obliged to bail him out, and with the check would come a scolding.

This time Temple's visit with his father and stepmother could not have been as pleasant as before. It is the rare youth who does not harbor some rebellious impulses toward his father; he knew very well that those books and pamphlets he had been sending the governor were not harmonious with his opinions. William still believed that most of his countrymen were opposed to independence, and that Thomas Paine's earth-shaking revolutionary pamphlet *Common Sense,* published in January, 1776, would backfire.

On March 28, Governor Franklin wrote again to Lord Germain. He reported that the committee bound for Canada to win the French over to the American side had just passed through Woodbridge, a town two miles north of Amboy on the Lower Post Road. The party included Dr. Franklin and three men from Maryland—Samuel Chase, Charles Carroll, a wealthy influential Catholic, and John Carroll, a priest. It almost certainly included Temple Franklin, because they first passed through Amboy. Naming his father among these official traitors was an unnecessary and even resentful gesture. Perhaps William felt slighted. It would not have been prudent for these gentlemen to visit the governor of New Jersey in house arrest, and they did not. The boy got out of their coach with his portmanteau, bade his grandfather goodbye, and made his way to his father's house on the hill.

Temple did not stay in Perth Amboy very long. His stepmother was not at her best, after her ordeal; and as the early flowers filled the air with pollen, her breath came with difficulty. The governor, too, was ill. He went over Temple's accounts with him, reiterated his expectations, and pointed out his son had the God-given qualities of diligence and prudence; he trusted him to improve. Before returning to Philadelphia on April 6, Temple had ten weeks' allowance from his father.

Before the end of April the money was all spent and William was exasperated. On May 8, he wrote the prodigal son that he "did not imagine (tho' I was willing to make the experiment) that you had prudence enough to make it hold out for the time it ought to have lasted." Having been given every necessity, Temple could only want money for trifles. "I cannot afford you money to fool away, nor would I if I could," William wrote, as surely this would lead to excesses that would ruin the boy's constitution.

This lecture made Temple so angry he did not respond until May 25. In his defense he wrote that he had purchased many items for his father and stepmother for which he had yet to be reimbursed: bottled mustard and Germantown brown-thread stockings (not exactly necessities); for Elizabeth, ruffles and edgings and lace borders from the dressmaker; indigo, snuff, and from the chemist pearl dentifrice, and an elixir for her asthma. William asked for an accounting to settle the matter, requesting at the same time a dozen copies of Charles Inglis's *The True Interest of America,* a new pamphlet attacking Paine's *Common Sense,* which he must send without anyone else's knowledge.

Temple seems to have gone so far in honoring his father's request as to avoid the bookshop altogether. His grandfather had returned from Canada on May 30, sick. As he and Uncle Richard Bache ran the postal service, it would not be at all seemly for young Franklin to be shipping multiple copies of a Tory pamphlet to his father in New Jersey.

William waited ten days before writing, "If you are not more punctual in obeying my orders, I must find some person who will." He would regret this petulant note almost as soon as he sent it, but he and his wife had been under an intolerable strain. Every newspaper that passed through the door bore a message of doom. The Third Provincial Congress had convened in New Brunswick, raising troops, issuing bills of credit, and otherwise managing the colony as if Governor Franklin did not exist. Many of his friends were there, including Francis Hopkinson and the lawyer Jonathan Deare, who was a vestryman at St. Peter's Church across the road. After a year of warfare, the Continental Congress was advising the provincial conventions to replace the royal governments as suited their constituents.

At the end of May the defiant Governor Franklin called for a meeting of his General Assembly in Perth Amboy on June 20, announcing he had news of another peace commission from Lord Germain: Agents were under sail from England to negotiate the longed-for reconciliation. For William's enemies, and many of his friends, this order was the last straw. On June 11, the newly elected delegates of the New Jersey Congress convened in Burlington chose Samuel Tucker as president and William Patterson as secretary. Four days later they passed three resolutions, 38 votes to 11, concerning William Franklin, Esquire: He had acted in contempt of the congress's resolutions by convening the old assembly; he had shown himself to be an enemy of the country's liberties, so measures must be taken to secure his person; and he would receive no more salary.

This time they did not send the good-hearted Squire Winds to call upon the governor and his lady. It was clearly a job for a younger, more severe officer. Nathaniel Heard from Woodbridge, a wealthy land-owner, had been made a colonel of militia in the First Regiment of Middlesex. Congress expressed confidence in his zeal and sagacity. In January, Colonel Heard had led a detachment of five hundred minute-men against a battalion of Tories in Queens County, Long Island. They disarmed the loyalists, took nineteen prisoners, seized a thousand mus-kets, and compelled 319 men to swear allegiance to the Continental Congress. His deeds inspired some doggerel in his memory composed by the bitter loyalists to the tune of "Yankee Doodle":

Colonel Heard has come to town
In all his pride and glory;
And when he dies he'll go to Hell
For robbing of the Tory.

After a similar campaign in Staten Island, Heard took over the royal barracks in Perth Amboy, across town from the governor's man-sion.

There, on Sunday the sixteenth, Colonel Heard received the Pro-vincial Congress's orders to execute their resolves with regard to Gov-ernor Franklin, and that this "be conducted with all the delicacy and tenderness with which the nature of the business can possibly admit." For tenderness he invited Jonathan Deare, Franklin's fellow parish-ioner at St. Peter's, to go along with him to call upon the governor. They were delicate enough to wait for the Lord's Day to pass. But it was no less nerve-racking for Elizabeth and her husband, both of them frightened and ill, to hear the knocking at the door on Monday morn-ing and behold the figure of Nathaniel Heard, the infamous scourge of Tories.

As a Christian neighbor and a fellow lawyer, Major Deare may have come to reason with William Franklin. But Franklin wasn't having any of it. He coldly asked them their business. The colonel handed him a copy of the proceedings in the congress concerning his offenses and the measures to be taken against him; they also showed him a form of parole with blank spaces for his signature and the date. The governor read these pages, nearly blind with fury. He cried out, he raged at these impertinent messengers in a storm of invective that they would try, and fail, to record.

"To be represented as an *Enemy to the liberties of my country* (one of the worst characters) merely for doing my duty in calling a meeting of the legal representatives of the people!" This was, he recalled, an insult fit to arouse indignation in any man. The governor did not curb his emotions. Refusing to sign the parole, which gave him a choice of detention in Princeton, Bordentown, or his own farm on Rancocas Creek, he rejected it and wished the lot of rebels in hell. He threatened Heard in particular if he continued to harass him in his own home, exclaiming, according to the colonel's recollection: "It is *your* turn now, but it will be *mine* another day!"

So the colonel turned on his heel and bade the governor good morning, Major Deare followed him out the door, and William went upstairs to comfort his wife. The Passaic waterfalls depicted in the stair hall, meant to evoke the beauty and gracious bounty of the New World, now rushed and roiled violently around him.

COLONEL NATHANIEL HEARD RETURNED to the royal barracks on the edge of town, and called up sixty soldiers to march down to the governor's mansion, surround it, and stand guard while he stayed behind to write a letter to the Provincial Congress. He informed President Tucker that he had asked the governor to sign the parole, which he refused to do, instead forbidding Heard, at his own peril, to carry out his orders. Expecting no change of heart, the colonel requested further instructions as soon as possible.

Heard's letter was read aloud in Burlington on Tuesday the seventeenth, and the congress immediately ordered him to bring Governor Franklin hither, under whatever guard he judged sufficient. Next they wrote to John Hancock, president of the Continental Congress, officially notifying him of what was going on in Perth Amboy. They asked, rhetorically, if it would not be best for the United Colonies if this Franklin were transported to some other colony, such as Connecticut, where he would be less capable of doing mischief than here in New Jersey. They would be happy to receive any advice the congress should think proper to give.

When this letter arrived on John Hancock's desk, the father of the accused traitor was not in his chair in the State House. He was home in bed recovering from the agonies of gout and pleurisy. The journey to and from Canada, on the failed expedition to court the French, had nearly killed him. On June 21, he wrote to George Washington that his gout was so severe it had kept him from congress and society ever since the general's departure on June 4, so that he knew very little of what was going on in the world. He had missed the reading of the letter from Burlington, and the congress's orders to go ahead and interrogate his son. They told the New Jersey delegates to question William, and if they believed he ought to be confined to say so, and then the congress would designate the place of confinement.

While Colonel Heard was waiting, he increased the security around the governor's mansion. Toward sundown he replaced the armed sentries with bombardiers (artillerymen), an infamously noisy gang. They kept up such a racket in the yard that the Franklins could not rest. The next day both were in need of the doctor, but no one was allowed to visit the house, neither physician, minister, nor friend. Servants were permitted to pass, but only in the presence of armed guards.

William Franklin sat at his desk and wrote an eloquent letter to the legitimate Council and Assembly of New Jersey pleading his case, appealing to them and every soul in the province to vouch that "in no one instance have I ever manifested the least inimical disposition toward this colony." The idea that his summoning of the Assembly was in violation of the orders of the congress was absurd. Anyone who read their letter of resolve could see the congress had recommended that the assemblies make new governments *where no governments sufficient to the exigencies of their affairs existed.* This was not the case in New Jersey! Where the governor had stepped aside, or neglected to call his assembly, of course things were different. But here, where they could have met, where the Provincial Congress prevented it, it was *they* who were in contempt, who were *Enemies to the Liberties of the People,* and not he.

And so the governor went on, under arrest, dipping his quill in gall.

How could these blackguards stop his salary? "An instance of mean-ness which I never expected to have experienced from any body of men in New Jersey." The money had hardly been enough to support the dignity of the office and they had been about to increase it. Now "a body of men are got together who . . . think to make a merit with the people of robbing me of even a pittance . . . which they have no more right to deprive me of, than to take my money out of my pocket book."

Finally he appealed to the best of them to defend their constitution, and avoid the traps of Independence and Republicanism that had been laid for them. "You can never place yourself in a happier situation than in your ancient constitutional dependency on Great Britain," he wrote. He admitted that his was not the language of the times. "But it is bet-ter, it is honest truth flowing from a heart that is ready to shed its best blood for this country. A real patriot can seldom or ever speak popular language. A false one will never suffer himself to speak anything else."

A knock came at the door. It was Colonel Heard and Major Deare come to get the real patriot and take him to Burlington. Under whose orders? Franklin inquired. The Continental Congress? That very con-gress indeed, Heard replied. And disagreeable orders, but they must be obeyed. No man, the governor advised, was obliged to obey illegal orders. Yet Heard and Deare stood firm while Franklin fumed and argued and warned the colonel once again that he would be held ac-countable, personally, for his treason.

At length Colonel Heard agreed to give the prisoner several hours to pack his bag, settle his affairs, and say goodbye to his wife. He then returned to the barracks. Elizabeth—with good reason fearing the worst—wept and cried out, clinging to her husband until Colonel Heard could be seen riding back up the winding path to the mansion, leading sixteen cavalry armed with rifles and bayonets, at three thirty that afternoon. It was a painful leave-taking, with Elizabeth "in a con-dition as affecting as can be imagined," William recalled.

So at last it had come to this. On a late afternoon in June near the solstice, when the farmers work late in the fields, Governor Franklin, surrounded by armed men on horseback, was led like a bear along the High Road through Middlesex County for all the world to see. Colo-nel Heard meant to make an example of him. To heighten his humiliation they chose the High Road, through Brunswick, Kingstown, Prince Town, and Trenton, the most populous areas, where crowds would be likely to gather and cheer the parade. They stopped for the night at a tavern in New Brunswick where William was guarded so closely in his room he was not even allowed outdoors to answer a call of nature but had to relieve himself in the chamber pot. The carousing of the sentries outside was so boisterous he hardly slept at all.

The next day, traveling the road to Burlington, news of the party ran ahead of them so that crowds gathered at every town and crossroad—Maidenhead, Crosswicks, Burdenstown—plowmen, yeomen, milkmaids, tradesmen, and mechanics in leather aprons all come to witness the disgrace of the Tory governor. By nightfall they were near Burlington. Passing Franklin's former residence, they made their way to a cottage owned by Josiah Franklin Davenport, Aunt Jane Mecum's nephew and William's cousin, a baker. There William would stay the night, under a heavy guard, awaiting his hearing. He was not allowed any visitors. He passed a fretful night, worrying about his wife, and with some physical ailment that needed a doctor's attention; it would be a week before one would be allowed to treat him.

At ten o'clock on Friday morning, June 21, two fellows from the New Jersey Congress came to call upon the governor at Davenport's. William told them he had no business with the congress and refused to leave his room. So the delegates went away, returning an hour later with twenty armed men. Unimpressed with the posse, Franklin demanded to see their orders. Handing him the paper, they allowed him to make a copy for his records. He protested the illegality of such instructions, repeating his refrain that the whole lot of them proceeded at their own peril. They proceeded anyway, removing him bodily from the cottage and into a coach, even though, as he recalled, many of the men looked dissatisfied with their employment.

So they paraded up Main Street in the spring light, past the market houses to the courthouse at the intersection of Broad Street, the grim procession of soldiers leading the coach, and the local officers following. In the Supreme Court chamber the congressmen, most of them well known to him, awaited the prisoner. As president, Samuel Tucker occupied the high seat. To his left sat the Reverend John Witherspoon,

President of Princeton. They invited him to be seated within the bar, a civility he afterward regretted accepting.

Tucker, humorously dubbed "the Governor" by his colleagues, stood at the head of the tribunal. The fifty-five-year-old wealthy landowner and Trenton merchant was known for finding his way into positions of power and holding them by sharp practices, speaking half-truths, and courting the winning side. The careful cut of his coat and sidelong glances let it be known that this former justice of the peace and high sheriff played to please those in the know. Tucker fixed his hooded eyes upon the captive and addressed him as Mr. Franklin—omitting his royal title.

When he had read the instructions from the Continental Congress, Tucker turned to his list of questions. Did Mr. Franklin call the Assembly to meet in June? No response. The silence was heavy. Franklin would answer no questions posed by an illegal assembly; he would not legitimize the goings-on by parleying with this group of men who had usurped the government. William Franklin recited his grievances: they had *falsely accused him* of being an enemy to the people; they had *imprisoned him* in his home; they had *robbed him* of his salary; and now they had *dragged him* before this unlawful court-martial. "Do as you please," Franklin said, "and make the most of it."

And so Samuel Tucker, with all the dignity at his command, continued with his list of questions. Did Franklin know of the congress's resolutions of May 15? By what authority did he call the Assembly? Why did he call them and what was his agenda? Tucker's voice resonated in the paneled chamber and made the long pauses seem to echo with mutual contempt. Had Franklin written letters to Parliament advising the use of force against the colonies? Another silence descended, so long and charged some of the hundred witnesses thought that it must break under the weight of their collective reprehension. But no, it went on and on as the clock ticked in the chamber and everyone fumed excepting the defendant upon whose lips the faintest of smiles had begun to bloom.

The president had one more question to ask. For reasons no one but the governor divined, this stirred him from his stillness. On June 17, had Franklin threatened Colonel Nathaniel Heard by saying "It is your turn now, but it will be mine another day"? Hearing those words Franklin bristled and leapt out of his chair. No one doubted it: This was the governor's arrogant voice precisely and the colonel had neither the need nor the ability to counterfeit it. Yet William, raging, objected to the accuracy, tone, or lack of context in the president's posing of the question. He demanded that he be faced by his accuser, Nathaniel Heard, in person—the man stood just outside the doors. He insisted that Colonel Heard enter and testify to his exact words.

William had not lost his sense of humor, and now he wanted to play. Like a brave man about to be hanged he knew he had little to lose in a battle of wits with Nathaniel Heard, and he meant to make a fool of him and the rest by making him repeat the ominous phrase over and over. The congress was of two minds whether to honor Franklin's request. "This occasioned a little debate among them, which I was sorry did not last longer, as it was the only amusement I had had for some days before," William recalled.

The Reverend John Knox Witherspoon was among those who wanted to let the colonel in, but his motion was denied. This Witherspoon, a Scot who had immigrated eight years earlier to become president of Princeton, was a powerhouse. Fifty-three years of age, bright-eyed and rosy-cheeked, the father of ten, Witherspoon was old enough to have fought the Catholic Jacobites at the Battle of Falkirk Muir in 1745. A Scottish nationalist and republican, he was naturally wary of the British Crown, and now had become an ardent friend of American liberty. In January he had proclaimed from the pulpit that it was not only a moral obligation for America to become independent, it was a duty to God.

William Franklin's words during the last minutes of the interrogation are nowhere recorded. He is reported to have made a brief speech, lofty, sarcastic, and patronizing, that summarized his complaints and reinforced his conviction that *his turn would come.* And Witherspoon, professor of moral philosophy, could stand it no longer. He shook his bewigged head in anger. President Tucker's restraint and decorum had been admirable in their way, but the situation and the prisoner's contempt cried out for a more passionate rebuke. Witherspoon, in his high Scots burr, condemned Franklin's pride, his vanity and impudence, his perverse pleasure in turning the occasion into a farce where all but he must appear ridiculous. The ex-governor "has made a speech every way worthy of his exalted illegitimate birth and refined grammar-school education." With sarcasm that equaled Franklin's, Reverend Witherspoon skewered him for his stiff-necked defense of the king, as the sworn enemy of American liberty. And that was the end of the hearing.

Franklin was escorted back to his cousin's house, while the congress voted him a malignant enemy to his country who should be imprisoned where it pleased the Continental Congress. Tucker sent the minutes of the meeting to John Hancock, calling the governor's behavior gross and insolent and begging the congress to take charge of him as soon as possible and send him away wherever they pleased, as long as it was outside New Jersey.

Under house arrest that weekend, and racked with fever, Franklin pondered his fate. Somehow he found the strength to keep writing to the extinct Council and Assembly of New Jersey. Certain now that the new congress's attack on him was personal rather than official, he observed their intent was thereby to intimidate every man in the province from resisting their evil proceedings. Just today they had threatened him with the news that they had discovered yet another letter he had sent to the ministry, even more compromising. And every effort he was making to publish his side of the story was frustrated by their intimidations. He had smuggled a letter of protest on the seventeenth to the king's printer, who promised to print it but then changed his mind, fearing for his safety. "Poor men," Franklin wrote. "They can no more bear the light of truth, it seems, than owls can endure the light of the sun!" He was pleading not for privileges as a royal official, but the fundamental rights of an Englishman.

He could do no more. "*Pro Rege & Patria* was the motto I assumed when I first commenced my political life and I am resolved to retain it till Death shall put an end to my mortal existence."

JOHN HANCOCK RECEIVED TUCKER'S report on Monday the twenty-fourth. Congress unanimously ordered that William Franklin be transported to Connecticut, where Governor Trumbull should mercifully parole him; and if the prisoner refused to honor the Connecticut parole, Trumbull should treat him exactly as the congress had resolved respecting prisoners. Benjamin Franklin had been absent from the meetings for three weeks due to illness; and while he must have known what was going on in the State House, it is unlikely that he returned for this regrettable proceeding on Monday morning. Tact, and consideration for his friends, would have prevented it.

The orders came to William at the Davenport cottage the next morning. He was so weak from fever he could hardly rise. From his bed he wrote to his son:

Burlington, June 25, 1776

Dear Billy,

I was ordered this day to set out on a guard to Princeton, on my way, I hear, to Connecticut; but as I had a pretty high fever on me, their Low Mightinesses with great difficulty were persuaded by some friends of mine to postpone my departure till tomorrow morning, when I must go (I suppose) dead or alive. Two of their members, who are doctors, came to examine me to see if my sickness was not feigned. Hypocrites always suspect hypocrisy in others.

God bless you, my dear boy; be dutiful and attentive to your grandfather to whom you owe great obligations. Love Mrs. Franklin, for she loves you, and will do all she can for you if I should never return more. If we survive the present storm, we may all meet and enjoy the sweets of peace with the greater relish.

I am ever your truly affectionate father

Wm. Franklin

On Wednesday morning the feeble governor, under a guard of twenty-three cavalry, set out in a closed coach on the road to Princeton and Brunswick, upon the two-hundred-mile journey to Lebanon,

Connecticut. Passing Amboy the second day, he desperately wanted to see his wife, but his escort would not permit it. He had second thoughts about his position and wondered if his martyrdom was inevitable.

As the party reached Hackensack on Sunday, June 30, Franklin begged for a day of rest. Seventeen miles from the northern New Jersey border, he confided to Thomas Kinney, captain of the light horse troops—a former sheriff unaccustomed to such responsibilities—that he wanted to write a letter to the Continental Congress. He told Kinney that he had decided he would consider signing a negotiated parole. This seemed like a reasonable request, so the captain permitted his prisoner to post this letter to Philadelphia. Then the governor begged the captain leave to write a few words to his grieving wife, and—not insensitive to the family's troubles—Kinney consented to this, too.

This second letter, to Elizabeth, got no farther than the Bergen Meadows before it was opened and read by the courier. Alarmed, he turned it over to the Essex Committee of Safety. Along with his endearments to his wife, Franklin's letter assured her that during the time he had gained in Hackensack, "something will turn up to make my removal improper, and at any rate, to gain time will be of advantage." The committee wasted no time forwarding this letter, along with a report of Captain Kinney's progress, to George Washington, who was at his headquarters across the Hudson River, not fifteen miles away.

The general was surprised, and he was angry. But those words cannot begin to describe the swirl of emotions he experienced that Sunday as he read the letters and prepared his response to the Essex Committee. Washington was a complex man, to say the least. The last time he had seen William Franklin was three years earlier. He had stopped in Burlington and dined with the governor and his wife before delivering his stepson Jack to King's College in New York. The general and the governor had known each other for most of their lives, having first met at Braddock's camp in Virginia in 1754. William was always good company and a generous host, lively in conversation, and the two had a great deal to talk about, including land speculation, farming, memories of the French wars, and the growing tension over the tea tax. That was six months before the Boston Tea Party. Since then it seemed the

world had gone off its axis; or, if you happened to be an American patriot, England had gone mad just as America was coming to its senses.

William Franklin, son of the man Washington most admired
among the older patriots, seemed to have gone the way of the most
irrational Tories. Washington wrote to the Essex Committee censuring Captain Kinney's conduct and ordering him to escort Mr. Franklin
to Connecticut at once. "The circumstances you represent, his letter to
his lady, and the whole complexion of the case, afford . . . full evidence,
that he means to escape if possible." As Governor Franklin is no friend
to the American cause, he continued, and the provincial congress has
ordered him to Connecticut for refusing to sign the parole, the general
believes that the Essex Committee of Safety should intercede. Order
the guard to proceed. If there is any danger of the prisoner's being rescued, or the guard malingering, the Essex Committee should appoint
its own escort and command them to carry out the intentions of the
congress. Enclosed was a letter of orders to the captain: "Set off immediately . . . delays are dangerous," and a poignant aside: "Governor
Franklin once had his choice, and chose Connecticut." He might easily
have stayed at home.

Under a full moon the armed caravan made haste along the Post
Road to Boston, rolling through Bridgeport and New Haven before
crossing the Connecticut River at Hartford. There the local paper reported: "Governor Franklin of New Jersey passed . . . on his way to
Governor Trumbull at Lebanon. . . . A noted Tory and ministerial tool,
he has been busy in perplexing the cause of liberty. . . . If his Excellency
escapes the vengeance of the people . . . his redemption will flow not
from his personal merit but from the esteem and veneration which this
country entertains for his honored father."

Another day's journey east, twenty miles through the Meshomasic
Hills along the Salmon River, led to the town of Lebanon, the military
nerve center of Connecticut. Upon an immense village green, in the
shadow of the white belfry of the First Congregational Church, stood
the modest wood frame home of Governor Jonathan Trumbull. Nearby
stood a shingled building with a gambrel roof, once the family store
but now known as the War Office. In this humble chamber old Gov-

ernor Trumbull, a patriot only four years younger than Ben Franklin, convened his Committee of Safety. This was July 4, 1776, the very day William's father was listening to the Declaration of Independence in the Philadelphia State House.

Trumbull was a gentleman in every sense, a Harvard graduate who had studied theology before going into business with his father and entering into politics in his thirties. As Governor Franklin was escorted into the unadorned room with its plain table and chairs, Trumbull was as aware as any man might have been of the sadness, and awkwardness, of their situation. It did not matter at all what Franklin thought of Governor Trumbull; but it mattered enormously what Jonathan Trumbull thought of Governor Franklin. Although Trumbull was twenty years older, toothless, bald, and wizened, he was, like William Franklin, a man of conscience and sensibility. They were equals in everything but fortune and power bestowed by an accident of history.

An advocate of the Golden Rule, the governor of Connecticut would treat the governor of New Jersey as he himself would be treated in his place. Jonathan Trumbull and his committee had strict orders as to how to deal with William Franklin. Nothing was left to their discretion but manners and grace. William wanted to talk to Jonathan man to man, and he wanted to present his case in a formal, recorded appeal. So Governor Trumbull allowed him to speak. Tired, ailing, and sore from days on the road, Franklin talked all morning, until the church bells chimed the noon hour. He had nothing to say that the reader has not heard before, except that the Connecticut committee had no legal right to detain a king's officer from New Jersey. He demanded that they return him to his own province, to Perth Amboy, in fact. Trumbull explained to him that this was out of the question, but if he would sign the parole giving his word that he would not attempt to escape, he might have his choice of a comfortable residence nearby in Connecticut.

Near the end of his endurance, Franklin allowed that he might go to Stratford, a port town sixty miles to the south. Governor Trumbull shook his head. The town was Anglican and full of loyalists, including William's old friend William Samuel Johnson, whose father had founded the Tory King's College in New York. Denied this option,

Franklin said he would not cooperate any further, and at this point the members of the committee grew restless. They explained to the governor that he was a prisoner, with few rights at all. If he did not promptly sign the parole they would put him in prison; and the colonial prisons, regrettably, were unclean, unsanitary hellholes more fit for vermin than for governors. There was a jail like this in Litchfield he might have heard of, in the hills west of Hartford.

So Franklin signed the paper they set before him. He was then driven to Wallingford, a beautiful village on the Quinnipiac River twelve miles north of New Haven, known for its corn mills, and barrel hoops, and witches.

CHAPTER 15

Paterfamilias

W HEN SALLY BACHE HEARD that her brother had been transported to Connecticut, the news conveyed in his pathetic letter to Temple, she immediately invited Elizabeth to come and stay
with them on Market Street. Her father, as paterfamilias, must have
approved, but with all of his other responsibilities, Franklin may well
have been relieved when the poor woman declined his hospitality. She
was probably hoping that a miracle would restore William to his home
in Perth Amboy. And in the meantime she felt the need to stay there
in the house to protect their belongings and William's papers.

That summer the peaceable town on the Raritan, crowded with
rebel troops, had become bedlam. Soldiers spilled out of the barracks
into town, roistering at the King's Arms Tavern en route to Proprietary
House, where, for fun, they would shout insults and obscenities at the
governor's wife. "I can do nothing," she wrote to Sally, "but sigh & cry;
and even now my nerves are so weak that my hand shakes to such a
degree that I can scarcely hold a pen." Men sashayed on her lawn and
garden—ignoring General Hugh Mercer's orders to leave Mrs. Franklin alone—trampling flowers and raising hell. They picked green apples
from the trees and threw them at one another and at the dog, Temple's
Pekingese, whom they threatened to kidnap and hold for ransom.

IT IS DIFFICULT TO fathom the anguish Benjamin Franklin felt at
this time, impossible not to grieve with a father over the conduct and
fate of his only son. One day he would confess that nothing had ever
hurt him so much. From the time he returned from England he had
done everything to persuade William to change his course, or at least
trim his sails until he could withdraw gracefully. And now, for the rest
of his life Dr. Franklin would have to suffer the judgment of men like
Ambrose Serle, Lord Howe's secretary, who called William "a steady
honest man [whose] father is and has been every way his misfortune."
These would always believe that Dr. Franklin had forsaken the sacred
duties of parenthood regarding William and "thrown off all natural
affection for him." Even Strahan would call him to account.

He had given up trying to rescue William in November 1775. As
head of the household he was steering a delicate vessel through a violent storm. On board were his daughter and son-in-law, their children,
his grandson Temple, his sister Jane Mecum, Catharine Greene's boy
Ray, and also, it seemed likely, Elizabeth Franklin, his daughter-in-law.
There was no room for William Franklin, whose reckless behavior
threatened to drown them all.

From August through October 1776—his last months in America
during the war—Ben Franklin's feelings about family affairs are evident from his dealings with his grandson and his daughter-in-law.
Temple had grown to love his father and his father's wife, and now was
heartsick over the governor's detention as an enemy of his country. The
boy had yet to accept the principles of the new republic, as much as he
admired his grandfather. And naturally he felt a strong loyalty to the
woman who had embraced him as her son. She needed his attention
now, and he wanted to go to her.

So Temple's grandfather had to consider, very carefully, what was
best for everyone concerned. He wanted to encourage Temple to be a
dutiful son, yet he would prefer that the impressionable young man,
born and raised in London, avoid the influences he might encounter in
the Tory mansion. There was also the frightful possibility that William
Franklin's son might be taken hostage by extremists, of which there

was no shortage on either side of the conflict, as it might serve their purposes.

Taking all of these things into account, Franklin permitted his grandson to travel to Perth Amboy in early August to visit his ailing stepmother. Among other gifts for her, and necessities from the city, he brought a bottle of precious asthmatic elixir she had requested from the apothecary. He also carried an envelope from his grandfather to Elizabeth. The note, enfolding sixty dollars, has been lost, but her response on August 6 indicates that he advised her not to lose heart, and to take consolation in the knowledge that others were suffering more than she. It was cold comfort. Her letter of response is an appeal for mercy. "I will not distress you by enumerating all my afflictions, but allow me, Dear Sir, to mention, that it is greatly in your power to relieve them. Suppose that Mr. Franklin would sign a parole not dishonorable . . ." She wrote as if her husband had not had his chance, and his choice, as General Washington had put it, to stay at home. She had no idea of her father-in-law's dilemma, and that now he had no power to intercede on William's behalf.

Temple was a great comfort to his stepmother, and he stayed with her for the rest of the summer. He did return to Philadelphia for a few days in mid-August at his grandfather's request. The baby Sarah, nine months old, was deathly ill. Temple's presence was needed there, and in nearby Moreland, where Sarah's four-year-old brother, William, also ailing, was under the care of a family friend. In spite of a violent thunderstorm, Temple obediently stopped in Moreland on his way back to Amboy, via the Galloways'.

It is significant that Benjamin Franklin entrusted the youth with such duties, and that he was still on good terms with Joseph Galloway. Galloway had altered his position. He had purchased flags for a regiment of American militia and thrown a party for four hundred of them. The change of heart was instigated by the Parliament's Prohibitory Act of December 1775 authorizing the navy to plunder American ships. While he had not returned to politics, he did not wish to be a victim of his own opinions, and so for the time being the disillusioned lawyer posed no threat to the cause of liberty.

Franklin wrote to his grandson in Amboy on August 27 to say that the baby had died—her suffering was over. Little Will would return home the next day and help comfort them. Franklin also sent his love to Elizabeth and asked Temple to "let me know what you hear from your father."

Grandfather insisted that Temple write to him daily, as he was so close to the scene of action. The Perth Amboy barracks was a staging area for the defense of New York, and Franklin was eager for intelligence from that quarter. After driving General Howe and his redcoats from Boston, George Washington had moved his base of operations to the Kennedy mansion, No. 1 Broadway, New York. For four months he and his generals had been laboring in the uphill task of fortifying Manhattan, Staten Island, and Long Island against the likely invasion of British troops by land and sea.

Forty-five British ships were anchored inside Sandy Hook, just across Raritan Bay from Perth Amboy. They unloaded troops on Staten Island just days before the reading of the Declaration of Independence. And on July 12, two men-of-war, the *Rose* and the *Phoenix,* escorted by three tenders, boldly cruised up the Hudson River, unimpeded by a hail of artillery shells descending from redoubts and nests from Red Hook and Governors Island up to Fort Washington. By midafternoon the cloud of gunpowder smoke had nearly blotted out the sun. The *Rose* was damaged—an 18-pound shot hit the foremast, some shots pierced the sails and ruined the main topsail braces. But the ship's cannon gave more than they got, sending cannonballs through the walls of a dozen homes in Manhattan and creating pandemonium in the streets.

No one was killed except six artillerymen, some of them drunk, who were blown to pieces along with their overheated cannon. But in one day Washington had confirmed how hard it would be to defend this city against the British navy. Where two ships had passed, a fleet would eventually follow, delivering an army of ten thousand up the river. By the time Franklin wrote to his grandson requesting news, the British fleet in view of the lighthouse over Sandy Hook had swelled to two hundred ships. Forty-five had come up from Carolina bearing Generals Charles Cornwallis and Henry Clinton and their three thousand regulars. Another hundred warships, the first of Admiral Richard Howe's armada, arrived soon after from England. And they kept coming, until there were four hundred under sail in Raritan Bay and the Narrows, and thirty-two thousand British and Hessian troops were making camp on the banks of Staten Island. This was the greatest and best-equipped expeditionary array of the century.

In the last week of August, General Howe began moving soldiers across the marshes under cover of night, ten thousand men, light infantry with rifles and bayonets, and fourteen pieces of artillery. With a spyglass Temple might have seen some from the dormer of Proprietary House. They advanced through Jamaica Pass, a rocky road through a narrow gorge, past Bedford, and attacked the American lines at the Gowanus Road.

The first major battle of the Revolutionary War, in which British forces under Howe and Clinton outflanked the Americans, forced Washington to retreat and give up Brooklyn and Long Island. The Battle of Long Island took place on August 27, 1776, and the rout was thorough, horrifying, and humiliating. Three hundred Americans were killed and another thousand taken prisoner. According to Howe, he lost fewer than four hundred men: fifty-nine killed, 267 wounded, and the rest missing.

The British captured several generals, including Lord Stirling, who had fought valiantly, and Brigadier General John Sullivan, a brilliant young officer from New Hampshire. They released Sullivan upon the condition that he travel to Philadelphia and deliver a message to the Continental Congress from the Howe brothers. The Howes led the commission Governor Franklin had prayed for and promised his assembly, empowered to settle the conflict on terms agreeable to both sides and authorized to issue a general pardon.

Now General Sullivan appeared at the State House on Chestnut Street just after Washington reported the military catastrophe. General Washington wanted instructions. If forced to abandon New York—should he burn the city? And Sullivan delivered the seductive message from the Howes: Desiring an accommodation with America, the officers were willing to meet as soon as possible, wherever it suited the congress, with a delegation to discuss the prospects for peace. Many in the congress were cynical, John Adams calling Sullivan a decoy duck sent forth "to seduce us into a renunciation of our independence," but after lively debates they voted to arrange an informal meeting. On September 6, they appointed Benjamin Franklin, John Adams, and South Carolina's Edward Rutledge as the committee to represent them. Rutledge, twenty-six, was the youngest signer of the Declaration of Independence, and one who had to be persuaded; he would add balance to the entrenched republicanism of Adams and Franklin.

The three delegates rode out of town, Franklin and Rutledge in a carriage, Adams on horseback, arriving in New Brunswick on Tuesday evening. To ensure secrecy, Howe would divulge the meeting place at the last minute, delivering a sealed envelope addressed to Franklin either to the Tory Proprietary House or to the barracks in Perth Amboy. Rain had swamped the roads. Franklin wrote to Temple describing their plans and requesting his assistance: If a note from Lord Howe should be left for Dr. Franklin at his mother's, regarding the scheduling of a meeting "to night, or very early in the morning I could wish you would set out with it on horseback so as to meet us on the road." That way, if Howe insisted on meeting them in New York, the party would not go out of their way through Amboy. "Besides," he added, "I should be glad to see you. My love to your mother." If no letter came to the house, Temple was to ask at the barracks if any letter had come for Dr. Franklin—but to offer no other information. The meeting place was to be kept secret as long as possible.

Once again he was binding the boy to him, and his cause, by entrusting to him, secretly, a serious responsibility. Howe's letter of the tenth must have reached Perth Amboy quickly; Temple galloped off with it to Brunswick, not twelve miles away.

At daybreak they rode on to Perth Amboy, Temple and John Adams on horseback leading the carriage. Lord Howe in his letter had explained the conditions of their meeting. Weather was threatening, but if the sea was calm he would await them at the stone house across the bay from Amboy. First he would send a boat with a flag of truce. That British boat had already docked when the three delegates arrived, and they learned that an English officer aboard was to be left in their stead as hostage. All agreed this was silly—as gentlemen, none feared for his safety; the officer would return with them. Adams had forgotten his razor, so Temple went up the hill and got him a spare blade from the mansion so he could shave before meeting Lord Howe.

The parley on Staten Island on September 11 was cordial but aimless. Lord Howe led the conversation, which took up three hours including a dinner of mutton and bread, cold ham, tongue, and bottles of red wine. He said that he was confident their differences could be settled and that he personally felt for America as for a brother. He would grieve, he said, as for the loss of a brother if the colonies should be vanquished. To this, the witty Franklin replied, in his gentle, innocent voice: "My Lord, we will use our utmost endeavors to save your lordship that mortification," the most memorable phrase of the summit. At length the conversation moved in a circle, with Howe begging his guests to consider a peace and Franklin insisting this was out of the question so long as Britain called for an unconditional submission.

At a late hour on that moonless night, Lord Howe bade his guests godspeed at the dock. His ferryman, hanging the lantern in the bow, rowed the Americans a mile across the sound to the pier at Smith Street. The King's Arms Tavern lay just two blocks ahead, on High Street, and it would have served Adams and Rutledge for a good night's rest, but Franklin would not have refused his daughter-in-law's hospitality on that night, after she had begged him so often to visit her. Nor would he have passed up the chance to spend time with his grandson, in the mansion he would refer to, only a week later, as that "Tory House."

The next morning the commissioners returned to Philadelphia, to report to the Continental Congress.

ON FRIDAY THE THIRTEENTH, Franklin received an unsettling letter from his grandson. Temple wanted to go and visit his father in Connecticut. The governor had been removed from Wallingford to more hospitable quarters in nearby Middletown; Temple longed to see him before returning to college, and asked his grandfather's permission.

Also, he reported that his stepmother was distraught over her in-

ability to send or receive letters to or from her husband. She wanted
Temple to go there with her letters so she might "communicate the
situation of her family concerns" and "get that advice she is desirous of
having, and without which she knows not how to act." The only explanation Elizabeth ever gave for remaining in the mansion was that she
wanted to guard it from looters. But their most precious things were
not more important than each other's company and solace in such a
time. She must have believed he would return under parole, or even
that a prisoner exchange was in the offing. Perhaps she was too frail to
travel the hundred miles along the seaboard to Wallingford. But it
seems more likely that she was living from day to day, praying that the
next post would bring news of her "poor dear persecuted prisoner's"
deliverance.

Whatever the case, Benjamin Franklin was not about to allow his
grandson to go off on such a journey, for many reasons. These included
concern for the boy's safety—from enemies, and from so many sick
soldiers returning on that road. He also feared that Temple was losing
interest in his studies and that the trip to Connecticut was merely an
excuse for him to cut school. Neglecting his studies now, he said, would
be like "cutting off the spring of the year."

This was good advice and well expressed. But the stubborn son of
the Tory governor was not taking it, at first, and wanted to argue.
Grandfather had made a special point of conveying his "Love to your
good Mama"; and in a postscript he wrote that Temple's aunts, Jane
Mecum and Sally Bache, "desire I would express more particularly
their love to Mrs. Franklin." Yet Grandfather's advice concerning her
letters—which he had hoped to deliver himself—Temple wrote was
unkind. Benjamin had insisted that she should simply write and seal a
letter to her husband and send it under cover to Governor Trumbull,
promising there was nothing in it but private family concerns. If she
asked him to deliver it—reading it first if he liked—surely Trumbull
would forward the letter to William.

Temple expressed their sorrow that the journey did not meet with
his approval. As for sending letters via Trumbull, this had been tried
already, with no evidence they had ever been received. Furthermore,
Elizabeth found it awkward to enclose a letter to a gentleman with

whom she was totally unacquainted, particularly one who had been unkind to her husband. Ill fortune had not yet caused her to lose her sense of decorum. Dipping his quill with a sense of indignation, Temple told his grandfather what he thought: "In my going, you might perhaps imagine, I should give such intelligence to my father, as would not be thought proper for him to know." He denied any knowledge relating to military affairs apart from general conversation and what he read in the papers. Finally he explained that his father, in his last letter, had told Elizabeth to keep Temple with her in Amboy unless she should hear from her husband that she might leave. As winter was approaching and there seemed no likely end to the present troubles, he wanted to go immediately.

All of this sounded, to Dr. Franklin, more like a threat than a reasonable argument, and he exploded.

> You are mistaken in imagining that I am apprehensive of your carrying dangerous intelligence to your father, for while he remains where he is, he could make no use of it. . . . You would have been more in the right if you could have suspected me of a little tender concern for your welfare. . . . to send you on such a journey merely to avoid being obliged to Governor Trumbull for so small a favor seems to me inconsistent with your mother's usual prudence.

His real opinion was that Temple's motive was adventure, a reluctance to return to school, and "a desire I do not blame of seeing a father you have so much reason to love." The last phrase sounds a diapason of pent-up emotions. He could not blame the boy for loving his father any more than he himself could be blamed for his tormented affections. William Franklin had willfully put himself out of the reach of everyone who loved him. Grandfather closes his letter of the twenty-second with a promise to send franked covers for Elizabeth's use, addressed to Governor Trumbull, and sends endearments from the family to both of them in Perth Amboy.

From that day on, sensing the Tory House was doomed, Franklin was determined to rescue his grandson from it. On Tuesday, September 24, Franklin received instructions from the Continental Congress to negotiate a treaty of alliance with France. He and the other commissioners, Silas Deane and Arthur Lee, were to sail for Paris as soon as possible, after the various articles of the treaty had been determined.

By Saturday, Franklin had decided he would take Temple with him to France. He wrote to "Dear Tempe" (he usually addressed him as "Grandson" or "Billy"—"Tempe" was a grown-up nickname) just a three-sentence note, cryptic and alluring. "I hope you will return hither immediately, and that your mother will make no objection to it, something offering here that will be much to your advantage if you are not out of the way. . . . My love to her." If she had known more she would have objected, but the mission was top secret and neither she nor anyone else outside the congress would know much about it for months.

TEMPLE SAID GOODBYE TO his stepmother on October 2, not knowing when he would return. Entrusting him with her letter to her husband, under one of Benjamin Franklin's franked covers to Trumbull, she asked him to mail it from nearby Woodbridge. Somehow he neglected to mail the letter, misplaced or lost it; in any case when she discovered, on October 11, that it had not been posted, she wrote to Temple, furious: "I am truly miserable indeed, to be here in a strange country without a friend or protector, and that a letter from me to my husband is not allowed to pass."

She wrote to Temple several times that month, before his departure on the twenty-seventh, hoping to hear about the offer Grandfather had in store for him. Needless to say, Dr. Franklin made him an offer he could not refuse, but he was not forthcoming about it. Elizabeth would have to learn from Sally, whose eight-year-old son Benny shipped out with Temple, that she was to be even more forlorn in the coming winter.

Franklin did not leave the country without first having a discussion with his daughter and Mr. Bache about family and business matters. Bache was to be his agent and representative, guardian of his household and papers and property. If money or political favors were required they could rely upon the resources and discretion of that indispensable family friend, Robert Morris. Franklin was a great judge of character, and in Morris he had found a man with rare skills whose capability matched his own. Forty-two years of age, a large, ruddy, round-faced merchant with short-cropped sandy hair, Morris was a self-made millionaire with abundant charm and ingenuity—the greatest capitalist of his generation. He was devoted to Franklin, and to the cause of liberty.

Papers and manuscripts were to be shipped to Trevose, where Joseph Galloway would safeguard them.

What about William? It was necessary to keep William Franklin's name out of any correspondence with the American minister to France unless it was delivered by a personal friend, hand to hand. If anything was to be done for the governor's benefit, Benjamin Franklin's name must not be connected with the effort.

NEWS OF FRANKLIN'S ARRIVAL in Paris did not reach America until February 10, when a notice appeared in the *Boston Gazette*. During those terrifying, tumultuous months, not a scrap of correspondence passed between the Franklin household in Philadelphia and the chief of the secret commission to France—or the two grandsons he had taken with him. Elizabeth, Sally, and the rest of the family remained in the dark about their children while Tory rumors flew that the party had been hijacked, carried via New York to Bermuda, then to England, as Bache informed Franklin. No doubt the delicacy of Franklin's mission demanded discretion, but the long silence took its toll, in different ways, on the women in Perth Amboy and Philadelphia.

Now the good luck of one Franklin was the misfortune of the other. The British had gained the upper hand in battles from Fort Washington, New York, to Fort Lee and Paulus Hook. In mid-November their troops began the invasion of New Jersey and Eastern Pennsylvania, to Elizabeth Franklin's relief. So many Americans had been taken prisoner after the capitulation of Fort Washington that William Franklin's value in a prisoner exchange skyrocketed. On November 23, the congress ordered George Washington to propose an exchange of Governor Franklin for Brigadier General William Thompson; and on December 1,

Washington conveyed this message to enemy headquarters. John Hancock, alarmed, wrote to General Washington that an exchange of Governor Franklin was too risky. As the tide of the war turned, he was too prominent and dangerous a figure to be at large.

The chief justice of New York, recollecting the general despondency at the end of that year, wrote that Connecticut was so convinced that America had lost the contest with Great Britain that in December 1776 the General Court there released every prisoner in their power with the exception of Governor Franklin, "who was detained and most inhumanly treated." Actually William's circumstances in Middletown were comfortable. He rented rooms in a house overlooking the wharf, enjoyed the freedom of the town, and could even ride out in the countryside. He had whale oil for his reading lamp, good food and wine, green tea, and whatever clothing and stockings he needed to order from New Haven. According to the historian George Trevelyan, one night there was such howling and shouting at Governor Franklin's lodging in celebration of General Howe's bravery, and drinking the king's health, cursing the American soldiers as cowards, and roaring of catches, that it brought out the town constables. "Blows followed words, and in the end the whole party were marched off to the guard room."

Who paid for all of this? House rent and horses and a servant? Somehow in the welter of loyalties and betrayals, his chief benefactor was his old partner in the land deal, and sometime antagonist, Thomas Wharton. As soon as he heard of Franklin's arrest, Wharton had contacted a Quaker friend in Connecticut and directed him to advance William whatever money he needed, and he would cheerfully pay the tally. Wharton's generosity is intriguing; one can only surmise that there was enough blood left in the Walpole Company that the partners could still bail out one of the founders.

Discouraged by his everlasting captivity, but emboldened by the news of General Howe's success, William entered into a secret correspondence with Howe. A rich Irish trader in New York delivered their messages back and forth. The British general had come to America as a peace commissioner whose greatest desire had been to offer a general pardon to any of the king's subjects who would pledge his loyalty. After the fruitless meeting at Staten Island, and the bloody battles of Fort Washington and Trenton, Howe recognized that a general pardon was hopeless. The next best thing would be a plan of divide and conquer, under which pardons might be issued individually, in towns and counties that were receptive, with a view to building consensus. Supposedly a third of the people were against independence and another third remained neutral. In a province like New Jersey, a campaign to enlist loyalists could reverse the balance of power in their favor.

Howe wanted Governor William Franklin, the premier loyalist, to endorse individual pardons. Given the war's progress, William felt that he had little to lose; security in Middletown was lax and he felt no obligation to honor an illegitimate parole. Using private lines of communication he began soliciting and issuing pardons to loyalists in New Jersey and Connecticut. As the British army was on the move north and south, burning and looting, a farmer or merchant bearing a letter of royal pardon might see his house and property spared from confiscation or the torch.

This is what things had come to in the winter of 1776–77 when Richard Bache wrote to his father-in-law in France. Ben Franklin had been gone more than three months, and since, Bache observed, "our common cause has undergone a variety of interesting changes and events." Only through the intervention of Divine Providence and the efforts of the militia had Philadelphia resisted an English occupation. Yet Bache saw that it was inevitable. The enemy already occupied Brunswick and Perth Amboy, a result cheered by Elizabeth in the Tory House, the Skinners, and other relics of the Empire in New Jersey. She had reason to hope. And by then she must have been in touch with her husband. William's former physician, their neighbor Dr. John B. Lawrence, was one of his confederates in the plot to distribute royal pardons.

So Elizabeth's spirits revived that month, even as darkness and terror descended upon the household in Philadelphia. As the British advanced toward the city, Bache packed up Franklin's precious books and sent them to friends in Bethlehem for safekeeping. He sent his wife and children up to the village of Goshen, twenty-five miles to the west in the hills of Chester County. The enemy was expected, by land and sea, in the spring. Franklin's papers and letters had been entrusted to Galloway, a fatal mistake: a month after Franklin's departure for France, Galloway left Trevose forever, fleeing behind the British lines. When the house was plundered, twenty years of Franklin's correspondence was scattered to the winds.

Elizabeth Franklin's elation was short-lived. So was her husband's undercover role as a pardoner—which in New Jersey was an ill-kept secret. The new governor of the province, William Livingston, informed General Washington in March that Franklin was violating his parole by dispensing pardons, and on March 23, the particulars of Livingston's accusation were relayed from headquarters to Governor Trumbull in Lebanon. Trumbull was not so much surprised as he was embarrassed, having heard already that William Franklin had granted thousands of certificates in Connecticut alone. Counterespionage agents had depositions to prove it in Philadelphia.

Trumbull wrote to Washington on April 16 to confirm his understanding that William was working for the Crown. Washington said that he was "amazed that under such engagements he should not be more regardful of the ties of Honor" and condemned Franklin's violation of the generous parole as truly reprehensible. A week later, the congress informed Trumbull that Franklin was dispersing protections and aiding the enemies of the United States, and ordered him to remand the governor into close confinement, prohibiting him the use of pen and ink or access to anyone not given permission by Governor Trumbull.

Governor Franklin's spirits, at the time, were buoyed by news of fighting in nearby Danbury, where American troops tried and failed to destroy the British rear guard. But on the second day of May 1777, a Friday morning, while he was taking his ease in his rooms in Middletown, his servant came to tell him the sheriff was at the door.

When William went out to greet the men he recoiled as one of the deputies discharged his musket. The guard later said that the firearm went off by accident. In any event William heard the zing of the bullet that missed his head by only an inch, and realizing these constables were not to be bargained with, he led them inside, as he was told. There in the parlor they read aloud the charges against him. He was not permitted to respond. His servant, Thomas Parke, stood by, wide-eyed, helpless. The prisoner was ordered to leave his dwelling with no more than the clothes on his back—not so much as a razor or a change of linen.

Later William would lament that the bullet had not killed him. As he was led outside and mounted the spare horse, he did not know at first where they were taking him, so ill provided, or how many hours he might be gone.

Litchfield, he heard one of the riders say. The news could hardly have been worse. The Litchfield Gaol was infamous, a destination of the last resort for outlaws condemned to be hanged, convicted murderers and sodomites, reprobates and traitors who had dishonored their parole. The little town stood on an eminence in the foothills of western Connecticut athwart the Bantam River. A strategic depot for military supplies on the route from New York to Canada—safe from British encroachments—it was also a safe place to detain prisoners of war. Despite the threats, Franklin had never really believed he would end up here. Now, in the month of May, as the fruit trees were blossoming on the roadsides and the songbirds trilling, he was on his way, surrounded by armed guards, through the hills and valleys of Mattatuck Forest, forty miles northwest to the godforsaken village of Litchfield.

On arriving he was delivered into the custody of the high sheriff of the town, also master warden of the prison, Captain Lynde Lord. Captain Lord, the same age as William, was a hard man. Apart from his dealings with Franklin he would be known to posterity as a lawman scrupulous in exactly enforcing the corporal penalties of the day: hanging, branding with red-hot irons, ear clipping, and flogging especially. He kept records of these accomplishments in a neat hand, so no one would ever accuse him of shirking his duty.

Without ceremony Franklin was led to his new quarters off the village green. The jail, a brick building on East Street, catercornered to the Meeting House, was two stories high. The cells, a dozen or more, each with a narrow four-paned window, partitioned the level above the street. The ground floor was occupied by a tavern that was open to business most hours of the day and night, a watering hole for American soldiers and provisioners.

A narrow, dim stairway led to a narrow hall. It smelled awful. The turnkey showed him the cell, and he might have thought this was a joke or a ruse to frighten him on his first night in the patriot outpost. The room was empty except for a stoneware chamber pot. The plank wood floor was strewn with straw. In the twilight from the high little window the prisoner searched the four corners in vain for a chair to sit in or a pallet to lie upon. "A most noisome, filthy room of I believe, the very worst gaol in America." A dungeon, he called it.

And Franklin was not permitted to leave that space for any reason, not for exercise or worship, not even to answer a call of nature, for six months. Food and water were provided for the prisoner through a hinged trap in the heavy door. Through the same aperture he passed the chamber pot to be emptied. The jailers were not inhuman, but they had orders not to converse with the wily Tory; and so "in short," as he recalled, "I was in a manner excluded human society, having little more connection with mankind than if I had been buried alive." He had no company apart from the brown rats and mice who came and went as they pleased, flaunting their liberty, scuttling across the floor in the darkness, or the prisoner's body as he tried to sleep, raking his flesh to mitigate the gnawing of the inevitable fleas and unkillable lice. Soon it was summer and there were houseflies, too, mosquitoes, and black flies in July that stung like the furies and drew blood.

After a few days or weeks of crying aloud to God and one's captors in anger and disbelief and finally for mercy, it is natural for a prisoner in such extremity to enter a benevolent trance, a self-induced hypnosis. The beard and nails grow long, untended, the teeth loosen and leave the gums inflamed; one's clothes grow loose also, tattered, unlaundered. The sense of smell abates. A man like William would pace and exercise. One forces oneself to eat without gagging whatever bread or gruel or offal comes through the trap at regular times of the day. These are the only markers of time apart from the daylight, the moving shadow of the sash-bars of the window casting a black cross upon the floor. Sleep, day and night, is the prisoner's best friend, and dreams of freedom; night and day mingle in a measureless twilight. Franklin's sleep was often disturbed by the strident laughter, singing, and shouting of the revelers in the tap house below his cell.

BENJAMIN FRANKLIN AND HIS grandsons arrived in France on December 2, staying in Paris three months before moving from the Hotel d'Hambourg in the Rue de l'Université on the Left Bank to the village of Passy, two miles away.

That spring he and the boys lived in a villa there on the grounds of the palatial Hôtel de Valentois. The eighteen-acre estate of the French magnate Jacque-Donatien Le Ray de Chaumont included the main château and three outlying houses on a hill overlooking the Seine. One of these houses, a two-story structure upon an Italian garden pavilion, stood a few hundred yards from the castle. Franklin and his family set up housekeeping and lived there, for the time being, rent free. Chaumont had a vital business interest in the American's success. Young Benny was placed in the village school, and Temple had tutors.

They were welcome to dine at Chaumont's table with his wife and four daughters. Or, if they preferred, they could take their meals in their own dining room, prepared by their cook, and draw from a well-stocked wine cellar. Franklin's collection soon included more than a thousand bottles of Bordeaux, Burgundy, Champagne, port, and sherry. From the dining room he looked out upon a terraced garden with linden and chestnut trees, and roses and dahlias in season. In mild weather he strolled the garden path from the great house to the villa with a view of Paris beyond the Seine to the east, the towers of Nôtre Dame and St. Eustache, Sainte-Chapelle and St. Étienne du Mont, and the purple colored hills of Saint-Cloud. He walked from the pavilion to the door of his villa, which opened upon a gallery where precious oil paintings and marble sculptures graced the way.

Franklin had accepted Chaumont's invitation and moved there in March after several months of overwhelming attention in the French capital. It had been flattering and distracting. Dr. Franklin was one of the most famous men in the world, and in that city of fads and fashions, among powdered wigs, hoop skirts, and macaroni trousers, the large American at once became a fashion plate, idol, fetish, and guru. He appeared to them in the Rue du Bac wearing an outlandish fur cap and curious spectacles, his thin silver hair showing beneath the hat brim, as plainly dressed as any Quaker. He carried a walking stick instead of a sword.

He had not been in Paris very long when fashionable households began to display an engraving of his likeness over the mantelpiece. Chaumont himself invested in terra cottas cast in Franklin's image, bankrolling the Italian sculptor Giovanni-Battista Nini, who fired medallions of the American philosopher by the score, shipping them all over France and returning half of the profits to Chaumont. Franklin's colleague Silas Deane observed his reception by the populace at an important meeting of the French parliament. The meeting hall and the streets leading to it were swarming with people, and when Dr. Franklin appeared they made way for him most reverently. As he passed through the crowd to the seat reserved for him, the people cheered and saluted him, "an honour seldom paid to the first princes of the blood," Dean observed. At the opera Franklin received the same treatment. This must have been gratifying to the American, and beneficial to his country's image and cause, but the social whirlwind of Paris, the salons, the drawing rooms, and cafés, and balls—was not conducive to delicate and discreet diplomacy.

Franklin's mission was elementary, but the means of accomplishing it was devilishly complex. He and his fellows, Silas Deane and the sullen Arthur Lee, had been instructed to obtain arms and a treaty of alliance with his most Christian Majesty of France, Louis XVI. England and France had been at peace since the end of the Seven Years' War in 1763. So the French foreign minister, the comte de Charles Gravier Vergennes, faced a prospect that held in equilibrium a fabulous gift and a formidable threat. Since his appointment in 1774, Vergennes had dreamed of restoring France to its rightful grandeur, the supremacy of its empire before the Treaty of 1763. He had begun building up the nation's military might, with particular emphasis on the navy. Successful collaboration with America could tip the balance of power in France's favor and ruin England. But if the colonies succumbed to the British forces or decided at any point to reconcile with the mother country, Vergennes and his sovereign would have thrown away a tolerable peace and a great deal of money in the effort to gain a false ally at war.

Secretly the French minister had encouraged the Americans. Money and munitions had already found their way from France to Congress. Silas Deane, a sharp-featured, shrewd lawyer and businessman, had gone to Paris in advance, arriving in July, to test the waters. He went in the frock-coated guise of an American merchant, with letters from Franklin and the plan to meet with Vergennes as soon as possible. Franklin advised Deane to tell Vergennes he had come on business of the American congress and to stress the need for arms and ammunition—to be precise: uniforms and guns for twenty-five thousand men, ammunition, and a hundred cannon. He must assure the minister that France was the first nation to be solicited, and if America were to arrive at a complete separation from Britain, France would be the power whose friendship it would be most beneficial to nourish. What had been England's commercial bounty might now belong to France, if America gained its independence.

Deane learned that France was prepared to advance one million livres (a hundred million of today's dollars) to be conveyed to the Continental Congress via a fictitious trading firm, Roderigue Hortalez and Company. Arrangements were already under way in London, concocted by the French dramatist and undercover agent Pierre-Augustin Beaumarchais, to perfect the delivery system.

To get more money, guns, and cannon, Franklin would have to play a tricky and perilous game. The ship that delivered Franklin to France carried no news that favored George Washington's army. The news that autumn of 1776 was that American troops under Benedict Arnold had failed in the Canadian offensive, and that the British, having defeated Washington's army in the Battle of Long Island, occupied New York. Somehow, in spite of this gloomy outlook, the commissioners had to convince Vergennes that the Continental Army could prevail if France would only increase its support.

On Christmas Eve, Franklin and Deane sent Temple Franklin to Versailles with a letter for Vergennes requesting a meeting to discuss a treaty of amity and commerce. A formal alliance between France and America had grave implications. So King Louis granted Vergennes permission to meet with Franklin—but only under strict conditions.

The Americans were advised to admit to the world only that they had come to France on family business. And should they visit the palace in Versailles, they must go there in disguise.

So on the Saturday following Christmas the three commissioners went to call upon Count Vergennes at the royal château of pink marble. It must be left to the imagination how each was disguised. Vergennes received them with due diplomatic courtesy in the south wing, where the king's family dwelt. They must have been struck with Vergennes' appearance. Fifty-eight years of age, tall, with piercing blue eyes and chiseled features, he resembled no one more than George Washington, a less rugged, older, and more idealized figure of the general. And Vergennes was charming, flattering all three of his visitors. A career diplomat, first as a minister in Germany, then as ambassador to the Ottoman court, Vergennes had been so successful in that difficult post that in 1771 he had been charged with a crucial mission to Sweden. From there he was summoned on short notice to return home, where he would assume the office of secretary of state for foreign affairs.

Son of a wealthy family in Dijon, "country aristocracy," Jesuit-educated, Vergennes was an uncharacteristic courtier. Diligent, prudent, thorough, he was at his desk, an immense rosewood confection, every morning at eight o'clock; often he would be found there, by candlelight, at ten at night. Self-effacing, even-tempered, he was not considered brilliant but rather incisive and wise. Most significant, Vergennes was incorruptible—a quality that was considered at the time extraneous to public service on the Continent. In this, his innate honesty, he resembled Benjamin Franklin.

At the meeting the Americans humbly requested that French ports remain open to their ships; they diplomatically inquired whether it would be proper to approach the Spanish ambassador as a potential ally. Vergennes was agreeable. Franklin offered to prepare a memorandum on the state of American affairs as well as a proposal for the treaty. Vergennes said he would consider it. Then he got up and graciously bade his visitors good day. He came away from that meeting impressed with Dr. Franklin's intelligence and diligence, informing his ambassador in London, the Marquis de Noailles, that Franklin's conversation was gentle and forthright and that he appeared to be a gentleman of considerable talent.

If Franklin's surprise materialization in France produced no other benefit to his hosts, it struck fear in the hearts of those English lords who had enjoyed his humiliation in the Cockpit only three years before. That terrible scene, the Marquis of Rockingham recalled, haunted his memory. Rockingham, leader of the opposition in the English Parliament, wrote of Franklin, admiringly, "he boldly ventures to cross the Atlantic in an American little frigate, and risk the dangers of being taken and being once more brought before an implacable tribunal. The sight of Banquo's ghost could not more offend the eyes of Macbeth than the knowledge of this old man being at Versailles should affect the minds of those who were principals in that horrid scene." To be sure, Franklin would plead powerfully. The British ministers, pretending to minimize the dangers of his appeal, would inwardly tremble at it.

Franklin's memorandum, composed during the closing days of 1776, was delivered to Versailles in the new year. Vergennes found it bold, straightforward, and practical, just as he had expected. In a nutshell Franklin explained the present balance of power and the benefits that would come of an alliance among France, America, and Spain. As the enemy had already enlisted the Hessians, England would have no just complaint if France aided America; but should England declare war on France, the united powers of France, Spain, and America would prevail. Britain would lose all its islands in the West Indies and be reduced to the state of weakness and disgrace warranted by her treachery. North America was prepared to guarantee to France and Spain all those properties in the West Indies now in their possession—plus any they might acquire in a war.

All of this was agreeable to Vergennes, with the exception of entering a war allied with an unproven republic. Republics were notoriously fickle. What was troubling, as resonant with complications as any figure multiplying its reflection in the Hall of Mirrors, was the menace spelled out in Franklin's description of the British navy. As long as that navy could move soldiers from port to port along the coast, unchecked, "We may possibly, *unless some powerful aid is given us,*" Franklin wrote, "be so harassed and put to such immense expense" that America would have to make an accommodation with the enemy. In keeping with instructions from the congress, Dr. Franklin was sounding a note of caution—that might be construed as intimidation—but the situation demanded it. John Hancock had advised him to press for the immediate declaration in America's favor by the French, lest their delay force America to make peace with Great Britain.

The American memorandum and request for a treaty lay upon Vergennes' rosewood desk for months. The foreign minister publicly avoided the Americans, referring all of their requests for further meetings to his assistants. Neither he nor the Spanish ambassador, whom Franklin had approached, had any desire to provoke the English while America was making such a poor show in the war, no matter what their commissioners promised. Hoping they would succeed, Vergennes and the king privately, and under cover, continued to funnel money and arms to the colonies, kept French ports open to them, and even ignored American privateering in nearby seas. Franklin reported to the congress optimistically, trusting that delay would only make the alliance stronger when it came.

And so things stood during that spring and summer of 1777, as the Franklin family settled into their villa overlooking the gardens at Passy—Temple at his secretary's desk, and little Ben enrolled in grammar school in the village.

Of all the woes that beset Temple's father as he paced the dim cell in Litchfield, Connecticut, probably the least of his concerns was the fate of his son during those harrowing years. Learning that Temple had gone on the ship to France with his grandfather, William Franklin mildly speculated: "If the old gentleman has taken the boy with him, I hope it is only to put him in some foreign University."

CHAPTER 16

Dark Night of the Soul

For Elizabeth Franklin, life in Perth Amboy was not greatly improved by the arrival of the British soldiers. Regardless of politics, one army of occupation was much like another. They stabled horses in the church; they took over private homes for lodging and leveled the trees for firewood. Infantrymen and dragoons caroused in the taverns and streets at all hours and flirted with the maids.

In early May 1777, Joseph Galloway went to visit Mrs. Franklin. A few blossoms clung to the apple boughs outside her windows. He found her depressed—desperate, in fact—on account of her husband. At that point she had not heard the worst of it, his being buried alive in the Litchfield jail, but the news would not be long in coming.

The success of American forces under General Nathanael Greene and Colonel Daniel Morgan in Somerset County, New Jersey, made the British presence in the province impractical. So in the last week of June, Howe's men quit Perth Amboy in order to focus on Philadelphia. Mrs. Franklin packed up her husband's books and papers in trunks and barrels; servants stacked the furniture, rolled-up carpets, and crates of china upon wagons headed for New York City with a caravan of worried New Jersey loyalists.

New York City was a garrisoned shambles in the summer of 1777.

Many houses were charred, reduced to rubble; others were over-crowded, filthy, disease-ridden. There was so much cholera and ty-phoid, a dozen burials in an evening was not uncommon. Elizabeth was grateful to find rooms at the house of William Hick (not to be confused with William's dueling enemy, William Hicks) at Dock Street, overlooking the East River, but they could not accommodate half of her belongings. She had to store most of her treasures in an army warehouse.

The strain of that exodus was more than Elizabeth's constitution could bear, and her spirit was nearly broken. She grew weaker by the day, struggling for breath. But in mid-July she summoned the strength to devise a way to get word to her husband in Litchfield. Young Joseph Webb, Jr., a member of the Connecticut Assembly and brother of George Washington's former aide-de-camp Samuel Webb, kindly agreed to convey an open letter from landlord Hick to Governor Franklin through a relay of British officers.

THE LETTERS THAT CAME through the crack in William's cell door on or about Sunday, July 20, were heartbreaking. Mr. Webb wrote that upon a recent visit to New York he had heard from friends that all the doctors in Perth Amboy had given up on Elizabeth Franklin as past recovery. It is fairly certain that she was suffocating from obstructive pulmonary disease—hers was a chronic case and there was no cure for it. Opium could ease the pain, but the suffering of such patients in those days was awful. William Hick, reporting at greater length, ob-served that Mrs. Franklin was in such poor health, and so weak, she was unable to hold a pen.

When William begged the high sheriff of Litchfield, Lynde Lord, for a pen and paper so he might compose a letter to George Washing-ton, Sheriff Lord partially relented. He had reason to believe this pris-oner was still dangerous. Any man who could receive a letter through such a bipartisan chain of citizens, including Webb, was worthy of guarded consideration. He did not grant Franklin the freedom of pen, ink, and paper, with the dangerous apparatus of a knife to trim the quill. Instead he called up a clerk from town to take dictation from the prisoner, who then would be allowed to put his signature to the letter he had authored.

And so it was that William Franklin composed his long and sorrow-stricken epistle to General Washington, aloud, through the locked door of his dungeon. It is a superb work. The letter, more than twelve hundred words, might have melted a heart of iron, not to speak of the fellow-feeling of General Washington, known for compassion, and one who had visited this man and his wife in their own home in a time of peace.

> Sir,
>
> I am sensible that you must have so much employ of your time & attention, in the great business you are engaged in, that you can have a very little of either to spare for an individual. But as the peculiarly distressing circumstances and urgency of my case will admit of no delay, I have such confidence in the generosity and humanity of your disposition, that I cannot but flatter myself you will take it into consideration, and grant me such relief as may be in your power.

Humble yet dignified, the writer's words have the compelling merit of being absolutely true. He was wise to trust the general's humanity in a situation where there was no sign of humanity to be seen anywhere else.

He explained that Elizabeth had always had a frail constitution, and for several years had required his constant care and tenderness to maintain tolerable health. Her distress, heightened by his long absence and her flight to New York, was now so great that only his attention might keep her alive. He would not trouble the general with details.

"Your own heart," he dictated, "will suggest the necessity she must be under of my assistance." So he asked Washington's permission to go and visit her.

Then he promised he would enter into any kind of agreement or oath that he would do nothing to oppose the congress in the war, mentioning this oath as an occasion to assure the world that there was no truth in the charge he violated his parole to Governor Trumbull. Franklin wanted only pen, ink, and paper to testify—to the satisfaction of General Washington and the congress—that the appearance of violating his parole, granting pardons, and other offenses was a distortion, an invention, a myth! As soon as he was given the chance he would provide his unassailable proof.

Perhaps General Washington could not properly honor the writer's request without the congress's approval, since he was a prisoner at their pleasure. Unfortunately, the delay this would cause might "put it out of my power, by being too late, to be of any service to Mrs. Franklin." So he begged Washington to skip that formality in lieu of the promise that should they later object, he would leave New York at once and return to Litchfield. "All I request is to be allowed to visit my poor dying wife, and to endeavor to recover, or . . . at least contribute all in my power to comfort her in her last moments."

This letter, unfamiliar to previous biographers, concludes with the only recorded appeal from William Franklin invoking his father. "I am likewise certain that an indulgence in my present request will be thankfully acknowledged by my father both to you and the Congress; for he has great esteem for my wife, who has ever shewn a dutiful & respectful regard to him; and I trust and believe that though we differ in our political sentiments, yet it has not lessened his natural affection for me, any more than it has mine for him, which I can truly say is as great as ever."

The sheriff saw to it the letter went out that day, and that the messenger would wait upon General Washington for his reply. Headquarters was a village called Sidman's Clove in the Ramapo Mountains, the northeast tip of New Jersey, across the Hudson's North River. It was ninety miles of rough riding down through the Connecticut hills over Croton Bridge, but the horseman covered the distance by Friday morning, July 25, saluting the sentries outside the rustic tavern where the general slept.

At this point in his life the forty-five-year-old Washington had reasons to be proud of his leadership as commander in chief, whatever the world might think of his chances for victory. His decisive campaign to rescue Trenton and Princeton in the winter of 1776–77 had wiped away the stigma of the defeats at Long Island and Fort Washington and would always be regarded as a high point of his military career. It had changed the course of the war. General Howe was obliged to withdraw his forces from the Delaware River back toward the Raritan. He had not yet acted upon his obsession to occupy Philadelphia; and Washington, in Morristown and Ramapo, was positioned to keep the redcoats' northern army, under Burgoyne, and the southern army from uniting to attack Philadelphia by way of the Delaware.

This would be a long day for George Washington. He was about to decamp from the Clove and head for Pompton Plains, above the great falls of the Passaic, moving his army toward Philadelphia. The day before, he had received word that Howe's fleet had sailed from Sandy Hook, heading seaward rather than up the Hudson as expected. This could only mean that the British commander had set his sights upon the capital and planned to invade the city by way of Cape May.

When the general read William Franklin's letter at eight o'clock in the morning, he was deeply moved. At eight thirty he wrote to John Hancock. He told the president of the Continental Congress that he had the honor of enclosing Governor Franklin's letter, but as Mr. Franklin was confined by an order of the congress, Washington did not think himself authorized to answer his request. Nonetheless he argued forcefully on William's behalf, saying, "His situation is distressing and must interest all our feelings." Washington had no doubt that Mrs. Franklin was gravely ill, and after hearing the governor's vow to be bound by any restrictions the congress might impose, he felt he ought to be allowed to see her. "Humanity and generosity plead powerfully in favor of his application," he urged, and he asked that if they should approve it, they should let him know at once, or Mrs. Franklin might die before her husband could see her.

The letter was dispatched by express rider. Next, General Washington wrote to William Franklin a brief but compassionate message. "I heartily sympathize with you in your distressing situation." As strongly as he wanted to comply with William's request, he had no power to override the congress. He had forwarded the request with his own recommendations, and he could do no more. He would be happy, he said, if the delegates would honor Franklin's wishes, and hoped sincerely for a quick restoration of Mrs. Franklin's health.

This message would have reached Franklin soon after the first letter reached John Hancock, three days later. As Elizabeth Franklin lay dying in a sweltering room in New York, the congress discussed her husband's request and the general's plea. On July 28 they resolved that after his flagrant violation of the sacred bond of honor, they thought it contrary to the country's safety to allow Franklin "an opportunity of conferring with our open enemies under any restriction whatsoever." They enclosed a copy of one of the pardons William had endorsed, to one Robert Betts, as proof that the traitor could not be trusted, and sent it along with their resolution to General Washington at Coryells Ferry on the Delaware, a day's ride to the north.

Reading the contents of the sealed packet, George Washington's reaction would have encompassed pity, embarrassment, and rancor. Summoning his faithful aide-de-camp, Tench Tilghman, he ordered him to take a letter to William Franklin in Litchfield Gaol. This would be brief, little more than a note covering the resolution and the pardon of Robert Betts. Yet Washington struggled with the wording, mastering his anger, so that the young aide was required to start over, again and again. He wrote, at first, "I am sorry that an act of your own, so contrary to the tie of Honor under which you stood engaged has laid Congress under the necessity of refusing your request." But this was cruel, and the man in jail was helpless, grief-stricken. One must somehow soften it. At last he asked Tilghman to write, tersely: "It appears that this Act has laid Congress under the necessity ... etc. I am & ca."

General Washington was not yet finished with the son of Benjamin Franklin. On August 5, one week later, in Philadelphia he would be introduced to a remarkable young Frenchman whose claim to attention was a letter of recommendation from his admirer, Dr. Franklin, who praised the young man's charm, his bravery, and his burning desire to distinguish himself. The nobleman with family connections and vast wealth was the Marquis de Lafayette. The marquis was the last person of Washington's acquaintance to have seen the elder Franklin, back in the spring. Lafayette and Washington instantly connected, and they were inseparable until the Frenchman was wounded at Brandywine on September 11. Lafayette wanted to know everything about his mentor's relations, and he soon would.

ELIZABETH FRANKLIN PASSED AWAY the same day in July that the congress ruled her husband could not visit her. She was buried the next morning, Tuesday, July 29, 1777, at forty-three years of age, in the chancel of St. Paul's Church on Broadway. The funeral in the pale chapel with the classical portico was "attended by a number of the most respectable inhabitants of the place," according to *The New-York Gazette*. "She was a loving wife, an indulgent mistress, a steady friend, and affable to all."

William would not have heard of her death until the second week in August, unless someone believed it was worth the expense of notifying him by express—which is unlikely. And George Washington had informed him he could not leave prison, so he was already resigned to not seeing Elizabeth again in this world. A paid obituary, in the form of a mortuary inscription, appeared in *The Pennsylvania Gazette* on August 13, for "a lady dignified by a refined education, a peculiar sweetness of manners. . . . She filled her station in life with a dignity that commanded respect and an affability that engaged the love of all." The subscriber is identified only as a friend paying a tribute "and embalming her memory with a tear."

Jane Mecum heard that the author was the poet/composer Francis Hopkinson, who—despite his differences with the governor—had always loved his wife. Mrs. Mecum sent Benjamin the sad news on August 18, saying she knew no particulars of Betsy's death but sincerely grieved for her. "She must have suffered much. . . . I loved her greatly, Temple will mourn for her much." Jane Mecum alone had the temerity to scold her brother and nephew for not staying in touch. "We have never had a scrape of a pen from him, nor have I received more than one letter from you which was from Nantes," dated December 8, 1776.

Word of Elizabeth's death would have reached Litchfield by regular post not much later than it came to Jane Mecum. Hardly a surprise, the news was still devastating to a man who had no comfort left in the world. The weekend of September 13 he requested paper, pen, and ink from the sheriff so he could write to Trumbull—and this time received them. He wrote, on September 15, that having learned of the sad death of his wife in New York, he requested permission to send his servant Thomas Parke to take charge of his personal belongings that had been stored there. He needed Parke to bring him linen, soap, and other necessities he could not procure in prison. Also there had been business records in his wife's possession concerning not only him but his father; he wanted to convey these documents to Benjamin's attorney "before I die, an event that I am convinced cannot be far off, unless there should be some speedy relaxation of the unparalleled severity of my confinement."

He told Trumbull he was wasting away, so weak he would never recover. His anxiety about his wife had been unbearable, but now the actual news of her death—this, the best of women—had caused such dejection of spirits that, with his constant fever and other complaints, life had become quite a burden to him. "In short, I suffer so much in being thus, as it were, buried alive, having no one to speak to day and night, and for the want of air and exercise, that I should deem it a favor to be taken immediately out and shot—"

Once more he begged permission to write a full vindication of his conduct and requested lodgings in some private house so he might collect his thoughts and write in peace. The sheriff had agreed to monitor Franklin's use of pen and paper in such a place, with Trumbull's leave—and it might be made as secure as this jail, which must soon be the death of him.

The day William wrote his letter to Trumbull, his sister Sally and her husband were in flight from Philadelphia just ahead of the invading British army. The city could not be defended, so the delegates held their final session there on September 18. On the tenth, Sally had given birth to a daughter she would name Elizabeth after William's late wife. Just four days later the family packed up the bare essentials needed for personal comfort—beds, clothes, linens—two weeks before the redcoats swarmed over the town. The family moved a hundred miles west to Manheim, near Lancaster, where their friend Robert Morris had found them a house. Congress was reconvening in York, twenty-five miles to the south and west of Manheim, across the Susquehanna River.

And it was there in Manheim that Richard Bache received the let-

ter that would lead eventually to William Franklin's deliverance from
the dungeon in Litchfield. Until then the Baches had not known William's plight. On a round of inspections, Washington's deputy commissary general of prisoners, Captain Daniel Clymer, found his way up the
noisome stairway to the cell block where Governor Franklin lay in
squalor, more dead than alive. Clymer had gone there, that second
week in October, to be sure that Franklin's quarters were suitable to his
station, and he was shocked at what he saw. Writing at once to Bache,
on October 11, he described the horror, and conveyed William's message: "He requested me to write to you that he may be permitted to be
confined in a private house in the town. . . . He complains of his loss of
strength—he is very much emaciated and appears to me to be in a bad
state of health. Dictates of humanity have induced me to write to
you. . . . He desired his respects to you and his sister."

This letter reached the Baches in Manheim within the week, and
Richard lost no time getting it to the York Court House, where it was
laid before the Continental Congress on October 22. In this he enjoyed the cooperation of his intimate friend—and Benjamin's closest
political colleague—Robert Morris of Manheim, whose capital by
now was financing the war effort. Morris was commuting daily to the
meetings of the congress. And on that day, the congress ordered that
the Clymer-Bache letter be referred to the Board of War. The secretary
of the board was Richard Peters, Jr.—another family friend and nephew
of the rector of Christ Church; and Trumbull's son Joseph was appointed to that body in November. Their exact deliberations are not
known, but before Christmas, William Franklin was delivered from
the Litchfield jail.

Richard Bache informed his father-in-law that William's release
had come about as a result of an application he had made to the congress. In the same letter of January 31 he said that William had recently asked if he, Bache, would work for his exchange, or if that was
impossible, arrange parole, under Bache's supervision, or in New York.
Bache informed Benjamin by letter that he intended to try, with Robert Morris's aid, to see what could be done. As Morris was the most
powerful civilian in America, a member of the Secret Committee of
Correspondence, treasurer of the Continental Congress, and a finan-

cier who had given a million pounds ($130 million today) to pay the Continental Army, he could indeed do something for William. Bache would not have dared to enlist such support, and inform his father-in-law of it, if he thought Franklin would object.

Learning of William's confinement in the winter of 1777–78, in a miserable jail, and that his wife had died in New York of a broken heart, William Strahan was appalled. He informed every person of influence he knew in Parliament of the scandal, in case someone might find a way to come to his rescue. He wrote to Benjamin in Passy, bitterly. "I know not what may have brought upon him this severe treatment; but I think, whatever his demerits may be ... the son of Dr. Franklin ought not to receive such usage." And after all, Dr. Franklin was now one of the chief agents of prisoner exchange.

There was a great deal that Mr. Strahan did not understand about William's recent history, and more that he might never know about the father's predicament. But if he had seen a certain letter that passed between two gentlemen on the periphery of Franklin's drama, two patriots with no interest apart from relieving "the distresses of others," he might have glimpsed the sword that hung above Ben Franklin's head. The writer was the Quaker lawyer James Kinsey, the chief justice of New Jersey. On February 11, he wrote to his friend James Duane, a delegate to Congress from New York. Unaware that William had already left the jail, he composed a letter describing the haggard governor's circumstances. If no relief was afforded, he averred, these would lead him to his grave in a short time. Kinsey insisted that he had no attachment to the man—who had never done him any favors—and no justification for his conduct. Yet common decency and the instinct of humanity plead for his relief. He urged Duane to do what he could. And if he would be so kind, *please* keep the writer's name out of it.

And this is the part of the letter that would have enlightened Strahan, that worldly, good-hearted man. Kinsey understands that even the most optimistic of Governor Franklin's friends and relatives cannot expect that he, or they, will be granted the slightest concession. In his own words: "The most sanguine of his friends cannot expect any favor to be shown to him," not the slightest gesture that might challenge the measures that had been taken to guard the liberties of America.

The conflict between patriots and loyalists was stark and cruel. Americans convicted by provincial courts-martial were denied due process, arraigned as criminals, and often treated no better than murderers and horse thieves. Litchfield was not the worst prison. In East Granby, traitors were kept below ground in cells carved from the shafts of a copper mine. Kinsey mentions the inhuman treatment of unlucky patriot prisoners in New York, recently reviewed and censured in the congress, and how this might justify harsh retaliation if it could fall only upon the perpetrators. But that would be madness, barbaric, just as wrong politically as it was morally. Kinsey was appealing to his friend to put an end to the cruelty, beginning with Franklin's case—but the Quaker judge was rowing against the tide.

No one was exempt from the righteous fury of the Sons of Liberty—not even Benjamin Franklin's children. Kinsey had written of William: "He is the only son of a man to whom America owes so much he seems to be almost entitled to some indulgence." Strahan thought so, and so did Francis Hopkinson and other friends on both sides of the ocean. Few could measure the agony of Benjamin Franklin, the paterfamilias, who had seen the disaster looming years before and been powerless to stop it. Now Dr. Franklin, the envoy to France upon whom the entire enterprise of independence depended, must prosper there without inviting the least doubt concerning his loyalties.

From the day he and Jane Mecum rode away from the governor's mansion in Perth Amboy, November 1775, Benjamin had been forced, against his nature, to break off all communication with his son. The risk William posed to the whole family—not to mention the cause of American independence—was too great for him to consider any other policy.

Indeed, William was not the only Franklin with adversaries. His father, like all successful men, had fierce enemies. As Dr. Franklin understood, and explained candidly, these were animated mostly by the green-eyed monster. One of his two colleagues in Paris, Arthur Lee, hated him with a passion that drove Lee mad; his letters, and Franklin's efforts to appease him, are hilarious. Envy can find many excuses and pretexts—political differences, perceived slights or injustices. But in Franklin's case, after a long and extremely social career, few men had cause to complain about his manners. The mature man had made a study of being ethical and agreeable, and people in their right minds went to great lengths to cultivate his friendship. There was simply no benefit in alienating him.

Yet there was angry Arthur Lee, and his brother William, who had been sent as envoy to the courts at Berlin and Vienna but was received at neither, and shadowed Arthur in Paris. There was their brother Richard Henry Lee, the great orator from Virginia. He hated Franklin cordially and kept the home fires burning against him in the congress. There was the frustrated Ralph Izard of North Carolina, who had been appointed commissioner to Tuscany with insufficient funds from the congress to leave France; thus he awkwardly became dependent upon Franklin there. Izard disliked Franklin because he shut him out of diplomatic affairs and would not pay him enough to support his pregnant wife and five children in the manner to which they had become accustomed in Paris.

All of these people hated Franklin and would do their best to damage him in France and America, although, as he wrote to Bache, he had never done any of them the slightest injury, or given them any offense. His great reputation, and the goodwill the people at large entertain for him, their respect and praise, "all grieve those unhappy gentlemen; unhappy indeed in their tempers, and in the dark uncomfortable passions of jealousy, anger, suspicion, etc." Benjamin Franklin, to their eternal vexation, was thoroughly happy! How was it possible, at his advanced age, and with such responsibilities? Temple Franklin wrote to his aunt Sally on November 25, 1777, that he had never seen his grandfather in better health. "The air of Passy and the warm bath three times a week have made quite a young man of him. His pleasing gaiety makes everybody in love with him, especially the ladies, who permit him always to kiss them."

His enemies: first the spies, French and English, who haunted him trying to catch him in double dealings; then the American diplomats who resented his control and tried to wrest it from him. All of these lay awake nights scheming to belittle him. Dr. Franklin was so candid and outspoken, so contemptuous of the very idea of espionage, that he virtually disarmed the system. He had nothing to hide. He declared that if everyone was a spy, including his valet, he did not care. (His valet *was* a spy.) He was too clever and nimble to allow his American colleagues to botch the treaty, working with Vergennes around the other commissioners or playing one against the other while all accused him of secrecy and stealth. At their wits' end they set their sights upon those reliable hostages to fortune, the man's children and grandchildren. The Lee brothers, scheming on both sides of the ocean, and Ralph Izard, recalled to Philadelphia in 1779, promulgated the doctrine that no Franklin could be trusted in public office—particularly in diplomacy—because William Franklin was an archtraitor and his son was Ben Franklin's confidential clerk.

This ugly rumor had several unhappy results. It eventually put an end to Temple's career in the diplomatic corps. What Temple did for the embassy in Paris during the war would be his only contribution to the United States of America; his grandfather's efforts would never succeed in securing him any official place in government. When Richard Bache wrote to Franklin in October to congratulate him on being appointed minister plenipotentiary to the court of France, he and Sally felt it was necessary to inform him of Izard and Lee's abuse. The men were loudly complaining that Dr. Franklin employed as his private secretary his grandson, a youngster not fit to be trusted because of his father's principles. The Continental Congress's vote to appoint Franklin was unanimous with the exception of Pennsylvania, his home, and the argument used against him was Izard and Lee's. Robert Morris cast the lone Pennsylvania vote in his favor.

After all he had done to protect his family from the ill effects of William's damnable obstinacy, this talk wounded Benjamin Franklin. It pained him that there might be some plot under way for removing Temple. "Methinks it is rather some merit that I have rescued a valuable young man from the danger of being a Tory," he wrote crossly. He praised Temple for his integrity, early sagacity, and business acumen, which would in time make him of great service to his country. "It is enough that I have lost my *son*, would they add my grandson!" Note that he lays no blame upon William, but charges the loss to fate or the cruelty of politics. "An old man of 70, I undertook a winter voyage at the command of Congress, and for the public service, with no other attendant to take care of me. . . . If I am sick, his filial attention comforts me, and, if I die, I have a child to close my eyes and take care of my remains."

No one would take Franklin's grandson away from him. He would not have to suffer that loss, as the boy's father had. The worst of the rumormongering, the most far-reaching and damaging, too libelous to be written, was the rumor of a pact between Franklin and his son—the patriot and the renegade. Each would cling to his principles. They would go their separate ways until the countries were reconciled or the war was over, then the man on the winning side would use his power to rehabilitate the other and preserve the Franklin fortune. There was all that wealth tied up in the Walpole grant to support this theory for anyone who wished to subscribe to it. And there were plenty who would.

At the end of a bitter meeting with the British spy Paul Wentworth on January 6, 1778, Wentworth had the gall to ask Franklin to reconsider an imperial union in which America would enjoy rights similar to the Scots'. They were dining at the long table in the great castle at Passy, joined by Silas Deane and another spy, Edward Bancroft. As the bottle of wine passed around and the men put aside their differences, Wentworth was charmed by the Americans' confidence—and a specific wager. They were laying odds that America would gain its independence; that the new colony of Vandalia was to be paradise on earth; and that Chaumont and his wife and children would emigrate there. Wentworth recorded this for the undersecretary of state, William Eden, the head of British intelligence. Parliament was always interested in that Hydra-headed beast of immeasurable riches, the land grant company under any of its names, Grand Ohio, Walpole, and now the colony of Vandalia. William Franklin had started the business back in America a decade ago, and his father had brought it to fruition in England. A few men would become very rich if the company survived the war.

THAT VERY DAY, TWELFTH Night in America, William Franklin lay in a feather bed with fresh linen, clean-shaven and clipped, convalescing in the Connecticut home of Lieutenant Joseph Diggins. A widower in his late sixties, Diggins owned a country house a mile south of East Windsor, a mile measured from the old Congregational Church in the village center. The house was situated on the Podunk River that flowed past Hartford.

William was literally in Podunk, a name now synonymous with "nowhere" in America, a place unworthy of notice. Yet it must have seemed to him like paradise after the place where he had suffered for two hundred thirty days. Sometime before the solstice in December the high sheriff of Litchfield, Captain Lynde Lord, received orders from the War Board via Governor Trumbull to let William Franklin out of jail. He was to be transported to East Windsor, on the Connecticut River, forty miles to the northeast, where old Captain John Ellsworth supervised a number of prisoners in various degrees of security. He would take custody of Governor Franklin upon his arrival, and Captain Lord would be well rid of him.

Captain Ellsworth, eighty-one years old, and his kind wife, Ann Edwards, took one look at the new prisoner and decided he presented no threat to anyone apart from the vermin and fever that came with him. The governor was driven out of town to Lieutenant Diggins's home in Podunk, where he would receive medical care suitable to his rank. As far as security was concerned he would be assigned a juvenile guard, namely two fourteen-year-old boys who were more likely to play checkers with the governor, or take him fly-fishing, than point a gun at him.

That winter William Franklin was utterly subdued as he struggled to recover his strength. He was forty-seven years old and looked as old as Diggins, his bookish, companionable host, who was nearly seventy.

The war news, if accurately reported in East Windsor, was not discouraging to a Tory. General Howe and his redcoats still occupied Philadelphia, where Joseph Galloway was made Tory superintendent general of police. Major John André had taken over the Franklin home in Market Street. As yet no one in America knew just how much Benjamin Franklin had capitalized on the American victory at Saratoga the previous October. Even as the American commissioners were signing the crucial French alliance on February 6, George Washington had retired to Valley Forge for the winter, to freeze there.

It was cold in Connecticut, too. But by the fireside William wrote what letters he pleased, to Trumbull, Bache, and others. He informed his sister and brother-in-law that he was comfortable, but that his health had been greatly injured by close confinement. That is, his limbs had atrophied, he had lost some teeth and some of his olfactory nerves, and his digestion was ruined, perhaps forever. Yet he did improve that winter, with good care and a diet of fresh bread and meat, butter and cheese, and farm-fresh eggs. He read books and newspapers. He walked the country roads winding through snow-covered tobacco fields to build up his legs. From other prisoners he learned of the atrocities committed against loyalists, violence that reminded him of the Indians. He got new clothing and teeth of gold and ivory. His servant Thomas attended him.

There were other prisoners in easy confinement here, lodging in the homes of any families who were willing to board them. There were both British and Hessian soldiers, some of high rank such as General Richard Prescott, quartered in the Ebenezer Grant mansion. Franklin enjoyed their company, at cards and modest entertainments. In this gentle backwater it appears that the convicted loyalists were treated with the same courtesies as the military prisoners of war who stood under the king's protection. Captain Ellsworth seems to have regarded the men under his surveillance as victims of circumstance rather than criminals.

In the spring they learned that the British army, now under command of General Henry Clinton, had fled Philadelphia after news of the alliance between France and America changed British strategy. Philadelphia, a symbolic trophy, had little military value. Clinton was obliged to march his soldiers up through New Jersey to New York. Galloway, after enjoying months of power in his native city, was so disgusted by Clinton's arrogance and shift in focus that he made plans to leave America.

According to oral tradition, the Marquis de Lafayette briefly resided in South Windsor during the spring or summer of 1778. He stayed in the house of the merchant Nathaniel Porter, a quarter mile north of Diggins's home in Podunk, where William was lodging. The timing and the location of the Frenchman's visit—bridging military headquarters in Albany and White Plains to the west and Lafayette's command in Rhode Island—make it likely that the story is true. Major General Lafayette crossed Connecticut several times that year in obedience to General Washington's orders.

In the absence of good wine, William had become fond of sour punch, a drink made of lime juice, sugar, Barbados rum, water, and nutmeg. In a little bower verging on the brook behind his house, in fair weather the governor took pleasure in mixing this rum concoction for special visitors. The French soldiers called the drink *"une grande contradiction,"* a phrase that needs no translation; one of the drinkers was the twenty-one-year-old hero the Marquis de Lafayette.

The world was very large then; Windsor was a tiny village. And the proximity of the Porter House to Diggins's house is arresting. Lafayette, a man upon whom nothing was lost, a soldier whose honor in America had been promoted by Benjamin Franklin's recommendation, would have been eager to meet his son and hear his curious story.

Assuming that Lafayette was sojourning in Windsor that year—and there is no reason to doubt it—his alleged encounter with William Franklin opens up an intriguing possibility concerning William's French connection to his father in Passy. In October, Lafayette would be granted leave to return to France to visit his family. He went by way of Philadelphia, where he made a point of meeting with Richard Bache so that Bache could entrust to him letters to be delivered directly into Dr. Franklin's hands. One was from Bache, and the other was from Sally. The first knowledge of William's exchange for an American prisoner came to his father in Bache's letter of October 22, 1778. It arrived, with due courtesies, upon the person of the Marquis de Lafayette. The Frenchman was the last person of Benjamin Franklin's acquaintance to have seen his son the governor in the flesh.

NOT LONG AFTER LAFAYETTE discovered William Franklin in Connecticut, John McKinley, the governor of Delaware, traveled from New

York to Philadelphia on parole. McKinley had been a prisoner of the British for almost a year. Now they were giving him a month to see if he could persuade the Continental Congress to exchange him for Governor Franklin. He laid his appeal before the delegates on August 20, and they debated it for three hours before tabling the motion.

The dispute over Franklin's release was bitter and nearly endless. There were many, like Richard Henry Lee and Daniel Roberdeau, who distrusted the whole Franklin family and could not imagine that freeing William would be anything other than a menace to the United States. There were slightly more who, like the formidable Robert Morris and the tenderhearted Francis Hopkinson, believed that the governor was weary, defeated, and toothless in every sense, and that he wanted nothing more than a chance to go back to England where he belonged. These made up the majority. And after some more wrangling over the technicality of his being a prisoner subject to rules of exchange, or not, the congress moved, on September 11, to approve Franklin's exchange for McKinley. Not until mid-October were the details fully worked out.

As William prepared to leave his rooms in South Windsor on October 24, he wrote a formal note commending Captain Ellsworth and his wife for their kind treatment of all the British prisoners during his detention. With mild irony he recommended them and "their family and property, to the civilities and protection of all British officers, and other of His Majesty's loyal subjects"—roughly the language of the pardons that had been his undoing.

In the secret letter that Bache wrote to his father-in-law on October 22 and handed to Lafayette, he explained that the same argument that had bruised Dr. Franklin's appointment as minister plenipotentiary had been used against Governor Franklin's release: *"he had a son [Temple] living with you, and much evil might ensue to the United States."* Bache hastened to excuse "your friend Mr. Morris from the imputation of suffering such weak reasons. . . . Governor Franklin however is exchanged, and I expect is gone, or will shortly go for England." *He would leave for England!* This is what Richard and Sally, and Robert Morris, and Lafayette in all likelihood, had schemed and prayed for. The news would be welcome in Passy among the family members there who loved William in spite of everything. If Benjamin Franklin had not interceded for his son, his nearest kin and most powerful friends had done so instead.

On the last day of October, a Saturday, William Franklin left Connecticut under guard and was delivered to Kingsbridge, the gates of New York City, on Sunday, All Saints Day. Bells were ringing the faithful Tories to churches all over the damaged town. It smelled of wood smoke, charred brick, and sewage. Franklin would offer up thanks that he was at last a free citizen of the British Empire, at liberty to book passage on the next ship bound for Portsmouth. If he had sailed, it would have been the last scene of a sad drama: the martyrdom of a high-principled, courageous British governor during a civil war. It would have been best for all concerned—for William and his family, for the United States, and even for England.

But Governor Franklin had other plans, chivalrous, astonishing, hatched perhaps in the dingy cell in Litchfield and nursed in the sunnier rooms and on the country lanes of Windsor. He had written to General Howe as an experienced soldier requesting a commission. Arriving in New York, where Henry Clinton had replaced Howe, it took him a few days to ascertain that there was nothing for him. Many able-bodied loyalists also found they were not welcome in the British army. Broke, he applied to the British Peace Commission for relief. Bereft of his wife, his friends, and his possessions, he considered leaving for England. But only briefly.

On November 16, he wrote to Galloway, who had left for England in October, "An unwillingness to quit the scene of action, where I think I might be of some service, if anything is intended to be done, has induced me to remain till I can discover what turn affairs are likely to take."

PART FOUR

Danse Macabre

CHAPTER 17

The Scene of Action, 1778–81

DURING THE YULETIDE SEASON in New York, William Franklin was embraced by the influential and wealthier American Tories, who admired his courage, integrity, and willingness to suffer any indignity rather than give up his allegiance to the Crown. They still called him Governor and looked to him for leadership. It was generally assumed that Franklin was staying there simply to learn everything he could about the living conditions on the island and the army's plans; then he would depart for England.

He certainly feared for his safety, to have been so secretive about his street address. Letters are discreetly headed "New York." He probably stayed in rooms let by William Hick, in the dwelling formerly occupied by his late wife, on Dock Street. Used to confinement, the governor now moved within a triangle of streets in lower Manhattan whose vertex was St. Paul's Church at the upper end of Broadway, where Elizabeth was buried, down to British headquarters, the Kennedy mansion, at the foot of Broadway near the western battery, over to Dock Street on the southeastern quay.

One could walk the whole perimeter in an hour looking up at the spires of half a dozen churches saved from burning. Fires here started just after the British occupation had destroyed the northwest quadrant of the city. Five hundred houses burned north of Broadway, as well as the nave and bell tower of Trinity Church south near Wall Street. Loyalists believed the fires were set by rebel incendiaries under orders from General Washington. The most recent blaze, in September, had leveled the warehouse where Governor Franklin's furniture, books, and papers had been stored.

At the head of Broad Street stood City Hall, a three-story building with wings that now quartered the Main Guard; the Royal Exchange crouched upon immense stone arches at the foot of the same street, at the city's center. There were four enormous sugar houses: one now used to dry tobacco, another as a prison. Broadway was the raised backbone of New York and there were markets and theaters all up and down it, taverns and coffeehouses, and the famous Fly Market stood at the foot of Maiden Street. This market, whose name comes from the Dutch word *vly*, "meadow," sold meat and fish, and so was aptly named.

Manhattan was crowded with loyalist refugees, tens of thousands who lived wherever they could find a bed. The poor pitched tents upon the foundations of burned and gutted buildings, so the ruined quarter northwest of Broadway became known as canvas town. High-ranking soldiers had commandeered the best houses, and the wealthier American Tories were able to afford rooms in homes where the rent quadrupled in two years. Inflation was rampant, and food, clothing, and fuel were often difficult to find at any price. Rebels surrounded the city, controlling supply lines, holding New York hostage.

So Franklin was fortunate to find himself in a place where he was revered, and grateful for any hospitality. He had lost nearly everything. Gaunt yet handsome, he was the image of the counterrevolutionary, a man capable of anything because he has nothing to lose. In this character he walked the streets: across the island from Dock to Broadway, past the portico of St. Paul's, down Broadway to General Clinton's headquarters and the fort with its turreted barbicans, its battlements, overlooking Bowling Green. Safe here, a British citizen under protection of the king's army, he could not venture outside the stronghold of New York without risking his life.

Of course he was free to board a ship and sail for England, following in his friend Galloway's footsteps. But his reluctance to leave the scene of action compelled him to remain tethered to this stubborn, dwindling British colony. Arriving with well-tempered hopes and a prospect that the empire he had long served would prevail against the rebels, he envisioned a plan of collaboration between the American loyalists and the British army.

The war itself had moved eight hundred miles south, to Georgia and South Carolina. In the New York winter of 1778–79 it would be, for all purposes, invisible. This was as frustrating to Henry Clinton as it was to William Franklin and the rest of the loyalists who longed to fight the rebels in New Jersey and Connecticut. They milled about the streets and taverns grumbling, bored, and frustrated they were not allowed to fight for their own country.

What Benjamin Franklin had accomplished at Versailles in February 1778, the treaty of alliance with France, England's greatest enemy, had swift and far-reaching results. On March 13, England declared war on France, the alliance automatically took effect, and Lord Germain ordered Major General Clinton to transform his military strategy in America. Clinton quit Philadelphia in May, leading a caravan of fifteen hundred wagons bearing military supplies and booty from patriot homes. The army marched to New York past vicious defiance at Monmouth and began preparing the campaign in the south, certain of strong loyalist support there.

General Clinton understood the danger of a French, American, and Spanish coalition in the south, but he hated shipping such huge battalions to the region as Germain had ordered. This would weaken his main army in the mid-Atlantic, troops that had been battered at Monmouth, where only the bungling of Washington's generals had saved Clinton from a crushing defeat. He offered up his resignation—it was refused. The arrival of the French admiral Charles Henri Hector, comte d'Estaing, that summer, in command of sixteen ships off Sandy Hook, blockading Lord Howe's little fleet in the Bay, deepened Clinton's despondency. He knew this was only the first of a parade of French and Spanish armadas that would bear down upon his dispirited soldiers.

Foreign wars are terribly costly when the invaders are not quick to prevail. At the close of 1778, no one knew who would win this sprawling war for independence, but certainly the Americans had time, and now international support, on their side. What remained uncertain was the slant of public opinion. Clinton's advantage in the south was groups of colonists and some Indian tribes that remained loyal to the Crown. But communication was slow and dispatches from the front were maddeningly vague, so New Yorkers did not know what to make of a battle fought at Port Royal Island, South Carolina, or Kettle Creek, Georgia, in February. The news took weeks to arrive, by which time it might be irrelevant. It was possible to live in New York City as in a bubble, surrounded by Tories who seized upon every rumor of victory as fuel for their faith that the rebellion would fizzle out.

Tories might also grow discouraged by the leadership of the military government in the British-occupied city, as William soon learned. The generals' condescension toward the American loyalists—the very patriots they were charged to defend—was astonishing.

Power and authority resided at No. 1 Broadway, the two-story English mansion of whitewashed brick overlooking the Hudson. There Major General Clinton had his headquarters. Governor Franklin paid his respects early in November 1778, at the first opportunity. Walking down Broadway he could glimpse the square cupola and widow's walk surmounting the steep roof of tiles. One admired the symmetry of the Kennedy mansion: beneath the gable of the central section a Palladian triple window duplicated the entrance beneath.

Guards saluted. The governor was expected. The carved doorway led to wide halls. The drawing room, where the general held his war councils, was fifty feet by thirty, hung with crystal chandeliers that cast rainbows on the wainscoting. A recently knighted Member of Parliament, Sir Henry Clinton was Franklin's age, forty-eight, a fair-haired, blue-eyed officer with large features and a pouting lower lip. His long, delicate hands looked more artistic than military. He was shy but also very brave, having sustained saber wounds in Germany during the Seven Years' War that would have crippled a lesser man. His conversation swung from sullen taciturnity to overwhelming bluster. Suspicious, reserved, given to spells of melancholia, the general nevertheless had a first-rate military mind that was too often ignored by the ministry.

Clinton was one of three so-called peace commissioners at the long table who welcomed Franklin in November, the others being William

Eden and Sir Frederick Howard, Earl of Carlisle. Their admiration for the governor upon his arrival that day was fulsome and explicit.

Franklin's first appeal had to do with money. He had nothing, and his debt to Thomas Wharton had mounted into the thousands during his captivity. Knowing the governor's sacrifice and his influence, the officials were eager to oblige, promptly granting him £1,200 in New Jersey currency (about $100,000). Soon to sail for England after a fruitless peace mission, Eden and Carlisle promised to acquaint Lord Germain with Governor Franklin's situation, with a view to getting him a pension. That was the easy part. He would have enough to get by, and to rent a small house in a city where inflation had made a coat more costly than a horse had been.

Everything else Franklin wanted to discuss met with resistance. While the commissioners welcomed his aid as a propagandist, willing to pay him to keep the newspapers full of essays inviting Americans to forsake the cause of independence, Clinton was reluctant to discuss the military potential of the loyalists. A few Tories had been organized into Royal Provincial Regiments and had seen action; some served in the New York militia, guarding Manhattan. But the British regarded the Americans with so much distrust that they mostly declined to deploy them. To Franklin's wonderment, the British army held the American Tories in low esteem for some of the same reasons their countrymen did. They saw the refugees as renegades who had fled for safety, forsaking their neighbors—they could not be trusted. Even if they could, these were not soldiers fit for the British mold, lacking the requisite training and character. It was this monstrous prejudice the governor discovered between the lines of his conversation with Henry Clinton.

Yet Franklin was not discouraged. When he returned to his lodgings he drew up a plan to create a Board of Loyal Refugees, men from six colonies who would work together to procure intelligence of the plans and movements of the enemy. The board would interview every refugee and prisoner who came through British lines and inspect captured letters. These members would be issued passes to move through the British lines and infiltrate the Continental Congress and the rebel army; then of course they would report to General Clinton.

Franklin sent this proposal with Eden and Carlisle when they sailed for England on November 27. He also gave them a letter to the colonial secretary, Lord Germain, a narrative of his own trials, hardships, and losses during the years since he was abducted from his home in Perth Amboy.

FRANKLIN'S LIFE DURING THE next two years was dedicated to getting American loyalists into the field. The British had come to put down a rebellion, but if they failed it would be the American Tories who would suffer, deprived of their homes, their property, their influence—and driven into exile. To William, the condescension of the British establishment, the very thing that had driven his father away from the motherland, seemed insane. At first he would not accept that it was systemic, instead attributing the attitude to Henry Clinton.

By this time General Clinton did not have much faith that his army and navy could put down the rebellion. And beyond a twinge of vanity, he did not care. Soon after his meeting with Governor Franklin at No. 1 Broadway, Clinton sent his aide-de-camp, Lieutenant Duncan Drummond, to England in order to present the general's petition to be recalled. The king refused, declaring that no man but Clinton could save America. These flattering words brought him small comfort when they came in the spring of 1779. His command was listless. Governor Franklin had arrived with momentum at a time when the stagnant military government had left the refugees feeling helpless and hopeless.

So Franklin planned his board, essentially an intelligence agency, and next, with the aid of the grant he had received, he began reaching out to assist all "suffering friends of government," families in the city, in Staten and Long Islands, and Tories in Connecticut prisons. He quickly got everyone's attention by negotiating the release of some harmless Tory lumbermen who had been captured on Long Island and then faced trial for treason in Connecticut. Franklin had succeeded in spite of the doubts, fears, and meddling of the commander in chief. William had demanded that an equal number of rebel prisoners in Connecticut should be selected and retained as hostages for these unfortunate woodcutters, and Clinton was worried that British prisoners elsewhere would be endangered in response.

William got his way by pressuring General Clinton with lawyer's logic and a startling, irrepressible authority. He demanded that those eight rebel prisoners be released into his custody, then he told the Connecticut court that if they did not free his eight woodmen, he would force the rebel hostages to dig a dungeon beneath the New York prison and live underground there on half rations. Within days the prisoners were exchanged.

Clinton's pleasure that the loyalists had come home did not equal his vexation that Governor Franklin had upstaged him. He had succeeded in saving the prisoners' lives, and in showing a determination that had long been missing—that the government would no longer stand by idly while some of the king's best subjects were slaughtered with impunity. Many thought that Franklin deserved an appointment as superintendent of refugees. The man was perfect for the role, but Clinton wanted no such office and was naturally opposed to a newcomer who threatened the established order.

One of Franklin's first political acts upon his arrival in New York had been to sign a petition to restore civil government. New York City under martial law was viciously corrupt. Civilians had no protection against British soldiers and bureaucrats, and violent crimes were everyday occurrences. A German officer wrote of "theft, fraud, robbery, and murder by the English soldiers," excited by their love of drink, and as they received little money, they resorted to robbery and rape to get what they wanted.

A wartime army's chief concern is for its survival; the rights of civilians come second. In a colonial city like Philadelphia, martial law was beside the point because the army was mostly kin to the civilians. But British and Hessians together might prey upon the Americans of Manhattan—and martial law enabled them, being a system not of justice but of maintaining the army. The punishments handed down by courts-martial for capital offenses—flogging, fines, jail time—were designed to restore the offender to active duty. It was terrifying to see a man who had been convicted of rape or theft back at his post, armed with a rifle, thirty days later.

The rebels' blockade of the city created perfect conditions for bribery and a black market: a scarcity of wheat, beef, firewood, and other necessities. The city that had thrived upon the produce of the surrounding farms now depended solely upon imports for its staples. New York had rum and molasses aplenty, and these things were scarce beyond the blockades, so smugglers were eager to trade them in New Jersey for beef and meal. The illegal trading, essential to the military and civilians alike, was acknowledged by authorities with a nod and a wink; and of course a great deal of money greased the wheels at every turn of the merchandise.

Governing the city was the military commandant, a coveted position shared in turn by several British generals. Continuity was provided by the superintendent general, Andrew Elliot, a civilian Clinton appointed to oversee day-to-day trade and police operations. Elliot regulated prices, rents, and wages, and supervised the night watch. Every tavern keeper, peddler, auctioneer, distiller, and stable keeper—anyone who wished to do business—required a license from the police. Trollops and smugglers paid their dues under the table. In 1779, a commandant tried to limit the number of taverns to two hundred, not for any moral purpose but to increase kickbacks from unlicensed tapsters.

This was the garrisoned city that Franklin discovered in 1778, a power pyramid that rested upon illegal trade, blackmail, bribery, and authorized vice. In the middle of the structure stood quartermasters, barrackmasters, naval commissaries, clerks, hay inspectors, wood inspectors, rum inspectors, ration deliverers, and police of the night watch. Everybody wanted a piece.

And at the very top, with authority over all, was the commander in chief, Major General Henry Clinton.

Clinton had little interest in Governor Franklin's crusade on behalf of the refugees, so William began to work around him. With his charm and organizational skills he started a club of refugees from many provinces that met at the City Arms, Hicks's tavern on the west side of Broadway, next to the ruins of Trinity Church. Two blocks from Clinton's headquarters, the place was popular with the soldiers, as this stretch of Broadway now made a promenade for the women of the city to display their finery in all kinds of weather. At the corners of the balcony and the piazza below were special tables for gentlemen of rank and reputation. At the head of his table, Governor Franklin hosted the Refugee Club. They drank rum, claret, and Madeira, smoked superb tobacco and Turkish opium, shared their stories of loss and defiance, and schemed for the future. They had nothing to hide from the British soldiers, as all had a common goal to put down the rebellion.

The idea of loyalists from many provinces banding together was novel and empowering. The refugees were impatient for a more aggressive strategy in the central colonies—a blockade of American harbors, bold guerrilla tactics, "one capital stroke," as Franklin advised Lord Germain. Such talk irritated Clinton, who despised the overly optimistic refugees whose zeal had often outrun their prudence. He had no idea how frustrated they had become, stranded in New York, unable to march against the rebels.

That year the club plotted to create a force that would succeed where the British army was failing. The idea was to empower William's planned Board of Loyal Refugees not only to gather intelligence but also to muster guerrilla units, terrorize rebel ports, free loyalist prisoners, and block rebel raids upon the Long Island Tory settlements. William's petition to General Clinton went unanswered. Knowing Franklin's intention, Clinton would not formally approve it; on the other hand, he made no effort to discourage any action that might trouble the enemy as long as it did not disrupt his command. Opposed to terrorism as a matter of policy, he was aware of the effects of it in the hands of an enemy. As Clinton's adviser, Justice William Smith, once said, "Sir Henry wished the conflagrations, and yet not to be answerable for them."

The loyalists did not wait for authorization. They began ordering retaliatory strikes in New Jersey and Connecticut. On March 27, one of the board, John Mason, sent out a letter headed "Warning to Rebels" promising that if they continued their murders and cruelties, six of their men would be hanged for every loyalist killed. Lord Germain approved, acknowledging a change in the conduct of the war. It had become what General William Tryon called "desolation warfare," that final lawless paroxysm when arson, rape, and murder prosper under the lex talionis, an eye for an eye, the Golden Rule gone to the devil.

Tryon, former governor of New York, was now Major General Tryon, Commander of Provincial Forces in America under Clinton's direction. Tryon was one of two men in Clinton's inner circle who liked Franklin and served as a broker between them. The other was the head of British secret intelligence, the stage actor, painter, and poet, twenty-nine-year-old Major John André. One of the most fascinating men of his time, the major burned brightly and would not live long in its welter. Franklin knew him in 1779, near the end of his tragic life. They had a curious connection: During the occupation of Philadelphia, John André had the honor of taking over the Franklin-Bache house in Market Street. Galloway figured the young poet, a man of refinement, would appreciate and take care of his friends' valuables. The fact that André made off with Ben Franklin's portrait, his harpsichord, and his spyglass does not seem to have stood in the way of his friendship with William, who was as charmed by the major as everyone else was.

First John André and then William Tryon represented Governor Franklin in the war room at No. 1 Broadway. With so many old contacts in New Jersey, Franklin quickly established a network of spies behind rebel lines, and he reported directly to Major André. His secret intelligence encompassed troop movements as well as loyalist sentiment regarding a counterinsurgence. George Washington, writing from headquarters in Middle Brook, New Jersey, on April 28, said he had heard that Governor Franklin had been appointed major general and commandant of new loyalist militia, and that already he was nominating civilians to replace the American government once Perth Amboy surrendered. The rumor was overblown, but founded upon the fear of what Franklin actually wanted to do.

André liked Franklin's plan for a Board of Refugees, and he hoped the general would fund it. On May 29, Franklin wrote up the details in a letter to André meant for Clinton's consideration. But the next day the army began a major offensive upon the rebel garrison at Strong Point, a strategic bridge over the Hudson. Clinton was so busy with this, and his campaign on Long Island, that he had no time, he explained, to answer Franklin's petition. Years later he would admit that it was not the press of other business that diverted him but his belief that further plans to employ the loyalists would be a waste of resources.

Far from useless, Franklin's unchartered Refugee Club and its spy net-work were reporting the movements of rebel generals Anthony Wayne and Nathanael Greene in New York and New Jersey. And they mus-tered a militia at Lloyd's Neck, Long Island.

On June 11, Franklin informed Clinton that the club's militia at Lloyd's Neck was embedded there, provisioned and fully armed, await-ing his orders. Clinton should have enlisted them, but pride and a per-verse sense of failure deterred him. Angry and frustrated, Franklin then turned to his colleague Governor William Tryon, inviting him to intercede. A career soldier with a proven appetite for cold-blooded warfare and terrorism, General Tryon appreciated his friend's rage and realized how much energy was stored up in the idle loyalists of New York. Wanting to fight, they refused to join the British for fear of being shipped to South Carolina. These men wanted action here and now, rescuing their own people. So Franklin drew up a proposal under the heading "Regulation of Refugees" and gave it to Tryon at the end of June.

Tryon was intrigued. Under the command of "some capable gentle-man," as William phrased it, the Tories were to be armed, provisioned, and equipped. They needed gunboats and guns, and authority to un-dertake expeditions wherever General Clinton did not expressly forbid them; everything was subject to his approval. If he preferred, he might order this regiment to support his own troops, but in that case the Americans would receive equal pay and privileges. They would own any plunder they seized during forays; and what prisoners they took would be kept separate from the army's, to use in exchange for any of their own men captured.

William's proposal included a peculiar clause forbidding any "ex-cesses, cruelties or irregularities contrary to the general rules of war among civilized nations, *unless by way of retaliation.*" Qualified as it was, this provision was self-canceling. Already there had been so many atrocities on both sides that any cruelty might be justified as retalia-tion.

Tryon recommended the plan to Clinton the next day, specifying that the "capable gentleman" modestly mentioned must be William Franklin, of course. The force ought to be organized under the command of Governor Franklin with the title of Director General and Commandant of the Associated Loyalists, and he should have authority to appoint officers and give orders agreeable to General Clinton. General Tryon then rode off to command a campaign of terror in Connecticut, looting towns before setting fire to them. Franklin corresponded with John André, waiting for a response from General Clinton that never came, not that summer, fall, or winter.

At least William had money while he waited. He had received a cordial letter from Lord Germain saying the king was fully persuaded of William's commitment and would reward his merit. The Lords of the Treasury were granting Franklin £500 ($76,000) for his present use and £500 per year as of January 1780. He was to appoint an agent in London to receive the money for him—that would be Mr. Strahan, of course.

The official adoption of Franklin's plan for the Associated Loyalists was drawn-out and complex. André tried in vain to sway Clinton. The general's blundering warfare in New Jersey and New York, and his constant wrangling with his admiral, convinced him that British morale would be best served by mounting an expedition in South Carolina. Deciding to take personal charge of this distant campaign, he embarked with a legion of fourteen thousand soldiers on Christmas Day.

Left to themselves, William's club, or the Associators, as they came to be known, commenced conducting espionage and guerrilla warfare along the coast. Their ten vessels attacked ports in Connecticut and Rhode Island. After the British commander in chief sailed away without a word, a loyalist named George Leonard, who had been bankrolling the club's expeditions out of his own dwindling fund, got on the next ship bound for England. In his pocket was Franklin's plan that General Tryon had submitted to Clinton long ago. He would give it to Lord Germain when he got to London.

Lord Germain liked it, and he wrote to Clinton on April 21 ordering that Franklin's plan be put into effect. Leonard sent the good news to him on May 3, and their letters reached New York simultaneously, in June 1780, just before Clinton returned, in triumph, from South Carolina. He dodged Franklin for two weeks before ordering his secretary to show him Germain's letter, without commenting or hinting how he would respond.

Months passed. One day in September, William was at headquarters on an errand and Clinton approached him. Out of a clear blue sky he asked what had been done to establish his proposed board. William blinked. He replied that the group did not have a copy of Germain's letter, and they had received no official order to proceed. Calling for the letter, Clinton declared he was in favor of it, and turned the paper over to him.

And so began another game of cat and mouse, Franklin rewriting the damned plan to please the commander in chief, and Clinton nitpicking and stalling and caviling until there were so many restrictions upon Franklin's authority it all seemed useless. Finally there was a document that satisfied no one but would have to suffice. The final draft was completed on Christmas Day 1780 and submitted to Clinton. At last he signed the documents, on the twenty-seventh, forced by the order from Germain.

William Franklin was to be president of the Board of the Associated Loyalists, with powers limited by the commander in chief and unlimited liabilities.

In Clinton's war room that autumn, the Intercolonial Council that met at the long table discussed the terrible predicament of William's friend John André. Major André had gotten tangled up in Benedict Arnold's plot to surrender West Point to the British for £20,000. Returning from a meeting with Arnold on September 23 in civilian clothes, with incriminating letters from Arnold in his stocking, he was arrested by militiamen near Tarrytown and taken to Continental Army headquarters at Tappan. There he was held while George Washington went to West Point to question Arnold, who had just time enough to sneak away to the garrison in Manhattan before Washington confirmed his treason.

Major John André was left holding the bag. Washington convoked a board of American generals presided over by Nathanael Greene that included such luminaries as Lafayette, Von Steuben, Lord Stirling, and Henry Knox. As a court-martial, the generals saw no choice but to condemn André to death as a spy. Receiving this news the following day, September 30, General Clinton convened his council to consider what might be done to save his favorite aide from the gallows. Governor Franklin, outraged, distraught, advised challenging the evidence that André was a spy, but he was voted down. Instead, the council sent a letter to Washington condemning his ignorance of military procedures and threatening a stern reprisal if the major was executed. They announced that a commission was on its way there to discuss the matter.

The delegation, headed by General Robertson, sailed up the Hudson on Sunday, the first of October, to a meeting place near Tappan, bringing Major André his uniform and razor. George Washington had sent General Greene there to talk with the British. Robertson argued, as well as he could, the protocols concerning prisoners, the right to escape in civilian clothes, André's right to suborn an enemy officer, and other considerations. Besides, the major was young, and brave, a stalwart who refused to place the blame upon Benedict Arnold. Greene and the other generals were really sorry for the gallant, poised, and eloquent officer who reminded many of Lafayette—no one in his right mind wanted to see such a person die. But Washington could think of no way of sparing André without violating military justice and demoralizing his soldiers.

Benedict Arnold wrote to Washington that if André were executed, he swore to heaven that His Excellency would be made to answer for the torrents of blood that would be spilled in consequence. Arnold promised that he himself would retaliate against any one of Washington's soldiers unlucky enough to fall into his power, and that forty patriots in South Carolina would be hanged.

It is said that Washington's hand trembled as he signed John André's death sentence. On October 2, surrounded by a crowd of civilians and soldiers, the young man stepped up into a wagon. He drew two handkerchiefs from his pocket, knotted together. Removing his hat and scarf, he tied his own blindfold with steady hands, slipped the noose over his head, and tightened it around his throat, sparing his executioner. "I pray you bear me witness that I meet my fate like a brave man," he declared. The wagon lurched and pulled away and he hung in the air in his red regimental coat and black boots. Few witnesses could forbear weeping at the sight of the hanging man.

This was a crucial provocation in what Tryon had called the warfare of desolation. Washington was deeply disturbed by Arnold's betrayal and the chance of more defections. He wrote in distress about the fitful fluctuations of his army, and the importance of West Point, complaining on October 18 that his army was dwindling to nothing. It appeared to him then that the enemy was free to ravage the country whenever and wherever they liked. William Franklin hoped so. The execution of his friend André was appalling, and might have been his own fate but for the grace of God. He wrote to Strahan on November 12 calling the execution "a shocking, bungling piece of business." Franklin grew bitter.

But in 1781, Governor Franklin was authorized to retaliate; Clinton had signed the articles of organization at the end of the previous year. A circular had been issued announcing the charter of the Board of Loyalists, to be headed by President Franklin whose men enlisted not as British soldiers but as Americans answering to the board. The charter stated that their aim was to take arms and help suppress the rebellion by harrowing the seacoasts of the revolted colonies and upsetting their commerce. No innocent people were to be hurt. Loyalists who served would share in the captured spoils, and anyone who served for the rest of the war would receive two hundred acres as well.

By March the Board of Loyalists was in full swing. William played several roles for which his life experience had prepared him: military strategist, commander, and mediator between the American Tories and the British high command. All of his sacrifices on behalf of the Crown, his zeal and integrity over so many years, were an inspiration to many thousands of loyalists who stepped up to serve him. He had become the most influential, the most revered, and probably the most powerful American loyalist.

With his commission came a secretary, Sampson S. Blower, and a house at No. 4 Nassau Street, where the board made their headquarters. It stood in the center of the city on Broadway between City Hall and the towering New Dutch Church. In the little house on Nassau

Street, in the shadow of the great church tower, Franklin presided over the paramilitary organization, planning hundreds of missions. Most involved a ship or two and a dozen to three dozen men sent to capture stores, livestock, or prisoners. The time and labor involved in planning and documenting these missions—not to mention listing and managing the companies—was staggering. Plus, every detail had to be relayed to Clinton. Men drawn to guerrilla warfare are not always orderly, and President Franklin had his hands full in keeping these companies on task and under control.

What did they accomplish? There are glimpses in newspapers. On March 1, Captain Cornelius Hetfield and four other refugees under cover of night crossed the Raritan River from Staten Island to the village of Spanktown, five miles west of Rahway. There they dragged out of bed John Clauson, commissioner for selling confiscated property, and took him prisoner, along with an ensign who tried to rescue him. The two patriots were taken to Staten Island and never heard from again. Later that month a handful of Associators hatched a plot to kidnap one Josiah Hornblower, Speaker of the Provincial Assembly, who lived in Newark. A renowned mechanic, he had built the first steam engine in America, and worked such wonders of military engineering for the patriots that it would be useful for the Tories to capture him. They tried on March 29, but Hornblower outwitted and escaped them.

More typical was the raid upon the town of Closter, high up on the Hudson. During a two-day expedition in March the marauders robbed the village of everything of value that was movable. Almost weekly there were raids somewhere in New Jersey. Elizabethtown, across the river from Staten Island, was a favored target. On May 4, a party of refugees carried off forty head of cattle, and on June 2, a sniper there killed Private Richard Woodruff.

There is no evidence that Franklin ever left New York for active duty upon any of these errands. He surely would not have risked it. On the garrisoned island he was fortunate, at night, if some assassin did not dispatch him with a dagger; lucky, eating his breakfast, if he was not poisoned. He relied upon young soldiers like Thomas Ward.

Captain Thomas Ward commanded a corps of loyalists who foraged with axes in Bergen County to provide firewood for New York. Valiant and resourceful, the captain realized his feeble blockhouse at Bergen Point on the Hudson was not only vulnerable, it was too far south to serve the guerrillas as a base for raids upon the farms and forests of the Hackensack Valley. Fort Lee, across from Harlem, would be better. One of the memorable actions of the Associated Loyalists occurred on May 14, 1781, when a fleet of gunboats bearing two hundred troops landed near Fort Lee under Captain Ward's command. They quickly scared away the militia pickets and began building a new blockhouse upon the remains of this fort that George Washington had abandoned in 1776.

The rebel commanding officer there put out a call to the Bergen County militia, and three hundred patriots showed up to drive off the invaders. For five days the fighting was fierce. At his headquarters in New Windsor, George Washington got word of it and ordered Colonel Alexander Scammell and his corps to mobilize. General Clinton heard of it and got a thousand troops ready to sail away—Hessian riflemen, as well as loyalists from Bergen County. But a British colonel, arriving first to assess the action, ordered Captain Ward and his marines to return to their ships and give up the fort as they could not secure it.

While Fort Lee was not a major battle, it had been a costly diversion, worrying General Washington and wasting the energy of an entire corps of crack soldiers who came from Westchester County and crossed the river at Nyack. The patriots marched around from Closter to Tappan in the rain and mud before learning that the Tories had gone back to New York. Captain Ward was promoted to the rank of major.

THE EXPEDITIONS FRANKLIN PLANNED in his office on Nassau Street that summer and autumn were not glamorous. But an important post was established at Lloyd's Neck on the north shore of Long Island, with a well-armed garrison under the command of Colonel Joshua Upham and a warship named the *Henry Clinton*. From this point his loyalists in brigs conducted raids along the Connecticut coast, skirmishing with rebel guards and capturing horses, cattle, and sheep.

More damage was done in New Jersey. Up and down the coast from New Jersey to Rhode Island, foraging and looting—it was impossible to know exactly what went on. Given such license, the terrorists were not likely to inform upon one another. The tactics of terror were viewed as retaliation, and the reports of patriot atrocities were bloodcurdling. In early summer the Board of Associated Loyalists had sent unlucky agents down to Maryland to liberate prisoners in Frederick Town and Sharpsburg and raise a force that would aid Cornwallis as he moved up from the Chesapeake, dividing the rebel army, south from the north. In Frederick, one of William's men, mistaking an American officer for a disguised Tory, passed him letters detailing the plot. Seven Tory conspirators were brought up before a rump tribunal and summarily convicted of treason.

The sentence the judge handed down—for the crime of enlisting men to the service of the king—echoed the Dark Ages: "You shall be carried to the gaol of Frederick town, and be hanged therein; you shall be cut down to the earth alive, and your entrails shall be taken out and burnt while you are yet alive, your heads shall be cut off, your body shall be divided into four parts and your heads and quarters shall be placed where his Excellency the Governor shall appoint. So the Lord have mercy upon your poor souls."

Usually the cruelty was more random and spontaneous. General Nathanael Greene, observing the war in the south, wrote that the rebels seemed determined to exterminate the Tories, and the Tories the rebels, and if a stop was not soon put to the massacres, "the country will be depopulated in a few months more." Naturally William Franklin was most sensitive to rebel acts of terrorism in New Jersey. He was particularly alarmed by developments in Monmouth County, where an Association for Retaliation had been murdering Associated Loyalists in Freehold and Shrewsbury for three years. He kept count—it was more than a dozen killings. In the case of the loyalist Jacob Fagan, the man died of his wounds and was buried by his friends; then the rebels dug him up and carried his corpse to Colt's Neck, where they hung it in chains from a chestnut tree a mile from the courthouse.

The patriot "Retaliators" worked under the leadership of General

David Forman and Joshua Huddy, a vicious, disowned Quaker, troublemaker, and felon. After the Battle of Monmouth, General Forman's duty was to report to General Washington on British warships from New York to Little Egg Harbor, fifty miles to the south. In his spare time he was to suppress the Tory guerrillas, who called him Devil David. As for Huddy, the times and the task suited his temperament. As a captain of the New Jersey militia he had led raids upon merchants smuggling for the British, capturing and sometimes murdering loyalists as the spirit moved him. He liked to boast of his cruel deeds, and it is said that Huddy looked like a pirate with a black beard, a headscarf, and an earring.

Now both armies had a new adjective for what the war had become: "intestine." As Abner Nash, governor of South Carolina, put it, this was "a country exposed to the misfortune of having a war within its bowels." Back in September 1778, a newlywed New Jersey loyalist, Stephen Edwards of Shrewsbury, was in bed with his wife when Captain Jonathan Forman (no relation to Devil David) knocked at his door in Eatontown. The captain, leading a party of cavalry from the New Jersey militia at midnight, knew where to find the Tory because their families had known each other for years. His wife tried to hide Stephen under the blankets. That he was disguised in a maid's outfit and cap did not fool Captain Forman. Searching the house, he found papers that led him to believe the bridegroom in a gown was a spy.

The rebels took Stephen Edwards to the jail in Freehold on a Saturday. On Monday at ten in the morning he was hanged from an oak tree shading the portico of the Monmouth Courthouse. Joshua Huddy was proud to say he was one of the party that captured and hanged the first loyalist spy in Monmouth County. He told the world he was the man who had greased the rope and pulled it tight around Edwards's neck.

More than a year passed before William Franklin was able to orchestrate a reprisal in Huddy's hometown of Shrewsbury, on the river below Sandy Hook. On April 30, 1780, Captain William Gillian led a party of seven loyalist marauders on a mission there to capture the privateer brig *Elizabeth* and some prisoners—including Huddy, if he could be found. The loyalists, most of whom were from the area, included Richard Lippincott and Philip White, both of whom were relatives of young Stephen Edwards and wanted revenge.

The Tories made short work of the *Elizabeth*, capturing the vessel and its captain. But they ran into trouble soon after their door-to-door pillaging began. Entering the home of one John Russell, guns blazing in the night, the raiders met with rebel gunfire from sixty-year-old Russell and his son, and a surprisingly complex bloodbath followed. Captain Gillian, born and raised in Shrewsbury, grabbed the old man by the collar and was about to bayonet him in the face—though he was mortally wounded—when the fire suddenly blazed up, illuminating the scene. The younger Russell, who lay bleeding on the floor, took a bead on Captain Gillian and shot and killed him outright. John Farnham, a loyalist from nearby Middletown, then leveled his musket at Russell Jr. and meant to shoot him when Lippincott, suddenly recognizing a kinsman, knocked away the weapon, crying there was no need to shoot a dying man. He then got on with ransacking the house. Russell's widow, screaming, and John Jr.'s wife and five-year-old son were cowering in a back bedroom. Somehow in the confusion the child was struck by a bullet and wounded, but he managed, like his father, to survive.

Try as they would, the Associated Loyalists could not catch Joshua Huddy. In August, the Continental Congress issued him a commission to man a gunboat called the *Black Snake* to attack British shipping and loyalist strongholds. He was so destructive that in September, William Franklin ordered a surprise attack upon his sturdy house in Colt's Neck. An hour before dawn, sixty loyalists, led by the notorious commander Titus Cornelius, a runaway slave the British had given the honorific "Colonel Tye," surrounded Huddy's well-built wood frame home. A gunfight ensued. Huddy and his twenty-year-old mistress, Lucretia Emmons, somehow held the refugees at bay for two hours, firing from different windows as if they were five persons. Tye, badly wounded in his wrist, at last set fire to the house. Only then did Huddy agree to surrender on the condition they leave the girl alone.

When Colonel Tye and his men were returning to their ship with the prisoner and some livestock, the rebel militia arrived, muskets booming, to rescue Huddy. They killed six Tories before the rest made it aboard the vessel with their prisoner. As they weighed anchor, the militiamen kept shooting from the shore, wounding Huddy in the thigh. Then this cat with nine lives leapt overboard, shouting to his comrades, *"I am Huddy! I am Huddy!"* and swam ashore to live, and terrorize loyalists, another day.

While Captain Huddy's leg healed, gangrene set in to Tye's wound and he died of it. And the Committee of Retaliation, a shadow government in the lawless barrens and coves of Monmouth, arranged to plunder and butcher the refugees whenever they could, settling old scores with the Tories in the name of liberty. Franklin lobbied for gunboats and guns, with small success. In Freehold there was a vacant lot owned by General Forman that became known as the Hanging Place for the dozen Tories who had been lynched there without ceremony.

It was Devil David, and Captain Huddy, and the bloodshed in Monmouth County that troubled William Franklin's sleep during that terrible night, October 23, 1781, when all were awakened by the sound of cannon fire upon the Jersey Shore.

A celebration was under way. News of Cornwallis's surrender had come to New Jersey.

CHAPTER 18

Captain Huddy and the Dance of Death

DURING THOSE YEARS, WILLIAM Franklin's longing to maintain contact with his family in Philadelphia and France never
waned. A few unpublished letters between Sally Bache and her nephew
Temple that have come to light reveal how much effort to communicate was made on both sides, from the time William was exchanged
until his last days in New York.

Sally informed Temple on September 16, 1779, that she had received two letters from his father that summer. The governor was perfectly fine and always inquired affectionately about Grandfather's
health as well as Temple's. William sent his two-year-old niece Betty,
his late wife's namesake, the birthday gift of a little bonnet. Sally felt
free to write to William in New York, and whenever she received any
news from Temple in Paris she made a point of relaying it to his father.
Richard Bache felt no such freedom to correspond with the loyalist—
although he did inform Benjamin, on November 2, that "By a gentleman lately out of New York we hear that his [Temple's] father is well."
This is, significantly, the last we hear of William Franklin from Bache
until the war is over.

Letters were constantly being intercepted. Soon after Sally wrote
the one to Temple quoted above, she and William were advised to cor-

respond no more. It was dangerous. As Governor Franklin's activism in the war mounted, the family was under mortal pressure to avoid him. What could not be trusted to the mails had to be communicated by a faithful intermediary, behind closed doors. Answering Aunt Sally's letter on March 18, 1780, Temple was so bold as to write: "It gives me infinite satisfaction, to hear that my father enjoys his health. I have never wrote him since I left Philadelphia: for several reasons." His grandfather had warned him not to. "I certainly might have done it without injuring the American Cause, but I thought it might give suspicions: and I was desirous of avoiding them." He admitted he had not been wholly successful in this.

By the time Sally wrote to her nephew again, on October 30, the only news she could offer about his father was hearsay. A Mrs. Lewis who came to visit from New York had often been with him and said he was in fine spirits. William had asked Mrs. Lewis the name of Sally's newborn. "She told him Louis, after the King of France." He smiled but said nothing. Sally reassured Temple that his reasons for not writing to his father were sound, and that whenever she had news of Temple, or Grandfather, she would find a way of conveying it to William without paper. "I am sure it makes him happy. . . . I do not now write— Peace I hope will soon restore to us the pleasure of corresponding with, and seeing our friends, along with many other pleasures and comforts that this cruel war has deprived us of."

THE SURRENDER OF GENERAL Cornwallis at Yorktown on October 19, 1781, came as a surprise to most of the world—but not to General Clinton. He had begun to despair a year earlier, after a third of Cornwallis's army was routed at the battle of King's Mountain, South Carolina. He later wrote that that defeat was "the first link in a chain of evils" that resulted in the loss of America. Yet George Washington's own despair, expressed soon after King's Mountain, is also well known, so clearly there was fear on both sides.

Most Americans, weary of war, inflation, conflagration, and terrorism, were hopeful but hardly confident the Continental Army would prevail at the beginning of that year. In mid-January 1781, Richard

Bache had informed Benjamin of Benedict Arnold's march to Richmond, burning public buildings and destroying all the public records.
The war, Bache explained, had been so far away that the colony of
Virginia "almost forgot there was such a thing existing in America;
being long unmolested, she lulled herself into security and was thence
unprepared for an attack." This might be said of all the provinces north
of the Carolinas, with the exception of New Jersey and New York,
where hand-to-hand fighting was a daily reality.

In the summer of 1781, William had still been hopeful. He knew
General Clinton had decided to send a fleet of ships with reinforce-
ments to save Cornwallis in August, and William had confidence in
the plan. What no one knew, because of Washington's trickery, fake
dispatches, and lightning speed, is how rapidly his army of seven thousand soldiers would march from Newport to Philadelphia. It was mi-
raculous. While Clinton dawdled in the harbor, Washington and
Rochambeau began, on August 19, what came to be known as the
celebrated march, delivering the army to Philadelphia—two hundred
miles in two weeks. From there they would sail to Virginia. No one,
including his generals, could have predicted Washington's luck and ingenuity, or Clinton's folly and misfortune—the storm that delayed his
armada. By the time the fleet set sail, Cornwallis, overwhelmed, had
surrendered his troops at Yorktown—a defeat so crippling the British
would not recover from it.

The news of the surrender, arriving in England on November 25,
would put an end to British hopes for victory. By April 15, Benjamin
Franklin was in secret negotiations with Richard Oswald, a special
agent for Lord Shelbourne, the new secretary of state, to secure a peace.
In America these events were widely anticipated; Sally Bache, writing
to her father on November 29, was jubilant. "You have heard so much
of the late glorious news from all quarters, that I need not repeat it,
only congratulate you on an event that I think must procure us a happy
peace." She wrote that she was all dressed up to visit Martha Washington, in town celebrating with her husband and Congress.

William Franklin heard of the terms of surrender from the loyalists
who had escaped Yorktown, the lucky soldiers who shouldered their
way aboard the British ship *Bonetta* moored in the York River. One

could hear their mournful voices in the City Arms Tavern. Cornwallis had thrown over his American brothers in arms, sold them to the rebels to save his English regulars and Hessian mercenaries! Clinton himself wrote of the horror and dismay with which the American refugees who had joined forces with his troops or expected their protection read Article X of the surrender. This denied American loyalists the immunity from punishment that was guaranteed to foreign soldiers. They were to be treated as criminals. General Washington—to ease his own conscience and appease Cornwallis—had included one little sentence, a loophole about the *Bonetta:* "It might sail without examination, with such soldiers as he may think proper to send to New York." There were hundreds of loyalists, and not room enough on the *Bonetta* for half of them. Men who rowed after the ship in boats, crying for their lives, were beaten back with curses, and many were soon seized by the patriots. Some faced the gallows and others were whipped. Most lost their property.

William Franklin wrote to the colonial secretary on November 6: "Of far more consequence than the loss of ten such generals, and ten such armies, is the confidence of almost every rank and denomination of people throughout the British Provinces." One high-ranking Associator, Colonel Joshua Upham, wanted to know if he and his men were also to be sacrificed.

The Board of Associated Loyalists asked Governor Franklin to sail to England at once and plead their case. He agreed to go. But at the last minute General Clinton talked him out of it, promising that if Franklin would stay and keep the peace among his people, he, the commander in chief, would issue a public order that the loyalists would never be treated any differently than the king's troops. Taking Clinton at his word, Franklin answered his ranking officer, Colonel Upham, at Lloyd's Neck, reassuring him that this new order was in effect.

When General Clinton heard that Franklin had informed Upham of the promised order of protection, airing the substance of their private conversation, he was furious. William protested that the order that might restore the faith of thousands was worthless if only the two of them knew of it. Clinton stalled. He wanted a formal petition from the board and insisted on waiting for Cornwallis's return to New York to explain, or apologize for, the odious Article X. Cornwallis came and went, sailing for England on December 15 without explaining his choice to anyone's satisfaction. William wrote to Lord Germain that if the blunders committed in the management of the king's affairs in this country were not yet plainly obvious, he was at a loss to know what could convince Parliament. On January 23, Clinton agreed to issue the order against any discrimination between the loyalists and the British regulars. But he never did. He just wanted to go home, to follow Cornwallis to England, to be anywhere other than this hellish place. In March he authorized Franklin to publish the order as president of the Board of Associated Loyalists.

Desperate to gain some tool of leverage for his refugees, William begged Clinton to issue a public letter addressed to General Washington and the congress vowing retaliation. If any American taken prisoner at Yorktown was executed, the British would square accounts by hanging a rebel prisoner in New York. At the very least, he pleaded, Clinton might authorize the Associated Loyalists to deal with their own prisoners as they saw fit, an eye for an eye. Nothing less than retributive justice, he advised, would restore confidence and a sense of security among the Tories.

Clinton would do nothing of the sort. He would not publicly criticize his own general for the conditions of his surrender, nor would he make a public policy of the Mosaic *lex talionis*. General Clinton knew very well that retributive justice would follow, inevitably, from civil war. As so many suffering patriots and loyalists would live to tell—soldiers driven mad by violence and privation, innocent men and women caught in the crossfire, widows and orphans—the war of rebellion was over but the civil war would rage on.

While Benjamin Franklin was in France negotiating the peace, William Franklin was fighting for his life and the lives of the king's good subjects. They had no choice, these men with prices on their heads. And despite General Clinton's cynicism and gloom, the Associated Loyalists had not given up hope that the British might win the war after all. If this seems irrational, so it was. Sane men were out of their element. News traveled unreliably and distant battles offered seeds of hope. At Clouds Creek, South Carolina, a troop of two hundred loyalists crushed a company of patriots on November 17; only two rebels survived the massacre. On January 25, 1782, Rear Admiral Samuel Hood commanding twenty-two British battleships defeated a larger French fleet at the sea battle of St. Kitts. This was a significant victory. And William Franklin was plotting an uprising in Duchess County; he was strengthening the garrison at Lloyd's Neck and designing a stronghold at Sag Harbor as a base for spring campaigns in Maryland, Pennsylvania, and New Jersey.

Governor Franklin reported to Lord Germain on March 23 (not knowing Germain had been replaced) that Cornwallis's failure had resulted not from military disadvantage but from blundering, delay, and failure to cooperate with American loyalists. He believed he and his men could do better. That very day a convoy of Associated Loyalists was under sail from Lloyd's Neck down to Toms River, deep in Monmouth County, under orders to destroy a nest of rebel pirates, the garrison of the infamous Jack Huddy.

Captain Huddy commanded a small fort guarding Dover, a coastal hamlet seventy miles south of New York. On the hill overlooking Toms River, the fort was a square palisade of logs seven feet high garrisoned by twenty-six rebels, who manned cannon mounted on the four corners. The deep harbor there, camouflaged by marsh grasses, made perfect anchorage for privateers, like Huddy himself, who could lie in wait for British vessels sailing north to New York with provisions, arms, or treasure.

By the end of the winter, March 1782, Huddy had caused such loss of life and property along the coast that the Associated Loyalists vowed to put him out of business. The expedition deployed three armed whaleboats bearing eighty seamen, under guard of a brig, the *Arrogant,* shipping its crew and thirty more soldiers ready to fight.

The convoy sailed from Lloyd's Neck on the vernal equinox, arriving near the mouth of Toms River on Saturday, March 23. A sentry spied their landing at midnight and ran to awaken Huddy. When the Tories attacked at dawn, the rebels behind the notched palisades were armed with muskets, pistols, and long pikes. In the fight that ensued the sailors swarmed over the fort and its cannon, losing nine men to bullets and bayonets while killing seven rebels.

Huddy escaped to look for shelter in the village, running from house to house as the Tories set fire to one after another. They burned the warehouses and tavern, and every house in Dover except for two dwellings belonging to Tory relations, before finding Joshua Huddy barricaded in Randolph's mill, with Justice of the Peace Daniel Randolph. The two men laid down their arms, and were led in irons to the *Intrepid* bound for New York.

At last Captain Jack Huddy, the man who had greased the noose for Stephen Edwards, was a prisoner of war. Arriving in New York on April 1 under guard, he was held in a British military jail.

That same day rumors drifted up from Monmouth County that the loyalist Philip White had been captured near Snag Swamp, off the coast, and tortured. White reminded everyone of the late Stephen Edwards, his loyalist kinsman from Shrewsbury. Twenty-six years of age, he, too, had a wife, a son, and a baby daughter. A carpenter by trade, he also commandeered a privateer called *The Wasp*. This was the same man who had joined the raid on Shrewsbury that killed rebel John Russell's sixty-year-old father and wounded his little boy. White's ship had been anchored off Long Branch and he was about to board her when a party of rebel cavalry took him by surprise. One of these was John Russell, Jr.—the son of the man he had killed. As Russell chased Philip White over the sedge and dunes, White turned to fire his musket and dispatched one of his pursuers. The others overtook him.

John Russell, Jr., rancorous, and vengeful, commanded the guards that conducted the Tory White from Snag Swamp to Freehold, where he was to be held in the jail at Monmouth Courthouse. It satisfied Russell's desire for revenge that Philip White did not get to Freehold alive or even in one piece. Russell and two other militiamen pierced him with swords until he ran; Russell then overtook White three miles from Freehold, at Pyle's Corner, and murdered him piecemeal. What remained of the young husband and father lay bleeding upon a long table in the Monmouth Courthouse for the gaping mob as a public show and a warning to traitors. So grisly was the sight that when the victim's sister drove over from Shrewsbury with a coffin to bury him, she was turned away.

The agonizing martyrdom of Philip White in Monmouth coin-

cided with the loyalists' worst fears of persecution. They wanted revenge, and as news of White's murder reached Governor Franklin, so
did demands for Joshua Huddy. So Franklin agreed that as soon as he
had custody of Huddy, he would hand him over, to one Captain Richard Lippincott, who had a formal commission from the Board of Associated Loyalists.

John Tilton was one loyalist passionately concerned in the affair,
because his brother Clayton Tilton, and his friend Aaron White, the
late Philip's brother, were in the Monmouth jail in danger of hanging,
and Huddy's life might be exchanged for their freedom. So Tilton
spoke to Captain Lippincott, who Governor Franklin said "would be
fond of going"; both knew Captain Richard Lippincott took a hearty
interest in Huddy's fate, having been both a lifelong friend and a kinsman to Philip White.

When Lippincott reported to the board on Nassau Street on the
morning of April 8, 1782, William Franklin was absent. Captain Lippincott told the board that Clayton Tilton was a prisoner in Freehold
about to be hanged. He requested an order to remove Joshua Huddy
and two other rebels in chains down to Sandy Hook, where he would
use them to bargain for Tilton's freedom. A little later Governor
Franklin entered, greeted the company, and glanced at the document
on the table. Lippincott had in his pocket a piece of paper that unfolded to the size of a man's heart with some writing upon it. He
pressed the note upon the governor and asked him to read it, inquiring
if it would do. At this, Daniel Coxe, the vice president of the board,
angrily objected, telling him to put it away.

So the captain went away with his orders to Provost Jail. There the
marshal bound Huddy, and two other prisoners, over to Lippincott and
his company of loyalists, headed for the bay in a schooner. But instead
of running the three men straight to Freehold to negotiate a prisoner
exchange, Captain Lippincott stowed them safely aboard an armed
ship, the *Britannia,* anchored off Sandy Hook, where the captain
agreed to hold them. Lippincott then set off with his soldiers to free
Tilton and White by force of arms from Freehold Prison. Failing in
the attempt, Lippincott returned to the *Britannia* in a rage and asked
for one prisoner, Joshua Huddy.

What happened in the next few hours on the beach at Gravelly Point, was witnessed by no fewer than twenty-four men, the April sunlight on the Navisink hills behind them, strong light upon the sand and sea. They would never forget the weirdness of the scene. Carpenters hammered up a gallows of several stout planks above a barrel and fastened a noose to the top brace. The rope, which had come from the *Britannia*, made a curious shadow on the sand. Joshua Huddy was given a quill and paper and invited to write his last will upon the barrel head. He wrote it, maintaining an admirable composure. Then most of the men stood back to watch Huddy, Lippincott, and a black slave in a queer pantomime against the sea and sky.

Huddy and Lippincott were conversing softly. There was no sign or sound of anger, no pleading or condemnation. The slave put the noose around Huddy's neck and tightened it. Huddy climbed up on the barrel. He put his hand out to Richard Lippincott for him to shake it, and he did. The black man pulled the rope tight, fastened it, and kicked over the barrel.

THERE HAD BEEN HUNDREDS of murders just as barbarous on both sides of the conflict. But this is the one beyond all others that got the attention of George Washington, Henry Clinton, America, and all of Europe.

The paper that Captain Lippincott had unfolded at the board meeting on Monday morning was pinned to Huddy's shirt as he hung on the gallows on Friday the twelfth.

> We, the Refugees, having long with grief beheld the cruel murders of our brethren and finding nothing but such measures daily carried into execution, we therefore determined not to suffer without taking vengeance for the numerous cruelties; and thus begin having made use of Captain Huddy as the first object to present to your view; and we further determine to hang man for man while there is a refugee existing.
>
> UP GOES HUDDY FOR PHILIP WHITE

The body was discovered the next morning, still hanging. The rebels cut him down and marched with the corpse the seventeen miles to Freehold, gathering mourners along the way and delivering Captain Huddy's remains to the courthouse, where he lay in state for three days. The two loyalists, Tilton and White, for whom Lippincott had come days before were released from the Freehold jail in exchange for Huddy's two fellow prisoners aboard the *Britannia.*

Retaliation, Aaron White swore, had saved his life and Tilton's.

Whatever sins Joshua Huddy had committed in his troubled life, in death he was a hero to his countrymen. The crowd of mourners was so enormous that no building in town could hold a quarter of them. The eulogy for the military martyr concluded with a thundering condemnation of the hanging—and an appeal to General Washington for justice.

George Washington was properly outraged. On April 21, he wrote a letter of protest to General Clinton enclosing testimonials from the people of Monmouth, who believed Clinton had ordered the hanging. Washington called Huddy's death "the most brutal, unprecedented, and inhuman murder that ever disgraced the arms of a civilized people" and demanded that Captain Lippincott be given up. Do it speedily, he added, or he would consider himself justified in the eyes of God and man for the measures he would then take—in other words, Washington would hang an English officer in retaliation.

Sir Henry Clinton was also provoked: first, by the unauthorized execution of a prisoner of war, and second, by Washington's insinuating that he, General Clinton, would authorize such a "barbarous outrage against humanity." As soon as he had heard of the deed he had ordered an investigation. Lippincott was already under arrest and would soon be tried by a court-martial. Clinton could not resist some moralizing of his own: Washington's threatening to sacrifice an innocent man to prevent further bloodshed would be to magnify barbarity. Furthermore, if one wanted examples of cruelty, there were plenty of those in Washington's own jurisdiction, worse, in fact, and probably inciting this recent horror.

Clinton had written to William Franklin on April 20, a polite letter reporting the murder and enclosing a copy of the note that had been pinned to Huddy's shirt. He asked for an inquiry and a report, at once. He waited for five days for a response before writing again on the twenty-fifth, demanding an answer. The general informed President Franklin that he had just appointed a Board of Generals to investigate the hanging. When taken into custody, Lippincott claimed he had orders from the Board of Loyalists dated April 8 to carry Huddy and other prisoners to Sandy Hook and arrange a prisoner exchange.

This time Governor Franklin replied, explaining that as soon as he got the first letter he had read it to his board, who directed Captain Lippincott to prepare a report. This took him a few days, as he had to take depositions from people living in different places; and by the time he had gotten it all organized and copied fair—just yesterday evening—he was seized and carried to the Provost Jail. Now Lippincott was powerless to make his report, and so the board was powerless to comply with His Excellency's request. He enclosed the letter that had informed Clinton's adjutant of the planned expedition, and the original instructions that had gone to Captain Lippincott.

For General Clinton, this would not do. In light of the furious threats from General Washington, this would not do at all. Clinton insisted on having every bit of information the Board of Associated Loyalists could provide by ten o'clock the next morning.

The letters that followed may be summed up in a sentence of Franklin's statement on behalf of the board: "The three prisoners delivered to Captain Lippincott on the 8th were not exchanged according to the intentions of the Board, but . . . they were nevertheless disposed of in a manner which the Board are clearly of opinion was highly justifiable." The board denied giving orders to Lippincott to kill Huddy. Yet, given that hundreds of British subjects had been murdered without their government's lifting a finger to defend them, no wonder they felt justified in retaliating. Men placed in such dire circumstances will act out of emotion rather than reason.

It is quite simply, Franklin declared, a law of nature and self-preservation that justifies such measures, and in the present case no other means could address the purpose. Such an argument, written in blood, was unanswerable. It was probably for the best that Franklin's words were not included in the public discourse, or in the transcripts of the court-martial that commenced on May 3. Clinton would not have to answer Franklin's letter, or the board's objections to the court-martial of Lippincott, which they said was illegal and offensive because Captain Lippincott was not a British officer but an American loyalist. Clinton would not have to deal with any more of this, because he was mercifully relieved of his command the very day, Saturday, April 27, that he received the terrible letter—terrible because it was sad, unanswerable, and true—from William Franklin.

One of Clinton's last acts as commander in chief was to summon Philip White's brother Aaron, and two other loyalists, William Murdock and Isaac Alyay, to headquarters. Under oath, these Tories testified as eyewitnesses to atrocities committed by rebel soldiers. Their depositions were meant to accompany a letter to be composed by Clinton's successor as governor, General James Robertson, to George Washington.

Washington found himself in the worst political predicament he had ever faced. On April 19, he had promised the citizens of Monmouth, and his own generals at a council of war, that he would retaliate. If Captain Lippincott was not surrendered, then some British officer of equal rank must die in his place. Washington's sensibilities shrank from the heartless lunacy of such an action, but the people had given him no choice. After Huddy's funeral the citizens of Monmouth had issued the Monmouth Manifesto, threatening to act on their own and "open to view a scene at which humanity itself may shudder."

General Robertson did write to Washington on May 1, begging him to agree that each man would punish war crimes in his own camp—and renounce retaliation. He pointed to the gruesome testimony of Aaron White concerning his brother. Then he called attention to an incident in Westchester County that had become notorious, of great interest to William Franklin because he knew the parties involved. Loyalists Alyay and Murdock testified that they were among five civilians brought before a major general in the rebel service upon suspicion of treason. The commander asked the guard who the men were. Told that they were prisoners, the general said, "Damned rascals, they shall every one be hanged," and, pointing to Daniel Current, said, "You shall be hanged first."

Without further discussion apart from the order "See him kicking on the tree," Daniel Current was led to a locust tree next to the house. An aide-de-camp put the noose around his neck and bade him stand upon a cart, as the general stood by under the tree giving directions. Current begged to speak in his defense but was silenced by the general, who cursed him. Current cried out he wanted a priest and a little time to prepare for such a great change, but those requests, too, were refused—likewise when he pleaded for time to say his prayers. The order was given for him to be hung up and the cart was kicked away.

Either the rope was tied too loosely, or in stretching caused the hanged man to fall on the ground, where they let him lie until he came to his senses. Realizing where he was, Daniel Current cried out again, piteously, for a little time and a clergyman; he was no spy, only a man who came out of the British lines to visit his wife and child in the country. But once more the noose was tied and the prisoner commanded to mount the cart, "and he was accordingly executed." The entire proceeding took less than half an hour.

It pained George Washington to read these depositions all the more because the major general who had presided over this procedure was none other than William Alexander, Lord Stirling, one of his most valiant and trusted generals. General Washington had given away Stirling's daughter at her wedding. At one time William Franklin's honored friend—turned mortal enemy—Lord Stirling was considered to be among the most civilized gentlemen in the colonies, a mathematician, astronomer, and master winemaker. War had unhinged him.

The Lippincott affair caused General Washington considerable grief during a season when it seemed likely that peace was at hand. Governor Franklin and his infernal Board of Associated Loyalists had wrecked the channels of reconciliation. Washington answered Robertson on May 4, saying that far from retreating from his previous decision, he had designated a British officer for retaliation. "The time and place are fixed." Yet he told the general he still hoped that the result of the British court-martial would prevent this awful alternative.

Actually, he had lied—the place and time had not been fixed. Washington had written to the commander of the prison camp only the day before ordering him to select an officer to be hanged, and legal technicalities delayed the process until May 25. That Sunday, all the British officers held captive at Little York across the Susquehanna were summoned to Lancaster to meet with British major James Gordon at his quarters. There were thirteen of them. The major explained to the young men at his dinner table that "Washington has determined to revenge upon some innocent man the guilt of a set of lawless banditti."

The next day the men were ordered to report to the Black Bear Inn on the cobblestone square. Indoors in the dim light the American commandant awaited them; by his side stood an aide-de-camp, the commissary of prisoners, and a drummer boy. The aide and the commissary each held out a hat: in one were slips of paper with thirteen names, the other with a dozen blanks and one that read "unfortunate." The drummer boy drew a name out of one hat, read it aloud, then drew a blank from the other and handed it to the lucky prisoner.

Ten times the boy read names and drew blank papers from the hat. Three names were left. On the eleventh drawing the unfortunate lot fell to Captain Charles Asgill, nineteen years of age, the youngest of them all. "Lively, brave, handsome—an only son—and an especial favorite with his comrades," wrote Samuel Graham, one of the lucky twelve.

WHAT BENJAMIN FRANKLIN DID not know about his son's business in New York he gratefully relinquished. He had a great deal to do in the year 1782, negotiating with Richard Oswald and other peace emissaries. A treaty lay within their grasp.

But the Asgill affair and William Franklin's likely part in the sordid events were too prominent for anyone to ignore—especially the American minister whose duties it affected. Like no other incident of the war, this fatal lottery appealed to the French sense of melodrama, thrilling the public from the palace of Versailles to the back streets and cafés of Paris.

It took seven weeks for word of the young soldier's predicament to reach the ones it most concerned, his mother, Lady Theresa, his father, Sir Charles Asgill, Baronet, knighted as Lord Mayor of London, and his sisters, Amelia and Caroline. One can imagine their horror in July upon learning that the boy had been marked for death in May. After appealing first to the English ministers, Lady Theresa wasted no time in composing a very moving letter to the French foreign minister, Count Vergennes, sending it across the Channel on July 18:

> My son (an only son) and dear as he is brave, amiable as deserving to be so, only nineteen, a prisoner under articles of capitulation of York-Town, is now confined in America, an object of retaliation! Shall an innocent suffer for the guilty? Represent to yourself, Sir, the situation of a family under these circumstances . . . distracted by fear and grief . . . my husband given over by his physicians a few hours before the news arrived and not in a state to be informed of the misfortune; my daughter seized with a fever and delirium, raving about her brother. . . . Let your own feelings, Sir, suggest & plead for my inexpressible misery.

She begged Vergennes to write to General Washington asking for her son to be released.

A week passed, ten days. Newspapers all over the Continent illustrated the story with images of the distraught mother and mad girl, the young man gazing through bars at the gibbet, General Washington sternly raising his sword. Every ship that made port was greeted with the cry: "What news of Captain Asgill?" For the time being there was no news, which was good news, for Washington was awaiting the outcome of the Lippincott trial.

Time was of the essence, yet the days passed without action in Europe. Vergennes shared the mother's letter with Marie Antoinette and King Louis at Versailles. He later said they were deeply moved by Lady Asgill's trouble and wished she might be relieved. Yet nothing was done. Vergennes also shared the letter with his counterpart Benjamin Franklin as soon as it came to him, for the American was the man whose business was most affected by this terrible turn of events. French sympathy was vital to his success, and he was also the man most likely to know how to deal with this crisis in the New World.

On Sunday, July 28, Franklin met with Richard Oswald at Passy. Both were deeply concerned with the Asgill family's plight as well as the political implications of the son's fate. Everyone hoped that something might be done to save him, but no one had a plan. "The situation of Captain Asgill and his family afflicts me," said Franklin, "but I do not see what can be done by anyone here to relieve them." He did not think for one minute that General Washington had the least desire to take the gentleman's life. His goal was to punish a cold-blooded murder of an American prisoner by Captain Lippincott. Franklin knew that his son was president of the board that supervised Lippincott. "If the English refuse to deliver up or punish the murderer," Franklin continued, "it is saying that they choose to preserve him rather than Captain Asgill." So he advised Oswald to apply to the English ministry for a command to surrender Lippincott to General Washington.

The orders must go out immediately on the swiftest sailing vessel at His Majesty's service. No other means could produce the desired end. Franklin explained that the English had committed so many cruel murders without retaliation that Washington had finally yielded to what his people demanded, for their common security. "I am persuaded nothing I could say to him on the occasion would have the least effect in changing his determination."

Scientist, conjuror, hoaxer, Benjamin Franklin pondered. He did not want this boy Asgill to die on the gallows because of his own son's recklessness. He told Oswald to send a courier to London—the post was too slow. Now, if he might be excused, he had other urgent business nearby which "I would not give a moment's delay." What this was, exactly, Dr. Franklin would not divulge for fear of being caught in a lie. There *was* in fact a thing that could be done here in France that might possibly relieve the Asgill family, and he would not rest until that, too, was accomplished.

The road from Passy to Versailles, Vergennes' residence, was thirteen miles. A man could walk it in three hours. An old man with gout in a painted horse-drawn carriage could make it painfully in one. The innocent youth sweating in the shadow of the gallows, his mother and father and sisters, the general's conscience, the very peace itself—all might be saved by a timely appeal launched from Versailles. But it required an argument so subtle, passionate, and forceful that Count Vergennes might not think of it.

The very next day, July 29, 1782, a courier galloped out of Versailles with a letter bound for Le Havre, with orders to put it on the fastest ship sailing for New York and gold enough to induce the captain to weigh anchor. This letter to George Washington was a masterpiece of the epistolary art. There were not five men in France who could have composed such a letter, and one of them was a foreigner. Franklin's friend Voltaire had been dead three years; and Vergennes, for all his eloquence and good sense was no match for Voltaire or Franklin when it came to the art of letters.

> Sir.—It is not in quality of Minister of a King, the friend and ally of the United States (tho with the knowledge and consent of His Majesty) that I now have the honor to write to Your Excellency— It is as a man of sensibility and as a tender father who feels all the force of Paternal Love . . .

And so the writer addressed his "solicitations in favor of a mother and a family in tears—her situation seems the more worthy of notice on our part as it is to the humanity of a Nation at War with her own that she has recourse for what she ought to receive from the impartial Justice of her own Generals." This sentence so distinctly expresses Franklin's intelligence that it is difficult to believe anyone else wrote it. How well he knew the strained humanity of a nation at war with her own! How deeply had he known the heartache in his own house, and the senseless cruelty of the British!

The writer drew attention to Mrs. Asgill's letter, which he enclosed. Not Lady Asgill or Madame, he called her, but *Mrs.* Asgill. His Excellency General Washington would not read this letter without being deeply moved, he averred it had had that effect on the king and queen when he read it to them. Marie Antoinette wept. The king expressed his desire that the poor mother might be calmed and reassured. The general's character was too well known, the letter went on, for the writer to believe he desired anything more than a pretext to avoid the unpleasant necessity.

And so the king's minister held out the lifeline that would, if it traveled swiftly enough across the ocean, save them all. Rochambeau, commander of the French army, had let General Washington know in June (and probably Vergennes) that of *course* Captain Asgill was Washington's prisoner, but he was one whom the French king's army had assisted in capturing at York Town. Rochambeau had signed the Articles of Surrender, protecting prisoners. And His Majesty preferred that Charles Asgill, Lady Theresa's only son, not be hanged in violation of those articles.

That was the pretext, and it would suffice if Washington used it. Nothing more was required. The letter went on, diplomatically, passionately, to appeal to the general's humanity and common sense. Count Vergennes put his name to it and handed the papers over to the messenger. No historian has ever suggested that the famous document was not, from beginning to end, the work of the French minister of foreign affairs.

GEORGE WASHINGTON FOUND PLENTY of excuses not to hang Captain Asgill during the spring and summer of 1782. When Clinton, and then his successor as commander in chief, Guy Carleton, refused to surrender Lippincott, General Washington agreed for the time being to await the outcome of the court-martial. For the next two and a half months he publicly displayed his impatience at the court's delay, his anger that the British command was trifling with him. Privately he was grateful for every day that passed without a verdict. Asgill was confined in a log hut in a prison camp near Chatham, New Jersey, not far from the site where Huddy had been executed. His suffering in the shadow of the gallows was harrowing, and there was very little the general could do, at first, to comfort him.

When at last General Carlton informed Washington on July 25 that the court-martial was concluded, Washington quibbled over the messenger's passport to the Newburgh headquarters, buying more time. The verdict was kept secret, then the official papers did not reach headquarters until August 13: Captain Lippincott had been acquitted. Although Joshua Huddy had been executed without proper authority, what Lippincott had done was not malicious; he had acted out of a sense of duty to obey the orders of the Board of Associated Loyalists.

In an accompanying letter, Carlton stated that both he and Clinton had denounced the hanging as a barbarity. He was ordering the judge to conduct a further investigation and prosecute others who may have been complicit in the crime. He also reminded Washington of the fact that General Clinton had stripped the Board of Loyalists of every power that had enabled them to act independently. Now Washington had two more pretexts not to hang Asgill: General Carlton's promise to pursue the real murderers, and the fact that the terrorist organization had been dismantled. Above all, Washington informed the Continental Congress, on August 19, the Asgill affair was no longer a regional matter, it had become a grave national concern, too important for any one person to decide. So he was leaving it up to the congress. They referred the matter to a committee, who quarreled over it, and set it aside, and picked it up to quarrel again, then ignore, for months while Charles Asgill paced, perspired, and tossed and turned upon his pallet in Chatham.

General Washington hoped for a miracle. At last it arrived, in that envelope posted from Versailles, the tear-jerking letters from Mrs. Asgill and Count Vergennes. In the way that history sometimes mirrors the style of melodramas and Highland ballads, the miracle descended upon George Washington at his Newburgh headquarters on Friday, October 25. The timing was eerie. His own note enclosing the letters went out at once and arrived upon the desk of John Hanson, president of the Continental Congress, five days later, just in time to disrupt the scheduled vote upon the motion to execute Asgill. It would have passed. But first that morning those pleas from Europe were read aloud in the State House. According to Elias Boudinot of New Jersey, the power of the messages was "enough to move the heart of a savage.... This operated like an electric shock." Congressmen examined the envelope, and Washington's signature. They interrogated President Hanson. They looked at one another in wonder.

"In short, it looked so much like something supernatural that even the minority, who were much pleased with it, could scarcely think it real." When everyone was fully convinced that the letter was legitimate, "a motion was made that the life of Captain Asgill should be given as a compliment to the King of France."

That is how General Washington escaped his dilemma. And indeed it seemed to all involved that this had been the work of a conjuror.

Months would pass before William Franklin heard of Asgill's good fortune—which would affect him, probably, more than anyone outside Asgill's immediate family. By then William would be long gone, in England, upon his own mission of mercy. Although Charles Asgill and the Lippincott trial had been the talk of New York in the summer of 1782, news had arrived then from England that cast all other matters in its shade. King George had ordered the peace commissioners to treat with America as an independent state. General Guy Carlton called a public meeting at the foot of Broadway and read aloud a letter he had sent to George Washington notifying him of the momentous developments in Paris and London and preparations for an exchange of all prisoners. After seven years of suffering, destruction, carnage, and incalculable loss, the war was over.

Nowhere was the shock and burden of this news felt as strongly as in New York City where the colony of American loyalists perceived themselves in grave danger. Officers of the martial government urged them not to panic. As the living symbol of the loyalist cause, William Franklin was the obvious choice to plead for their community in England, and on August 10, at a meeting of a few dignitaries in Manhattan, he was formally deputed to present their concerns to Parliament. His long residence in America as a public figure, his knowledge of the people, and the passion which he had shown affecting the king's loyal subjects had induced them to place full confidence in him.

Some did not agree. Franklin's alleged role in the hanging of Captain Huddy might weaken him at the royal court. The verdict and the transcripts of the Lippincott trial were not made public until August 13, but William Franklin knew every detail of the proceedings by the time the court adjourned, and he knew even more about the underlying events. While he was never officially indicted for complicity in the murder, it seemed possible that his friend Guy Carleton—investigating Huddy's murder—would soon be obliged to arrest him.

And so on Sunday, August 18, 1782, as church bells tolled from the towers of St. Paul's, St. George's Chapel, and the New Dutch Church, William Franklin packed up his trunks and crates and sent them to the wharf. He had received Carlton's permission to sail that day, on the *Roebuck*, for England. He asked the general to settle the rent on the house where he had lived. He wanted it paid through October so that he might leave his furniture and other valuables there until he could sell them at the best price. He was leaving in haste, attended by his servant Thomas Parke. Their ship was one day out to sea at the moment General Washington was forwarding Carleton's letters—about Lippincott's acquittal and the plan to punish the true culprits—to the president of the congress. Later, the committee that considered Asgill's case discussed sending to England for extradition of the "absconded" Governor Franklin to try him for murder; but this was never formally resolved, and the matter was relegated to an undated footnote in the minutes.

A MAN ON A sea voyage of thirty-five days, in fair weather, has leisure to reflect, to grieve, scheme, and worry. By day on the windswept quarterdeck with no sound but the breeze in the cracking, brilliant topsails and the sight of the earth's curve above the glittering waves; by night beneath the stars of Sagittarius, and Capricorn, and those tragic heroes Perseus and Hercules.

William had lost nearly everything but his pride, his wits, and his will to live. At the age of fifty-two, he was utterly disillusioned. He was justly satisfied with his conduct as royal governor and servant of the king during the last twenty years—not excepting his work for the Board of Associated Loyalists. He was just as sorry as the generals that Asgill was condemned, but that had not been his intention or his fault. His conscience—expressed in his letters to Clinton—was clear. If the man died on the scaffold, the world would seize upon the president of the board for a scapegoat. This was inevitable. Although there was no longer any court with jurisdiction to convict or exonerate William

Franklin, there was always the court of public opinion. So if some miracle did not deliver Charles Asgill from the hangman in the next few weeks, Franklin's name would be blackened even in England, where for the time being he was a hero.

William looked forward to being back in London. He had fond memories of living there with his father in Craven Street; of glittering Northumberland House on Charing Cross, where he had met his bride-to-be, Elizabeth Downes; of studying at the Inns of Court. He had been young and happy and altogether fortunate to marry such a woman, and to be appointed a royal governor.

Two of his best friends lived there, William Strahan and Joseph Galloway, with whom he had continued corresponding. And there were many others in and out of government who knew and admired him. In fact, there was a good deal to hope for in his last years of life. He had his pension and reason to believe it would increase. As chief lobbyist for Tory reparations he intended to give full attention to his own claim, losses that amounted to more than £48,000 sterling ($6.5 million). As far as his family was concerned, he had the unflagging devotion of his sister as well as of the entire Bache family, who would visit him as soon as they could. His son still loved him. Temple had found ways of communicating during the years when it was forbidden, when no mail was safe. He would entrust notes to personal messengers bound for New York, or he would encrypt endearments in letters to his aunt Sally, who had her own private line to Governor Franklin.

That very summer, Temple had confided to Benjamin Vaughan, Prime Minister Shelburne's agent in Paris, that he had "hopes to see something done for his *father* . . . something in the corps diplomatique . . ."

Aunt Sally's letter to Temple informing him of his father's departure for England is the most poignant of their long dialogue, as that brave and wise lady flouts the cruel hand of censorship that has come between them. "Your father was well the 18th of last month when he sailed for England. You must not mind what Bradford put in his papers about him." Thomas Bradford, publisher of the *Pennsylvania Journal* and a long-standing enemy of both Franklins, had pinned Huddy's murder on William, as well as the fate of Asgill, who was still confined. Whether Asgill lived or died, William Franklin might be forgiven but never vindicated. She turns to Temple:

> It's a long time since I have had a letter from you. When your
> dear father was in England, and a very young gentleman, he
> found means of writing to me very often, and long entertaining
> letters. I should hope the son had as much affection for me; I feel
> no less for him than I did and now do for the Father—I care not
> into what hands this letter falls, nor who sees it for I should de-
> spise the person who could not make a distinction between a po-
> litical difference and a family one.

A wise woman to think such thoughts, and a brave one to write them in a letter. She had seen such sad confusion in other houses, "and hope and believe will never happen in ours, I ever held those people cheap, who were at variance with their near connections." Somehow Sally still hoped and believed that her father and brother would rise above their differences, that love would prevail over fear and fury sooner or later; and if she would not give in to despair, then there was hope for Temple.

And what did William Franklin dare to hope from his father, who for seven years had been so antagonistic and distant? The healing would take time. No communication was possible at present, for fear of ap- pearances. Enemies suspected a sinister partnership. Not until peace was finalized, and well established in America, might father and son rebuild their cherished relation.

CHAPTER 19

Going Home

WILLIAM'S ARRIVAL TOOK LONDON by surprise and can be said to have caused a mild sensation in certain quarters. It was reported in *The London Courant, The Daily Advertiser,* and other journals the next morning, Wednesday, September 25, 1782. A letter to Benjamin Franklin conveying the news shows one old friend's reaction: "I see, by the papers, the arrival of Governor Franklin [and here the letter is torn] . . . as it is I feel angry he should bear a name I have long learned to love and respect."

There were many others, however, who welcomed William with open arms. First among these was Mr. Strahan, now nearing seventy years of age. It was this old friend of the family who had taken charge of William's finances in England when the Treasury granted him an allowance. Since the spring of 1779, Strahan had received the funds four times a year, arranged the transatlantic bank drafts to meet Franklin's needs, and invested the rest. William was eager to thank him, and to examine his accounts.

He needed a place to stay, and he was drawn to Charing Cross, Northumberland House, and Craven Street, where he had lived in his youth. The city had grown. There was more traffic and noise. He could hardly resist a stroll down Craven Street to take a look at the old row house and the view of the river from the wharf. In Suffolk Street, a few steps from the home on St. James's Street where his wife had once lived, stood well-built brick houses, fading in grandeur. There he settled upon quarters at No. 16 Suffolk, near the Haymarket Theatre, just north of Charing Cross. Then he went looking for Joseph Galloway.

Galloway and his daughter lived at the north edge of the city, in Marylebone, a block south of the famous gardens. The air was fresh in the new streets around Queen Anne's Square as the autumn breeze came down out of the pastures above Tottenham Court.

Grace Galloway had passed away in February, and William would convey his condolences. The marriage had been troubled from the beginning, and her melancholy deepened in middle age with the decline of Joseph's fortunes. When Galloway sought asylum in London he still believed that the British would crush the rebellion. Joseph, a public enemy, had virtually abandoned Grace at Trevose, where she remained in the vain hope of saving their property; she could not imagine that any government present or future could take it away. Husband and wife were both terribly wrong. Their large estate was confiscated, and Grace was evicted to live out her days in poverty. In her diary she wrote: "I am determined to go from this wicked place as soon as I hear from Joseph Galloway and not by my own impatience." She awaited the summons from England that never came. Sometimes she cursed him.

Such memories and reflections might have occupied these old friends for an hour or two in late September, in a smoky tavern on Cavendish Square. They had made mistakes and paid dearly. Maybe they had learned something. There was still vital work to be done here, and no time for self-pity. Galloway knew the political forces in the new ministry, and where he might find sympathy and support. Lord North's party had collapsed after Yorktown, then Lord Rockingham had died suddenly of the flu and Lord Shelbourne—more opposed to independence—became prime minister. Here was a ray of hope.

Unfortunately, Joseph Galloway had lost credibility. Calling the Howe brothers and General Burgoyne incompetent, he had insisted that four-fifths of the Americans remained loyal and that Britain would win the war. His poor judgment could not be concealed. Viscount Sydney dismissed Galloway as one who "remembered every military maneuver that had, as well as those which had not taken place" but who seemed to have forgotten he was once a member of the American Congress. There would be no more serious discussion of the American loyalists' fate until Benjamin Franklin dispatched the Treaty of Paris to Parliament in the autumn. While Galloway remained an important figure among the refugees, it would be left to Governor Franklin, who had the gravitas, and the focus, to lobby for funds to relieve them.

He had no difficulty getting an appointment with the prime minister. Lord Shelbourne received William warmly in October. Temple Franklin had spoken up once more on his father's behalf—upon hearing he was in England—and the prime minister was reminded that a favor to Governor Franklin would be timely. Temple's logic is odd. Benjamin Franklin would not have approved of any such overtures. He was so ill that summer and autumn that Temple may have believed his grandfather would die; in any case, Dr. Franklin was too feeble to discourage Temple's well-intentioned intrigue.

Lord Shelbourne heard Governor Franklin's account of the sufferings, the sacrifice, and the predicament of the American loyalists and assured him he would do everything in his power to persuade Parliament to address their plight. But as Richard Oswald sailed back and forth from London to France, from Lord Shelbourne to Benjamin Franklin, refining the terms for a separate peace, the needs of the American loyalists stood as low on the list of priorities as did their esteem in the eyes of most Englishmen. They believed the loyalists' selfish advice had prolonged the war.

When preliminary articles of peace were signed in late November 1782, there was no promise that the United States government would pay restitution to British subjects. To William Franklin's surprise, the greatest enemy of reparations was his own father. John Adams was amazed at his severity, finding Dr. Franklin far more decided on this point than John Jay or himself. Dr. Franklin demanded Canada. If they wouldn't give him Canada in fee for reparations, then what about this? In his pocket he had folded a bill of damages: towns sacked and burned, women raped, babies scalped, mills and plantations reduced to rubble, livestock rustled, ships sunk or stolen, libraries pillaged. Would they talk of reparations? They might compare claims.

WHEN THE PACKET *Swallow* dropped anchor in the Thames two days before Christmas and Charles Asgill stepped ashore, there were few people as happy as his mother and father, his sisters, and William Franklin. The governor would not be welcome at the king's levee at the Court of St. James's, where Captain Asgill paid his respects to George III. But at least he would never be accused of murdering Asgill, and the American loyalists could pursue their claims without that particular handicap.

William's £500 annual pension ($75,000) was guaranteed in January 1783. In February he joined delegates from other American provinces heavily populated with refugees, forming a committee to lobby Parliament. These included Lord Dunmore from Virginia, William Bull of South Carolina, and Galloway for Pennsylvania. A smaller agency including Franklin as representative of New York, New Jersey, and Connecticut was deputed to meet with Lord Shelbourne.

Shelbourne received their petition on February 6 and agreed to present it to the House on February 12. There it met with the squabbling that usually attends a new demand upon the Treasury. The cost of the war had been staggering to the exchequer. Yet Franklin was undaunted. He and Galloway argued the loyalist case all that winter and spring, in Whitehall and in the press, declaring "The claims of the American Loyalists . . . stand upon the highest ground of national honor and national justice—the fundamental laws of the British Constitution." King George himself agreed. In June, Parliament passed a bill appointing commissioners to evaluate the losses and services of every person who had suffered during the war as a result of his loyalty to the Crown. They were supposed to wrap up the business within nine months. It was still grinding on seven years later, when two-thirds of the 3,225 claims were honored.

While waiting for his own claim to be heard, William stood as witness for hundreds of Americans with cases for damages and pensions— his main occupation during those years. In his leisure time he enjoyed the company of Mr. Strahan and his circle, and longtime friends such as Joseph Priestley and Cortlandt Skinner; his former neighbor on Craven Street, the wine merchant Caleb Whitefoord; and his father's paramour, the green-eyed and free-spirited sculptor Patience Wright.

It was very curious, this web of Franklin relations between London, Paris, and America and the idea that they were supposed to ignore one another. William explained his own boundaries to a British army officer who had begged him to ask Temple to use his influence to get him released from parole: "As I have avoided all correspondence, either by letter or otherwise, with both him and my father, ever since they went to France, and as I have still strong reasons for observing the same conduct, I must beg you will excuse me on this occasion."

That was during his first winter in London. But it is not to be supposed that Governor Franklin had no communication with his son. Temple had been lobbying the ministry for his father via Joseph Priestley's best friend, Benjamin Vaughan, who, along with Caleb Whitefoord, was one of the agents working for Lord Shelbourne in shuttle diplomacy from Paris to London. Secret communication across the Channel was routine.

As for Patience Wright, poet, sculptor, prophet, and self-styled madwoman, she held herself to a standard of conduct beyond the judgment of anyone but God—and sometimes Benjamin Franklin. She regarded him as God's apostle on earth. Her passion for him had remained unslaked since the early days of their intimacy, in his rooms in Craven Street, in 1772. Widow Wright had a gift for molding lifelike figures of men from wax, which she first softened by kneading it between her thighs. Magically she would produce a head from beneath her petticoats as if it were a newborn. She referred to these doings as her "performances." Abigail Adams, a stern judge of character, called Patience "the queen of sluts." Benjamin Franklin had been her greatest patron in London.

She saw no reason why she should not be good friends with Temple's grandfather and Benjamin's son as well, living as she did a few doors from his lodgings, just around the corner on Cockspur Street. Patience wrote to Benjamin in Passy in February to tell him that William lived nearby and was petitioning Parliament for aid to the Tories.

"His health is bad, he looks old," she reported, but William neverthe-less excited in her the old passion for friendship.

Next to Patience Wright, William Franklin, and the Stevenson family, no one was more eager for Dr. Franklin's return to London than William Strahan. After Ben's departure for America in 1775, the men's political difference had put a terrible strain on their friendship. Stra-han, as a Member of Parliament, found himself under constraints sim-ilar to those William Franklin endured in corresponding with his father. Yet the affection never diminished. One can see this in the dozen letters from Strahan to Benjamin Franklin during the war, and Ben's are no less cordial and hopeful. Their most serious disagreement was over William's fate. Strahan's complaint that "the son of Dr. Frank-lin ought not receive such usage" is well known. Dr. Franklin did not respond, and years passed before there was another letter in either di-rection.

Then it was Benjamin Franklin's turn to extend the olive branch. In early December 1781, soon after news of Cornwallis's surrender, Frank-lin felt he could resume his correspondence and renew the intimacy. His letter of December 4—after a five-year silence—is gentle and charm-ing. He requests an edition of Tully's treatise on old age, and praises the beautiful new typography in Paris and Madrid. Congratulating Strahan on his daughter's marriage, he presents respects to his wife and love to all the children. And, "tho' at present divided by public circumstances," he cherishes *a remembrance of our ancient private friendship.*" Strahan was overjoyed, answering that he was glad to see that Franklin did him the honor of continuing to recall their amity. "I begin now to flatter myself that we shall soon meet again." Yet the day Governor Franklin arrived at Strahan's door, in September 1782, the communication be-tween him and Benjamin, so happily resumed, ceased again.

Nearly a year later Benjamin wrote to "My dear old Friend, whom I shall probably never have the pleasure of seeing again," a letter of only three lines. It enclosed a longer letter from Sally Bache concerning the welfare of a woman the Franklins had sponsored in America at Stra-han's request. Not until February 1784, after the peace treaty, did Stra-han write again, thanking him and the Baches for their kindness. He kept up his hope of seeing Franklin again, soon. "You have so many friends here whom you must love because they love you." In all sincerity, he wrote, and uncompromised by Madeira, their favorite wine, he begged him to spend the rest of his life in England.

The swiftness of the thawing is evidenced in the quick response—two weeks later—from Passy. Ben found Strahan's arguments for his visit to England powerful, "but there are difficulties and objections of several kinds which at present I do not see how to get over." That is, he was still loathed by a faction there, he risked arrest, and his son William was now living in Westminster. Regarding the chaos in Parliament, he comically advises that they should dissolve their crazy government and send representatives to the American Congress. "You will say my advice smells of Madeira. You are right . . . more chitchat *between ourselves,* over the *second* bottle."

When news of the treaty's ratification came from America and the friendship between Strahan and Dr. Franklin had fully recovered, William at last felt the time had come that he, too, could write to his father. He wrote from Marylebone, No. 28 Norton Street, a new house owned by an Irish widow named Mary Johnson D'Evelin. It appears that the two were intimate before his move from Suffolk Street, having been introduced by mutual friends—perhaps Galloway, or Edward Gibbon, who lived nearby.

Strahan encouraged both Franklins to resume their correspondence, but he must have known that Dr. Franklin would not write first. William had no idea what to expect when in July he began composing a careful letter. He put his signature to it on Thursday, July 22. Even at this late date he was anxious about the missive's falling into the wrong hands. For two weeks he tried to find a friend who was going to France who might deliver it in person to Passy, and at last, finding no one, he sent the letter out by the night mail on August 6.

William's long letter to his father is one of the most eloquent apologies of all time. "Ever since the termination of the unhappy contest between Great Britain and America, I have been anxious to write to you, and to endeavor to revive that affectionate intercourse and connection which till the commencement of the late troubles had been the pride and happiness of my life." He has, he says, postponed writing for several reasons. First, he fears that his actions may have alienated his father forever. Second, it is possible that the minister plenipotentiary might still be prohibited from corresponding with a counterrevolutionary. Finally, there is the danger that such correspondence might arouse suspicions of collusion.

William explained that he had been waiting for a sign that a letter would be welcome. Also, he had heard that his father would soon be returning to America and would stop in England first. Mr. Caleb Whitefoord had shown him a note from Temple, a year earlier, that promised as much, so he had reason to hope for a personal interview. As for complaints of collusion—the Franklins should pay no heed. "I am happy that I can with confidence appeal not only to you but to my God, that I have uniformly acted from a strong sense of what I conceived my duty to my King, and regard to my country, required. If I have been mistaken, I cannot help it. It is an error of judgment that the maturest reflection I am capable of cannot rectify." If the same circumstances occurred tomorrow, he declared he would do the same, notwithstanding the scandalous ill treatment the poor loyalists had suffered.

A disagreeable subject—and he would drop it. Now was the time to renew their affectionate relation. "Encouraged by what passed lately between you and that good-hearted man Colonel Wadsworth, I flatter myself . . . that my advances . . . will be as acceptable to you as they are agreeable to myself." Colonel Jeremiah Wadsworth of Connecticut, admired for his wit and his magnanimity, had visited the Franklins in Passy in the summer. Commissary for the French troops in America, he had gone to submit an accounting, stayed in France throughout the winter, and then sailed to England to pursue his own business ventures, where he met William in the summer. Wadsworth brought good news of Temple's accomplishments, as well as charitable greetings from the patriarch.

William later informed the claims commission that Wadsworth told him Benjamin had been surprised "that I had never wrote to him, nor made any overtures towards a reconciliation, and that he (my father) had said he could not see any reason, now all differences between the two countries were settled, why those of individuals who had taken opposite sides in the controversy should not likewise be accommodated." Caleb Whitefoord had also been encouraging, visiting William several times in June 1784 and relaying detailed messages from his son. On June 30, Whitefoord reported to Temple that he had conveyed his words, and that Governor Franklin promised to write to Temple of his intentions to visit him in Passy.

And so, at the end of that lengthy letter to his father, William apologized for its limits. "Now that I have broken the ice many things occur," he suggested, things of a private nature, family matters that called for a meeting face-to-face. "I shall therefore, if you are not to be soon in England, be happy to have your approbation to wait on you at Paris."

Franklin did not keep his son in suspense. Ten days later he replied in a letter from Passy that was probably years in the making.

August 16, 1784

Dear Son,

I received your letter of the 22nd past and am glad to find that you desire to revive the affectionate intercourse that formerly existed between us. It will be very agreeable to me. Indeed nothing has ever hurt me so much and affected me with such keen sensations as to find myself deserted in my old age by my only son; and not only deserted, but to find him taking up arms against me, in a cause wherein my good fame, fortune, and life were all at stake.

If he had left it at that, the wayward son would have known the full burden of chastisement. But there was more.

I ought not to blame you for differing in sentiment with me in public affairs. We are men, all subject to errors. Our opinions are not in our power; they are formed and governed much by circumstances that are often as inexplicable as they are irresistible. Your situation was such that few would have censured your remaining neutral, tho *there are natural duties which precede political ones, and cannot be extinguished by them.* This is a disagreeable subject. I drop it. And we will endeavor as you propose, mutually to forget what has happened relating to it, as well as we can.

The lecture goes on, bitterly, nearly as long as William's. But that is the heart of it. "I send your son over to pay his duty to you. You will find him much improved. He is greatly esteemed and loved in this country, and will make his way anywhere." Benjamin complained that Congress would not accept his resignation—so he could not go home as yet. Another year in France and "I may be too old and feeble to bear the voyage. I am here among a people that love and respect me . . . and perhaps I may conclude to die among them."

As for William's coming to visit, the answer is curt: "I shall be glad to see you when convenient, but would not have you come here at present." If William wished to discuss family matters, he should confide them to Temple.

Only three days later, Dr. Franklin wrote to Strahan that his grandson Temple was setting out the next day to visit to his father in London, and that Temple would deliver this message to Mr. Strahan by hand. All of this happened so fast that William and his mistress, Mary D'Evelin, would scarcely have had time to schedule the longed-for visit or make up a bed. There must have been great eagerness on Temple's part, and confidence on Grandfather's, that William would be at home. Indeed, Temple was escaping a scandal in Passy. He had been carrying on an affair with the wife of the famous actor Joseph Caillot, and Madame Blanchette Caillot had just learned she was pregnant with Temple's child.

Before that letter, and Temple, the bearer of it, could reach London, Strahan wrote to Franklin in Passy—one more invitation for the doctor to visit England. And he mentioned William: "The Governor spent a day with me lately. He is quite well, and tells me he had just writ to you, which I am glad of; for there is surely now nothing to interrupt your correspondence."

It would be surprising, then, if William did not share with his trusted friend his letter to his father, as well as the one Benjamin had written in reply. Those two letters exchanged in the summer of 1784 come as close as any documents could to explaining the rift that remained between father and son. And they produced an iridescent gleam of hope. That would have to satisfy Strahan in lieu of knowledge. Those letters are crucial, as much for what they express as for what they conceal.

What the letters mask on both sides is a piteous misunderstanding. Those who had witnessed the lives of these two Franklins—Mr. and Mrs. Richard Bache, Robert Morris, George Washington, Jane Mecum—must have grieved over it. What did Benjamin know of the Litchfield jail, the rats, the reeking bed of straw, and nearly a year in solitary confinement? What did he care—the man who had deserted his wife and left her to live and die without him—about Elizabeth, William's beloved? Did he know of his son's efforts to go to her, to save her, or of William's grief upon being denied parole, in learning that her breath had stopped while the Continental Congress debated the matter?

What did the father comprehend of his son's efforts, his sacrifices, his mounting obligations in the service of the Ohio Company and Vandalia? William had been too proud to tell him the whole truth.

Finally, what did Benjamin Franklin know or understand about that hell on earth, the charred and teeming Sodom of New York City under the yoke of martial law, the cruelty and neglect of the British commanders, or the civil war in New Jersey? What did he care about the desperation of ten thousand refugees? What did the illustrious diplomat know of living in squalor and in constant danger of assassination on the island of Manhattan? What could he possibly have understood about the war of desolation, the hangings and rapes and dismemberments in Shrewsbury that led to the Asgill affair? Who, living in Passy in 1781, could really understand the frenzy for retributive justice?

It was a vast continent, the old man's ignorance, as great as Europe. But it was certainly no larger than William Franklin's unfamiliarity with his father's struggles. If ever Dr. Franklin had done *anything*—from the day William was arrested in Perth Amboy—to help his son it would have required the most elaborate contrivances of secrecy. So even now, after the war, such efforts could not be acknowledged but in a closed room, face-to-face. What did William know of the intercession of the Marquis de Lafayette, or of his father's friend Robert Morris, in 1777, before and after William was released from the Connecticut prison? Did he really believe that Captain Clymer's inspection of his cell and the subsequent actions of Bache and Morris were a mere happy coincidence?

In all likelihood, William had no idea of these interventions. The channels of communication that might have brought such understanding were closed to him. The individuals involved in William's release were sworn to secrecy. Bache, Morris, Lafayette, all knew Benjamin Franklin's wishes regarding his wayward son, and none would have defied him. History keeps its secrets, and the role of Dr. Franklin in his son's rescue is as well guarded as his mother's name. The fact is that Governor Franklin was released from the dungeon in Litchfield, and then he might have sailed to England with Galloway, as the entire family prayed he would.

Instead he went to New York and remained there for four years—as another kind of captive. What he did then, as his father learned from prejudicial sources, was so appalling he could not possibly forgive him. That had been the turning point. What did William Franklin know about *L'Affaire d'Asgill*, as it was called in the Paris salons, and how that debacle threatened the peace process his father was nurturing? The president of the Board of Associated Loyalists knew a great deal about the hanging of Joshua Huddy on the shore of Sandy Hook. But what did Governor Franklin know about the efforts of Asgill's mother, Richard Arnold, and Dr. Franklin in Passy, and Count Vergennes at Versailles, to rescue the boy from the gallows three thousand miles away? It had been considered a miracle. It is not an act that Dr. Franklin could ever explain to his son, any more than William could account for his violation of parole, or his leadership of Tory marauders. They could not, either one, appreciate the other's point of view.

TEMPLE CAME TO VISIT his father that summer and stayed until December. It was all very pleasant once he recovered from his journey. The twenty-four-year-old voyager got seasick crossing the Channel, came down with chills and fever, and took to his bed on arriving at William's lodgings in Marylebone. Temple wrote to his grandfather on September 2 that his father and the lady of the house were extremely attentive, and that they had gotten him the best possible medical care.

He had rented rooms in a fine house nearby, two blocks to the west, at the corner of Portland Road, on the edge of town, and planned to move there as soon as he felt better. Five days later, Temple reported to Grandfather that he was well and taking on the long list of errands and personal interviews the old gentleman had assigned him. He had lost so much time to illness he begged for an extension. His father had invited him to the seashore for ten days. He wished to go, and besides, Lord Shelbourne and other nobles to whom he had letters of introduction were at the seaside.

It took about eight days for a letter to pass between London and Paris, and Grandfather insisted on Temple's writing by every post. He consented to the boy's request to go with his father to the seashore, as well as to his staying in England until mid-October. Affectionate greetings passed back and forth between Benjamin Franklin and his son via Temple, yet it is clear by early October that the youth's absence was a strain to Benjamin. Not hearing from Temple made Ben irritable and plaintive. He had given him so much to do, so many commissions and duties to visit old friends, that the boy scarcely had time to spend with his father, and this, it would seem, had been the point. Benjamin had written to William, high-handedly: "I trust that you will prudently avoid introducing him to company that it may be improper for him to be seen with."

Temple's assignments included book buying and shipping, attending all the scientific clubs, shipping a letterpress to France, and calling upon dozens of Benjamin's friends. His most important mission was peculiar. Franklin's former landlady and surrogate spouse, Margaret Stevenson, had passed away the previous year, which grieved him, but he took comfort in his ongoing communication with her daughter, Polly Stevenson Hewson. When she married Dr. William Hewson in 1770, Franklin had led her to the altar. Widowed four years later after giving birth to three children, Polly never remarried. Now forty-five, she responded to her friend's invitations to visit him in Passy gratefully and with affection. For a variety of reasons—the cost, and her hope that he would visit her in England, she resisted, yet she kept changing her mind. At last, after Polly confided to him that she had nearly planned the journey in July 1784, but the gentleman who was to have escorted her and her children to Paris had backed out, Franklin decided to take action.

Polly's letter about her frustrated travel plans arrived in the same post as William Franklin's momentous letter of apology. Benjamin answered Polly's letter first. "I wish you had executed your project of taking a little trip to see me this summer. You would have made me very happy, and bathed your children here as well as Southampton," for he had baths in his house in Passy. Congress had denied his request to retire, "and I must stay another winter. Can you not come and pass it with me here?"

He told Polly that Temple was setting out right away to deliver this letter, and Temple would explain how she and her children would be accommodated. If she would agree to come, he would bring her to Passy. "Come, my dear friend, live with me while I stay here, and go with me, if I do go to America." Privately Franklin instructed Temple to use all of his charm and powers of persuasion to plead his grandfather's case and he was not to return to France without Polly.

Temple found her in a little house in the ancient village of Cheam, where she lived with her daughter and sons, south of London. It was a long way from Marylebone, a seventeen-mile ride through the traffic of the city, crossing Westminster Bridge. He called upon Polly's family for the first time on September 10 and wrote to his grandfather two weeks later that he had dined twice at Cheam, and Mrs. Hewson had not said no. "I follow your instructions, on that and every other head, very exactly." He was not to force the issue, nor was he to take no for an answer. Polly, a swan-necked, elegant woman with fine bright eyes and delicate features, was nothing if not coy, and she would make the most of Temple's flattering attention.

She wrote to Benjamin: "We are all pleased with our old friend Temple changed into young Franklin." She pretended the grandson was not quite so good-looking as his grandfather, "but then you never were so genteel; and if he has a little less philosophy he has more polish. To have such a young man ready to run off with one, and yet to stay behind, argues great virtue or great stupidity." On October 5, Temple wrote that he did not yet have an answer from Mrs. Hewson. On the twelfth she consented. Ten days later she changed her mind, although

Temple had booked the journey. He advised his grandfather not to give up hope: "When persons once change, there's no reason for their not continuing to do so." Meanwhile, he promised he would call upon Bishop Shipley and his family in Chilbolton.

October passed. Polly's vacillations bought him more precious time in London with his father. On November 3, Polly wrote to Temple that he had stayed so long, he had given her time to change her mind again. So when Temple boarded the ship at Dover on November 28, after saying farewell to his father, he was proud to take charge of Polly, her children, and their baggage.

The group arrived safely in Passy on December 2. Benjamin Franklin was delighted. He later told Polly that the winter they lived together in Passy was the shortest he had ever known in his life.

While Temple was in London, William might have believed that his exclusion from the family circle was about to end. It pleased Temple to think so, and his grandfather had voiced no opposition. Temple had written from Calais upon landing, and he wrote from Paris the next day to say they had safely arrived there. But from the hour he arrived at his grandfather's villa in Passy, not a single line came from Temple to William. He felt again the old chill. In an affectionate note to his son on December 16, he expressed his pleasure at hearing of his safe arrival and also of his father's good health. This particular letter was bound to be treasured, entrusted, as it was, to a scientist embarking on Jean-Pierre Blanchard's balloon to France and thus history's first air mail delivery across the Channel. Doubtless it was cherished, but it was never answered. And word must have reached William soon thereafter to cease writing to Temple, for there were no more fatherly letters passing from London to Passy, either.

Temple Franklin's future was at stake. Benjamin's happiness during that winter of 1784–85 was a victory over three circumstances. His health, at seventy-nine, was poor; Congress, for mysterious reasons, refused to let him retire; finally, he had failed to secure an appointment for Temple as secretary to the American embassy in France—then called the "peace commission." This he considered gross ingratitude. Yet he still hoped his influence and Temple's talent would get him a place in the government. The trouble was that the Franklins had so many powerful enemies in Congress (Richard Henry Lee had been elected president) that any pretext to veto Temple's promotion might suffice.

So in the new year the family resumed that habit of silence toward the governor that they had practiced during the war. In May 1785, a Dr. Thomas Ruston, traveling from Paris to London, was entrusted with a packet of letters including one from Temple Franklin to his father, and some contraband goods. Temple advised him to conceal the contraband at the bottom of his trunk, promising him he would not be searched. If they were discovered, he was to pay the duties, for which Dr. Franklin would reimburse him in Temple's name.

The next day, May 3, Franklin's grandnephew Jonathan Williams, who had escorted Polly and her children back to London, reported to Ben that they had arrived safely, and that he had just seen William Franklin looking well. Three days later Temple informed cousin Jonathan he would be hearing soon from Dr. Franklin that finally he had been granted permission to retire. He would sail to America via the Isle of Wight, and he wanted Jonathan's advice about sailing ships.

In light of Dr. Franklin's travel plans, that letter going with the contraband in Ruston's trunk was evidently extremely important. On May 19, William drew up a legally precise formal indenture conveying all the property he owned in New York (the Otago Patent) to Temple for £1,500, to be paid by Benjamin Franklin. This was what now would be called a purchase agreement, witnessed on both sides of the Channel, to be executed later.

According to William's testimony to the claims commission mentioned previously, this purchase agreement represented a compromise he had made with his father by an exchange of letters in late March. It has been noted that Dr. Franklin kept a strict accounting of every dime his son had ever borrowed from him. And so he proposed that William give all of his property in New Jersey and New York to Temple, "in consideration of which," William recalled, "I was to receive a full discharge of the Bond and Debt mentioned. . . . This proposal hurt me greatly, as I never imagined he meant (unless his necessities should require it) to demand any payment of that Bond." And as William's land in either province was worth far more than what he owed his father, he couldn't help telling him so. Benjamin was not pleased. But William had been persuaded that the old man was satisfied with the compromise. "Although this transaction convinced me that he preferred my son's interest to mine," William wrote, "and that I held not an equal place in his affections, yet I cheerfully acquiesced in hopes by thus complying with his wishes," that he might "re-establish harmony in the family."

WHILE IT WAS NOT a difficult decision for Franklin to return to America once Congress had given him leave, it was a painful one. His physical discomfort during those final years in Passy was hardly to be endured without opium, on which he would soon depend for relief. He suffered the agonies of gout (inflammation of all the joints) and recurrent kidney stones that were so excruciating he could not travel in a jolting carriage or take more than a few steps from bed to chair in his room. So he doubted that he could weather even the crossing to the Isle of Wight.

Add to his physical complaints his sadness at leaving a country where he was adored by so many friends and virtually worshipped by millions of strangers. He wrote to the Baches on May 10 of his qualms. Fearing the packet crossing the Channel might be overcrowded, he had asked Jonathan Williams to find a ship that might sail directly from Le Havre to Philadelphia with him and his grandsons and baggage. (There was no such ship.) "Infirm as I am, I have need of comfortable room and accommodations . . . or I shall not be able to hold out the voyage." His friends were so worried that they begged him to remain in France, offering him asylum in their homes.

They assured him that he was now among a people who universally loved and honored him; that death had diminished the number of his friends in America; and that there he "might meet with envy and its consequent enmity," while in France he was free of such furies. These fears were well founded. So was the likelihood that he would not survive this voyage in his eightieth year. "The desire however of spending the little remainder of life with my family, is so strong, as to determine me to try at least whether I can bear the motion of a ship." If not, he would disembark somewhere along the coast and be content to live his last days in Europe.

At last they prepared to leave France on July 12, 1785. Benny Bache, a promising youth of sixteen, returned from Geneva, where he attended boarding school. Franklin had sent Sally his regrets that her son now spoke French more fluently than English. Benny was eager to see his parents.

The departure of Franklin's entourage from Passy was magnificent, an affair of state; Thomas Jefferson later commented that it was as if the village "had lost its patriarch." The party included grandsons Temple and Benny, servants, friends, and neighbors including his landlord Chaumont, and M. Le Veillard, who was charged with returning them to France if the ship proved impossible. Franklin had wanted the ease of a barge gliding on the Seine, but the river was too dry in places to allow it, so Queen Marie Antoinette lent him the use of her royal litter borne between two enormous mules known for sure-footedness. The king had made him the customary gift to departing ministers, a portrait of his royal self; but as Dr. Franklin was no typical foreign minister, it was no typical royal portrait, but a pretty miniature framed with two bezels of glass encrusted with diamonds—four hundred eight brilliants in all. The historian James Parton in 1864 valued the brooch at $10,000, which would be a quarter of a million dollars today.

They advanced through green valleys toward Normandy and the coast at eighteen miles per day, stopping now and then to rest, and to be entertained and applauded: the village of St. Germain the first night, Mantes the next. At Rouen the distinguished Academy came to present their compliments, in the form of an elaborately drawn magic square coded to spell the Doctor's name; he later confessed he could not make head nor tail of it. After nights with the Cardinal de la Rochefoucauld in his castle and another in the market town of Balbec, they arrived at Le Havre port on the afternoon of the eighteenth. They spent three days there gathering strength for the crossing.

The weather was threatening, the winds cross and the tides rough. Franklin, of all the passengers, was the only one who was not seasick. At last he would be seeing Mr. Strahan. The tide was so unruly off

Cowes, the Isle of Wight, where they were to meet their ship, that the captain preferred to sail on and land at Southampton.

Arriving at the Star Inn at eight o'clock on the morning of July 24, Franklin wrote to Benjamin Vaughan informing him he had arrived that minute with his family from Le Havre. He would stay here until the captain arrived at Cowes to board them. He had weathered the voyage from Le Havre very well. Dr. Franklin was uncannily buoyant and the journey had actually rejuvenated him. Writing the next day to Bishop Jonathan Shipley, he begged him to bring the rest of the Shipleys at once. He was just putting pen to paper to summon his cousin Jonathan Williams, his factotum in London, when Williams rang the bell at the Star Inn—just on the heels of Governor William Franklin.

William had arrived at Southampton the night before, having planned to meet his father and son across the strait at Cowes. He appeared that morning about the same time as Jonathan, and an old friend of Dr. Franklin's, the Scottish banker who would attend to some of the financial transactions.

A heavy curtain of secrecy has been drawn over the scenes between Benjamin and William Franklin during those four days at July's end. There is no record in anyone's letters or journals that does more than acknowledge, as does Temple's journal, that Franklin "had the satisfaction of seeing his son, the former Governor of New Jersey." Business documents show that they met daily at the Star Inn or in the ship's cabin to negotiate and execute contracts. William had traveled from London longing for the reconciliation he had requested a year earlier: a resumption of open communications that would allow him freedom to return to America and to the bosom of his family in Philadelphia if he liked, for a month, a year, or forever. His father kept him in suspense about all of that.

First there was important business to settle. The indenture to sell the New York land had already been drawn up. They had to sign it in the presence of witnesses and the town clerk of Southampton. In addition, there were properties in New Jersey belonging to William that would be of greater use in the future to Temple, including two lots on Pearl Street, a wooded plot of five acres in Burlington, and the beautiful 577-acre farm, farmhouse, and outbuildings on Rancocas Creek outside town that had been William and Elizabeth's first home in America. The men discussed the value of these properties on Sunday and Monday, and drew up a bill of sale and conveyance. After a long, sleepy soak in Martin's saltwater hot bath ("Water is the easiest bed that can be!"), Benjamin read the documents aloud to Temple. The next day, July 26, the New Jersey properties were transferred to Temple for 48,000 livres, or £2,000 sterling, about $300,000 in current dollars. It was also agreed that the 48,000 livres would be released to William only upon the surrender of the New York land in satisfaction of his former debts to his father.

It was a hard bargain. William supposed the old debts would have been forgiven, but not much was forgiven. There were other minor transactions. Before the war Benjamin had promised to grant some lands in Nova Scotia to William; now he could have them for what little they were worth—if he would give half to Sally. Powers of attorney for William to settle on that property and to collect Ben's debts from the British government, and the agreement to include Sally in the land sale, were witnessed and signed by passengers and the ship's captain, Thomas Truxton.

Any words of a personal nature that Benjamin Franklin had to say to his son before the ship sailed were not recorded. William's testimony to the claims commission in 1788 says that his father appeared to express "no dissatisfaction to me whatever, but seemed nearly as affectionate as formerly." But the results of what passed between them admit no doubt as to their meaning. The men were never to see each other again in this world. Even beyond the grave, Benjamin Franklin would reach out in his last will and testament to strike at his son. Not a word was ever to pass again between them, and William was instructed not to correspond with Temple. There was no reconciliation.

TWO DISAPPOINTMENTS CLOUDED BENJAMIN Franklin's bright view of the horizon that week. Polly Stevenson surprised him with a letter—instead of her company—in Southampton. He had been so certain of her decision to move to Philadelphia with him that he had booked several berths "that would have accommodated you and yours . . . I took the whole cabin that I might not be intruded upon by any accidental disagreeable company." He had written to her in June and July renewing the invitation, which she had promised to accept. Yet she waited until now, wavering, before writing to explain that she was unprepared, promising to make the voyage at a later date. "I am not so easily moved as I am kept from moving," she wrote, in a manner that was pure Polly, with all her vacillations. "All happiness attend you!"

This was not irremediable. Polly had been known to change her mind. The other shadow on his passage was darker and more deeply disheartening. William Strahan had died on July 9, only three days before they left Passy for Le Havre.

Strahan was gone, the friend whose heart and spirit had been great enough to embrace all of these cantankerous Franklins. He was the only man who might, perhaps, have brokered a quiet accord, a generous peace.

EPILOGUE

1785–1823

Joseph Galloway worked alongside Governor Franklin for the rest of the 1780s in the effort to secure loyalist claims, writing several persuasive pamphlets and testifying before the commission for American claimants. When Franklin's own case was heard in 1788, Galloway was one of a dozen witnesses, along with Cortlandt Skinner, fellow Tory governor Philip Skene, and General Henry Clinton himself. William's statement of services and claims totaled £48,245 sterling, representing restitution for lost wages, property in New York, New Jersey, and Indiana, twenty million acres of "Vandalia," debts owed him, splendid furniture, and an expensive library.

Franklin needed those witnesses. Much to his dismay the commissioners heeded rumors that the governor had benefited from collusion with Dr. Franklin. Temple's efforts to get his father a position in the diplomatic corps in 1782 looked suspicious, providing ammunition to anyone who wished to avoid paying the governor tens of thousands of pounds in reparations. They demanded that the witnesses substantiate his services to the Crown and testify to his loyalty. Finally they awarded the claimant £1,800 as the value of his furniture destroyed in the New York fire, and that was all. Acknowledging his poverty, they increased his pension to £800 per year.

Galloway had to settle for an annual pension of £500. Unaccustomed to poverty and inconsequence, he was sad in England. He tried and failed to secure the post of chief justice of Nova Scotia. In 1790, he petitioned the government of Pennsylvania to drop the charges of war crimes against him, begging to be repatriated. He argued that he had been driven to loyalism against his better judgment.

He died in the market town of Watford, north of London, in 1803, in obscurity.

IN AUGUST 1788, SOON after receiving his grant, William Franklin married Mary D'Evelin. They lived well, dividing their time between the house in Marylebone in the winter and autumn and a cottage by the sea in warm weather. They enjoyed traveling in Ireland, where Mary had relatives, and Scotland, where William had so many friends. Mary's adolescent sister came to live with them soon after they were married.

William continued an affectionate correspondence with his sister for the rest of his life. He urged Sally to come to England, which she could not do while her father lived, because the Baches could not afford the trip, and Benjamin would not agree to it. He needed her attentions at home there on Market Street. In that shrine to greatness, with its books and stoves, lightning rods, bells, medals, and harpsichords, children and pilgrims, Sally waited upon him as Deborah had once done. In this she had the devoted cooperation of Polly Stevenson, who—as good as her word—followed her mentor to Philadelphia with her brood a year after he arrived.

Franklin's contribution to the federal Constitutional Convention in 1787, his campaign for abolition, and his painful demise eased by opium during his last years have been well chronicled. He died of pleurisy on the evening of April 17, 1790, at the age of eighty-four, and is buried beside his wife in Christ Church cemetery, Philadelphia. In his last will and testament he had—in sensational fashion—the last word in the tragic dialogue with his son. He bequeathed William land in Nova Scotia that no longer belonged to him to bequeath, as well as books and papers of his that were already in William's possession. Finally, he forgave all outstanding debts.

There were no outstanding debts.

"The part he [William] acted against me in the late war, which is of public notoriety," Benjamin wrote, "will account for my leaving him no more of an estate than he endeavored to deprive me of." He left his son nothing but a sentence so shamefully cruel in a sacred document that there were some who considered it the dead man's curse.

His wealth passed to the Bache family and Temple Franklin. Temple, who inherited all of his grandfather's papers, made arrangements to travel to London with a view to finding a publisher. The Baches would follow in the spring of 1792, with funds courtesy of the king of France. Defying a prohibition in Franklin's will against disposing of the fabulous brooch or any of its diamonds in Sally's lifetime, her husband pried out a few dozen brilliants and sold them to the local jeweler. They sailed for England and stayed there half a year, wintering in London with William and his wife, and Temple, in 1792–93.

Temple managed to disappoint everyone. Perhaps no one was more disappointed than the women who fell in love with him. But let us first consider his father and grandfather. It is no exaggeration to say that Benjamin Franklin worshipped the ground Temple walked upon. He spoiled the boy, flattering and indulging him to a degree that was sometimes an embarrassment to his friends and a comfort to his enemies. No tailor or bootmaker was too dear, no fabric or wig too rich or costly, no wine of Burgundy or Bordeaux too fine for his cellar.

He must have not only the best dog and horse but also the best portrait of the thoroughbred painted by the best horse painter to hang on the wall. His grandfather would see to it there was money for women, too, when it was called for. The youth was a veritable Adonis, and the husbands of the French neighborhood—including a rich Scots lord and a famous actor—were on constant guard against him. His inhibitions, if not his morals, were agreeably relaxed by generous doses of Champagne and French beer. The amounts of alcohol the family consumed in Passy, proudly itemized in Temple's hand, were gargantuan.

Nonetheless, Benjamin judged this grandson as one "who has no vices." To John Adams, Franklin boasted of Temple's "sagacity beyond his years, diligence, activity, fidelity, genteel address, facility in speaking French." Adams disagreed. So did Thomas Jefferson, who got to know Temple later.

In a letter introducing Temple to Bishop Shipley in the summer of 1784, Franklin confided: "My grandson, a good young man (who as a son makes up to me my loss by the estrangement of his father) will have the honor of delivering you this line." The parenthesis betrays him. Nothing could make up to Benjamin Franklin what he had lost, and yet he would live and die in hopes that Temple would redeem all of it.

Polly, who liked Temple when she first met him, might have informed her mentor about his grandson's imperfections. After two months in Passy she wrote to her sister: "He has such a love of dress and is so absorbed in self-importance and so engaged in the pursuit of pleasure that he is not an amiable nor a respectable character; he is just fit to be employed in a court and to be the gallant of the French ladies, nothing else."

Perhaps Benjamin Franklin did not live long enough to give up hope of Temple's redemption and success. But as the decade wore on he must have doubted it. Approaching the age of thirty, the no longer young man had been unable to get a position in the new government, nor any other gainful employment. He was exactly as Polly Stevenson had described him, a French courtier with no formal education or skills. He owned the farm his father had started in New Jersey, on Rancocas Creek. Adrift, with no other choice, he briefly played at being a gentleman farmer, and was in the course of failing at this, too, when his grandfather died and left him his inheritance.

In the spring of 1791, Temple Franklin arrived in London in pursuit of a publisher. He did not notify his father in advance that he was coming, but William, now in his early sixties and a distinguished man of leisure, was happy to see him. Temple rented a new house in fashionable Manchester Square, seven blocks east of his father's home.

Temple's arrival—and the offending articles of his grandfather's will—had erased any desire William may have had to return to Amer-

ica. He enjoyed his son's company, despite what he perceived as shift-
lessness, indolence, and self-indulgence. London bored Temple. He
preferred Paris, and sailed back and forth across the Channel as if
money was inexhaustible.

The winter of 1792–93 was particularly enjoyable for the family, as
the Baches lived nearby in London the entire season. William was able
to introduce Richard and Sally to his circle of friends, men such as
Andrew Strahan, Edward Gibbon, and Dr. Johnson. After returning to
Philadelphia, the Baches would send their son William (his uncle's
namesake) to England to complete his medical studies, in the summer
of 1794. The difference in the cousins' temperaments was evident. William Franklin wrote to Sally in August to tell her of young Bache's
meeting with Dr. Johnson, who held a high opinion of the student's
medical skills.

Temple had no profession. Sometime in the middle of that decade
he developed an attachment to Ellen Johnson D'Evelin, the "younger
sister" and ward of Mary D'Evelin Franklin, William's wife. "Younger
sister" belongs in quotation marks because, although that is what the
Franklins called her, the women's names tell a different story: The girl
was probably not Mary's sister but her illegitimate daughter; otherwise
they would simply have called her the child of Mary's former marriage.
If Mary had a sister, she would be named Ellen Johnson, not D'Evelin.
Ellen was the same age as Sally's daughter Elizabeth Bache, with
whom she corresponded, and was almost eighteen when she went to
bed with Temple.

As soon as this liaison was known it must have been the cause of
terrible strife in the house on Norton Street, and scandal when the girl
stole away to Temple's lavish rooms in Manchester Square. She became pregnant with his child in the summer of 1797. No one could
prevail upon the profligate American to marry the Irish Ellen D'Evelin,
who had no dowry to recommend her. Temple closed his house in
London and moved to Paris soon before the baby's birth. William
wrote that this rift caused "more trouble of mind than I had ever before
experienced," echoing his father's words to him in 1784.

The baby, christened Ellen Franklin, was born on April 7, 1798.
What is most remarkable is that the child's mother, Mary D'Evelin's

sister, or daughter, vanished from history without a trace—not a tombstone, letter, or diary entry. This brings a gothic chill to the record. She became as invisible as those other unwed mothers, the sad women who brought William Franklin and Temple Franklin into the world. But here is a disturbing difference: Those mistresses of the 1730s and 1760s were anonymous before and after giving birth to Franklins. Ellen Johnson D'Evelin was not only known by name, she was a family member.

So what became of Ellen D'Evelin, Ellen Franklin's mother? There is no one to tell us. Perhaps she returned to Ireland to begin life anew, under an assumed name. One thing is certain: Secrets of this nature beget more secrets and trouble in a family. In this case the chronicler is obliged to relate the mysterious circumstances of Ellen's disappearance to the dreadful demise of Mrs. Franklin. In her fifties, William's second wife lost her mind. Illnesses real and imaginary racked her frame and eventually confined her to her bed. The king's best physicians could do nothing for her. Refusing food and drink, Mary was kept alive for a while by force-feeding. At last, on September 3, 1811, she succumbed to whatever demons had been pursuing her.

"Happiness has received a stroke which cannot be remedied at my advanced period of life, and I must resign myself for the remaining days of my existence to that solitary state which is most repugnant to my nature," William Franklin wrote to his cousin Jonathan. After Mary's death, Temple wrote to his father expressing his renewed interest in publishing Benjamin's works and visiting London. He was living beyond his means in a house in Paris and another in the country with his mistress Hannah Collyer. William said he would be happy to see Temple whenever it was convenient; he hoped "to bury in oblivion all past transactions," and desired that if Temple would not leave Paris and live in London he might at least manage a visit to his truly affectionate parent. He told Jonathan Williams he could not bear the thought of dying at odds with his son. But he was never to see him again. Although Temple visited London from time to time, he did not call upon his father.

Still, William was not alone. He had Ellen, an intelligent and charming girl, age thirteen when his wife died. She reminded him of his father, and William said she "showed every promise of making a fine woman." He was right. She had been raised in the Franklins' house in Marylebone as their daughter, and was sent to a finishing school thirty miles from London. During the last years of his life, Ellen Franklin cared for her grandfather with all the tenderness and devotion that Sally had reserved for her father. William enjoyed life until the end, reporting to Jonathan Williams in July 1812 that his health—considering the fact that he was eighty-one—was generally good, and that he retained, praise God, his usual flow of spirits. His hobbyhorse during the nineteenth century was the tantalizing pursuit of lands, interest, and debts in relation to his real estate adventures in America. He engaged lawyers including Aaron Burr to bring suit against the Croghan estate for £12,000 owed him. It was never quite clear to anyone that the effort was futile. When William was too feeble to put pen to paper, young Ellen served as his amanuensis, not much caring what came of the knotty lawsuit, wanting only to be of service to her surrogate father.

She was richly rewarded. William left Ellen the lion's share of his estate, real property and investments probably valued at £20,000 sterling at the time of his death, November 16, 1813. He was buried in the churchyard of St. Pancras Old Church in London. Like his father before him, William left his son nothing but invalid titles to land and the right to claim uncollectible debts. He did not curse Temple. Ellen's fortune he put into a trust, and when she came of age it made an attractive dowry for officer Capel Hanbury of the Royal Scots. They were married in June 1818. In 1820, Ellen gave birth to Maria, the first and last legitimate child to be born in that crooked branch of the family tree. They lived in Nice, in the Mediterranean sunshine.

THE WORST FATE THAT could have attended the papers of Benjamin Franklin—after being abandoned by Joseph Galloway—was for them to fall into the hands of Temple Franklin. Greed ought to have served him better, for they were priceless. He wandered and delayed publishing the *Autobiography* for nearly thirty years while a dozen unauthorized versions were published lucratively in French and English. When he finally published his edition in London in 1818, the *Autobiography* included only three of the four parts. Temple had somehow been duped into trading the original complete manuscript in his grandfather's hand for some other copy that comprised only the first three quarters. Not for fifty years would readers see the book in all its glory, when the diplomat John Bigelow purchased the holograph manuscript in France and published an accurate text in Philadelphia.

As for the rest of Franklin's letters and writings? Before Temple left America, he hastily went through his grandfather's papers and grabbed twenty-five hundred pages that seemed interesting to him. The greatest part of the archive, fifteen thousand letters at least, were nailed up in hogshead barrels for his friend George Fox to store in a garret over his stable in Champlost, outside Philadelphia, as collateral for a loan. Years passed, the debt went unpaid, and Temple bequeathed the papers to Fox in his will. They meant nothing to Fox or his family. They gave some away as party favors. As late as 1862, Fox's daughter Elizabeth ordered that the barrels of letters should be sold to the mill for old paper. One keg had gone forever and others were being rolled out the door when a visitor asked what was going on and put a stop to it. What remained of the American archive landed, eventually, in the vaults of the American Philosophical Society and the University of Pennsylvania.

The papers Temple took with him to London he culled, publishing half of them, haphazardly edited, in several volumes between 1808 and 1819 in London and Philadelphia. Subsequently the manuscripts were held by Temple's London banker, Herries and Company. In 1840, an anonymous fellow lodger of the late Temple Franklin tried to sell the Franklin papers to the British Museum. When asked how they had come into his possession, all he would say is that he had discovered bound parcels of them on the top shelf of a tailor's shop in St. James's Street, near Herries's bank. The innocent tailor had been using this sturdy rag stock to cut shirt patterns. There was one sheet of foolscap snipped neatly into the shape of a sleeve.

No buyer stepped up to purchase the collection until 1850, when the insightful American book dealer Henry Stevens bought the entire lot, more than two thousand pages, for an undisclosed sum. In 1881, Stevens sold it to the U.S. State Department for $35,000 ($850,000 today).

William Temple Franklin died in Paris in 1823, at sixty-three years of age, penniless, nineteen days after marrying his patient mistress, Mrs. Collyer. She was the only woman he did not disappoint in that way; but he left his widow nothing but those papers deposited with the London bank, which she clearly mismanaged even worse than he had.

He is buried in the ornate garden cemetery of Perè Lachaise beneath an expensive obelisk.

ACKNOWLEDGMENTS

AMONG SEVERAL PROJECTS I proposed in 2011, my agent, Neil Olson, expressed a preference for this book—one I approached with reservations, considering the distant historical period and the perplexing character of Benjamin Franklin's family. Without Mr. Olson's confidence I would not have gone ahead. My editor at Random House, Susanna Porter, showed great enthusiasm for the book from the beginning.

Ms. Porter provided guidance throughout many drafts of this manuscript, and invaluable advice on every aspect of the work. She has been an imaginative and tireless collaborator. The eighteenth century is worlds away from the twenty-first, and my editor helped me to bridge the gap. Emily Hartley, Ms. Porter's editorial assistant, worked capably with me to gather the artwork for the book.

As always, I am grateful to the staff in the Manuscript Division of the Library of Congress, especially Jeffrey M. Flannery, who helped me locate the copies of William Franklin's correspondence and records as photocopied from the Public Record Office in England and other sources, and Bruce Kirby, who is a wizard at finding what seems to be nowhere to be found. Travis Wesley in the Newspaper and Periodical Room helped me locate obscure eighteenth-century newspapers, navigate the digital files, and obtain original copies of what was not available online. In the Geography and Map Division I had the insightful assistance of the Franklin scholar Ed Redmond, and of Mike Busher, head of the division, and Michael Klein who helped me to find the perfect maps of Philadelphia and New Jersey in the eighteenth century, and the great John Rocque map of London in 1769, and to copy them full size to hang on the walls of my study.

Special thanks go to Robert Frankel, associate editor of the magisterial papers of Benjamin Franklin at Yale, for sharing with me the discovery of the "Abstract of Vouchers" William Franklin submitted to the British claims commission in 1788.

Manuscripts, collections, and entire libraries can migrate or vanish altogether in a generation. One example will serve: The William Franklin letters and manuscripts that for many years were said to be filed in the Sterling Library of Yale University were no longer to be found there when I went looking for them. It took the assiduous efforts of Kate Woodford, editorial assistant for the Benjamin Franklin Collection, to determine that those papers had been moved to the Beinecke Library and to find and copy for me the exact catalog cards for the items in the collection. The good news then was that the papers had been located; the bad news was that the Franklin papers at the Beinecke were being processed and were, for the year that I wanted them, declared off-limits to researchers. Through the extraordinary kindness and intervention of Elizabeth Frengel, Research Services Librarian at the Beinecke Rare Book and Manuscript Library, I was provided with access to every item I needed, and with copies of the letters.

A sadder story is the fate of William Franklin's important letter to Margaret Abercrombie in 1758, mentioned in my chapter notes. For a century it had rested in the files of the Historical Society of Pennsylvania. Now it cannot be found. If anyone has a copy of that letter (whole or in part), it would be a great service to scholarship to forward it to the Society.

At the Historical Society of Pennsylvania, which now houses documents formerly held by the Library Company of Philadelphia, I had the advantage of working with research librarians Steve Smith, David Haugard, and Willhem Echevarria. Janet Bloom, reference librarian at the

Clements Library at the University of Michigan, provided important advice concerning the Clinton Papers. Earl Spamer, at the American Philosophical Society in Philadelphia, helped me find many documents and letters of the Franklin family and associates that cannot be found in other collections. Joseph Dillullo advised me about artwork in the APS collection. Mary Ellen Parlosky of Proprietary House provided the portrait of William Franklin by Danuta Wyszynski.

At the American Philosophical Society and elsewhere I had the thoughtful assistance of my partner, Sarah Longaker, in organizing and copying original manuscripts. For her support and care during the researching and writing of this book I am deeply grateful. Rosemary Knower, with whom I have had the privilege and the pleasure of working on all of my books of history, gave more than the usual attention to this one, which presented narrative challenges we had not encountered elsewhere. She is a gifted reader and editor and I was lucky, once more, to have her judicious advice.

In the 2013–14 academic year I had the honor to serve as the Patrick Henry Fellow at the CV Starr Center for the American Experience at Washington College in Chestertown, Maryland. One of the benefits was the pleasure of living in the Patrick Henry House, an eighteenth-century dwelling on Queen Street in the heart of the historic district. I had no idea, before accepting the fellowship, that the charming Georgian house also serves as quarters for the Leo LeMay Library of Americana, one of the finest collections of books about Benjamin Franklin and colonial and revolutionary America anywhere. J. A. Leo LeMay, a legendary Franklin scholar whose work is cited in my book, left his books and notes to the Starr Center with the stipulation that they be kept together there. Readers may note the effects of my having lived night and day within reach of every single issue of *The Pennsylvania Gazette*, the paper Franklin founded.

I owe a debt of gratitude to the Starr Center, to the college, and to the late Leo LeMay for inspiration and support. Thanks especially to Director Adam Goodheart and Interim Director Ted Maris Wolf, and to Jenifer Emley, the Center Coordinator. Ms. Emley provided invaluable daily attention in facilitating my research and the organization of my materials while I was writing in Chestertown. Assistant Director

Jean Wortman also helped me keep track of research materials, and Michael Buckley, Program Manager, was tireless in providing every kind of logistical support during my residence in Chestertown. At the college library I had the imaginative services of Amanda Kramer, who helped solve research problems; Carol Van Veen, who procured rare books on interlibrary loan; and Dr. Ruth Shoge, the library's director.

Benjamin Franklin has had excellent biographers, beginning with James Parton in 1864 and including Carl Van Doren, whose Pulitzer Prize–winning book in 1938 remains the gold standard. Until 1975, however, with the publication of *The Private Franklin* by Claude-Ann Lopez and Eugenia Herbert, Franklin's personal and family life was, if not neglected, underexamined. The reasons for this are interesting, and too complex to be addressed here. Suffice it to say that those reasons have to do with long-standing habits and predilections in American historiography, and with the contrast between the character depicted in Franklin's famous *Autobiography* and the complex person who emerges from his vast and revealing correspondence. His relationship with his son, in particular, has been passed over as an inconvenience, an embarrassment—an unseemly feature—that does not fit the profile that has long served our beloved founding father.

So it is remarkable that in the 1950s a graduate student at the University of Pennsylvania should choose as the topic for his Ph.D. dissertation the life of William Franklin, a history that would inevitably confront the relationship between Benjamin Franklin and his bastard son. William Herbert Mariboe's thesis was presented and defended in 1962, and he was awarded the Ph.D. degree in Modern History from the university Franklin founded.

Dr. Mariboe should have been awarded the Pulitzer Prize in biography—which was not given that year. He did not get that prize, or any other prize, because his dissertation was never published. It is the best biography of William Franklin ever written, and one of the most significant contributions to Franklin scholarship of the twentieth century. The man Mariboe remains completely unknown.

William Herbert Mariboe ought to be named the patron saint of unsung biographers. It will be clear to the reader of this book just how much we owe him, and how stunning Mariboe's achievement was. In those days before word processors—not to mention the digitalization of books from the eighteenth century to the present and the ability to "word-search" sources—Mariboe mastered all of the primary and secondary sources from New York to Ann Arbor to New Haven, from Washington, D.C., to Philadelphia, from Newark to Trenton. He read everything on-site, with primitive copying facilities. This must have taken him more than a decade. Then he wove the material into a readable, intelligent narrative.

And so, you graduate students, scholars, historians, toiling in the libraries and archives here and abroad, look upon the example of William Mariboe and be humbled and consoled. Your work matters whether it gets published or not.

SOURCES AND NOTES

Abbreviations and Short Titles Employed in the Notes

BF	Benjamin Franklin	DF	Deborah Franklin
WF	William Franklin	SF	Sarah Franklin
GW	George Washington	RB	Richard Bache
WTF	William Temple Franklin	JM	Jane Mecum
JG	Joseph Galloway	EF	Elizabeth Franklin
WS	William Strahan		

APS: American Philosophical Society

Autobiography: Leo LeMay, ed., *Benjamin Franklin: Writings* (New York: Library of America, 1987)

Brands: H. W. Brands, *The First American: The Life and Times of Benjamin Franklin* (New York: Doubleday, 2000)

Chronology: Bud Hannings, *Chronology of the American Revolution: Military and Political Actions Day by Day* (Jefferson, MO: McFarland, 2008)

Docs: Frederick W. Ricord, ed., *Documents Relating to the Colonial History of New Jersey* (Trenton: John L. Murphy Publishing Co., 1893), sometimes cited as "New Jersey Archives"

Gazette: *The Pennsylvania Gazette*, facsimile edition (Philadelphia: Historical Society of Pennsylvania Microinsurance, 1968), citations by date of issue

HSP: Pennsylvania Historical Society

JCC: Worthington C. Ford et al., eds., *Journals of the Continental Congress 1774–1789* (Washington, DC: Government Printing Office, 1912)

LC: Library of Congress

Letters: Paul H. Smith et al., eds., *Letters of the Members of the Continental Congress 1774–1789* (Washington, DC: Library of Congress, 1776–2000)

Mariboe: William H. Mariboe, *The Life of William Franklin, 1730(1)–1813: "ProRege et Patria* (University of Pennsylvania Ph.D., 1962) Unpublished dissertation.

PBF: *The Papers of Benjamin Franklin* (New Haven: Yale University Press, 1959–). The apparatus (prefaces and footnotes) to the published papers, the work of many hands, is masterful, and constitutes the most important single source of information on Franklin's life apart from the papers themselves.

PRO: Public Record Office, Colonial Office, Archives, England. Transcripts of William Franklin papers in PRO are in the collection of the Library of Congress.

Skemp: Sheila L. Skemp, *William Franklin: Son of a Patriot, Servant of a King* (New York: Oxford University Press, 1990)

Van Doren: Carl Van Doren, *Benjamin Franklin* (New York: Viking, 1938)

V&P: *Votes and Proceedings of the General Assembly of the Province of New Jersey, 1682–1775* (Woodbridge: James Parker, 1754–), New Jersey State Library via Internet Archives

THE FRANKLIN FAMILY'S GENERAL correspondence is consolidated in *The Papers of Benjamin Franklin*, published by the Yale University Press, a multivolume work in progress. While the complete papers are not yet published, nearly all are available online in a searchable database by courtesy of Yale and the Packard Institute. Included is the entire correspondence of Benjamin, Deborah, and Temple Franklin, and of Sarah and Richard Bache. Many of William Franklin's letters are also included, but some are located elsewhere. Unless otherwise indicated, all letters quoted may be found in *The Papers of Benjamin Franklin*. If dates appear in the text, these letters are not footnoted. All letters not dated in the text are given full citations in the chapter notes.

Where a section or topic relies heavily on a single source, such as Anne Ousterhout's biography of Elizabeth Graeme Fergusson, I will cite it once to apply passim rather than repeating the citation opus citatum or ibid. with page numbers.

The details of the Revolutionary War's progress herein are so numerous and long established that I have not annotated them. My references for military events include W. J. Wood's *Battles of the Revolutionary War 1775–1781* (Chapel Hill: Algonquin Books, 1990), Hanning's *Chronology of the American Revolution* cited above, and Benson Bobrick, *Angel in the Whirlwind* (New York: Simon and Schuster, 1997). George Washington's widely published letters are listed by date only.

Sources clearly cited in the text are not repeated in the chapter notes. I have avoided annotating the obvious. The following chapter notes are limited to citations necessary for locating important sources, and to acknowledge the work of other historians.

PREFACE: A NIGHT JOURNEY, 1731

As the preface is not formally a part of the history, it is not annotated.

CHAPTER 1: AMERICANS IN LONDON: SEPTEMBER 22, 1761

In addition to contemporary newspaper accounts, descriptions of London during the coronation and quotes from the ceremony are recorded in Richard Thomson, ed., *A Faithful Account of the Processions and Ceremonies Observed in the Coronation of the Kings and Queens of England* (London: Printed for John Major, 1820), 98 pp.

"Since then, great Prince": *London Chronicle* for 1761, Sept. 29–Oct. 1.

"Your son I really think": WS to DF, December 13, 1757. The chief source of information on William Strahan, apart from his many letters to the Franklin family, is J. A. Cochrane, *Dr. Johnson's Printer: The Life of William Strahan* (Cambridge, MA: Harvard University Press, 1964).

"a most awkward ridiculous appearance": *Autobiography of Benjamin Franklin*, hereafter *Autobiography*, 1329.

"would be more convenient": Ibid., 1340.

"That hard-to-be-governed passion": Ibid.

"project of arriving at moral perfection": Ibid., 1383–94.

the gossips of Philadelphia: My understanding of the circumstances of William Franklin's birth is influenced by the late J. A. Leo LeMay's *The Life of Benjamin Franklin*, vol. 2 (Philadelphia: University of Pennsylvania Press, 2006), 4.

William marched north to Albany: John F. Folsom, "Col. Peter Schuyler at Albany," *Proceedings of the New Jersey Historical Society, New Series*, vol. 1, 1916, 161.

"As peace cuts off his prospect": BF to WS, October 19, 1748.

"Brethren . . . some of you have": Reuben Gold Thwaites, ed., *Early Western Journals, 1748–65*, by Conrad Weiser, George Groghan, et al. (Cleveland: Arthur H. Clark Co., 1904), 39.

"the country back of us": BF to Peter Collinson, October 18, 1748.

"the moment you leave": Paul Wallace, *Conrad Weiser, 1696–1760: Friend of Colonist and Mohawk* (Philadelphia: University of Pennsylvania Press, 1945), 270.

"As to your grandchildren": BF to Abiah Franklin, April 12, 1750.

"the daily opportunities": WS to DF, December 13, 1757.

CHAPTER 2: COLONIAL CONTEMPORARIES, 1753

"according to the rights": William Penn, "Charter of Privileges for the Province of Pennsylvania, 1701," APS.

"You have asked us the reason": *Journal of the Congress at Albany,* Collections of the Massachusetts Historical Society: Third Series V, 41–43; Van Doren, 221.

"Look about your country and see": Ibid.

nothing important . . . transacted: BF to Cadwallader Colden, July 14, 1754.

JOIN OR DIE: Cartoon published in *Gazette,* May 9, 1754.

In the meantime, the French: BF cited by Leo LeMay, ed., *Benjamin Franklin: Writings* (New York: Library of America, 1987), 376.

summit was moved to Alexandria: Lady Matilda Ridout Edgar, *A Colonial Governor in Maryland* (London: Longmans, Green, 1912), 40–45.

Mingo chief Tanacharison: see Joseph J. Ellis, *His Excellency: George Washington* (New York: Alfred A. Knopf, 2004), 3–16.

The French could rely: Fred Anderson, *Crucible of War: The Seven Years' War and the Fate of Empire in British North America, 1754–66* (New York: Alfred A. Knopf, 2000), 51.

"If you do not come to our assistance": W. W. Abbot, Dorothy Twohig, and Philander Chase, eds., *The Papers of George Washington: Colonial Series* (Charlottesville: University of Virginia Press, 1983–95), *Diaries* 1:189–90.

"Tu n'es pas encore mort": Contrecoeur to Duquesne, June 2, 1754; Fernand Grenier, ed., *Memorial Containing a Summary View* (London and New York: H. Gaine, 1764), 69; see also *Papiers Contrecoeur et Autres Documents Concernment le Conflit Anglo-français sur Ohio de 1754 à 1756* (Quebec: Les Presses Universitaires Laval, 1952) and George Robitaille, *Washington et Jumonville* (Montreal: Le Devoir, 1933).

"The volley fired": Walpole, *History of the Reign of King George II,* quoted in Thomas A. Lewis, *For King and Country: George Washington, the Early Years* (New York: John Wiley, 1993), 147.

"the cannon shot fired in the wilderness": James Wilford Garner, Henry Cabot Lodge, et al., *The United States* (Philadelphia: J. D. Morris & Co., 1906), 172.

foully assassinated: Henry Cabot Lodge, *George Washington* (Boston: Houghton Mifflin, 1895), 1:72.

a hero in Virginia: William Rasmussen and Robert Tilton, *George Washington: The Man Behind the Myths* (Charlottesville: University Press of Virginia, 1999), 55.

"He had too high an opinion": *Autobiography,* 1440.

"The English should inhabit": Matthew C. Ward, *Breaking the Backcountry: The Seven Years' War in Virginia and Pennsylvania, 1754–65* (Pittsburgh: University of Pittsburgh Press, 2003), 40–41.

if his people weren't free: Ibid., 39–41.

"My son *William Franklin*": *Autobiography*, 1437.

"These savages may indeed": *Autobiography*, 1441.

"the hero of the Monongahela": Joseph Ellis, *His Excellency George Washington* (New York: Alfred A. Knopf, 2004), 23.

"Who'd have thought it": *Autobiography*, 1442.

"succeeded in setting against the English": Wallace, *Conrad Weiser*, 385.

"husband looking on while": Ibid., 410.

"Why should they not act": Thomas Penn to Richard Peters, March 30, 1748, and June 9, 1748, PBF, vol. III, 185–86.

"Tho' I did not conceive": *Autobiography*, 1445.

"my son who had in the preceding war": Ibid.

CHAPTER 3: DEFENSES AND ENGAGEMENTS

"We shall endeavor": BF to DF, January 15, 1756.

"the narrow pass": Thomas Lloyd's "journal" remarks are located in PBF under the dates January 30–31, 1756, in an unaddressed letter from Fort Allen.

"All round appears nothing": PBF 6:380–82.

Elizabeth Graeme: Anne M. Ousterhout, *The Most Learned Woman in America: A Life of Elizabeth Graeme Fergusson* (University Park: Penn State University Press, 2004), 60–61.

Betsy was in pathetic distress: Ann Graham to Mrs. Campbell, May 13, 1756, Stauffer Collection of HSP.

"much more fit to command": *Autobiography*, 1449.

"1200 well-looking men": *Autobiography*, 1450.

"twenty officers of my regiment": BF to Collinson, ut supra.

"The city is in infinite distraction": Richard Peters to Thomas Penn, April 25, 1756, HSP.

"He had been advis'd . . . solicitations and promises": *Autobiography*, 1456.

"the same unfortunate instructions": Ibid., 1457.

Teedyuscung: Background comes from Flick, *The William Johnson Papers*, ut infra, and from Kendra Whitaker Yates, "Ye Land Affair Which Is Dirt," *Historia: The Alpha Rho Papers* (Salt Lake City: University of Utah Press, 2011), 116–41.

the Assembly at last: *Autobiography*, 1457.

"That William Franklin have leave": PBF, February 18, 1757.

"like the new fell snow": Elizabeth Graeme, "On the Fate of a Lottery Ticket," December 30, 1752, *Poemata Juvenilia*, doc. 0519 HSP.

"a certain elevation of soul": Elizabeth Graeme, *Commonplace Book,* HSP.

the most learned woman in America: Ann H. Wharton, *Salons Colonial and Republican* (Philadelphia: J. B. Lippincott, 1900), 13.

"Ye Ladies! Who are now": William Franklin, August 16, 1753, *Poemata Juvenilia,* 160, doc. 0509, HSP.

"Rude Winter comes to end": Ibid., 161, doc. 0510.

"Whether the feeling or insensible": Ibid., doc. 0520.

"the weight severe . . . dispersed by wind": Ibid., November 1, 1753, 140–49. "Sylvia" was the pseudonym of Rebecca Moore.

"Guess what that one thing": WF to Elizabeth Graeme, February 26, 1757, HSP.

"But now O Love!": WF, *Poemata Juvenilia,* 173, doc. 0513.

"made a jest of Cupid's Power": EG, ibid. 175, doc. 0534.

"There's various Reasons . . . forgetting me": Ibid., 177, doc. 0517.

"long in distant Climes": Ibid.

"dear Tormentor": WF to EG, February 26, 1757, ut supra.

"repeated acts of civility": WF to Margaret Abercrombie, October 24, 1758, Gratz Collection, HSP. N.B.: This important letter, cited by historians until the twenty-first century as being in the HSP, has vanished. I will continue to cite it by reference to any biographer who quotes it, in this case Ousterhout, 63.

"is still overcast . . .": WF to EG, April 7, 1757.

"Mr. Franklin's popularity": Penn to Peters, May 14, 1757, HSP.

CHAPTER 4: CHALLENGES, 1757

"Let the pleasures": WF to Elizabeth Graham, July 17, 1757.

"Were I a Roman Catholic": BF to DF, July 17, 1757.

"For my own part": WS to DF, December 13, 1757.

daughter-in-law: BF to WS, WS to BF, passim, n.d., 1750.

"You Americans have wrong ideas": *Autobiography,* 1465.

"He assured me . . .": Ibid., 1466.

"They are first drawn": *Autobiography,* 1465.

"a complete electrical apparatus": Van Doren, 160.

"to refuse his assent": *"Heads of Complaint"* op cit.

"We now appeared very wide . . .": *Autobiography,* 1466.

"A violent cold . . . nursed me kindly": BF to DF, November 22, 1757.

"Billy was also . . .": Ibid.

"To the Printer . . ." and passim; September 16, 1757, PBF.

"To the Proprietors . . .": *Autobiography,* 1467.

had "conceived a mortal enmity": Ibid., 1466.

"*expressly* says . . . his father's character" and passim: BF to Isaac Norris, January 14, 1758.

"power and privileges": "Pennsylvania Charter of Privileges," October 28, 1701, www.constitution.org/bcp/penncharpriv.htm.

"where it lay unanswered": *Autobiography,* 1467.

"The whole town . . .": BF to DF February 19, 1758.

"From this experiment . . .": BF to John Lining, June 17, 1758.

"collection of party malice . . ." and passim: WF to Margaret Abercrombie, October 24, 1758, cited in Ousterhout, 66–68, and Mariboe, 89–91.

"We are ready . . . for that purpose": Ibid.

"I need not point out": BF to Isaac Norris, January 19, 1759.

"The proprietors will be gibbeted up": BF to JG, February 17, 1758.

CHAPTER 5: TRIUMPHS

"open and communicative": J. Bennett Nolan, *Benjamin Franklin in Scotland and Ireland, 1759 and 1771* (Philadelphia: University of Pennsylvania Press, 1938), 63.

"a Lady distinguished": Francis Hopkinson, from his obituary of EF, *Gazette,* August 13, 1777, quoted in Vernon O. Stumpf, "Who Was Elizabeth Downes Franklin?" Notes and Documents, *Pennsylvania Magazine of History and Biography,* vol. 94, issue 4 (October 1970), 2.

"victories come tumbling": James Parton, *The Life and Times of Benjamin Franklin* (Boston: Houghton, Mifflin, 1864), 393.

"he was then too great a man": *Journal of the Peace Negotiations,* May 9, 1782, PBF.

"being in odium . . . fairly & equitably": *Autobiography,* 1467.

"Do you really believe": Ibid., 1468.

no more exemptions: Van Doren, 287.

"which protects and encourages": *The Interest of Great Britain Considered,* April 1760, PBF.

"It would be no small pleasure": BF to Edward Tilghman, William Murdock, et al., November 26, 1761.

"six weeks of the densest happiness": BF to Lord Kames, January 3, 1760.

"mind thirsty after knowledge": BF to Mary Stevenson, September 13, 1760.

"dear preceptor . . . ever dear saint . . . dear good girl": Corr. BF and Mary (Polly) Stevenson 1760–61, PBF.

"dear little philosopher": Ibid.

"After writing 6 folio pages": BF to Mary (Polly) Stevenson, September 13, 1760.

"whom he once": Ibid., August 11, 1762.

"we almost idolize": Ezra Stiles to BF, December 30, 1761.

"who knows your affair": BF to Edward Tilghman, William Murdock, et al., November 26, 1761.

"Be assured that the Address": BF to Tilghman ut supra.

"to carry us to see": WF to SF, October 10, 1761.

"in time enough": Ibid.

Garter King of Arms in his tabard: The details of the coronation of King George and all quotes passim from the ceremony are recorded in Richard Thomson, ed., *A Faithful Account of the Processions and Ceremonies Observed in the Coronation of the Kings and Queens of England* (London: Printed for John Major, 1820), 98 pp. See also *The Letters of Horace Walpole* (Oxford: Clarendon Press, 1904), vol. V, 1760–64, Horace Walpole to Horace Mann, September 28, 1761, 121.

"It was mere chit-chat": WF to SF, October 10, 1761.

"full of the best company": Frederick Albert Pottle, ed., *Boswell's London Journal 1762–1763* (New Haven: Yale University Press, 1950), 70, December 7, 1762.

"was quite a fairy scene": Horace Walpole to George Montagu, June 8, 1762, op cit.

"incomparably sweet": BF to Giambattista Beccaria, July 13, 1762.

he would marry Betsy Downes: See PBF, vol. 10, 108n.

"My son stays a little longer": BF to John Morgan, August 16, 1762.

"He stays in England": BF to Lord Kames, August 17, 1762.

"I feel like a thing out of its place": BF to WS, July 20, 1762.

"George the Third by Grace": Hardwick Papers, British Museum; also LC Mss. 36132, folio 125.

"Your friend is this moment": WF to WS, September 4, 1762, C. H. Hart, ed., "Letters from William Franklin to William Strahan," *Pennsylvania Magazine of History and Biography*, vol. 35, 1911, 421ff.

CHAPTER 6: AMERICA, 1763

"thank God, perfectly recover'd": WF to WS, December 14, 1762, Ibid.

"a jolly, lively dame": BF to DF, September 6, 1758.

"The river was hard and firm": BF to DF, February 24, 1763.

"double swearing": My sources for the seventeenth- and eighteenth-century history of New Jersey include Samuel Smith, *The History of the Colony of Nova Caesaria, or New Jersey* (Burlington: James Parker, 1765) and John W. Barber and Henry Howe, *Historical Collections of the State of New Jersey* (New York: S. Tuttle, 1845).

seat of residence: *Gazette*, March 10, 1763.

"wherever I may reside": Ibid., March 3, 1763.

"And if we presume": Ibid., March 10, 1763.

"He was received": Ibid.

"with the utmost respect": BF to WS, March 28, 1763.

"the lady is of so amiable": BF to Jane Mecum, November 25, 1762.

"no good understanding" and passim: WF to WS, April 25, 1763, Hart, "Letters," 424.

"If an Indian injures me": "Narrative of the Late Massacres," *Writings,* 546.

"The only crime": Ibid.

"fifteen hundred men": Benjamin Kendall quoted, Pennsylvania Assembly to John Penn, February 11, 1764, V&P, 43.

"I chose to carry": BF to John Fothergill, March 14, 1764.

"my rest [was] so broken": BF to Jackson, ut supra.

His recollection of events: Ibid.

"I became less a man": BF to Lord Kames, June 2, 1765.

"barbarous . . . Donegal": "Narrative of the Late Massacres," *Writings,* 546.

"All regard for him": Ibid.

"take the people of this province": Pennsylvania Archives, Eighth Series, VII, 5595.

"As some physicians": "Cool Thoughts on the Present Situation . . ." April 12, 1764.

"The want of union": New Jersey Archives, 1st Series, vol. IX, 429.

"than all the other colonies": BF to Richard Jackson, May 1, 1764.

"seem to be in a state of anarchy": WF to WS, May 1, 1764, Hart, "Letters," 436.

"Here lies the man . . . kitchen wench": PBF, vol. II, 382–83.

"canvassing among the Germans": John Penn to Thomas Penn, October 19, 1764, Penn Papers, HSP.

"by about 25 in 4000 voters": BF to Lord Kames, June 2, 1765.

"the utmost anarchy": WF to WS, September 23, 1764, Hart, "Letters," 439.

"O LORD our GOD arise": PBF, vol. 11, 447–48 notes.

CHAPTER 7: A FRENZY OR MADNESS

For background on British politics during these years, see Walter A. McDougal, *Freedom Just Around the Corner* (New York: HarperCollins, 2004), 202–38.

"a sort of frenzy or madness": John Hughes to BF, September 8, 1765.

"Between ten and eleven": *Gazette,* September 5, 1765.

"solemn knell": Ibid., September 12, 1765.

"By the many significant nods": Ibid.

"But as is usual with mobs": WF to BF, September 7, 1765.

"broke all the windows": *Gazette,* September 12, 1765.

"well-armed with fire-arms": John Hughes to BF, September 8–12, 1765.

"Cousin Davenport (Josiah) come": DF to BF, September 22, 1765.

"Towards night": Ibid.

"nothing [was] talked of but the Stamp Act": David Hall to BF, June 22, 1765.

"Caesar had his Brutus": John Burk, *History of Virginia* (Petersburg: Dickson and Pescud, 1805), Book III, 309.

"very amicable. . . . The utmost harmony": New Jersey Archives, 1st Series, vol. IX, 490ff.

"*strong efforts* to subdue": Skemp, 68, quoting James Biddle.

"There was great reason": N.J. Archives, 1st Series, vol. IX, 524–26.

"My father is absent": Docs, William Nelson, ed. (Paterson: Call Printing and Publishing Co., 1902), vol. XXIV, 643.

"Q. What was the temper . . . respect and affection": "Examination by the Commons," PBF, vol. 13, 135–36 and 142–43.

"late unprecedented, irregular": V&P 65B:10.

European and East India goods: advertisement in *Gazette,* June 5, 1766.

"bore a long and lingering fit": Ibid., September 4, 1766.

"for at this distance": BF to DF, May 23, 1767.

"the amount is greater": WF to BF, n.d. (May?) 1767.

"had often attempted to deceive him": Ibid.

"I am obliged to you": BF to RB, August 5, 1767.

"to brother Bache": SB to RB, May 14, 1767, Claude-Anne Lopez and Eugenia W. Herbert, *The Private Franklin: The Man and His Family* (New York: W. W. Norton, 1975), 141.

"would not occasion a delay": BF to DF, May 23, 1767.

"Reasons for Establishing . . . terrestrial paradise": Clarence Edwin Carter, *Great Britain and the Illinois Country* (Washington: American Historical Association, 1910), 172–81.

"The company shall consist": WF to BF, April 30, 1766.

"This is an affair . . . interest here": BF to WF, September 12, 1766.

"glass, china ware": BF to JG, June 13, 1767.

"English history affords": Dickinson, "Letters from a Farmer in Pennsylvania III," in Albert Bushnell Hart, *American History Told by Contemporaries: Building of the Republic, 1689–1783* (New York: Macmillan, 1901), vol. 2, 424.

"the sight of the *Romney*": Mark Puls, *Sam Adams: Father of the American Revolution* (New York: Palgrave Macmillan, 2006), 77–81.

"the country shall be independent": Ibid., 78.

"**tore their clothes and bruised**": Hutchinson to Jackson, June 16, 1768, Bernhard Knollenberg, *Growth of the American Revolution* (New York: Free Press, 1975), 68.

"**utmost influence to defeat**": Hillsborough to the Governors of America, April 21, 1768, Docs, vol. X, 14, 15.

"**to enter into any unwarrantable combination**": WF to Hillsborough, June 16, 1768, Docs, vol. X, 34–35.

further uniting: WF to Hillsborough, July 11, 1768, Docs 10:36, 37.

"**to draw in question**": Hillsborough to WF, August 16, 1768, ibid., 45–46.

"**but what either believes**": WF to Hillsborough, November 23, 1768, ibid., 64–69.

"**There must be an abridgment . . . should be broken**": Hutchinson to Whately, January 20, 1769, PBF, vol. XX, 549–50.

"**Your good Mrs. Franklin**": Bond to BF, June 7, 1769.

"**(such a helpless family) . . . never seen so much changes in me**": DF to BF, November 20, 1769.

"**I am in hopes**": DF to BF, ibid.

"**I came to town**": WF to BF, September 1, 1769.

"**He is not so fat**": Ibid.

"**I was well enough**": DF to BF, August 31, 1769.

CHAPTER 8: BLOOD AND MONEY

"**no force on earth**": WF to Hillsborough, November 23, 1768, Docs, vol. X, 70.

"**against the *Right* of Parliament**": WF to BF, January 31, 1769. WF is reporting hearsay.

"**first adventurers who have proposed**": Franklin, Walpole, et al., "Petition to the King," PBF, vol. 16, 166–68.

"**One half of England**": A. C. Flick, *The Papers of William Johnson* (Albany: University of the State of New York Press, 1927), vol. V, 128ff.

boatloads of presents: Sam Wharton to BF, December 2, 1768.

Great Arbiter of Justice: See N.J. Archives, 1st Series, vol. X, 56–58.

"**If the boundary is speedily**": Ibid., 96.

"*ask for enough*": BF to WF, July 14, 1773.

"**Dear Son, I have ever**": *Autobiography,* 1307.

"**account against you . . . our satisfaction**": BF to WF, April 20, 1771.

"**We are under an absolute**": Mariboe, 321.

"**About six o'clock on Friday**": Affidavit of Stephen Skinner, New York Collection of Mss., vol. XCV, 46, State Library at Albany; Docs, vol. X, 37.

"**to impeach the conduct**": V&P, 69:74.

"for want of that security": Ibid., 70B:21.

On February 22: This account is informed by Hiller B. Zobel, *The Boston Massacre* (New York: W. W. Norton, 1970), 148.

"Come out, you": *Boston Evening Post,* February 26, 1770.

"the ardor of the people": L. H. Butterfield, ed., *The Diary and Autobiography of John Adams* (Cambridge, MA: Harvard University Press, 1961), vol. I, 349–50.

"Lousy rascal . . .": Zobel, *Boston Massacre,* 186.

"Kill him": Knollenberg, *Growth of the American Revolution,* 79.

"Fire if you dare . . .": "Case of Thomas Preston, March 13, 1770," Historical Doc. 751 in Merrill Jensen, ed., *American Colonial Documents to 1776* (1955), vol. 9 of *English Historical Documents.*

"the late tumultuous and riotous" and passim: Archives of the State of New Jersey, 1st Series, vol. XXVII, 113ff.

"did, by their threats": Ibid.

"Rebels and traitors" and passim: BF to [Charles Thomson], March 18, 1770.

"the colonies were a rope": BF to JG, March 21, 1770.

"The public affairs of this nation": Ibid.

"Your father could not stir": WS to WF, April 3, 1771.

"This then is the *spirit*": Marginalia in a pamphlet by Josiah Tucker, PBF.

"To oppress, insult, and murder": Ibid.

"Of this he is himself so sensible": WS to WF, ut supra.

"It is imagined here": Ibid.

"I am sensible that what": WS to David Hall, April 7, 1770, *Miscellaneous Americana: A Collection of History, Biography, and Genealogy* (Philadelphia: Dando Printing, 1883), 126–27.

"Mutual provocation will thus": BF to WS, November 29, 1769.

"a majority readily confided": Cooper to BF, November 6, 1770.

CHAPTER 9: REBELLION, 1772–73

"a singular conversation": Margin note on ms. PBF, vol. 18, 16.

Dialogue between Hillsborough and Franklin: Ibid., 12–16.

"He threw me away": BF to WF, August 19, 1772.

"Therefore let us beware": BF to WF, August 17, 1772.

"I am glad . . . and I think": BF to WF, October 7, 1772.

distressed circumstances: V&P, 71A:12.

"Controversy . . . really disagreeable": Ibid., 92.

"violent contest . . . much degraded": Ibid., 74:138–39.

"I pretend not to infallibility": Ibid.

"I wish I could succeed": WF to BF, October 13, 1772.

"made in a fashionable taste": Ibid.

"Whilst others in my station": WF to Dartmouth, January 5, 1773, N.J. Archives 1st Series, vol. X, 389–93.

the great corridor between: Ibid., 392.

"a convenient house": John G. Wait Associates, Architects, *The Proprietary House Historic Structure Report* (Albany: Revised 1998), 3. This is the source of all architectural details of the governor's mansion.

a House committee condemned the act: See Bernard Bailyn, *The Ordeal of Thomas Hutchinson* (Cambridge, MA: Belknap Press of Harvard University Press, 1974), 203. Bailyn's book is a chief source of information on Hutchinson as well as the dramatic events in Boston during his tenure there. Bailyn is citing the *Report of the Committee of the Assembly* in July 1772 as quoted in the *History of Massachusetts Bay*, vol. III, 405.

"as men, as Christians": "Votes and Proceedings of the Freeholders of Boston," November 20, 1772.

"There must be an abridgment": Thomas Hutchinson to Thomas Whately, January 20, 1769, PBF.

"those heats are now cooling": BF to Cushing, December 2, 1772.

"were projected, advised . . .": Ibid.

"Anyone familiar with the situation . . .": PBF, vol. 19, 405.

"he was not thinking clearly": Ibid.

"It was thought": BF to Cushing, June 4, 1773.

"Upon convening the General Assembly": Samuel Cooper to BF, March 15, 1773.

"perceived the minds of the people": *Journals of the Honorable House of Representatives of His Majesty's Province of Massachusetts Bay* (Boston: Edes and Gill, 1773), 26, June 2.

"had a natural and efficacious": Ibid., May 26–June 29, 55–56, 58–61.

"footsteps stained with blood": *Boston Gazette*, June 21, 1773.

"Vile serpent": Bailyn, *Ordeal*, 243.

"nothing could have been": Cooper to BF, January 14, 1773.

"that no person besides Dr. Cooper": BF to Cushing, July 25, 1773.

"Rules by Which . . . Edict by the King of Prussia": *Writings*, 689–703.

"We were chatting": BF to WF, October 6, 1773.

"for his skill in casting": Valentine, vol. 1, 239–40.

Knights of St. Francis: Geoffrey Ashe, *The Hellfire Clubs* (Strouds: Sutton Publishing, 2000), 111–12.

the most careless: Sir Herbert Croft, *The Abbey of Kilkhampton* (London: G. Kearsly, 1780), 56–57. Croft's comments are by way of a mock eulogy.

"I had used all": BF to Jane Mecum, November 1, 1773.

"who wanted a jaunt": WF to BF, July 29, 1773.

"He always behaves himself": BF to WF, August 3, 1773.

"It is as well that it should continue": Ibid., September 1, 1773.

"precedent for every imposition": Knollenberg, *Growth of the American Revolution*, 95.

"I have told several": Ibid.

Background on the Boston Tea Party comes from Benjamin Woods Larabee, *The Boston Tea Party* (Boston: Northeastern University Press, 1979).

"I should have feared": Hutchinson to Dartmouth, January 24, 1774; Bailyn, *Ordeal*, 259.

"that the tea should not": Francis S. Drake, *Tea Leaves: Letters and Documents Relating to the Shipment of Tea to the American Colonies in 1773* (Boston: A. O. Crane, 1884), xliv.

"This meeting can do nothing": William V. Wells, *The Life and Public Services of Samuel Adams* (Boston: Little, Brown, 1866), vol. 2, 122–23.

"dressed and whooping": Rotch's Testimony to Privy Council, February 19, 1774, P.C. 1:56; Knollenberg, *Growth of the American Revolution*, 100.

"the candles were light": Ibid.

CHAPTER 10: A THOROUGH GOVERNMENT MAN

"infamous man of letters": Wedderburn, January 29, 1774, PBF, vol. 21, 37.

"written by public officers": BF to Printer of *The London Chronicle*, December 25, 1773, PBF.

Christian Schussele's rendering: circa 1859, Huntington Library and Art Collections, San Marino, CA.

"all the ill will": PBF, "The Final Hearing ... Wedderburn's speech," January 29, 1774.

"forfeited all the respect": Ibid.

"mark and brand the man ...": PBF, "The Final Hearing," January 29, 1774.

"conspicuously erect": Bancroft to WTF, circa 1810; PBF, vol. 21, 41.

"one of the best actions": WTF, ed., *Memoirs of the Life and Writings of Benjamin Franklin, LLD* (London: Henry Colburn, 1818), vol. 1, 185.

"traitor . . . old Doubleface . . . grey hairs": Brands, 481, quoting Catherine Drinker
    Bowen, *The Most Dangerous Man in America* (Boston: Little, Brown, 1974), 241.
    Bowen died before finishing the book or her footnotes.

"Judas's office in Craven": Ibid.

"a character of so much weight": BF to WF, August 19, 1772.

"just to acquaint you": BF to WF, February 18, 1774.

"no prospect of your ever": BF to WF, February 2, 1773.

"let them take your place": BF to WF, February 18, 1774.

"His majesty may be assured": WF to Dartmouth, May 31, 1774, Docs, vol. X, 458.

"that the parliament has no right": BF to WF, October 6, 1773.

"in insisting on their Independency": WF to BF, July 29, 1773.

"You are a thorough government man": BF to WF, October 6, 1773.

"the Committee is well disposed": *Minutes of the Provincial Congress and the Council
    of Safety of the State of New Jersey* (Trenton: Naar, Day and Naar, 1879), 4.

"with the most dangerous and alarming": Docs, vol. X, 456.

"consistent . . . when it is shut": WF to BF, July 3, 1774.

"But you . . . a thorough courtier": BF to WF, June 30, 1774.

"procure redress": Docs, vol. X, 456ff.

"and that the members consider": *Journals of the American Congress, 1774–78* (Wash-
    ington: Way and Gideon, 1823), vol. 1, 7.

"stop will be put": Docs, vol. X, 473–75.

"What shall I say with respect": Thomas Wharton to Samuel Wharton and Thomas
    Walpole, September 23, 1774, Wharton Papers #0542–0543–054848, PHS.

"as mean and despicable": Skempf, 134–35.

"I must just mention the horrid lie": Jane Mecum to BF, November 3–21, 1774.

"mention is made": *Boston Gazette,* October 3, 1774.

"to make peace with the Administration": the scene is recounted in detail in the
    Thomas Wharton Letter Book Mss., October 25, 1774, Wharton Papers, ut supra.

"circumstances were different . . . blissfully whole": Ibid.

"no importation into British America": Ibid.

"I have supposed it owing": BF to DF, September 10, 1774.

"we could put Great Britain": WF to WS, Hart, "Letters," 427.

"kind deportment and courtesy": *Gazette,* October 19, 1774.

CHAPTER 11: TWO ROADS

"as he has a good memory": BF to WF, August 1, 1774.

"I have in my eye . . . a drunken porter": BF to Charles Thomson, February 5, 1775.

the fragile vase: my paraphrase of Franklin's "that fine and noble vase the British Empire," first used in a letter to Lord Howe, July 20, 1776.

"few have the courage": WF to Dartmouth, December 6, 1774, in Larry R. Gerlach, ed., *New Jersey in the American Revolution* (Trenton: New Jersey Historical Commission, 1975), 99.

"without a groan": RB to BF, December 24, 1774.

"A very respectable number": WF to BF, Ibid.

"her death was no more": Ibid.

"Gentlemen of the Assembly": Docs, vol. X, 538–41.

"that any grievances": *Gazette*, March 1, 1775.

"to save appearances": JG to WF, March 26, 1775.

"And as he read the addresses": Jack Lindsay, ed., *The Autobiography of Joseph Priestley* (Teaneck, NJ: Fairleigh Dickinson University Press, 1971), 117.

"discoursing with so many": BF to WF, March 22, 1775.

"I do not find": BF to WF, November 28, 1768.

"nothing but submission": May 8, 1775, PBF.

He said he was pleased: BF to David Hartley, May 6, 1775.

"I have, neither directly": *Gazette*, May 17, 1775.

"It is whispered here": BF to JG, February 25, 1775.

"Alarms are spread": Docs, vol. X, 590–97.

"I have not heard . . . poison us also": BF to JG, February 25, 1775.

CHAPTER 12: TREVOSE, 1775

Sources for the lives of the Galloways are Benjamin H. Newcomb, *Franklin and Galloway: A Political Partnership* (New Haven and London: Yale University Press, 1972); John E. Ferling, *The Loyalist Mind: Joseph Galloway and the American Revolution* (University Park and London: Pennsylvania State University Press, 1977); and "Diary of Grace Growden Galloway," *Pennsylvania Magazine of History and Biography*, vol. 55, no.1 (1931), 32–94.

"I hope I have retired": JG to Verplanck, June 24, 1775, Newcomb, 278.

"Well, Mr. Galloway": Peter O. Hutchinson, ed., *Diary and Letters of Thomas Hutchinson* (Boston: Houghton Mifflin, 1884), vol. 2, 237.

"I can however (inter nos)": William T. Hutchinson and William M. E. Rachal, *The Papers of James Madison* (Charlottesville: University of Virginia Press, 1962–91), vol. I, 149–52.

"he hoped, if he [Benjamin] designed": Hutchinson, *Diary*, vol. 2, 237.

The king . . . was happy: *Gazette,* April 26, 1775.

"when that point": *Gazette,* May 24, 1775.

"at the expense of her blood": Ibid.

"It has been my unhappiness": WF to Dartmouth, February 1, 1775, Docs, vol. X, 537–38.

"The times are indeed greatly altered": Docs, vol. X, 638.

a committee of the whole: *Journals,* 59–60.

"accommodation of the unhappy": Ibid., 61.

"That where any person": Ibid., 67.

"made their claim of sovereignty": BF to WF, March 22, 1775. See Joseph Galloway, *Letters from Cicero to Catiline the Second* (London: J. Bew, 1781).

"against the corruption and dissipation . . .": Hutchinson, *Diary,* vol. 2, 238.

"tearing each other to pieces": Galloway, *Letters from Cicero,* 48.

"declared in favor . . .": Hutchinson, *Diary,* 237–38.

"parted as they had met . . .": Galloway, *Letters from Cicero,* 48.

CHAPTER 13: THE LAST WORD

"We shall give you": BF to John Sargant, June 27, 1775.

the only place in America: Charles Pettit to Joseph Reed, August 10, 1775, cited in Willard Sterne Randall, *A Little Revenge: Benjamin Franklin and His Son* (Boston: Little, Brown, 1984), 361.

The barometer plunged: The gale is reported in *Gazette,* September 6, 1775.

"strove zealously to draw": William Adee Whitehead, *A Biographical Sketch of William Franklin, Governor from 1763 to 1776,* Read before the New Jersey Historical Society, September 27, 1848 (Newark: Daily Advertiser Office, n.d.), 8.

"it would mortify me": WF to Dartmouth, September 5, 1775, Docs, vol. X, 658.

as he recalled Franklin's: Lord Stirling to WF, September 14, 1775, *Collections of the New Jersey Historical Society,* vol. II (New York: Wiley and Putnam, 1847), 114.

"a man ought to be damned": WF to Stirling, September 15, 1775, Peter Force, *American Archives: Documents of the American Revolutionary Period, 1774–76* (Washington, DC: Force, 1837–46), vol. 3, 657.

"for I make it a rule": BF to WS, October 3, 1775.

arrest and detain anyone: JCC, October 7, 1775, 149.

William Franklin's . . . not dangerous: Eliphat Dyer, quoted by John Adams in *Diary of John Adams,* October 6, 1775 [Notes of Debates].

sociable but not talkative: Abigail to John Adams, November 5, 1775.

Word of the treachery: BF to RB, October 19, 1775.

"My dear brother's conversation": JM to Catharine Green, November 24, 1775, in Mark Van Doren, ed., *The Letters of Benjamin Franklin and Jane Mecum* (Princeton: American Philosophical Society, 1950), 165.

motherly care: BF to JM, October 24, 1751.

"I expected Master Ray": JM to Greene, in Van Doren, *Letters*, 165.

"His Majesty laments": *Gazette*, November 22, 1775.

"evidence of His Majesty's gracious inclination": Ibid.

to prevent bloodshed: Docs vol. XVIII, 565–67.

"rope of sand": Notes of Dickinson Speech, New Jersey Archives, 1st Series, 10:689.

"Humble Address": *Minutes of the Provincial Congress,* 309.

"Your Excellency expresses": Ibid., 310.

"done their duty": Ibid.

"Their surprise that anyone": Ibid., 311.

"Your reply, Sir, though rather darkly penned": *Gazette*, December 13, 1775.

"That *some* have actually departed": Ibid.; also Docs, vol. 31, 229.

"But of this circumstance": *Gazette*, December 13, 1775; also Docs, vol. 31, 230.

CHAPTER 14: THE RECKONING, 1776

"About 37 ladies": *The Journal of Nicholas Cresswell, 1774–77* (New York: Dial Press, 1924), 53.

"I was not without apprehensions": WF to WTF, January 10, 1776, B.F. Papers, Mss. vol. 101, #10, APS.

"the will and pleasure": Docs, vol. X, 699.

"regardless of their duty": JCC, 89.

"Secret and Confidential": WF to Dartmouth, Docs, vol. X, 676–81.

perfectly indifferent: WF to Lord Germain, March 28, 1776, Docs, vol. X, 703.

"You may force me": Ibid., 706.

The chief justice was going and passim: Ibid., 704ff.

"Demogogue [*sic*] of Faction": Docs, vol. X, 576–77.

Elizabeth's nerves: WF to WTF, January 22, 1776, APS ut supra.

any of their friends: Ibid.

"Dear Sister: Your favor": EF to SB, February 5, 1776, N. J. Historical Society, Proceedings, 2nd Series, 5, 1877, 128.

"but let it not be your fault": WF to WTF, March 14, 1776, APS, 101:12.

said he was grateful: WF to WTF, January 22, 1776, APS, 101:12.

"If you are not more punctual": WF to WTF, June 13, 1776, APS, 101:12.

Congress expressed confidence: *Minutes of the Provincial Council,* 457.

"Colonel Heard has come to town": Docs, Series 2 (Trenton: John L. Murphy Publishers, 1901), vol. 1, 10.

"be conducted with all the delicacy": W. Woodford Clayton, ed., *History of Union and Middlesex Counties* (Philadelphia: Everts and Peck, 1882), 467.

"To be represented": Docs, vol. X, 721.

He informed President Tucker: V&P (Burlington: Isaac Collins, 1831), 16.

bring Governor Franklin: Ibid.

"in no one instance have I ever" and passim: Docs, vol. X, 722–24.

"body of men are got together": New Jersey Convention to President of Congress [Read June 24, 1776], *American Archives,* vol. VI, 1010.

"It is your turn now": Ibid.

"This occasioned a little debate": WF to N.J. Legislature, June 22, 1776, Docs, 2nd Series, vol. X, 730.

"has made a speech every way": Randall, 420.

thereby to intimidate every man and passim: WF to N.J. Legislature, June 22, 1776.

"Pro Rege & Patria": WF to N. J. Legislature, ut supra; also published in *Proceedings of the New Jersey Historical Society* (Newark: Office of the Daily Advertiser, 1847), vol. 3, 151–52.

"something will turn up": GW to Essex Committee of Safety, June 30, 1776, in *The Writings of George Washington* (Boston: Russell, Odiorne and Metcalf, 1834), vol. 3, part II, 447–48. Hereafter GW letters will be cited by date only.

"The circumstances you represent": Ibid.

"Set off immediately": Ibid.

"Governor Franklin of New Jersey": *Constitutional Gazette,* in Frank Moore, *Diary of the American Revolution* (New York: Charles Scribner, 1860), vol. 1, 268.

Lebanon: The events are recorded in WF to Lord Germain, November 10, 1778.

CHAPTER 15: PATERFAMILIAS

"I can do nothing": EF to SB, July 12, 1776, HSP.

"a steady honest man": E. H. Tatum, ed., *The American Journal of Ambrose Serle 1776–1778* (New York: New York Times, 1940), 49.

"I will not distress" EF to BF, August 6, 1776.

purchased flags: Newcomb, 285.

Desiring an accommodation: JCC, vol. V, 730–31.

"to seduce us": Ibid.

"to night, or very early": BF to WTF, September 10, 1776.

"My Lord, we will use": Francis Wharton, *The Revolutionary Diplomatic Correspon-*

dence of the United States (Washington, DC: Government Printing Office, 1889), vol. 2, 141.

"Tory House": BF to WTF, September 19, 1776.

"communicate the situation": WTF to BF, September 21, 1776.

"poor dear persecuted prisoner's": EF to WTF, October 11, 1776.

"cutting off the spring": BF to WTF, September 19, 1776.

"no evidence they had ever been": WTF to BF, September 21, 1776.

"In my going": WTF to BF, ut supra.

"Dear Tempe": BF to WTF, September 28, 1776.

"I am truly miserable indeed . . .": EF to WTF, October 11, 1776, HSP.

Tory rumors flew: RB to BF, February 28, 1777.

"who was detained": Thomas Jones, *History of New York During the Revolutionary War* (New York: New York Historical Society, 1879), vol. 1, 134–35.

historian George Trevelyan: George O. Trevelyan, *The American Revolution* (London: Forgotten Books, 1912), vol. 4, 48–49.

cheerfully pay: Mariboe discovered this from Wharton's letter book in the HSP.

"our common cause": RB to BF, February 5, 1777.

"amazed that under such": GW to Trumbull, April 16, 1777.

into close confinement: JCC, vol. XII, 291.

zing of the bullet: WF to Germain, November 10, 1778, PRO 654, Colonial Office 5/1002, 20, LC.

"in short . . . I was in a manner": Ibid.

My sources for Franklin's experience in France include Stacy Schiff's *The Great Improvisation: Franklin, France, and the Birth of America* (New York: Henry Holt, 2005); Carl Van Doren's *Benjamin Franklin*, cited above; and H. L. Brands, *The First American*, cited above.

"an honour seldom": Charles M. Andrews, "A Note on the Franklin-Deane Mission to France," *Yale University Library Gazette*, II (1928), 53–68.

Vergennes: Orville T. Murphy, *Charles Gravier: Comte de Vergennes* (Albany: University of the State of New York Press, 1983).

Franklin's conversation: Ronald Clark, *Benjamin Franklin* (New York: Random House, 1983), 306.

"he boldly ventures": George Thomas, earl of Albemarle, *Memoirs of the Marquis of Rockingham* (London: Bentley, 1852), vol. 2, 302.

state of weakness: BF to Vergennes, January 5, 1777.

"We may possibly, *unless*": Ibid.

Hancock had advised: John Hancock to BF, September 24, 1776.

"If the old gentleman": WF to EF, November 25, 1776, APS.

CHAPTER 16: DARK NIGHT OF THE SOUL

He found her depressed: *Diary of Ambrose Serle*, 221.

as past recovery and passim: WF to GW, July 22, 1777.

"Sir, I am sensible": Ibid.

"His situation is distressing": GW to President of Congress, July 25, 1777.

"I heartily sympathize": GW to WF, July 25, 1777.

"an opportunity of conferring": JCC vol. III, 583.

"I am sorry that an act": GW to WF, July 29, 1777.

"It appears that this Act": Ibid., revision.

letter of recommendation: BF and Silas Dean to American Committee on Foreign Affairs, May 25, 1777.

"She was a loving wife": *Gazette*, August 13, 1777.

having learned of the sad: WF to Trumbull, September 15, 1777, "Governor Franklin in Litchfield Jail," *Proceedings of the New Jersey Historical Society*, New Series (1918), vol. III, 45–47.

the bare essentials: RB to BF, January 31, 1778.

"He requested me to write": Daniel Clymer to RB, October 11, 1777, Randall, 457–58, quoting papers of the Continental Congress, M247, reel 93, 111.

This letter . . . was laid before the Continental Congress: JCC, vol. 2, 299: "A letter from Daniel Clymer to Richard Bache respecting the confinement of Mr. William Franklin was laid before the Congress and read. *Ordered*, That it be referred to the Board of War."

"I know not what": WS to BF, July 14, 1778.

"the distresses of others": James Kinsey to James Duane, February 11, 1778, *Publications of the Southern Historical Association* (Washington, DC: The Association, 1906), 307–8.

"all grieve those unhappy gentlemen": BF to RB, June 2, 1779.

Izard and Lee's abuse: RB to BF, October 22, 1778.

"Methinks it is rather some merit" and passim: BF to RB, June 2, 1779.

They were laying odds: Van Doren, 502.

juvenile guard: Henry Reed Stiles, *The History and Genealogies of Ancient Windsor, Connecticut 1635–1891* (Hartford: Case, Lockwood and Brainard, 1891), 660.

There were other prisoners: John Werner Barber, Henry Howe, *Our Whole Country, or The Past and Present of the United States* (Cincinnati: Henry Howe, 1861), vol. 1, 348.

Marquis de Lafayette: Ibid.

"une grande contradiction": Ibid.

"their family and property": Mariboe, 484, quoting ms. in New York Public Library.

"An unwillingness to quit . . .": John Ward Dean et al., eds., *Historical Magazine and Notes and Queries* (New York: Charles B. Richardson, 1861), 271.

CHAPTER 17: THE SCENE OF ACTION, 1778–81

Franklin was embraced: Dean, *Historical Magazine,* 272.

My main sources for occupied New York City in 1779 are William A. Polf, *Garrison Town: The British Occupation of New York City* (Albany: New York State Bicentennial Commission, 1976) and Oscar T. Barck, Jr., *New York City During the War for Independence* (New York: Columbia University Press, 1931).

aid as a propagandist: Eden to Clinton, November 19, 1778, Mariboe, 487.

to procure intelligence: PRO, Colonial Office 5.82, 53–55 LC, copy.

"suffering friends of government . . ." and passim: Isaac Ogden to JG, November 21, 1778, Galloway Letters, LC.

"theft, fraud, robbery": Polf, *Garrison Town,* 22.

"one capital stroke": WF to Germain, November 12, 1778, PRO 654, Colonial Office 5/1002, 20, LC, copy.

"Sir Henry wished the conflagrations": Paul David Nelson, *William Tryon and the Course of Empire* (Chapel Hill: University of North Carolina Press, 1991), 169.

"Warning to Rebels": John Mason, March 27, 1779, Clinton Papers, Clements Library, Mariboe, 491n.

"desolation warfare": Thomas B. Allen, *Tories* (New York: Harper, 2010), 307.

"some capable gentleman": PRO, Colonial Office, ut supra, 45–47 LC.

"excesses, cruelties": *Trial of Capt. Richard Lippincott of the Associated Loyalists for Hanging Joshua Huddy, April 1782, Provincial Archives of New Brunswick,* 492. This document, which exists in a few longhand copies, running to hundreds of pages at the LC and elsewhere, has recently been digitized in part. Online it runs 28 pages, and I am citing the document pages as they appear there. Hereafter I will refer to this source as *Trial.*

under the command: Mariboe, 494, citing Clinton papers.

the king was fully persuaded: Germain to WF, January 22, PRO Audit Office, Class 13, vol. 109, 310–311; available from Online Institute for Loyalist Studies.

a document that satisfied no one: PRO, Colonial Office 5.82, 37–44, LC.

he swore to heaven: Benedict Arnold to GW, October 1, 1780.

"I pray you bear me": James Thacher, M.D., *The American Revolution from the Commencement to the Disbanding . . .* (New York: American Subscription Publishing House, 1860), 226–28.

his army was dwindling: Jared Sparks, ed., *Writings of GW,* vol. 7, 282.

"a shocking, bungling piece": WF to WS, November 12, 1780, Hart, "Letters," 457.

The charter stated: October 28, 1780, Mariboe, 507.

for the crime of enlisting men . . . "You shall be carried": John Thomas Scharf, *History of Western Maryland: Being a History of Frederick, Montgomery, Carroll . . .* (Philadelphia: Louis H. Everts, 1882), 143.

"the country will be depopulated": Greene to Col. Wm. David, May 3, 1781, in Charles Sumner, *Recent Speeches and Addresses* (Boston: Ticknor and Fields, 1856), 361.

"a country exposed to the misfortune": Allen, *Tories,* 283.

Stephen Edwards of Shrewsbury: *Historical Collections of the State of New Jersey,* op. cit., (John W. Barber and Henry Howe, NY: S. Tuttle, 1845), 367n.

Captain William Gillian led: Franklin Ellis, *History of Monmouth County, New Jersey* (Philadelphia: R. T. Peck, 1885), 247; Edwin Salter, *A History of Monmouth and Ocean Counties* (Bayonne: F. Gardner and Son, 1890), 171–72.

In August, the Continental Congress issued: John Barber and Henry Howe, ut supra, 364–65.

"I am Huddy!": Benson J. Lossing, ed., *The American Historical Record* (Philadelphia: Samuel P. Town, 1873), vol. 2, 169–71.

CHAPTER 18: CAPTAIN HUDDY AND THE DANCE OF DEATH

"the first link in a chain": Allen, *Tories,* 290.

"almost forgot there was": RB to BF, January 16, 1781.

horror and dismay: William B. Willcox, ed. *The American Rebellion: Sir Henry Clinton's Narrative of His Campaigns* (New Haven: Yale University Press, 1954), 352.

"It might sail": Allen, *Tories,* 324; see Edward Lengel, *General George Washington* (New York: Random House, 2005), 342–43.

March 1782: William Scudder Stryker, *The Capture of the Block House at Toms River, New Jersey* (Trenton: Naar, Day and Naar, 1883), 10–14.

armed whaleboats: *Historical Collections,* ut supra, 328–29.

So grisly was the sight: Affidafit of Clayton Tilton, April 23, 1782 PRO, Colonial Office 5:108.

"would be fond of going": *Trial,* 18.

angrily objected: Ibid., 11.

What happened: Barber and Howe, *Historical Collections,* 366; also Edwin Salter, *History of Monmouth and Ocean Counties,* 185–87.

"We, the Refugees": *Independent Gazetteer,* Philadelphia, Saturday, May 4, 1782, 2.

"the most brutal, unprecedented": GW to Henry Clinton, April 21, 1782.

"barbarous outrage against humanity": Clinton to GW, April 25, 1782.

"The three prisoners": WF to Clinton, April 27, 1782, quoted in *Trial*, 17.

"open to view": "Monmouth Manifesto," included in GW to Clinton, April 21, 1782.

"Damned rascals": deposition of Isaac Alyay, April 27, 1782, included in Robertson's letter to GW, May 1, 1782.

"The time and place are fixed": GW to Robertson, May 4, 1782.

"Lively, brave, handsome": Ibid., 444.

the Asgill affair: Background comes from Katherine Mayo, *General Washington's Dilemma* (Port Washington, NY: Kennikat Press, 1938, 1970).

"Washington has determined": *The Military and Naval Magazine of the United States* (Washington, DC: Benjamin Homans, 1835), 441.

"My son (an only son)": *The Scots Magazine* (1782), vol. XLIV (Edinburgh: Murray and Cochran), 696. This was probably edited by James Boswell.

"The situation of Captain Asgill": BF to Oswald, July 28, 1782.

"Sir.—It is not in quality": Vergennes to GW, July 29, 1782.

Rochambeau, commander: Ibid. See also Mayo, 185–88, re Rochambeau's letter of June 16, 1782, to Chevalier de la Luzerne, French minister to the United States.

complicit in the crime: JCC, October 17, 1782, vol. XXIII, 662.

"enough to move the heart": Elias Boudinet, *Journal or Historical Recollections . . .* (Trenton, C. L. Traver, 1890), 63–64.

"In short, it looked so much": Ibid.

He asked the general: WF to Lieut. Gen James Robertson, August 9, 1782, *Report on the American Manuscripts in the Royal Institution of Great Britain* (Hereford: Anthony Brothers, 1907), 61.

"absconded": JCC, ibid., 662n.

"hopes to see something done": Benjamin Vaughan to Lord Shelbourne, July 31, 1782, Benjamin Vaughan Corr. Mss. APS.

Note: All correspondence in PBF after August 16, 1782, is unpublished.

"Your father was well": SB to WTF, October 1, 1782.

CHAPTER 19: GOING HOME

"I see, by the papers": Georgiana Shipley to BF, October 2, 1782.

"I am determined to go": Grace Galloway, *Diary,* June 30, 1778, 88.

"remembered every military maneuver": William Cobbett, ed., *The Parliamentary History of England* (London: Longman, Hurst et al., 1814), XX, 818.

Shelbourne received William: Vaughan to Shelbourne, December 10, 1782, ut supra.

John Adams was amazed: Adams, November 26, 1780, "Journal of Peace Negotiations, continued," Wharton, *Diplomatic Correspondence*, 84.

"The claims of the American Loyalists": Joseph Galloway, *The Claim of the American Loyalists Revived and Maintained Upon Incontrovertible Principals . . .* (London: G. & T. Wilkie, 1788), v–vi.

"As I have avoided": WF to Richard England, December 27, 1782, enclosed in letter from Richard England to WTF, December 29, 1782, unpublished, PBF.

madwoman: Patience Wright to BF, March 19, 1783.

"performances": Ibid., March 29, 1778.

"the queen of sluts": Abigail Adams to Mary Smith Cranch, July 25, 1784, in C. F. Adams, ed., *The Letters of Mrs. Adams* (Boston: Charles C. Little and James Brown, 1841), vol. 2, 33.

"His health is bad": Patience Wright to BF, February 22, 1783.

"the son of Dr. Franklin": WS to BF, July 14, 1778.

"I begin now to flatter": Ibid., May 27, 1782.

"My dear old Friend": BF to WS, July 29, 1783.

"You have so many": WS to BF, February 1, 1784.

"but there are difficulties": BF to WS, February 16, 1784.

"that I had never wrote to him": "An Abstract of the Vouchers, with Observations respecting the Memorial of Governor Franklin delivered to the Commission for enquiring into the Losses and Services of the American Loyalists on the 25 of March, 1784. February 14, 1788. No. 21—Letters between Dr. Franklin my Father and me in [1784] and Extracts of two Letters from my Son in 1786." This document from the United Kingdom Archives was digitized by Ancestry.com and came to the attention of Robert Frankel, associate editor of the Papers of Benjamin Franklin at Yale University. I am indebted to the editors of the Franklin papers for many services and kindnesses, but especially to Dr. Frankel for sharing this important document with me soon after it was discovered. While it does not include the letters themselves, the passages I quote bear significantly on the relationship between father and son.

"The Governor spent a day": WS to BF, August 26, 1784.

"I trust that you will": BF to WF, August 16, 1784.

"I wish you had executed": BF to Mary (Polly) Hewson, August 15, 1784.

"I follow your instructions": WTF to BF, September 26, 1784.

"We are all pleased with our old friend" Hewson to BF, October 25, 1784.

Temple advised: WTF to Ruston, May 2, 1785.

"in consideration of which": "Abstract of Vouchers," ut supra.

"Although this transaction": Ibid.

"had lost its patriarch": Jefferson to Rev. William Smith, February 19, 1791, *The Letters of Thomas Jefferson*, Papers, 19:113 (Princeton: Princeton University Press, 1773).

"had the satisfaction of seeing his son": WTF, ed., *Memoirs of the Life and Writings of Benjamin Franklin* (London: Henry Colburn, 1818), vol. 2, 165.

"Water is the easiest bed": Carl Van Doren, ed., *Benjamin Franklin, Autobiographical Writings* (New York: Viking Press, 1945), 653.

"no dissatisfaction to me": "Abstract of Vouchers."

"that would have accommodated": BF to Hewson, July 26, 1785.

"I am not so easily moved": Hewson to BF, July 23, 1785.

"the only man who might": William Willcox, *Portrait of a General: Sir Henry Clinton in the War of Independence* (New York: Alfred A. Knopf, 1964), 263.

EPILOGUE, 1785–1823

"The part he [William] acted against me": BF Will and Codicil, July 17, 1788, PBF.

"who has no vices": Lopez and Herbert, *Private Franklin*, quoting BF to Mme. Brillon, n.d., 276.

"sagacity beyond his years": Adams, *Diary*, vol. III, January 11, 1783, 102.

"My grandson, a good young man": BF to Shipley, August 22, 1784.

"He has such a love of dress": Mary Hewson to Barbara Hewson, January 25, 1785, in Lopez and Herbert, *Private Franklin*, 269.

"more trouble of mind": WF to Jonathan Williams, July 24, 1807, microfilm APS.

"Happiness has received a stroke": WF to Jonathan Williams, October 28, 1811, microfilm APS.

"to bury in oblivion all past": WF to WTF, July 3, 1812, WF mss, Beinecke Library.

"showed every promise of making a fine woman" and passim: WF to Jonathan Williams, May 26, APS.

William enjoyed life: WF to WTF, July 3, 1812, WF mss, Beinecke Library.

Franklin's letters and papers: Herbert Baxter Adams, *The Life and Writings of Jared Sparks* (Boston and New York: Houghton Mifflin, 1893), vol. II, 521; another source for the fate of the letters is John W. Jordan, *Colonial and Revolutionary Families of Pennsylvania* (New York: Lewis Historical Publishing Co., 1911), vol. 1, 329–30.

ILLUSTRATION CREDITS

1. Ben Franklin in London, circa 1760: Engraving courtesy of the Library of Congress.
2. Deborah Read Franklin, circa 1759: Engraving courtesy of the Library of Congress.
3. Sally Franklin, in 1793: Catharine Lorillard Wolfe Collection, Wolfe Fund. The Metropolitan Museum of Art.
4. Governor William Franklin, circa 1785: Painting by Danuta Wyszynski after a portrait by Mather Brown.
5. Benjamin and William Franklin's London Residence on Craven Street: Benjamin Franklin House, Courtesy of Friends of the Benjamin Franklin House.
6. Joseph Galloway, circa 1760: Courtesy of the New York Public Library.
7. Benjamin Franklin with "friend" on Craven Street, circa 1761: American Philosophical Society.
8. Thomas Penn, proprietor of Pennsylvania, 1752: 125th Anniversary Acquisition, Gift of Susanne Strassburger Anderson, Valerie Anderson Readman, and Veronica Anderson Macdonald from the estate of Mae Bourne and Ralph Beaver Strassburger, 2004, Philadelphia Museum of Art.
9. Glass armonica, 1762: Franklin Collection, Yale University Library.

10. Lord Stirling (William Alexander), 1770: Engraving courtesy of the Library of Congress.

11. George Washington in 1772: Washington-Custis-Lee Collection, Washington and Lee University.

12. Benjamin Franklin being interrogated by the Privy Council, 1774: The Huntingdon Library, Art Collections and Botanical Gardens.

13. Marquis de Lafayette in 1790: Portrait by Jean-Baptiste Weyler.

14. The great diplomat in France, 1778: The Friedsam Collection, Bequest of Michael Friedsam, Metropolitan Museum of Art.

15. William Strahan in 1780: Engraving of the painting in the National Portrait Gallery (U.K.), courtesy of the Library of Congress.

16. Benjamin Franklin returns to America, 1787: Engraving courtesy of the Library of Congress.

17. William Temple Franklin, 1790: Trumbull Collection, Yale University Art Gallery.

INDEX

ABOUT THE AUTHOR

DANIEL MARK EPSTEIN has published twenty books of poetry and biography, including the international bestseller *The Ballad of Bob Dylan*; *Lincoln and Whitman*, which received an Academy Award from the American Academy of Arts and Letters; and *The Lincolns: Portrait of a Marriage*, named one of the top ten books of 2008 by *The Wall Street Journal* and the *Chicago Sun-Times*. His honors include the Rome Prize from the American Academy of Arts and Letters, and a Guggenheim Fellowship. He lives in Baltimore, Maryland.

danielmarkepstein.com

ABOUT THE TYPE

This book was set in Caslon, a typeface first designed in 1722 by William Caslon (1692–1766). Its widespread use by most English printers in the early eighteenth century soon supplanted the Dutch typefaces that had formerly prevailed. The roman is considered a "workhorse" typeface due to its pleasant, open appearance, while the italic is exceedingly decorative.

6/26